Supreme Court

THE ASCENT TO POWER

A HISTORY BY
Lantz McClain

Copyright © 2022 Lantz McClain
All cover art copyright © Lantz McClain
All Rights Reserved

No part of this book may be reproduced or transmitted in any form or by any means, electronic or mechanical, including photocopying, recording, or by any information storage and retrieval system, without permission in writing from the author.

lantzemclain.com

Publishing Coordinator – Sharon Kizziah-Holmes

Published in the USA

ISBN -13: 978-1-956806-65-6

FOR RUTH

"So that in the first place, I put for a general inclination of all mankind, a perpetual and restless desire of Power after power."

– Thomas Hobbes, *Leviathan* (1651)

CONTENTS

Chapter 1 - The Institution of the Court 1
Chapter 2 - The Power of the Court 21
Chapter 3 - Judicial Review at Inception 45
Chapter 4 - The Paradigm of Dred Scott 65
Chapter 5 - The Logic of Reconstruction 85
Chapter 6 - The Invention of Substantive Due Process 106
Chapter 7 - The Enactment of Segregation 129
Chapter 8 - An Institutional Defeat 151
Chapter 9 - The Moral of Brown 178
Chapter 10 - The New Model Judicial Supremacy 201
Chapter 11 - Religion 230
Chapter 12 - The Judicial Revolution 262
Chapter 13 - The Judicial Revolution Continued 285
Chapter 14 - Judicial Ideology 310
Chapter 15 - A Summing Up 331
Index 365
Footnotes 376

CHAPTER 1

The Institution of the Court

What holds together the great and famous cases in the history of the U.S. Supreme Court? Over the more than two hundred years, the justices have changed ideological fronts more than once, sometimes radically. In their turn, present legal scholars have endeavored to fit these changes together into an ideological evolution, explained as progress, what has been called a march of liberty. But another side of the cases forces a way upon the mind, and most prominently, two observations intrude: First, over this same history, the Court has repeatedly differed with and overruled Congress: and second, the Court has as repeatedly re-interpreted so as to increase its own power. None of the expressed ideologies appear to account for these repeated occurrences, which when fit together occur so regularly as to suggest a course attracted by influences left so far not explained.

The constant conflicts with Congress – The crucial significance of the Court's constant conflicts with Congress leaps out looking back at the example of Reconstruction. During that tragic era, Congress enacted three great Reconstruction Amendments (the 13th, 14th, and 15th Amendments), which guaranteed the freedmen the franchise and their other civil rights, as well as the Civil Rights Act of 1875, which prohibited segregation. But the Court will shortly interpret away the intent of this massive legislative effort, making the promises a dead letter on the face of the Constitution. Then with Plessy v Ferguson (1896), the Court interprets into the Constitution the legal doctrine of "separate but equal," opening the way for legal segregation. In effect, the Court replaced the congressional program for Reconstruction with a judicial program. Rather than equal rights, the freedmen end up with segregation.

The currently dominant explanation blames "racism," a mistaken and evil ideology, seen as gripping the whole nation, not just the Court. Yet that explanation forgets the facts and so misses the point. Congress proposed and the people ratified the Reconstruction Amendments, and Congress also passed the Civil Rights Act of 1875. The Court threw the whole thing out. Then actually, racial ideology cannot have triumphed in Congress, but rather only in the Court. Then what explains this conflict between Congress and the Court? What explains why Congress did one thing and the Court the reverse?

Wherever our casebook on constitutional law falls open, the pages reveal a similar divide, the Court against Congress, each arriving at diametrically opposed policy solutions. We must begin to wonder about some underlying, systemic cause in the very nature of the two institutions, transcending the ideological issues of the day and worthy of our interest for its own sake.

The Court's ascent to power – Looking back across these institutional conflicts, we also notice the Court repeatedly emerges victorious. Just as they won over Reconstruction, they keep winning. Since the political marketplace works on power, the ability to impose one's will, such a run of success must reflect a predominant power. And turning to that calculation, we find that the wins do reflect the Court's superior institutional power, moreover, a superior power that keeps growing, especially in relation to Congress. So for example, during industrialization the Court will strike down a series of "progressive" reforms, laws aimed at the accompanying ills, such as child labor, dangerous workplaces, and faulty products. But the Court enjoys the power to strike down those laws only through having themselves previously invented a new doctrine called "substantive due process." This new doctrine let judges void as unconstitutional laws they deemed "unreasonable." Since that standard lacked hard edges, this legal innovation let the Court intervene much more widely. Matters initially reserved to the legislative calendar became matters pending on the judicial docket. Yet we find nothing more routinely neglected than tracing the Court's ascent to power, never squarely faced and dealt with on its own terms.

Through long-stranding judicial caution, the Court contributes to this gap, the justices preferring to speak about their power only in the most circumspect language. On their face the opinions generally rule clearly enough, holding for or against the parties. But in the subtext, without explicit discussion or even acknowledgement, these same opinions subtly re-define and expand judicial power. To grasp the significance requires an effort of exegesis and putting the pieces together. In 1803 in Marbury v Madison, Chief Justice John Marshall will claim that great power of judicial review, which lets judges declare congressional laws unconstitutional and hence void. But we must turn to other cases for the precise contours, these supplemental texts hedging the doctrine with narrow limits, the judges pledging never to declare an act unconstitutional except in a clear-cut case beyond a reasonable doubt. In fact, the Court never held another congressional statute unconstitutional for over fifty years. Then finally, in 1857 in the Dred Scott Case, Chief Justice Roger Taney would declare the Missouri Compromise of 1820 unconstitutional. That law prevented the spread of slavery into free territory, and Taney voided it. But since such a conclusion hardly clear-cut, reaching that ruling forced him to abandon those original restraints on judicial review. Not only did he utterly fail to acknowledge this, but wrote as if he were doing nothing unusual. Despite this reticence, in effect Dred Scott created a new paradigm for judicial review. No longer would the justices be limited to clear-cut cases, instead enjoying a much more wide-ranging power. And so it goes throughout the history of the Court. We must continually engage in a somewhat complex endeavor to sort out and add up the implications, which obscures the movement of the power.

The ideological explanation – The present scholarship continues to ascribe the Court's motivations to ideologies. Just as we heard them blame the rise of segregation on racism, they ascribe the rise and fall of other legal doctrines to the rise and fall of other underlying ideologies. But this approach suffers from another besetting defect. Since ideologies ultimately rest on ethical values, such assessments of the Court ultimately amount to ethical assessments. Good judicial performance is seen as resulting from good values motivating the hearts and minds of the judges and vice versa. Much reason looks to reside with this outlook. After all, our overriding concern calls for justice, outcomes that square with our ethical notions. Then if good ethical values motivate the judges, surely that should lead to good judicial opinions. Except the usual problem occurs with such ethical evaluations. The consensus on ethical norms breaks down over the details. Thus, in these ideological or ethical assessments, the image of the Court must necessarily shift with the ideological or ethical perspective of the viewer. Rather than a stable picture we are left with no more than an ongoing ideological and ethical conflict between rival factions.

The familiar controversies between "liberal" versus "conservative" demonstrate this failure. In the 1930s, liberals attacked the Court for declaring virtually the whole New Deal unconstitutional. More recently and in their turn, conservatives attacked "judicial activism." But neither do more than applaud or denounce the Court on a partisan bias, as shown by running over the litany, going from affirmative action back to abortion. Both sides demand outcomes in keeping with their agendas, support or condemn by that measurement. Surely we need a better way to describe the Court than to say in essence: It's good when liberals win or bad when conservatives lose.

How get beyond this stalemate? Both liberals and conservatives ignore an initial difficulty: How fairly weigh their competing claims? In arguing about the Court, both sides strain every fiber of rhetoric like lawyers desperate to win before the court of public opinion. Only as any lawyer worth his salt can tell you, fair judicial procedure fundamental to a just verdict. Even before you begin a trial, you must first set up the legal forum to render impartial justice. But in controversies over the Court, neither liberals nor conservatives show any inclination to face this preliminary question. Instead, each takes the stance summed up by the King of Hearts to Alice: "Verdict first and trial afterwards." Each insists on their outcomes, rather than honestly asking: Is the procedure in place to fairly judge between us? Just here we should avoid such an error in method. Instead, we should begin by asking the right initial question: Is the institutional forum properly constructed to render a just verdict, even-handedly to decide such disputes as those between liberals and conservatives? Setting up a fair process should stand as the precondition to the discussion.

Such a move seems obvious and looks down an avenue that promises to bypass the deadlock in the ideological or ethical approach. The success of scientific method furnishes a clear analogy. Scientists continue to differ over theories, but eventually learned to agree upon method. This shift in emphasis led to progress across the board. Almost an obsession with similar tactics serves as a marker of modernity and often allows a similar progress. Dialogue in all spheres relies upon a pre-accepted methodology, participants acquiescing as they enter. Scholarly controversy may rage in the academic journals, but all submit to the crucible of peer review. It has come to be widely recognized that reliable method stands as a preliminary problem, stands at the start of any intellectual endeavor, and we are more successful by settling those preconditions upfront. Unable to agree on what the tests will verify, we are more able to agree on what tests will prove validity. The rules come before the game, and however much the lust for victory, all must agree to play by the rules.

From what has been said, then, certain considerations emerge, suggesting a new approach to understanding the Supreme Court. We must account for the constant institutional conflicts between the Court and Congress. We must account for the Court's ascent to power. We should not let the agenda of any political faction predetermine our judgment. Rather we should start by directing our attention toward the processes, asking if those fairly judge between the factions. By keeping all these concerns in view, we may hope to reach a more adequate and coherent explanation about the Court, that is, one flowing from a central set of premises and explaining the completeness of the data.

Classic political science – At least since Aristotle, classic political science has centered on analyzing political power in relation to political structure. Brief reflection will show that the suggestions made with reference to the Court no more than a return to that traditional method. This coincidence reinforces the notion such an approach has much to offer applied to the Court. Other governmental institutions face interrogation phrased in terms of their power and structure all the time, studies yielding useful answers about Congress, the presidency, or the bureaucracy. To put the judiciary through a similar inquiry looks in order.

Also at least since Aristotle, classic analysis began by dividing government into three basic forms: monarchy, aristocracy, or democracy, that is, rule by a single individual, rule by a select group, or rule by the people. Constitutions ancient and modern show considerable ingenuity mixing and matching these elements into more complex combinations. But the distinction between the types ultimately rests on who possesses the power, the ability to impose one's will. Within each type a political process controls the flow of power. Speaking of a political institution's structure refers most significantly to this process, which keeps power in certain hands.

The internal structure of these basic political forms all operate upon two strong and interconnected forces: First, individual self-interest, the tendency of individuals to seek power or equivalents such as money or prestige. Second, the institutional will-to-power, this same tendency manifested on the institutional scale. These forces variously aligned bind together the institutional structure of all the types. To take an early example, in ancient kingship the personal self-interest of the king runs throughout, giving coherence to the system. Whatever else the king's government may accomplish, maintaining his own interests stands primary. Nor does he willingly brook rivals, attracting all authority to himself.

This same self-interest and institutional will-to-power crucially influence the function of any political institution, exerting an irresistible attraction within the system. As a result, if we plug the same political, social, or ethical problem into one type of government institution, we likely get an entirely different answer than from another type of government institution. The gravitational tug of individual and institutional interest warps any issue passing through the system, altering the course. Those wielding power within the process will change outcomes in subtle and not so subtle ways toward their own ends. To stick with the example of kingship, despite any platitudes to the contrary, we expect such a system to reach outcomes favorable to the monarchy. History amply proves how widely these may vary from the public good. A benevolent monarch is almost as much an oxymoron as a dictatorship of the proletariat. Absolute power at least tends to corrupt absolutely.

At bottom such recognition foundational to the American belief in democracy. Long ago Americans perceived only democratic institutions function in the public interest. Elections serve as an overriding, effective mechanism, redirecting self-interest to work in the public interest. Since an elected official must at least appear to serve the people, this mechanism refracts his self-interest to work in the public interest. One cannot forebear quoting Hume's well-known aphorism: "[I]n contriving any system of government, and fixing the several checks and controuls of the constitution, every man ought to be supposed to be a knave; and to have no other end in all his actions, but private interest. By this interest, we must govern him, and by means of it, make him co-operate to public good, notwithstanding his insatiable avarice and ambition."[1]

The Founders sought to employ the institutional will-to-power in another familiar way as well, setting up the separation of powers and system of checks and balances. They divided the power of government between the competing branches and balanced the power of each against the other. Under their theory, the institutional will-to-power of the legislature, the executive, and the judiciary relentlessly collides. But since none can overcome the others, this tension maintains a stasis, preventing tyranny, giving room to freedom.

A well-built democracy depends upon the same care to institutional design throughout. Just as elections hold officials responsible, all aspects of the system must incorporate effective mechanisms of accountability. It is not enough to elect Congress, if later the internal rules of procedure let a few members dominate the body, and generally speaking, the party and committee system have passed through the will of the majority. It is not enough to assign mandates to the bureaucracy, rather Congress, the chief executive, and the courts need to constantly hold bureaucrats accountable, carrying out as well as limited to those mandates. Appropriate controls must extend through every line of the political blueprint.

It would seem doubtful the Supreme Court somehow exempt from these fundamental rules of political science. It would seem self-interest and the institutional will-to-power must play some part in how the Court functions. In other words, these factors must affect outcomes. It then becomes important to study the Court's institutional structure, seeing how these forces apply, if at all.

Other influences of political structure – However, to say interest says much, but not all. While political institutions strongly tend to serve interests, other aspects of their structure also influence their function. Analysis needs to pay careful attention to the devil in these other institutional details.

To develop the significance, let us return to ancient kingships, noticing how the very nature of the institution results in strengths as well as weaknesses. Kingship offers the prospect of unanimity, dispatch, and secrecy. Kings can centralize national resources and aims; they can respond rapidly; they can hold their purposes close. These features serve extremely useful purposes, especially in conducting foreign policy and warfare, and in early history gave kingships a comparative advantage over less organized nations. But in other contexts these same strengths serve as liabilities. A king's tight control crushes freedom and free-markets, leading to the age-old story of oppression and economic stagnation, the people miserable and impoverished. Other besetting flaws appear a creeping senescence, the leadership cadre clinging on unto death, and frequent quarrels over the succession leading to civil wars.

The Roman Senate gives a striking instance of an institutional nature that decisively influenced institutional function. An aristocratic element in a republican constitution, senators held their seats for life, but promotion came only at the culmination of a long career, the final tier after winning a series of offices by election before the Roman assemblies. A senator had run a gauntlet of public service, training him in a harsh school of practical experience, testing his ability and stamina. Within the Roman state, this august body exercised considerable power, and in particular, over foreign policy. And it is a remarkable fact that for some two hundred years the Senate plotted a consistent course in foreign policy, steered upon four guiding principles: First, Rome never fought any except just wars, which they interpreted as eliminating all potential rivals. Second, Rome never quit on a war regardless the cost, relentlessly doubling down on loses, which forced opponents into a zero sum game, facing catastrophe as the price to stay in. Third, despite some well-known exceptions to teach an object lesson, Rome treated the vanquished with unusual generosity. Rather than enslaving conquered peoples, they promoted them to allies and left them largely autonomous. Fourth, Rome scrupulously honored her treaties, allowing reliance upon her word. In combination, Rome meant to conquer, and she put to other nations a stark either-or choice: Either negotiate an early out, taking easy terms reliably kept, or face ceaseless war to annihilation. This formula applied naked power and self-interest to both ends of the equation, and most made the necessary calculation. Many surrendered without a real contest; Rome built a network of loyal alliances, which further increased her strength; the recalcitrant suffered obliteration like Carthage. With this foreign policy Rome conquered the then known world. And it must be noticed none of this could have happened without the very nature of the Roman Senate. Senators had extensive, practical experience of affairs, forming them into exactly the sort of men to come up with such a hard-headed, long-sighted policy; their elevation above day-to-day politics took much factional strife out of the process, facilitating a consensus; their life-time offices, fresh senators gradually added as others died off, gave the policy long-term stability. The institutional structure decisively influenced the institutional function, charting a course otherwise unimaginable.

We have only to contrast the foreign policy of ancient Athens or for that matter U.S. foreign policy to see the effects of other institutional structures. In the Athenians' highly direct democracy their turbulent popular assembly constantly intervened in foreign affairs. Faction raged and momentary enthusiasms often prevailed, disregarding prudent counsel, dragging foreign policy back and forth, undermining firmness, contributing not a little to defeat in the Peloponnesian War. While far more stable than Athenian democracy, American foreign policy depends up political institutions much less firm than the Roman Senate. The presidency and Congress constantly sail into the headwinds of party politics, and so foreign policy usually makes way against a fierce gale of criticism from the party-out-of-power. During President John Adams undeclared Quasi War against the French, running from 1798 to 1800, the Jeffersonians tirelessly assailed him. During the Iraq War, beginning in 2003, virtually their same speeches and articles, recycled and updated, served virtually the same purpose. Whether good or bad, we cannot but notice the influence of the institutional set-up on how the institution function.

Social facts – The modern social sciences second the teachings of classic political science. Partially in an effort to leave behind the vagaries of ethical dispute, sociologists early developed a descriptive method to discover reliable social facts, observations and predictions about aggregates of individual choice or behavior. At the same time, they paid careful attention to the structure of social systems and institutions. Among other things this methodology provides a basis for modern economics and management theory, whose successes demonstrate accuracy and usefulness. This newer approach has given a further confirmation to the older tradition of political science.

Emile Durkheim pioneered the descriptive methodology in his *Suicide*, published in 1897. By a careful study of suicide statistics, Durkheim showed a correlation between the suicide rate and other factors, say good or bad economic times. This technique avoided the notorious difficulty inherent in the study of individual motivations, instead describing more identifiable general trends and influences. To open a city phone book and pick out the future suicides embarks upon an endless inquiry into individual motivation. Yet past behavior safely predicts a suicide rate, the rise and fall tied to measurable indicia. The same can be done for the divorce rate, the crime rate, much economic behavior, and so forth. This move translates from the realm of chaos to the realm of almost science, to the social sciences. We distill the incomprehensible welter of individual motivations into clearer social facts, reliable observations and predictions about aggregates of individual choice or behavior. At the same time this route avoids the shifting sands of ethical argument, ethical norms becoming no more than an item in the observed data. This is the essence of the descriptive method.

Undoubtedly economics became the most successful of the social sciences. In economics the role of money permits statistics as a tool of analysis, achieving a precision denied sociology, psychology, or political science. Yet economics, too, finally rests on social facts abstracted in the same manner as the other disciplines. Just as political scientists posit political systems operate on interest, economists posit that economic systems operate on the profit motive. Buyers and sellers in a marketplace may display a wide variety of behavior. Some may show concern for ethical values such as fair dealing or environmental impact, while others could care less. But we expect the bottom line to decisively reflect the profit motive. Otherwise, the bottom line would elude all calculation. This social fact of profit seeking makes the marketplace comprehensible. It gives economics a foundational principle.

In their next move economists structure their system around this principle. Free-markets outperform socialism by working with rather than against the profit motive. Yet as is well known, free-markets suffer from market failures, such as recession or unemployment. These equally solid facts compel economists to constantly tinker with their economic model. Market systems and institutions require not only set up, but continual supervision and even intervention. Such devices as regulatory control and fiscal and monetary policy give some of the means. Today's high standard of living marks the level of the economists' success, but persistent shortfalls attest a lack of utter expertise. Yet compared to the past, their achievement impresses, and the same methods look the best avenue down which to search for further advances.

Modern management theory revolves around the central notions of information flow and accountability within a corporate model. That business form represents an innovation essential to modern economies. But almost like living bodies, corporations must constantly respond to changing environments and function efficiently. These require the quick interchange of accurate information and the enforcement of performance standards throughout. Management must hear the message from all reaches of the enterprise, not merely dictate down, and hold employees at all levels promptly accountable. Successful management must structure the business to respond agilely and attain maximum goals. Mechanisms like detailed and timely accounting, customer surveys, or regular performance reviews work as feedback. The black or red ink at the end of the ledger dictates the ultimate reality, continued corporate existence or demise.

Presenting in another context, economics and management theory deal with the same issues as political science. If we take the purpose of government as the public interest, then democracy attempts to set up and run a system much like a free marketplace, working on the same principles of information flow and accountability as a business corporation. Elections serve as the overriding mechanism to sort out competing interests, force information from bottom to top, and hold officials accountable. Other government designs such as monarchy choke off the people's voice and place accountability outside their control. Just as the dead hand of bad management can stifle creativity and doom a business corporation, excessive power in government's leaders cuts the people out of the process and disregards their interests.

Modern sociology in all branches follows such a pattern, striving for social facts and stressing the importance of system and institutional structure. In effect, these methods take over the techniques first applied in classical political analysis. In traditional political science, self-interest and the institutional will-to-power amounted to what we now call social facts. These forces reliably predicted aggregate behavior and the performance of political systems and institutions. In the social sciences similar social facts such as the profit motive predict the performance of systems and institutions such as the marketplace or the business corporation. This perception focuses attention at all levels upon the structure of social systems and institutions to achieve desired results.

Beginning from so similar a start, classic political science and modern social science have come to intertwine and cross-pollinate. Recent studies of bureaucracy exemplify this trend. While bureaucracy is nothing new, mass societies of necessity generated equally massive bureaucracies. This phenomenon in government has naturally attracted the attention of scholars deploying all the weapons in the present day arsenal. As an instance, the "capture theory of bureaucracy" holds that bureaucracies demonstrate a strong tendency to serve the interests of those regulated over the public interest. In other words, over time interests placed under an agency somehow manage to "capture" the agency, turning it to their purposes. The Interstate Commerce Commission (ICC) early set up to regulate the railroads is often cited. While intended to prevent monopolistic practices, the ICC quickly came to favor the railroads over the public. Exactly how such subversion occurs may prove difficult to trace in detail, which replicates the trouble sorting out individual motivations in other social settings. Yet the capture theory articulates a well-accepted social fact. The response must again come from attention to institutional design. The bureaucracy must be structured so as to maintain accountability to the public. Here we find the purpose for such rules as forcing agency employees to wait a period before going to work in the firms they regulate. This limits the "revolving door" where the bureaucracy and private firms exchange staff, setting up a comfortable and profitable relationship between the two enterprises. On the larger scale the Congress, the chief executive, and the courts must hold the bureaucracy accountable. In all of this we see applied the methods jointly developed by political science and the social sciences.

This same sort of analysis is widely applied to Congress, the presidency, and the bureaucracy, but for some reason not the Supreme Court. Yet why should techniques yielding useful information about the other branches not do the same for the judiciary? It would appear time to extend contemporary methodology to the Court.

An aristocracy of merit – To begin with structure, then, the Supreme Court runs as an aristocracy, albeit one of merit. However the sound may grate upon some sensibilities, the simple need for accurate definition must serve to excuse the offence, which amounts to no more than an accurate application of the classic terms of political science. The merciless requirement for correct description presents no other ready alternative. Since governmental form influences governmental function, we must start by proper identification of the form, taking the other steps as they come, letting the consequences fall where they may. The method forces the beginning.

In traditional political analysis "aristocracy" is a term of art, an aristocratic institution being defined as no more but no less than vesting control of office in a select group. Periodic elections serve as the defining characteristic of democracy, and in turn, lifetime tenure marks a clear transition, either to monarchy or aristocracy, assuring as it does office in the hands of a single ruler or select ruling group. Descent by birth is not a necessary ingredient to an aristocratic institution, history offering numerous instances of quite other principles of selection. While held for life, membership in the Roman Senate came only as the culmination of a long career in public office won by balloting in the Roman assemblies. The key distinction lies not in the manner of selection, but in who controls the institution. In a democracy the people retain ultimate control. In an aristocratic form the officials control the institution, outside of intervention by the people.

Accurately described in these traditional terms, the Constitution does not create a pure representative democracy at all, but a mixed form of government. The Congress and the presidency are democratic elements, but the Supreme Court an aristocratic element. By the briefest inspection this conclusion becomes inescapable. Article III provides: "The judicial Power of the United States shall be vested in one supreme Court, and in such inferior Courts as the Congress may from time to time ordain and establish. The Judges, both of the supreme and inferior Courts, shall hold their Offices during good behaviour." This language effectively confers lifetime office on the justices of the Supreme Court, precisely fitting the classic definition of an aristocratic institution. The select group of the justices controls the institution.

Clearly the Founding Fathers preferred republican institutions over monarchy or aristocracy. Why then depart from representative principles in their construction of the Supreme Court? It appears that as throughout where feasible, they were imitating the English model. Not surprisingly, the English constitutional system having grown up under royal tutelage, the monarch appointed their judges, retaining a power of removal. In the events leading up to the Glorious Revolution of 1688, this royal authority worked against the parliamentary opposition, as in politically charged cases the judges ruled for the king or suffered the consequences, being stripped of their robes. After final triumph, Parliament responded by effectually cutting the judges' leading strings. While the monarch still elevated to the bench, judges now held office during good behavior. This reform rendered the judiciary independent of the executive. However, English judges did not and still do not enjoy supremacy over Parliament in interpreting their constitution. Since that constitution remains unwritten, Parliament retains the ability to alter the fundamental law by simply passing a statute, which leaves final control with that body rather than the judiciary.

In the U.S. Constitution the Founders adopted lifetime tenure for judges to assure a similar judicial independence. In almost the same breath they adapted the English device for judicial selection to their new framework. The president replaced the king as chief executive, and in so doing, inherited the prerogative to appoint the judges, but with a check inserted by requiring Senate approval. Looking to Article II: "He ... by and with the Advice and Consent of the Senate ... shall appoint ... Judges of the supreme Court." In other words, the president nominates and the Senate must confirm the justices to the Supreme Court.

The historical record conclusively shows this two-step method elevates eminently qualified candidates to the Court. The president by virtue of his own qualifications possesses an unusual degree of ability and experience in making such choices while benefiting from wide access to information and counsel. The nomination must pass scrutiny by a chamber with a similar unusual level of ability, experience, information, and advice. The outstanding legal attainments of those confirmed attest the excellence of this method of selection. Perhaps no Supreme Court justice has fallen below the leading lawyers of the day, and many rank among the great jurists of any age.

In the terms of classical political analysis, then, the U.S. Supreme Court must be classified as an aristocracy, albeit one of merit. But classic analysis also holds that institutional structure decisively influences institutional function. Generally, aristocratic institutions function in the interests of the select class who control the institution. In addition, all institutions display an institutional will-to-power, a tendency to acquire more power. To proceed in the tradition manner next requires disclosing the interests in play as related to the attraction of power.

Judicial interests – Whatever else they may be, all justices on the Supreme Court share a closely connected set of professional and institutional interests. All are lawyers and serve on the Court. No other significant characteristics unify them all. These affiliations suffuse their attitudes and values with two readily identifiable tendencies: As lawyers they tend to prefer arrangements that confer business on their profession; as judges they tend to prefer arrangements that confer power upon their Court.

It is certainly nothing new to remark that those engaged in a common commercial enterprise show a marked tendency to promote that business. As long ago as 1776, Adam Smith memorably observed in his *Wealth of Nations*: "People of the same trade seldom meet together, even for merriment and diversion, but the conversation ends in a conspiracy against the public, or in some contrivance to raise prices."[2] Lawyers cannot be supposed to vary from this maxim, nor have they. One need only attend a state bar convention and listen carefully to hear the proof.

In the general culture references abound reflecting a public perception and grievance against lawyer's self-interested behavior, all the way from Shakespeare's "first, let's kill all the lawyers" to present day lawyer jokes. The English philosopher Jeremy Bentham, who lived 1748 to 1832, noticed that lawyers much preferred highly technical procedures and laws, since such complexity enriched their business. In his novel *Bleak House*, published in the 1850s, Charles Dickens portrayed this same complexity in probate proceedings, which made settling estates endlessly drawn out and onerously expensive. Fast forwarding to the present, Chamber of Commerce types speak of the "lawyer tax," complaining any business of sufficient size steadily leaks revenue to ongoing lawsuits. America has been called the "litigious society," where almost anyone can be sued over almost anything. All these instances show a widespread and long-standing perception about lawyers possessing a distinct set of interests, which often leave others feeling aggrieved in their own interests.

Nor can it be doubted that lawyers' interests decisively influence their behavior, indeed, decisively come to suffuse their ethical values. These interests enter into their thoughts, attitudes, and values by a thousand gaping doors, many almost unconscious. Only superficial familiarity with legal culture confirms this observation. Trial lawyers spend their professional lives suing corporations and insurance companies, frequently coming to detest all corporations and insurance companies. The lawyers who defend such cases as routinely come to regard those same trial lawyers as the incarnation of greed and sharp practice. Criminal defense lawyers grow to hate all cops, while prosecutors grow to hate what they see as the amorality, dodges, and lies of the criminal defense lawyers. All across the legal profession this same motion occurs. Typically elaborate justifications accompany the process, more or less plausible. Trial lawyers claim to stand up for the average man against the excessive power of corporate America, while their opponents claim to defend free enterprise against the excesses of the trial lawyers. Criminal defense lawyers claim to defend the rights of the accused against government abuse, while prosecutors claim to protect victims against criminals. Advocacy quickly assumes the status of personal conviction. Their occupational requirements fit a pair of spectacles to the lawyers' eyes, and by peering through the slight distortion of these lenses, that outlook becomes fixed and normal. Rationalization of professional needs hardens into ethical and worldviews.

But far from irreconcilably divided as a class, lawyers share numerous interests. Tort reform to limit damages in medical malpractice cases finds few friends on either side of the legal aisle, since the lawyers on both sides benefit from the litigation. This may serve as an exemplification of the overriding general rule: Lawyers favor more litigation rather than less, as more litigation means more business. By an extension of the same rule: Lawyers favor more power in courts rather than less, as more power equates to more litigation. The underlying imperative constantly attracts almost all varieties of the legal mind, their attitudes and values being drawn on to follow. Whether we look to the origins of the common law or contemporary legal theory, we find the lawyers faithful advocates for legal theories compatible with these inclinations.

On the Supreme Court such interested motives find similar expression in the judicial will-to-power, a tendency to constantly increase judicial power. As seasoned lawyers, the justices arrive on the bench already fitted out with the usual professional outlook. Once inside the institution, most develop further along those same lines. The psychology here is only too familiar to anyone acquainted with the corridors of government. All officials tend to demonstrate a perpetual dissatisfaction with their share of the perquisites of power and the performance in all other departments and branches. All want more of everything and have a better idea about how things should run. At the lower pay grades, officialdom quarrel endlessly over precedence, office space, funding, and staffing. At the highest levels over matters of utmost national concern, these same struggles play out on a more epic scale, as witness the turf wars between cabinet heads and the White House offices. While the Court deliberates behind an opaque screen and action takes the form of highly reasoned documents drained of such references, yet the results indicate a similar determination to assume precedence and exercise power.

Throughout government the familiar aphrodisiac of power lures on, often for what seem the best of reasons. Given the chance, almost no one can resist the temptation to do good by conferring the benefit of their own views and solutions. Their pre-eminence puts the justices in constant danger of giving in to this call. In so doing they do not see themselves as power hungry, but as following their higher nature. To paraphrase slightly what Justice William Brennan will later say, "while a man can, he must." And so with this as the mantra, over the course of the Court's history, a familiar scenario has played out over and over. Becoming convinced of their cause, the justices then seize additional power to enforce their convictions. It makes no difference to what era or great and famous case we turn: Marbury v Madison in 1803, Dred Scott in 1857, the Reconstruction and segregation cases, the cases over industrialization, the New Deal litigation, or the judicial revolution in the last half of the twentieth century. In all we see the justices take that crucial mental leap: They develop an ethical certainty, often passionately held. But nothing in the Court's charter authorizes them to act, and so they ignore previously announced limitations on their power or invent new doctrines increasing that power.

But at some level it becomes a question of what comes first, the lust for power or the love of the good. Do the judges profess their love of the good in their lust for power or does their love of the good seduce them to the delights of power? Such passions and reasons intermix so that an individual can hardly sort them out in his own soul, let alone in an historical figure. But the Court's history will show the good repeatedly redefined, yet as repeatedly in such a way as to justify additional power. This suggests that the later remains the more stable factor in the equation rather than the former, and that predictions of judicial outcomes can be more reliably made on power relationships than professed ethical justifications. The judicial will-to-power operates inexorably through all vicissitudes of doctrine.

In traditional political analysis the identification of these tendencies is an effort to account for the operation of self-interest within any political system. It will be recalled the traditional approach posits a strong tendency of individuals to act in their self-interest and for institutions to demonstrate an institutional will-to-power. These forces exert an attraction upon any issue passing through a political system. The interests of those with the power will warp outcomes in their favor. Since lawyers make up the Court and the justices control power within the institution, we should then expect results in line with their interests. The lawyer' business and the judges' power should increase. In fact, that is exactly what we will see happen as the history of the Court unfolds.

To apply the methodology of the social sciences these same tendencies amount to social facts, reliable observations and predictions of the aggregate behavior of the justices on the Court. Thomas Jefferson was greatly disappointed in the rulings of some of his appointees. Chief Justice Earl Warren was a Republican appointed by Republican president Dwight Eisenhower, but those loyalties are not taken as explaining his course on the Court. Justice Henry Blackmun was appointed by Republican Richard Nixon, but once on the Court, Blackmun authored Roe v Wade, an abomination to most of his party. As a result of these constant changes, the attempt to describe the justices in terms of ideologies, parties, or factions catches only moments in time. But the avidity of professional and institutional interests operates across time, providing a social fact.

However, since today to use the term "interested" is almost to condemn, a moment must be taken to renounce that intent. Classic political science and social science do not indulge in the illusion of "disinterested" individuals such as philosopher-kings. Instead both accept interested behavior as a basic premise and endeavor to design social systems and political institutions putting that force to work in constructive ways, free-markets and democracy for example. In such an analysis to say that lawyers display self-interest or judges a judicial will-to-power is not to condemn, but merely to describe. It is not to say they are worse than anybody else, rather that they are no different. All individuals, groups, and political institutions demonstrate a similar self-interest and a will-to-power. But properly to account for interests first requires their accurate identification. The effort so far attempts to reach that stage in the discussion.

Other structural features – But as previously said, to say interest is not to say all. Political institutions also demonstrate other tendencies resulting from their structures, as monarchies enjoy the advantages of unanimity, dispatch, and secrecy or the Roman Senate promoted a remarkably stable foreign policy. Then with respect to the Supreme Court, what other structural features can we identify that help explain their performance?

First and foremost, under the separation of powers, the Court is forced to share power with the other institutions of government, most significantly with Congress and the presidency, but also to a certain extent with the states and the bureaucracies. Congress possesses the vast initiatives inherent in legislative power, the president the vast initiatives in executive power. The states and the bureaucracies possess powers as well. The law may claim to orchestrate all, and the Court may claim primacy as the *ultimo maestro*, but the justices aren't the only ones with a baton. A great many other composers are making up scores and a great many other conductors are leading orchestras at the same time. This rivalry leaves the Court limited in a great many ways.

Second, it has been mentioned the appointment process reliably elevates highly qualified individuals. Almost all have brought to the job not only solid legal credentials, but extensive experience of practical affairs. The Court's decisions affirm the justices' legal expertise, consistently demonstrating sound knowledge of the law combined with the ability to write logically well-reasoned opinions. In the past many of the most prominent justices had already participated in government at the highest levels. Chief Justice John Marshall's political career included service as Secretary of State. His successor Roger Taney had a comparable career including the cabinet. Chief Justice Earl Warren served as governor of California. In the last half century, the trend sets toward justices fielding resumes more confined within the legal profession. This shift probably reflects increasingly bitter Senate confirmation fights, which in turn reflect the higher stakes involved in the Court's present role. To better run that gauntlet, presidents avoid nominees with strong positions previously staked out in partisan strife or powerful enemies left over from those same battles. While such restrictions may eliminate a certain broadness of outlook, present day candidates still come with generally wide experience.

Third, as an effect of this selection process, we must notice that the Court has never been recruited from the ranks of the failed or disaffected, but rather from those already successful in life, fully integrated into the prevailing social, economic, and political order. In addition, while perhaps not as hidebound as in the past, the legal profession continues to instill respect for precedent, orderly procedure, and even tradition. As a net result, we would expect such a leadership cadre little inclined toward projects to throw everything out and begin anew; we would not expect an institution so composed to stray too far from accepted ethical norms or vested interests. At the most we might anticipate the justices siding with one or another strong running social tide; at the least we would not anticipate them operating on the radical fringe. Nor are these expectations disappointed, which has proved one of the Court's abiding institutional strengths. It has always ruled in keeping with not less than a sizable minority, if not the majority. It has been said that the justices "read the newspapers," that they do not depart too far from public opinion. This feature assures the Court never leaves behind strong reinforcements, which rally to disrupt the coalescence of successful counter-attacks. For example, for all the talk about a "judicial revolution" in the later part of the twentieth century, the justices' decisions always favored powerful, perhaps even majority blocks of support. These allies turned back all efforts to reverse the Court through legislation or amendments to the Constitution. Thus, the Court has shown no inclination to enter into a true revolutionary struggle, but is strategically placed to tip the balance between the factions. While in the long run this constant tipping may travel a considerable distance, society is not violently disrupted. The Court's intervention succeeds where an institution in the grasp of more extreme elements might well fail.

Fourth, we must also remark that the Court's personnel turns over at a slow rate, conferring considerable institutional stability. Once installed justices tend to pursue a steady course, making them bastions of predictability. While individual exceptions may be cited, yet overall, the Court remains remarkably consistent for long periods.

Fifth, this steadiness operating in conjunction with the high legal attainments of the justices renders the Court well equipped to assure "the rule of law," the important concept that requires the law be stated in a comprehensible and consistent way, be stable, be interpreted in keeping with commonly understood logic, and be fairly and impartially applied. The familiar phrase "a government of laws and not of men" encapsulates the idea; sometimes, too, we hear that "the judge followed the law." We will later see the rule of law not an entirely attainable ideal; law must remain interpreted by men, a process which almost invariably injects a personal ingredient. Yet insofar as able, the law needs a stable, objective existence to inspire trust and allow reliance upon fixed standards in making decisions and guiding conduct. While it must be confessed the justices have often infused their opinions with their own preconceptions, by any reasonably standard the record shows they well maintain the rule of law. We simply do not find gross departures from objectivity such as characterize the English revolutionary era, when king and Parliament, each in their turn of dominance, perverted accepted legal rules beyond recognition in persecuting opponents.

Finally, we must observe that as a judicial institution the Court necessarily little resembles a legislative body such as Congress. The nine-member Court hears cases. The much larger two-chambered Congress enacts statutes, laws of general application. This variation in functions results in large differences. Judges must wait for a case; legislators may leap to the occasion. Judges hear only the litigants; legislators hear from anybody and everybody. Before the bench only the lawyers in the case may speak; on the legislative floor any member may come forward. The judges sit in isolated audience; the public sits in audience on the legislature. The courtroom should shut out the bias of interest; almost any interest finds a way into the lobbies of the legislature. Judges rule in the specific case; the legislature passes laws of general application. Judicial remedies set forth rights; legislation can set up vast programs and bureaucracies as well as levy taxes. Under *stare decisis*, judges follow precedent; the legislature may alter or utterly repeal a statute the next session. Under the doctrine of double jeopardy only the convicted can of appeal; in the legislature victims of crime may complain about the law as well. Undoubtedly more distinctions could be listed, but these are among the most important.

All of these differences trace to the historic roots of the Anglo-American judicial system. English courts grew up in response to a need, enforcing the criminal law and protecting other legal rights. The English Parliament grew up in response to a separate need, passing laws to govern the entire society. Even down to the present day, this division of function continues, except gradually the judiciary assumed a wider and wider role. As part of this process, the courts burst the straightjacket of old-fashioned judicial procedure. Today the parties to a lawsuit can include vast constituencies, say all black children in a metropolitan school system. The "Brandeis brief" popularized legal arguments incorporating all sorts of data, say a sociologist's study about the negative impact of segregated schools on black children. Judicial remedies have expanded so far as mandating vast social programs, say busing to achieve racial integration. Judges have been known to take over and run bureaucratic agencies, even directing the levy of taxation. But even with these and other innovations, the trammels of judicial procedure still exert an influence. Without entering into the details of any examples, as compared to the legislature, judicial procedures remain more narrowly focused, limiting the issues presented, the interests heard, and the remedies ordered.

But any complete understanding of judicial function must await an exploration of judicial power, the ability to impose one's will. This will raise the initial question: What powers do judges possess? It involves a further and contentious question: What powers should judges possess?

CHAPTER 2

The Power of the Court

One often hears that judges should interpret rather than make the law. But throughout the long history of Anglo-American jurisprudence, judges have always made the law in the process of interpreting it. Even a brief consideration shows such judicial power both necessary and useful. Yet the judges themselves never profess to legislate, resolutely expressing their opinions as interpretations. Such a lack of clarity signals a need to sort out the terminology, distinguishing legislative from judicial power.

Judicial power – Article III says: "The judicial Power of the United States shall be vested in one supreme Court, and in such inferior Courts as the Congress may from time to time ordain and establish." Raised in the English common law tradition, the Founders' legal phraseology comes from that source. By the term "judicial power" they were referring to the power historically exercised by English courts.

Looking to that legacy, we may reliably consult Sir William Blackstone and his *Commentaries on the Laws of England*, published between 1764 and 1769. Throughout this era, American judges cited Blackstone almost like the law himself, and the nearer our lawyer forefathers had their Blackstone by heart, the better they knew their trade. He describes English courts this way: "In every court there must be at least three constituent parts, ... [the] plaintiff, who complains of an injury done; ... [the] defendant, who is called upon to make satisfaction for it; and the ... judicial power, which is to examine the truth of the fact, to determine the law arising upon that fact, and, if any injury appears to have been done, to ascertain and by its officers to apply the remedy."[1]

This careful description neatly sums up a court's basic structure and function. To unpack the language, we see three actors come together in the legal forum: the "plaintiff," the "defendant," and the "judicial power," this last, the judges, often operating with the assistance of a jury. The plaintiff "complains of an injury done," either a violation of the criminal code or some other legal right. The defendant is "called upon to make satisfaction" as the wrongdoer. Since "plaintiff" or "defendant" includes the plural, we can have several of each, as well as entities such as trusts or corporations. To resolve the dispute, the "judicial power" carries out a twin-headed function: "to examine the truth of the fact" and "to determine the law arising upon that fact," about both of which more in a moment. Finally, the judicial power may "apply the remedy," a punishment such as imprisonment, money damages, or an order directing conduct.

All this sounds familiar enough, but it is still far from familiar how their role thrusts on judges their mantle as lawmakers. To understand we must first notice any case starts with an alleged violation of the law. While also familiar, this beginning often involves an initial difficulty, which goes right past those un-baptized in the seas of legal complexity, but meat and drink to lawyers. The profession grasps that the law must remain stated in more or less in general terms, while every case must remain more or less a specific set of facts, leaving a more or less complex question: How does the general law apply to the specific facts of any case? The lawyers make their living in this interstice. While from the judges' perspective, giving the answers requires them, as Blackstone says: "to determine the law arising upon the fact." More commonly today lawyers simply say the judge must "interpret the law," that is, apply the law to the case. To the uninitiated ear, such sounds a mechanical exercise, as if the judge could merely "follow the law," but in practice works not at all that way, instead imposing considerable discretion. The power of English judges to make law flowed naturally, indeed inexorably, from this function.

Law may be defined as rules of conduct enforced by government and divided into five general types: customary, statutory, executive, case, and constitutional. Customary law describes no more than prior custom and usage. While this variety has diminished toward the vanishing point, in the late medieval ages Parliament passed few statutes, leaving a wide latitude covered by no more than prior custom and usage. But today the proliferation of statutory law has overgrown this older type, vast shelves of written laws enacted by legislatures, including Congress and the states. At the same time, executive law grew exponentially, laws created by the executive branch. Executive orders by the president form a subtype, such as President Truman's executive order desegregating the armed forces. Administrative regulations make up another huge subtype, such as the Nuclear Regulatory Commission's highly technical rules for nuclear reactors. Case law is judge made law, a genre developed below. Finally constitutional law, sometimes called organic law, sets up the government, as the unwritten British Constitution or the written U.S.

Constitution.

Since any case starts when the plaintiff "complains of an injury done," the initial hurdle requires pointing out a violation of some law from one of these sources. But frequently extreme controversy exists whether any law applies to a particular complaint, raising preliminary and crucial questions. To take an instance which will recur, in 1890 Congress passed the Sherman Anti-Trust Act, which provided that: "Every contract, combination in the form of trust or otherwise, or conspiracy, in restraint of trade or commerce among the several States, or with foreign nations, is hereby declared illegal."[2] Only what exactly constitutes a "contract, combination, or conspiracy in restraint of trade?" That question has ever since exercised the expensive talents of a large segment of the legal community.

The common law procedure – To answer such questions, the English common law developed a procedure illustrated by an interesting old case, Bushell's Case[3] of 1670, which still possesses vitality. In that year the young William Penn, whose American fame rests on other laurels, but we recall an ardent Quaker, together with a fellow enthusiast named William Mead, insisted on proselytizing their religion on a London street corner, preaching to some 400 to 500 listeners. Such public preaching deliberately defied the Conventicle Act, a statute favoring the official Church of England by closing non-conformist churches. The authorities promptly arrested and charged the two with unlawful assembly, but their trial before a London jury ended in a curious denouement. The vast majority of Londoners being religious non-conformists, the jury turned out friendly to the defendants. Although the trial judge, Sir Samuel Starling, instructed the jury to convict, they refused. Enraged, he held the jurors in contempt and jailed them. One jury member, an Edward Bushell, later appealed. Up at the higher court that judge, Sir John Vaughan, ruled jurors could not be held in contempt for their verdict, freeing Bushell and establishing an important principle of jury independence. Such the barebones of the story found in the old law reports. But looking inside the procedure shows how judges operate to interpret the law, in the process coming to make law.

Blackstone said that the "judicial power" carries out two functions: first, "to examine the truth of the fact," and second, "to determine the law arising upon that fact." In modern parlance, lawyers conveniently separate these tasks, dividing them into "factual issues" and "legal issues," the twin sides of any case. The distinction conceals a crucial significance. The factual issue always asks the question: What happened? Here the initial factual issue was whether Penn and Mead preached to the crowd. Obviously they did, but the jury refused to find those facts constituted the crime of unlawful assembly. In a jury trial, the jury decides the factual issues, in a non-jury trial the judge. Bushnell's Case firmly established the rule that a judge cannot compel jurors about this side of the case, leaving them free to reach their verdict.

By contrast the legal issue always asks: What is the law? Or as lawyers say: What is the applicable law? Since jurors cannot be learned in the law, this means that the legal issues must be decided by the judge, who is so learned. As a consequence, the judge possesses final authority over the legal issues. In a jury trial, the judge instructs the jury on the law, and they apply it to the facts. Here the judge instructed the jury on unlawful assembly, although they refused to apply those instructions as he perceived correct. On appeal to higher courts, those judges consider only legal issues. Rather than hearing new evidence, they review the written record from the lower court and determine if that judge got the law right. Here the appellate court reversed the trial court on a legal issue.

It should be seen, then, that the power of judges resides mainly in their authority over the legal issues. This authority requires them to interpret the law, and in the process, allows and often compels them to make new law. We see this when we ask: What was the law the appellate judge interpreted in Bushell's Case, holding against jurors being compelled to a verdict? In the rather lengthy opinion, we find cited a variety of sources, but none say in so many words what the judge concludes. He somewhat creatively stitches together these sources to reach his interpretation. In the process he actually made a new law. His opinion is a classic example of case law, the law made by judges and found in their written decisions. Recorded from the earliest times, such case law makes up a substantial and ever growing source of law. Once a particular issue decided, that sets a precedent, a new law, supposed to be followed in future cases.

The necessity for judge made law – Since we have seen numerous sources for the law, and since we have seen none may precisely fit the facts of any given case, we must see that the process of judicial interpretation has to stay open-ended. The judges must pick and choose among the sources of law, fit together diverse laws, and adapt the law to new and unforeseen situations. As an inescapable result, judges must constantly make new law. We should also see that as was said, the power of judges to make law is both necessary and useful. In innumerable ways the scenario in Bushell's Case replicates, endlessly demanding answers. Even with the proliferation of written sources, often set down in excruciating detail, the law must remain stated in general terms. Prolixity only leads to a natural as well as opening the door to an artful confusion. It might be a legal maxim that the more the verbiage, the more the litigation. There are always gaps; new and unexpected issues come up; human ingenuity invents schemes to edge around the barriers. If judges cannot interpret and apply the law to these situations, the letter of the law would be dead to the spirit. Law would fail to govern much conduct or provide a remedy for many wrongs. The judges must inevitably make law in the process of carrying out their judicial function.

Looking back over our history, we find our judges continually so compelled. Picking a topic, the rise of the business corporation served as an essential ingredient during industrialization. But as a relatively untried concept, corporate law emerged somewhat inchoate. State legislatures passed statutes using the corporate form, promoting ventures such as canal companies or railroads. But their experience and foresight could not account for all the contingencies, anticipate all the unexpected consequences. The courts were necessarily called upon to fill up much with interpretation.

For example, in the early and well-known 1819 Dartmouth College Case, the Supreme Court itself had to interpret the "contract clause" as applied to corporations. Created in 1769 by royal charter, early in the next century, Dartmouth became embroiled in an internal quarrel between rival factions. In 1815, the New Hampshire legislature took a side in this dispute, passing a law that abrogated the original charter for a new charter. This law transferred authority to appoint the college president from the board of trustees to the state governor. But the "contract clause" in Article I says: "No State shall ... pass any ... Law impairing the Obligation of Contracts." Did this prohibit a state from passing a new law altering the earlier grant of corporate status, since that created a contract? Justice Marshall ruled yes, which riled up considerable controversy as impairing state sovereignty, a jealously guarded realm in those days. If a state law creating a corporation made an unalterable contract, in essence the state had permanently alienated a degree of sovereignty to a private entity. Justice Joseph Story's observation in concurrence greatly lessened the impact, noting a state could easily edge around the rule, simply by inserting a reservation in the initial corporate grant, retaining a right to later amend the corporate charter. How all this played out falls outside our purposes. The point is to see how unanticipated questions demand answers, and the judiciary has to give a response.

Dynamic judicial law making – But for all the necessity and usefulness, judicial law making can become highly dynamic, nor is this a recent phenomenon. Legal history is replete with judge-made law leaving the fiction of mere interpretation behind. To take a well-known instance, we may look at the prominent 1916 case of McPherson v Buick Motor Company, an opinion authored by later Supreme Court Justice Benjamin Cardozo while he sat on the New York Court of Appeals. This decision dealt with products liability law, the liability of manufacturers to consumers for injuries caused by defective products. A long series of prior cases had denied liability without "privity of contract," that is, a direct contractual relationship between manufacturer and consumer. In the leading precedent, the 1842 English case of Winterbottom v Wright,[4] the plaintiff Winterbottom drove a mail coach under contract with the Postmaster General, and the defendant, Wright, maintained the coaches under a contract with the Postmaster General. The collapse of a coach under him injured Winterbottom, who sued Wright for not properly maintaining the coach. But the court denied recovery on the ground that no privity of contract existed between Winterbottom and Wright, rather Wright's contract was with the Postmaster General.

Whatever the earlier wisdom, as industrialization proceeded apace, the world increasingly filled with manufactured products, and such a rule came to seem less and less fair. As manufacturers poured their goods in the stream of commerce, they avoided responsibility unless sold directly to the buyer, and since they usually sold through middlemen, often escaped liability for shoddy or dangerous goods. So when we come to McPherson v Buick in 1916, we find an increasingly common occurrence. McPherson bought a Buick auto, but from a dealer, not directly from the carmaker. When a wooden wheel crumbled, injuring him, Buick denied liability, raising the accepted defense. But in his opinion, Cardozo changed the law, reasoning: "If the nature of the thing is such that it is reasonably certain to place life and limb in peril when negligently made, it is then a thing of danger. ... If to the element of danger there is added knowledge that the thing will be used by persons other than the purchaser, and without new tests, then, irrespective of contract, the manufacture of this thing of danger is under a duty to make it carefully."[5]

Thus, he abrogated the doctrine of privity of contract, creating instead a new doctrine of "products liability." In future, the obligation to manufacture safe products would pass through the original purchaser, here the dealer, to the ultimate consumer, here McFadden. Plaintiffs could now recover damages for such injuries from the manufacturer. We may conclude this new rule sensibility adapted to meet changing circumstances. But we must see this was done not by the legislature, rather by a judge through judicial interpretation. Cardozo had done more than fill in a gray area; he changed accepted law; he made far-reaching legal policy; he made new law. Nor had he done anything not done by many judges before and since.

The primacy of legislation – Then finally it must be asked: What draws the line between legislation and judicial law making? A purely formal definition must occur to us: The legislature enacts legislation; the judiciary makes judge-made law. And English jurisprudence attached a crucial significance to this very distinction: Legislation commanded primacy, trumping judge-made law. Certainly, when English monarchs still made their law, they expected judges to follow the royal command at the peril of the royal displeasure. This helps explain the concern of early English jurists to maintain that fiction about interpreting rather than making law, as medieval kings brooked little encroachment upon their prerogative. When Parliament eventually seized sovereignty from the monarchy, that included a thoroughgoing assumption of legislative power, including a similar claim to primacy; that body in turn expected and received judicial deference. The power politics stand out as obvious. As Parliament took power from the monarch, they had no purpose to cede a share to the judiciary. On both theoretical and pragmatic grounds, parliamentary supremacy could cite important considerations: The democratic nature of the system demanded parliamentary statutes control judge-made law, judges being unelected. Furthermore, lawsuits usually reflected the fairly narrow interests of litigants, whereas parliamentary laws consulted interests across society as a whole.

As is well known, the Founders modeled Congress upon Parliament. Article I says: "All legislative Powers herein granted shall be vested in a Congress of the United States." At the same time, it has always been well settled that American courts should defer to legislative intent, just as English courts did. Elaborate legal doctrines set forth the way in which judges consult that meaning, although it must be remarked these no more than words on the printed page, and numerous instances show American judges ignoring or simply overriding these rules. For instance, the previously mentioned Sherman Anti-Trust Act of 1890 attempted to outlaw monopolies. Yet in the 1894 E.C. Knight Case, the Supreme Court would openly frustrate that purpose, limiting the application of the Act to almost nothing. In such situations Congress has sometimes re-passed statutes in more forceful or specific language, although neither has that always proved effective. Nevertheless, the rule continues that courts should give effect to legislative intent.

Such was the power traditionally exercised by English judges and inherited by American, in essence allowing them to make law. The term "judicial power" in the Constitution meant at least this much. But gradually American judges would acquire still more potent powers. By these gains they became the final interpreters and indeed makers of constitutional law, attaining precedence over Congress. We must turn to these innovations for an understanding of the truly remarkable power won by the Supreme Court.

Interpreting constitutional law – We will recall that constitutional law sets up the government. Since all other law flows from government, constitutional law may rightly be thought the most fundamental and important law, the progenitor of all the rest, controlling their creation and operation. But in one respect constitutional law is no different than any other law: Any constitution requires constant interpretation to cover specific situations and interface with unforeseen circumstances. The 4th Amendment may guarantee against "unreasonable searches and seizures," only what exactly qualifies as "unreasonable?" Moreover, when the 4th Amendment was ratified back in 1791, no one imagined such things as automobiles, telephones, or radios. How would the Amendment apply to these technologies? The cases and commentary attempting to give the answers fill bookshelves. The Constitution is shot through with similar generalities; social and technological change is unrelenting. Once again, unless the letter of the law is to bind in futility the spirit, a dynamic process must fill up the spaces.

Nor did English judges lack power to interpret their constitution as well as their other sources of law, and by so doing, make constitutional law in the same way they made other law. Bushell's Case stands as a perfect exemplar, amounting to judge-made law of constitutional magnitude. American judges inherited this same power. Yet in England the constitution remains unwritten with Parliament able to work a change by merely passing a statute. This feature leaves Parliament in ultimate control over their constitution and may be called a system of "parliamentary sovereignty" or "parliamentary supremacy." But American circumstances called for a single act of creation to bring forth the national government, leading to a written constitution. Congress received no delegation of power to make alterations through ordinary statutes, rather amendments wend an almost unworkable course. By contrast, American judges did not lose authority to interpret the constitutional law. Over time this incommensurability between the two constitutional schemes let American judges claim final control over constitutional law, attaining precedence over Congress, exactly reversing the power of the two branches in the English and American systems.

Such "judicial supremacy" gave American judges a unique and impressive power not shared by their English forbearers. It is at this juncture that we finally encounter the true grounds of controversy over judicial law making.

The power side of law making – As judges went about making law in the Anglo-American tradition, a byproduct often included more power for their courts. When Justice Cardozo enunciated a new doctrine of products liability, he not only opened the courts to a new species of litigants, but simultaneously expanded the courts' power to cover those lawsuits. More legal rights automatically mean more to sue over, what lawyers call "a cause of action." The more causes of action, the more power for the judges and the more business for the lawyers. All of which goes far to explain the professional enthusiasm for inventing new causes of action, their ingenuity and persistence never abating, no wrong a lawyer can conceive worse than no right over which to sue, no right to sue being no fee. Even in the Founders' day, the law graphically exhibited the effects of this phenomenon over time. Through the accepted process of judicial interpretation, the judges had fashioned ever more legal rights, widening their reach, adding to the lawyers' client and fee base.

But in American circumstances this long-accepted procedure blended easily to become a more radical procedure: Judges not only interpreting the ordinary law in such a way, but interpreting the constitutional law so as to aggrandize power. All the cases marking the Court's ascent to power illustrate this method of judicial self-help, the connected doctrines of "judicial supremacy" and "judicial review" standing as potent testimony. Under judicial supremacy, judges possess final power to interpret the constitution, rather than the legislature. Judicial review is a necessary corollary, judges' power to declare legislation unconstitutional and hence void. And the judiciary definitively acquires both these powers by their own rulings, further rulings continually extending them. These doctrines are uniquely American and initiated a distinctive governmental form, the judiciary and the Supreme Court especially acquiring far-reaching control over the national agenda.

The rise of judicial supremacy – The Constitution contains no express grant of judicial supremacy, nowhere saying in so many words that the Court possesses final authority over constitutional interpretation. Nor does the Constitution specifically mention judicial review, nowhere saying judges can declare acts of Congress unconstitutional. Whether the Founders implied such authority continues a topic of endless legal and scholarly debate. But as a practical matter, these doctrines remain not in doubt. Today the Court possesses both powers in plenitude.

We may easily trace the inception and growth of these doctrines through a series of stages, beginning with the famous 1803 case of Marbury v Madison. From this fount flow all the rest. In that case Chief Justice John Marshall will persuasively and successfully claim the power of judicial review, that is, the power to declare laws unconstitutional and hence void. Without this first step, the journey could not have begun. Yet at this inception the concept was announced in a highly limited form, over and over the judges pledging never to void a law except in clear-cut cases beyond a reasonable doubt, where Congress obviously violated the Constitution. This may be called the "original doctrine of judicial review" and would not have amounted to that much, since Congress seldom lacks a good argument about constitutionality. And in fact, the Supreme Court never declared another congressional law unconstitutional for over half a century.

Finally, in 1857 with the notorious Dred Scott Case, this original, more limited doctrine of judicial review suffered an unacknowledged abrogation. But the present hostility expressed for that case relates only to part of the ruling, the holding the Constitution guaranteed a "right to slavery," not the concomitant expansion of judicial power. Commentators routinely flail the first, while failing even to remark the second. Yet since a "right to slavery" hardly stands clear-cut in the Constitution, reaching that conclusion required abandoning that restraint. While shortly thereafter in 1865, the 13th Amendment abolished slavery, the justices would never return to the original, limited doctrine of judicial review. From that day to this, any restraint to "clear-cut" cases disappears.

This momentous power shift would become fully evident during Reconstruction, stretching from roughly 1865 to 1876. During that era, rather than bound by "clear-cut" constitutional meaning, the justices began to freely interpret away clear constitutional meaning and as freely interpret in their own meaning. Congress proposes and the states ratify three great Reconstruction Amendments: In 1865 the 13th Amendment abolished slavery; in 1868 the 14th Amendment guaranteed the freemen's civil rights; in 1870 the 15th Amendment granted them the franchise; and for good measure, the Civil Rights Act of 1875 prohibited segregation. But the Court would shortly interpret away the intent of these great legislative initiatives, negating their obvious purposes. Finally in 1896 with Plessy v Ferguson, the Court would interpret into the Constitution the doctrine of "separate but equal," opening the way for enactment of segregation. Thus, the Court created and consolidated a new, much more potent version of judicial review. Rather than limited by clear constitutional meaning, judicial review could interpret away clear constitutional meaning and interpret in wholly unexpected constitutional meaning.

As the nineteenth century closed, the judicial invention of "substantive due process" still further increased judicial power. Under this doctrine, judges claimed power to declare laws unconstitutional which they deemed "unreasonable." And since nothing precisely defined "reasonable," this fresh authority let them void laws upon no more than their preconceptions, re-constituting the justices to sit as a sort of "super-legislature," reviewing every law, situated to replace the legislative judgment with their own judgment. Wielding this doctrine in the name of property and contract rights, the Court would strike down an array of laws aimed at ameliorating the ills of industrialization, such as wage and hour laws and workers compensation. Judicial supremacy acquired yet more potency.

However, during the crisis of the Great Depression, beginning in 1929, the Court suffered a serious institutional setback. Using substantive due process and a narrow reading of the commerce clause, the justices voided virtually the entire first round of New Deal legislation, President Franklin Roosevelt's blueprint for reversing the economic collapse. In response Roosevelt launched an unprecedented institutional counter-attack, his famous or infamous court-packing plan. Since the Constitution does not set the number of justices, he proposed adding one new member to the Court for every justice over 70, prospectively infusing appointees more favorable to his views. While savagely criticized and never enacted, yet in the face of this assault the justices beat a hasty retreat. The Court quickly began to approve new laws identical in almost all respects to those just previously declared unconstitutional, in the same breath publicly renouncing both substantive due process and a narrow reading of the commerce clause.

But this humiliation proved no more than momentary, commentators finding in the 1932 Carolene Products Case the germ of the idea which would regenerate the Court's lost powers. In writing this opinion, Justice Harlin Fiske Stone began by promising in future to "presume" the constitutionality of legislation, in essence a return to the original, "clear-cut" limits on judicial review. But then dropping down in the most famous footnote in judicial history, Footnote Four, Justice Stone expressed some hesitations and second thoughts: He mused such a presumption might not apply to cases involving the Bill of Rights, basic political processes, religion, or national or racial minorities. These prophetic hints forecast if they did not suggest the line along which the spring would recoil. If a presumption of constitutionality did not apply in these areas, what standards would apply? It would turn out a rebirth of substantive due process without the name attached.

In the last half of the twentieth century, the Supreme Court would take up this Footnote Four Program, leading a "judicial revolution," reclaiming the power lost during the New Deal and more. As part of this revolution the justices rewrote constitutional law across wide stretches, repealing their earlier doctrine of separate but equal, re-drawing the boundary between church and state, abrogating earlier restraints on obscenity, promulgating a new code of criminal procedure, carefully guarding rights to welfare, ordering a top to bottom civil service system, legalizing abortion, and more. As seen from the extent of the enumeration, the Court successfully asserted control over large reaches of the national agenda.

The Court not only re-asserted a dynamic doctrine of judicial supremacy, but further expanded the earlier version, developing broad techniques for mass litigation and direct supervision over legislative programs and executive departments. Through class actions judges assumed jurisdiction of lawsuits involving millions of litigants, including vast constituencies and causes. Through injunctions they directed the day-to-day operations of bureaucratic agencies. In this capacity they ordered massive busing to integrate the public schools, ran prisons, and redesigned the mental health care system, going so far in some instances as to command the levy of taxes, a power tradition scrupulously reserved to the legislature.

In addition, the Court invented new doctrines to further enhance their power, doctrines called "incorporation" and "preferred rights." Under the doctrine of "incorporation," they "incorporated" the Bill of Rights against the states. That is, since the Bill of Rights originally applied only against the federal government, now they applied those rights against the state governments as well, giving them much greater power over the states. Under the doctrine of "preferred rights" (also called "fundamental rights"), they could designate rights as "preferred," and then (under the doctrine) any government interference with the right had to withstand a "stricter scrutiny" and had to be in "the least intrusive way." Since nothing precisely defined either the "preferred" rights, the "stricter scrutiny," or the "least intrusive way," this doctrine possessed an easily facility for the Court, letting the justices interfere themselves whenever and wherever they preferred.

In sum, by its own decisions the Supreme Court has constantly conferred more power on itself. By this process and from uncertain beginnings, judicial review and judicial supremacy have undergone a relentless growth. While the justices proclaimed theoretical restraints and pragmatic obstacles sometimes intervened, no effective mechanism within the system of checks and balances prevented their re-interpretation of their own powers, which they constantly increased. Today the Court exercises utter hegemony over constitutional interpretation, which in effect includes authority to amend previously clear constitutional meaning. This story records a remarkable ascent to power.

Justifications for judicial supremacy – The Court's ascent to power coincides with a relentless growth of government at all levels, local, state, and federal, until today there is not much government is not called upon to do or does not take upon itself, filling up much more available social space than at the founding. In this wider context the Court's gains made up no more than a part, all the political subdivisions questing for power, conflicting over the share of each. Gradually the federal government has attained almost complete predominance over the states. Within the federal structure, the president has aggrandized largely in relation to Congress; the Court has aggrandized at the expense of Congress and the presidency. But what distinguishes the Court's rise involves a significant transformation in the very form of the government.

Americans have always and still conceive their government a democracy. As has been said, in the precise terminology of classic political analysis, that description never fit the actual facts. The Constitution creates a mixed institutional form, Congress and the presidency being democratic elements, the Court an aristocratic element. Yet despite this discrepancy, the judiciary began so narrowly constrained as left the overall design correctly regarded democratic, those institutions clearly preponderate. But the ascent of Court has as clearly altered the relationship between the parts. The unelected Court has come to exercise major control over much of the national life, supplanting the elected Congress or the president.

The upward arc of the Court's power has been briefly traced, but since Americans still think and speak as if their government a democracy, it must be asked: Under what rationale has this alteration been justified as harmonious with democratic principles? And generally we find three rationales advanced over time, all variations on the same theme: First, it is maintained the Court's powers part and parcel of the Founders' "original intent," included in their scheme to limit government, integral to the separation of powers and system of checks and balances. Second, it is maintained the Court protects "the will of the people" as expressed in the Constitution, preventing violations by

Congress or the president. Third, it is maintained the Court protects minority rights against the majority. However, none of these arguments square with traditional democratic theory, nor do any accurately explain how the Court's power arose or has worked in practice.

The first rationale rests upon an appeal to authority, describing the Court's role as the Founders' "original intent." Indeed, the Founders did mean to circumscribe government within delegated powers, divide those powers between the branches, and restrain the power of each against the other. But since as already seen, the Court's present powers acquired, not original, the current balance of power cannot be correctly described as "original intent," as built into the initial constitutional design. In any event, as usual with arguments from authority, conceding the point would still leave us searching for sufficient reasons upon which to rest the authority.

The second rationale attempted to provide such a sufficient reason: It argued that the Court would protect the people's will as expressed in the Constitution, preventing excesses by a momentary majority in Congress, in that cause enlisting judicial review to void unconstitutional acts. This does employ at the fulcrum a democratic principle, the will of the people, the Court keeping government within the terms of the people's original grant. But while plausible in statement, it has failed to describe performance. Over and over the justices have not defended, but changed constitutional meaning.

For a routine example, we may take the mentioned 4th Amendment guarantee against unreasonable search and seizure. Upon inquiry we find the original, well-understood rule still admitted improperly seized evidence at a criminal trial, leaving the remedy a lawsuit for damages against the offending officers. Then under the rationale as announced, if the people in 1791 had expressed their will by ratifying the 4th Amendment, the Court's task was to uphold that original, well-understood rule. But beginning with the 1914 Weeks Case,[6] the justices created a wholly new "exclusionary rule," prohibiting the use of improperly seized evidence. This rule may or may not rest upon sound policy, but cannot be claimed as part of the 4th Amendment as initially promulgated. Nor can it be claimed the justices consulted the people in mandating this new doctrine, rather their own notions about the need for reform.

Upon further inquiry, we find almost the entire Constitution has undergone a similar process, the original meaning continually changed by the Court. In fact, judicial review has almost never been used to defend the Constitution against the excesses of a momentary majority in Congress. Instead, the power has been consistently used to amend previously accepted constitutional meaning in keeping with the justices' own views. This record compels recognition that the practice fails to conform to the theory, cutting the ground from beneath the logic.

The obviousness of this situation has assisted a gradual shift toward a preference for the last rationale, that the Court protects minority rights against the majority. Yet as a justification consistent with democratic principles, this argument suffers from a largely unacknowledged difficulty: While in one sense democracy consists of a set of rights, including minority rights, yet on any view those rights include a right to democratic process. Then to leave that process behind must also leave behind a complete description of democracy. But such a maneuver has to underlie this argument. Before the Court can successfully defend minority rights against the majority, we must confer upon the Court power over the majority. This step necessarily switches from democratic process to aristocratic process, transferring control to the lifetime Court, away from the elected Congress. We must finally come to recognize and accept the consequences of this move. Such a delegation of power to an unelected judiciary simply cannot be defended as a democratic device.

Classical liberalism – If we are to appeal to the Founders' authority, about this issue they spoke clearly and eloquently. Whatever else their variety of opinions, first and foremost the Founding Fathers were classical liberals, that tradition advocating representative democracy. We may reliably consult them, then, about the central concern of that tradition to unify the concept of rights with democratic process.

The Declaration of Independence remains their most memorable and influential proclamation, indeed, accepted as setting forth the principles underlying the American system, a precursor to the Constitution regarded as more fundamental still. To re-quote that famous and well-known language: "We hold these truths to be self-evident: that all men are created equal, that they are endowed by their Creator with certain unalienable rights, that among these are life, liberty, and the pursuit of happiness. That, to secure these rights, governments are instituted among men, deriving their just powers from the consent of the governed."

We immediately discern a triad of general concepts, all expressed together: "equality," "unalienable rights," and "the consent of the governed," that last a set phrase for democracy. To work these out in brief detail reveals an essential inseparability, the ideas as conjoined as the sides of a triangle. To detach any idea from the other destroys the very nature of the intellectual structure, just as it would the geometric figure.

While "equality" may remain an elusive ideal, yet neither has it ever been that difficult to discern the essential shape, however difficult the details. At the outset we trip over the obvious inequities of birth, fortune, and the vagaries of economic, political, and social systems. The genetic lottery notoriously picks winners and losers randomly, the Newtons and Einsteins as compared to us ordinary drudges; some possess boundless energy or greater determination; others inherit wealth or the advantages of nurture and education; just being born in the developed world improves your odds. From such a deck of circumstances we can never hope to deal equality of results. Nor can we finally and forever list what qualifies as equality of results, ultimate realization constantly glimmering ahead and never entirely in reach, the concepts not completely stable but evolving, details extremely difficult. For instance, does equality mean race neutral admission to graduate school or affirmative action to remedy past discrimination? Our history should make us familiar with numerous conundrums of the like, convincing us such questions will never go away. Yet when all is said and done, equality surely amounts at least to this: At some starting point all individuals possess equal worth, which we may call the ideal of individual equality. In some way, then, we must strive for equality of opportunity, maximizing each individual's opportunity to develop full human potential. And this effort must include large freedom to make our own choices, since such freedom lies at the heart of individual autonomy and essential to personal development. In government such freedom must generate a counterpart, an ideal of political equality, the opportunity of all to participate and make their own choices. Among the available types of government, only democracy can hope to fulfill such a vision of equality.

In an exactly similar way consensus surrounds "unalienable rights," yet the concept continues controversial and evolving, the details extremely difficult. We may broadly think of "individual rights" as those with which government should not interfere, embarking with some success upon an enumeration, such as universal enfranchisement, freedom of speech, and so forth. Yet at the fringes a lot stays up for grabs. It does not appear finally settled: Does a woman have a right to choice for an abortion or the unborn a right to life against an abortion? A multitude of such complexities have presented, do present, and will relentlessly present. This recognition must inevitably throw us back upon political process, the method to find the answers to the questions. At some moment it always becomes: What should the law be? At that same moment it also always becomes: What institution should decide the law?

Here we find in waiting "the consent of the governed," that is, representative democracy. That process, too, is a right and surely among the most fundamental, flowing inexorably from the principle of "equality," from the "ideal of political equality." Then how can we properly establish or maintain any of our other rights while ignoring that right to democratic process? Just as the scientific method only accepts results tested by observation and experimentation, democracy only accepts outcomes validated through democratic process. Democracy is democracy is democracy; there is no other democratic process except democratic process. Historically that comprehension culminated in the Glorious Revolution of 1688, which in England finally established once and for all that form of government. The same demand motivated the American Revolution and Constitution. In those days recent and graphic experience enforced the lessons about autocracy. Classic liberalism perceived democracy as the fount and guardian of equality and all other rights.

The Declaration proclaims an indivisible trinity in government: equality, individual rights, and democracy. All are inseparably bound together. Either in theory or in practice, none can fully exist outside the presence of the others. This core describes the Founders' creed of classical liberalism. Such a summation not only appeals to their authority, but marshals their reasons.

The democratic contradiction – Then returning to the Court as a defender of minority rights, we must see that rationale demands some justification outside classic democratic theory. Nor do we find this wanting, in its place substituted an argument that in effect turns democracy against itself. The first step begins by observing that majorities may violate the rights of minorities, called the "democratic contradiction." In the next step, rather than regarding democracy as the source and mainstay of our rights, that process becomes suspect as a possible, even likely, source of oppression. Therefore, the logic concludes that the Court must serve as guardian, defending minorities against the majority. Historical instances adduce the proof, such as the laws outlawing seditious speech and the Court's line of cases gradually relaxing those laws. But proponents always offer racial segregation as the prime example, definitively illustrating majority oppression, the 1954 Brown Case conclusively demonstrating how the Supreme Court protects minorities.

Yet serious problems beset this argument. In the first place, the reasoning suffers from an inherent contradiction of its own. If the majority is not to rule, then some minority must rule. It would seem that minority just as inclined to oppress the majority as the other way around. So whatever the faults of the majority, minority rule can do no more than reverse the winners and losers. This may be called the "inherent contradiction of minority rights," that in the name of their rights, the minority may oppress the majority. In the second place, the historical proofs pick and choose among instances. If we replace such selectivity with the completeness of the historical record, a rival interpretation emerges not so favorable to the Court.

The example of segregation – The key example of segregation quickly serves to illustrate this weakness. Let us begin by giving every credit to the Court for finally in 1954 with Brown reversing the doctrine of separate but equal. As will later be developed, that case probably qualifies as the greatest ever handed down by the Court. Yet let us not fail to put Brown in historical perspective. Again to re-tell in brief outline about Reconstruction: In 1865 the 13th Amendment abolished slavery; in 1868 the 14th Amendment guaranteed the freedmen their civil rights; in 1870 the 15th Amendment granted them the franchise; the Civil Rights Act of 1875 prohibited segregation. But in the coming decades the Court decisively intervened, interpreting away all that legislative intent. This series of cases defeated congressional Reconstruction, permitting gradual black disenfranchisement and the enactment of segregation. In 1896, Plessy v Ferguson placed the capstone on this legal edifice, elevating separate but equal to constitutional status.

Let us consider: How does this fuller narrative demonstrate the Court as a superior guardian over minority rights? As for the "democratic contradiction," the majority oppressing the minority, if these constitutional amendments and congressional statute did not stand for the will of the majority, what did? Themselves democratically arrived at, these laws put democracy to work on the rest of the problem. With their rights, most importantly the ballot in hand, the freedmen would sort out their own place in society. Such an agenda hardly convicts the majority of oppressing the black minority, rather the contrary. But the Southern white minority objected under their own theory of minority rights, claiming freedom of association and contract, freedom from excessive government interference in their lives, leaving them room to socialize and do business only with whom they chose, in short a right to segregation. If this position does not show the "inherent contradiction of individual rights" in action, the minority in the name of their rights oppressing the majority, it at least shows a minority seeking to discriminate against a minority. While for its part, the Supreme Court did indeed defend minority rights, only not the rights of the black minority, but those rights advocated by the segregationist minority. As an added bonus, their victories before the Court rendered Congress impotent against segregation, unable to act for the foreseeable future. Under the doctrine of judicial supremacy, the Court has the final say, and the Court had spoken. Democracy suffered rejection and defeat at all levels. Only half a century later did the justices relent, at last in Brown overturning their own earlier rulings. When this legal dam at last burst, the democratic river could once more flow to the sea. Congress quite promptly passed the Civil Rights Act of 1964 and the Voting Rights Act of 1965, achieving goals originally sought during Reconstruction.

Looking back with full historical perspective, where does this longview leave the Court as *par excellence* defender of minority rights? Today those old notions about a right to segregation have suffered an utter rejection. Then don't we have to ask: If in the past democracy got it right, why now reject that process? If in that same past the Court got it so wrong, why in the present put so much trust in that institution? The answer cannot be because of something inherent about the democratic process; that has not changed. Nor can it be something inherent about the Court's institutional nature; neither has that changed.

Rights regardless – Thus in the end it is found that a justification for the Court's present power must rest on ideological or ethical grounds, amounting to an argument from ends rather than about means. Quite simply put, those who support the Court's present course, support the Court. Their logic is outcome driven, requiring we first accept the overriding value of certain ideological or ethical norms, pronounced or implied. On examination these center around protecting racial minorities, the Bill of Rights, and a new right to privacy. Accepting these predetermined ends, the Court may indeed be seen as defending them. And it must be confessed such a view enjoys widespread if not monolithic support.

This mirrors an attitude characterizing much modern political discourse, where we constantly hear democracy referred to as a set of rights, while concerns about democratic process recede toward the vanishing point. These preferred rights draw upon various sources, like the Bill of Rights or the Universal Declaration of Human Rights. And the contours steadily undergo revision and expansion. For example, the Universal Declaration of Human Rights states: "Men and women ... have the right to marry and to found a family," a family being described as "the natural and fundamental group unit of society." Current efforts would extend this coverage to same sex marriages and families. But whatever the rights included, democracy becomes seen not so much democratic process, a means, as the ideological or ethical goals, an end. If democracy fails to reach the preconceived outcome, it is simply rejected. People demand their "rights" period, any obstacle, even democratic process, being unacceptable.

Comparing institutional performance – The Court's ascent to power constantly brings us face to face with those as constant conflicts with Congress, one going along with the other. These institutional clashes demonstrate stark contrasts, Congress enacting laws then voided by the Court. We witness the spectacle of one political institution, the Congress, laboring to bring forth, while another political institution, the Court, declares that progeny stillborn. These diametric opposites seem to cry out for a comparison of institutional performances. In any particular controversy, did Congress or the Court do a "better" job? And overall, how does the record of these rival institutions stack up? Such a weighing against each other precisely describes the analysis just carried out with respect to Reconstruction.

But exactly here the discussion threatens to return to the beginning and become circular. At the start, we noted that the current approach to the Court overwhelmingly ideological or ethical. Those approving the Court's present course support the Court, and vice versa. But since ideological and ethical arguments remain intractable, the sides merely butt heads, lacking a method to reach consensus. It was suggested such impasse might be avoided by thinking first about political processes rather than political outcomes. However much we might differ over better solutions, yet it was hoped we might be able to agree on the better way to reach those solutions. In pursuit of that effort, we returned to classic political analysis, examining political structure, never forgetting the influence of interests, keeping a focus on the power shift. Yet it was also conceded that ethical performance amounts to an overriding consideration in judging any institution of government. What we want is a just government, results in line with our ethical values. So does it turn out the argument has just been chasing its tail? When we come to a question such as whether or Congress or the Court has done a "better" job, how can we judge except by applying some ethical standard?

It must be confessed this obstacle does not appear entirely surmountable. At some level, crucial ethical choices must be made. Yet the classic approach can legitimately assert to have clarified the circumstances in which those choices must be made. In the first place, it can now be seen that in the realm of politics certain ethical values compel acceptance of certain institutional forms. In particular, if classical liberalism's core ideal of equality commands our allegiance, that value forces democracy as the government. Only democracy lives up to the ideal of political equality by attempting to assure equality of opportunity for all to participate. Under whatever pronounced rationale, all the other governmental types turn their backs upon that principle.

Now the U.S. Congress is a quintessential institution of representative democracy. As such, congressional laws are by definition "majoritarian," reflecting the will of the majority through the processes of representative democracy. This principle of majority rule flows inexorably from the ideal of political equality, since no way exists to count individuals equally without awarding victory to the side with the most votes. This may be far from saying Congress neglects all minority interests or rights, since the votes to pass any measure depend upon coalitions. Nor can the ruling party ever banish the fear of their majority washing away in the next electoral tide, which generally encourages inclusion rather than exclusion of a broad range of views. Still and all, a congressional law stands as the expressed will of at least a temporary working majority, not a minority.

By contrast, Supreme Court rulings never represent the democratically expressed will of the majority, but the will of at least five out of the nine justices. While not to say those decisions may not coincide with the public will, this does say the process takes place outside popular control. But if congressional laws do stand for the will of the majority, then whenever the Court exercises judicial review to void a law, that definitely amounts to a minority outcome. Since most of the Court's famous cases exhibit exactly this feature, we must admit the justices rather frequently impose their will upon the majority.

In comparing the institutional performance, then, it must be conceded: If the right to democracy stands essential on our list of fundament rights, only Congress realizes that right. It follows only Congress embodies those ethical values gathered into the ideal of equality. Based upon those values, Congress must do a "better" job. By the same token, if we are still to prefer the Court, that preference must rest on some rights superior to the right to democracy and on some ethical grounds superior to the ideal of equality.

Thinking about the Court in institutional terms also discloses other factors that strongly shape performance and must be considered in any comparison with Congress. The professional interests of the lawyer class and the justices' institutional will-to-power tend to influence the Court, not necessarily attracting down a path coincident with the public interest. However, as a leadership cadre the justices are drawn from those with proven records of success in their profession and large experience of practical affairs, having already developed attachments to dominant social, economic, and institutional interests. As a result, they generally avoid radicalism, instead reflecting some large segment of established opinion. And their capacity combined with their lifetime tenure, which confers long-term stability, make the Court well adapted to uphold the rule of law, enforcing objective and rational legal norms. It also was seen judicial procedure and remedies remain somewhat narrowly focused. But none of these institutional characteristics appear to confer a decisive advantage upon the Court over Congress.

It should be recalled in making a comparison that the legislature and courts grew up in response to different needs, which may be seen by looking back at the English experience. Actually, the judiciary coalesced earlier, assigned by the monarch the onerous tasks of enforcing the criminal law and resolving other legal disputes. Parliament evolved more slowly as a source of statutory law of general application. In these origins neither evidenced much attention to precise theory about proper institutional functions, and the compartments between them hardly stayed airtight. Parliament sometimes conducted criminal trials, for example, in the unhappy reign of Charles I, condemning two of his ministers through the procedure called attainder, the Earl of Strafford and the Archbishop William Laud, executed in 1639 and 1645 respectively. Of interest, the U.S. Constitution prohibited attainder in Article I. But impeachment, another judicial procedure carried out by Parliament, was a power inherited by Congress and still alive in our constitutional system. As for the judiciary, we have already witnessed how from the earliest time the judges in effect made laws of general application.

Despite this lack of theoretical tidiness, a division of labor clearly appears, and no question arises about the preferability of courts to perform their more traditional roles, that is, enforcing the criminal law or resolving other legal disputes. It must also be accepted modern complexity expands lawsuits to sometimes enormous size, involving governmental bureaucracies, multi-national corporations, or thousands of similarly situated individuals. The legislative body is ill adapted to decide these specific legal cases. Several considerations make this obvious: The members are not for the most part learned in the law; size renders the chamber a clumsy device to develop detailed interpretations of law applicable to specific fact situations; deliberations are open to influence; time is taken up with other matters; the body meets in only one place and only for limited sessions. Whereas judicial procedure focuses upon the immediate case; the judges are learned in the law; improper bias may be largely excluded; the courts are spread across the land and open at all times. Nor should a real question come up about the power of judges to in effect make law in these cases, including even constitutional law. The reasons have already been discussed.

Instead, the conflicts all occur as a result of those powers assumed by the Court under judicial supremacy, which renders the justices the final arbiters and makers of constitutional law. Crossing that threshold judges leave behind deciding discreet cases and step forward as the ultimate lawgiver to the nation, supplanting the legislature. In terms of institutional power politics, the encounters between the Court and Congress all take place in this portal to primacy. At this highest level the attempt to sort out proper judicial and legislative functions turns into the question: Which should have ultimate power?

Dead controversies – In comparing the Court to Congress, we have seen the response can favor the Court only at the expense of democratic principles. Nor has anything about the Court's institutional nature tipped the scales decisively toward its side. Insofar as the methods of classic political analysis will carry us, this looks to have wrung the pith out of that fruit. The approach promises to yield no further information. But in making the comparison still another method may avail. History is the laboratory of political science, providing demonstrative evidence of how institutions actually work in practice. Conveniently for such historical studies, the passage of time often permits a consensus to emerge. Numerous once contentious issues exhibit such a state of resolution. Few today will espouse the divine right of kings once so dear to the hearts of France's Louis XIV or England's own James I. Nor will many argue against religious toleration, a notion once so little acceptable to either Catholic or Protestant. Speaking directly to Congress and the Court, we find all the great controversies before around World War II exhibit such a state of resolution.

These are "dead" controversies, which for that reason escape the ethical quandary. Embalmed in the history books, the cadavers from these old political wars await a post mortem. To examine them reveals a consistent pattern: Present opinion would overwhelming conclude Congress fought in better causes, not the Court. To run these briefly in review: While the Court held slavery implied in the constitutional text, Congress battled to victory in the Civil War, expunging slavery. During Reconstruction, Congress put in place a program for a democratic evolution, which would have allowed the freedmen to work out their own place in the society. The Reconstruction Amendments conferred the vote and their other civil rights, while the Civil Rights Act of 1875 aimed to prevent segregation. But the Court interpreted away all this great legislative effort, finally anointing the doctrine of separate but equal with their constitutional imprimatur in 1896 with Plessy v Ferguson. Adding to the effect, under judicial supremacy the Court had the final word, rendering Congress impotent to act further against segregation. During industrialization the Court invented the entirely new doctrine of substantive due process, permitting the justices to void as unconstitutional any law they found "unreasonable." Using that sliding scale they turned back numerous reforms aimed at the ills of industrialization. When Congress responded to the crisis of the Great Depression with the New Deal, the Court voided all the initial round of legislation, only relenting under the threat of Roosevelt's court packing plan. In all these conflicts the verdict of history has decisively gone with Congress and against the Court every time.

But this historical consensus only carries so far, say to the middle of the twentieth century. Beyond that cutoff date, we again enter the land of the living, where interests and factions warp attitudes. Over live controversies such as affirmative action, religion, abortion, and the rest, there are irons in the fire, careers and fortunes to be made, strongly held convictions. Whether cynical or sincere, the rhetoric never lets up. Yet we have good reasons to persist in the way of classic analysis. At the very least keeping a focus on institutional performance promises to disclose with additional clarity that side of these disputes. Since all political controversies must pass through an institutional process to reach resolution, and since we have seen institutional nature influences outcomes, accounting for these factors cannot but assist to explain much, throwing light on the actors' motivations to assume their roles in the present drama. At the same time, this scrutiny forces into the open their interests and claims to power, exposing a great many pretensions and rationalizations. Just as this approach sheds fresh light on topics like Reconstruction or industrialization, there is every reason to think it will reveal much about the here and now. It lays bare the persistent and underlying struggle for power, facilitating a more objective assessment of what is really going on.

It must, then, become our purpose to re-read those great and famous cases making up the history of the Court, having these considerations in mind. This is to trace the Court's ascent to power, which encompasses all the other topics. This upward arc begins with the origin and inception of the doctrine of judicial review, that initial and fundamental assumption of power leading to all the other powers.

CHAPTER 3

Judicial Review at Inception

The origins of judicial review put in mind the well-remember observation by Justice Holmes: "A very common phenomenon, and one very familiar to the student of history, is this. The customs, beliefs, or needs of a primitive time establish a rule or a formula. In the course of centuries the custom, belief, or necessity disappears, but the rule remains. The reason which gave rise to the rule has been forgotten, and ingenious minds set themselves to inquire how it is to be accounted for. Some ground of policy is thought of, which seems to explain it and to reconcile it with the present state of things; and then the rule adapts itself to the new reasons which have been found for it, and enters on a new career. The old form receives a new content, and in time even the form modifies itself to fit the meaning which it has received."[1]

Judicial review has followed a similar pattern over a shorter course. The power began life as a legal device of British colonialism, as a royal prerogative, as an authority to void laws passed by the colonial legislatures that conflicted with British laws. But with the American Revolution, this "necessity disappears." So in the early days of the Republic, "ingenious minds set themselves to inquire how" it might be "accounted for" in "the present state of things." And it occurred to some ingenious judges to account for it by assuming it unto themselves, turning it into a judicial power, turning it into the authority of judges to void laws passed by the legislature as conflicting with the constitution, that is, by assuming unto themselves a power to declare laws unconstitutional. In the process, the rule acquired "new reasons and enters on a new career," explained as a way to assure limited government, while doing double duty in sustaining federal supremacy over the states. In Holmes' terms, "the old form receives a new content, and in time even the form modifies itself to fit the [new] meaning."

Parliamentary supremacy – In the first place, English judges held no power to void parliamentary statutes. Parliament reigned supreme over their constitution, which we may call "parliamentary supremacy."

Returning to Blackstone's *Commentaries*, published between 1764 and 1769, that pre-eminent authority states their settled rule: "[Parliament] hath sovereign and uncontrollable authority in making, confirming, enlarging, restraining, abrogating, repealing, reviving, and expounding of laws."[2] The Founding Fathers knew their Blackstone, which leaves no doubt they knew Parliament supreme over the British constitution. All the long revolutionary strife in the mother country, culminating in the Glorious Revolution of 1688, had striven toward sovereignty for Parliament. After fighting free from monarchy, that great deliberative body made no move to thrust themselves beneath the judiciary as an alternative. Parliament decided about the constitutionality of laws; the judges held no veto. Since America took her jurisprudence almost whole from England, whence then came judicial review?

The origins of judicial review – Looking back, the origins trace to the needs of empire, which led to a legal device, a royal prerogative that later morphed, altering shape into judicial review. Empire was nothing new to the English, whose monarchs had ruled over foreign dependencies from medieval times, and they had time-tested techniques to keep a tight rein on far-flung possessions. In the American colonies, a crown charter gave legal existence to a government for each, although these charters later suffered abrogation, replaced with elaborate written instructions issued the royal governors. In either event, these instruments all set forth a plan of government, closely mirroring the English model, serving like so many mini-constitutions. The royal governor stood in for the king locally, and each colony was granted a two-house legislature, an appointed chamber and an elected assembly, reflecting the parliamentary division into Lords and Commons. But no purpose existed to let these colonial assemblies slip the lease, and one long-standing practice inserted a restraint against them, forbidding passage of any law that contravened the charter or English law. This interdict tied back to a royal override, reserving a right of appeal to the British government itself. When we see how this worked, we see how the procedure suggested the later doctrine of judicial review.

While the law reports from those days incomplete, the 1728 case of Winthrop v Lechmere illustrates. This lawsuit concerned the estate of an individual with a grand old Puritan name, Wait Still Winthrop, who died in 1717. Somewhat ironically, he served as chief justice of Massachusetts' Superior Court of Judicature, but his legal acumen failed to prevent his estate from falling into an unpleasant quarrel between the heirs. He left no will, considerable property in Connecticut, and two children, a son John Winthrop and a daughter Anne, the wife of Thomas

Lechmere of Boston. Under the English rule of primogeniture, all land passes to the eldest son, and with the usual generosity of heirs, John immediately claimed all his father's lands. But his sister Anne came forward and objected, citing a Connecticut law which modified primogeniture, giving the eldest male no more preference than a double share. Beneath this lawsuit simmered colonial hostility for the English aristocracy, since inheritance by the eldest male greatly assisted concentration of wealth in a few privileged families.

Not surprisingly, the Connecticut courts showed a preference for their colonial laws, ruling Anne entitled to a share in her father's land. Nothing daunted, John played his trump. Connecticut exists by virtue of her charter from the crown, his lawyer argued, and when the legislature altered the rule of primogeniture, their act violated that charter. "For," the argument as recorded in the reports reads, "by the Charter [the General Assembly's] power of making laws is restrained and limited in a very special manner (namely), such laws must be wholesome, and [not] contrary to the laws of the realm of England." Primogeniture being a venerable law of the realm of England, he maintained the Connecticut legislature could not change the rule. When John "threaten[ed] an appeal to the King in Council, [h]e was taken into custody for contempt; but escaped ... and went to England, where he brought his appeal."

In England such appeals went before the Privy Council. Not a typical court at all, centuries ago the Privy Council began as the king's private council, but by now these gentlemen sit as a very formal institution of the English state, including the exercise of certain judicial functions. Again not surprisingly, the Privy Council favored English law over colonial law, ruling as follows: "Their Lordships, upon due consideration of the whole matter, do agree humbly to report as their opinion to your Majesty, that the said Act [abolishing primogeniture in Connecticut] should be declared null and void, being contrary to the laws of England, ... and is not warranted by the Charter of that colony."[3]

Winthrop v. Lechmere shows how this device worked in the colonial legal system. A litigant who lost in the colonial courts could appeal to the authorities in England, claiming the local decision "contrary to the laws of England and not warranted by the charter of the colony." In other words, he could appeal to a higher authority and law. This will be seen very much like the later idea of judicial review, where a losing litigant can appeal against a statute to the judiciary, claiming the legislative act violates the higher law of the constitution.

What happens when the Revolution comes along? America severs the tie that binds across the waters, yet conveniently keeps the colonial charters, re-modeled into constitutions for the newly independent states.

Elections replace the crown as the source of office, but otherwise the governments stay largely the same. To use Connecticut again, in 1776 she declared her old 1662 charter as "the civil Constitution of the State, under sole authority of the People thereof, independent of any King or Prince whatsoever."[4] With the addition of some other well-recognized rights, this document served as the constitution for Connecticut until 1818. Other states did somewhat the same. The oversight of the monarchy disappears, the colonists assuming full sovereignty unto themselves, each state having a written constitution.

Pray tell where went that power to "void" colonial laws that conflicted with the charters or English law? The charters have been replaced with new state constitutions; the binding force of English law has vanished. Obviously one cannot appeal to the Privy Council anymore. But available political power never goes un-requisitioned for long and this a very valuable power. So perhaps not surprisingly in the interval between Revolution and Constitution, judges in some states reach out to seize on that former royal prerogative, claiming it for their courts. They draw an analogy, asserting since the new state constitutions stand in the place of the colonial charters, they stand in the place of the Privy Council. In other words, they claim a power in their courts to void legislative laws as violating the state constitutions, just as the Privy Council used to void colonial laws as conflicting with the charters or English law.

This not inconsiderable assertion of authority went down by no means without dissent. At least some saw anti-democratic tendencies. Writing of their Constitution of 1777, a commentator on the laws of Vermont named Swift, who speaks with more authority since he served as chief justice of that state, noted: "No idea was entertained that the judiciary had any power to inquire into the constitutionality of Acts of the legislature, or pronounce them void for any cause. Long after [that] period ... the doctrine ... that the judiciary have authority to set aside ... Acts [of the legislature] ... was considered anti-republican." In 1784 when New Yorkers perceived a court had overturned a law passed by their legislature, the indignation brought forth a public meeting, which declared in an Address to the People of the State: "That there should be a power vested in the Court of the Judicature, whereby they might control the Supreme Legislative power, we think absurd in itself. Such powers in courts would be destructive of liberty." In 1807 and 1808 the legislature of Ohio went so far as to impeach judges for holding acts unconstitutional.[5]

So the idea for judicial review is out there, but not everyone agrees a good idea. It is like a new byte of software circulating. Will it go on to run as part of the government program or end up deleted, leaving no more than a blip in history's footnotes?

Judicial review in the Constitutional Convention – The Constitutional Convention convenes in Philadelphia in 1787, and the Founding Fathers draw up the Constitution. What did they intend about judicial review? The Constitution stays persistently silent, not expressly delegating such a power to the Supreme Court. Nevertheless, does the constitutional text imply the power? This topic continues a matter of lively scholarly debate, with one school concluding definitely yea, another definitely nay, all striving to cloak their views in the high authority of "original intent." But the surviving records show the Convention really reached no consensus about this issue, leaving the outcome in the eye of the beholder.

The Convention deliberated in secret, which presents an initial problem with the sources. Yet some preserved accounts, and most notably James Madison, the Father of the Constitution himself, kept copious notes, published many years later. What does Madison's journal record? Judicial review surfaces only a tantalizingly few times and never directly, all the references coming as afterthoughts in the debates about a "council of revision," a plank in the "Virginia Plan" or "Randolph Plan.'" Drafted by Madison himself, these proposals were the first laid before the Convention, a service performed by Edmund Randolph, a member from and incidentally Governor of Virginia. Consisting of the executive and members of the judiciary, this council of revision would have had power to reject legislation, which the legislature could have overridden by re-passing the act. Obviously, the notion failed to survive the final draft, but lingers in the presidential veto.

The remarks of Elbridge Gerry of Massachusetts, one of the most brilliant speakers at the Convention, are often quoted by those who maintain the Founders intended judicial review: "Mr. Gerry doubts whether the Judiciary ought to form a part of [the council of revision,] as they will have a sufficient check against encroachments on their own department by their exposition of the laws, which involved a power of deciding their Constitutionality. In some States the Judges had actually set aside laws as being against the Constitution. This was done too with general approbation."

However, upon Gerry sitting down, Mr. Gunning Bedford, Jr., a delegate from Delaware, obtained the floor and took an entirely opposite line: "Mr. Bedford was opposed to every check on the Legislative, even the Council of Revision first proposed. He thought it would be sufficient to mark out in the Constitution the boundaries of the Legislative

Authority, which would give all the requisite security to the rights of the other departments. The Representatives of the people were the best Judges of what was for their interest, and ought to be under no external control whatever." Thus, Bedford advocated legislative supremacy and opposed judicial review.

Still in talking about the council of revision, Mr. John Francis Mercer of Maryland rose to observe: "He disapproved of the Doctrine that the Judges as expositors of the Constitution should have authority to declare a law void. He thought the laws ought to be well and cautiously made, and then to be uncontrollable." John Dickinson of Delaware went along with that sentiment: "Mr. Dickinson was strongly impressed with the remark of Mr. Mercer as to the power of the Judges to set aside the law. He thought no such power ought to exist. He was at the same time at a loss what expedient to substitute. The Justiciary of Aragon he observed became by degrees, the lawgiver."[6]

And so, looking through the records, it goes. No one really treats the subject exhaustively. Other topics such as apportionment of Congress absorb the delegates' main attention. Then where does all this leave the Founders' original intent about judicial review? In all honesty it leaves both sides a plausible, but neither a conclusive argument. Delegates who favored judicial review probably departed the Convention fairly satisfied. They could argue that power implied in the Constitution. Delegates opposed could depart equally satisfied. Judicial review not being expressly in the Constitution, they could contend that silence expressed purposeful omission. Whichever side they stood on, judicial review must have remained a somewhat vague idea in all their minds. It was not an old and tested mechanism of government. So far it had seen very little application in practice. The limited debate at the Convention has done nothing to develop the complete contours of the new theory. Like so much else about the Constitution, this situation left a great deal up to events and interpretation.

Nor did events standstill, and during the ratification controversy, judicial review picked up an important endorsement. Alexander Hamilton, writing in the *Federalist, Number 78* comes out for it. Since James Madison, the Father of the Constitution himself, together with the lesser known but still influential John Jay, later the first chief justice of the Supreme Court, collaborated on these essays, and due to the high level of their tone and reasoning, the *Federalist* occupies a special niche on the shelf of those who cherish the Founders' "original intent." Hamilton's *Number 78* is, then, a proof entitled to considerable weight. Yet all agree Hamilton wrote this number, and Madison would later publicly repudiate judicial review. So once again the argument appears inconclusive. Yet Hamilton would provide a persuasive rationale picked up and sounded to the echo by Chief Justice John Marshall in Marbury v Madison, the case which successfully claimed that power for the Supreme Court.

The facts of Marbury v Madison – In the famous 1803 case of Marbury v Madison, Chief Justice John Marshall will successfully lay claim to that great power of judicial review for the Supreme Court. After a contentious fight over ratification of the Constitution, the new government assembled itself in 1789. The very general terms of the foundational document left much to fill in, not least this question about judicial review. While no express language delegated judicial power to declare legislative acts unconstitutional and void, yet was this implied in the text? Chief Justice Marshall would answer with a ringing affirmative.

The case grew out of the hard-fought, bitter election of 1800, which witnessed the first hostile takeover of the presidency. In the campaign, challenger Thomas Jefferson and the Republicans soundly trounced incumbent President John Adams and the Federalists. This bygone political acrimony falls outside our present concerns, except for the piece that went to make up Marbury. In those days a wrinkle in the Constitution left the outgoing president and Congress in office until March 3rd the following year, a lengthy stretch of days. Not until 1933 would the 20th Amendment alter that to January 3rd for Congress and January 20th for the president, finally doing away with "lame-duck" Congresses. The Federalists seized on this discrepancy between defeat and departure, beating a retreat into the bastion of the judiciary, whose life-time offices offered to perpetuate the party's influence in exile. On February 13, 1801, they rammed through a law creating sixteen new federal judgeships, which President Adams promptly filled, nominating faithful party adherents, the Senate as promptly confirming. Then on February 27, Congress passed a statute creating justices-of-the-peace in the District of Columbia. Occupying a lower rung on the judicial ladder, these were not lifetime slots, but for five-year terms. Again President Adams quickly named faithful Federalists, one of his choices falling on a William Marbury, who would shortly lend his name to posterity as plaintiff in Marbury v Madison. The Senate confirmed on March 3, 1801, Adams' last day in office.

These "midnight judges" understandably outraged Jefferson and his Republicans. No sooner did they occupy the Capitol, than they repealed the Circuit Court Act which created the new federal judgeships. This repealer was a thorny legal thicket. The Constitution says federal judges hold office during good behavior, yet leaves Congress authority to create their judgeships. Then after Congress creates a judgeship, can they later abolish the creation, thrusting the judge out of office? In the event, the Jeffersonians' bold stroke prevailed by default. None of the ousted judges mounted a serious challenge in court. Apparently, they conceived discretion the better part of valor, and if subsequent events serve an indicator, they read the public mood correctly. However convincing their logic, they sensed they could not muster enough political momentum to carry the day. The Federalists never recovered from this electoral defeat in 1800, the very name of their party soon to disappear from all except the history books.

But while the defrocked federal judges folded their tents and disappeared into the night, those justices-of-the-peace refused to depart so meekly to the outer darkness. The Jeffersonians did not repeal the law establishing their offices, instead taking another tack. In the last minute rush, President Adams signed their commissions, the Secretary of State affixed his seal, but not all were actually delivered to the appointees. For this default Jefferson's administration chose to regard the appointments as void.

These facts set up the famous lawsuit of Marbury v Madison. William Marbury and three other appointees sue as plaintiffs, demanding delivery of their commissions as justices-of-the-peace for the District of Columbia, the Madison appearing as defendant in the caption being none other than James Madison, coincidentally the Secretary of State in Jefferson's new cabinet. Finding the commissions upon his arrival in office, he refused the delivery.

This type of lawsuit goes under the name of a petition for writ of mandamus and amounts to this: If a government official refuses to carry out a duty required by law, an injured party can bring suit to compel the official to carry out that duty. To use a modern and trivial analogy, suppose someone passes a driver's license test, but the examiner refuses to issue the license. Well, if the applicant passes the driver's test, the law requires the examiner to issue the driver's license. A petition for writ of mandamus would lie to force that official to perform his duty.

Marbury and the other plaintiffs filed such a petition in the Supreme Court. They alleged that President Adams signed their commissions as justices-of-the-peace; that his Secretary of State sealed the signatures; that Madison as Secretary of State refused delivery. They argued such delivery a duty the law required Madison to perform. They prayed the justices to issue a writ compelling him to do just that. Thus was the case made up.

The ruling in Marbury v Madison – These facts do not look to raise the issue of judicial power at all, yet the real question in the Marbury becomes: Does the Supreme Court possess the power of judicial review? But before turning to the opinion, let us recall our location in the historical progression. Judicial review is not yet an accepted power in the Court's possession. We heard the debates at the Convention, heard the reference in the *Federalist Papers*, but whether the judiciary should possess this authority far from settled. The Supreme Court has never yet declared a congressional law unconstitutional. Next let us recall that speaking about judicial review speaks about power itself, the power of one government institution over another, the power of the Court to declare laws void as unconstitutional. Then let us recall the influence of interest and power on institutional performance. Finally, having all these thoughts in mind, let us ask: If this case raises the question whether their Court should have that power, which way would we predict the justices to rule?

We cannot but conclude the tendencies all line up, pointing in the same direction. To begin with professional interests, all the justices are lawyers. They and their fellow members of the bar well knew: Such a power would immensely advance the influence and dignity of their profession. Such a doctrine would generate a whole new species of lawsuits, raising a business of utmost consequence, accompanied by suitable fees. Almost as gratifying, while the legislature might pass laws, if those officials had to come hat in hand before the courts, waiting upon a final approval, this spectacle would show who on top. This power would elevate the Court superior to the other branches, Congress and the president. Would it not amount to an astonishing act of self-effacement for the Court to renounce it?

We might also mention Chief Justice Marshall himself one of those the Jeffersonians labeled "midnight judges," being appointed in January, taking the oath as Chief Justice only on February 4th. By still another quirk of fate, before his last minute elevation to the bench, Marshall himself served as Secretary of State in Adams' cabinet, continued as such until the end of Adams' term, making him the official charged with affixing the seals and delivering the commissions. In other words, he was intimately connected with the very facts underlying the litigation. Modern rules on conflict of interest would have precluded his presiding, yet under the standards of that day, Marshall did nothing improper. However, we see him a Federalist, rather than a supporter of Jefferson. This allegiance must add another ingredient to his motives.

Coming then to his opinion, the Chief Justice writes for a unanimous Court. Legal scholarship has always considered it a mark of his genius that Marshall finds opportunity where none seems to appear, while performing a remarkable feat of multi-tasking. At first glance, he looks impaled upon the horns of a dilemma: Either swallow the bitter draught and rule against his own party or gird his loins and rule against the Jeffersonians, who in their hour of triumph perhaps of a mind and in sufficient strength to exact vengeance. But Marshall's acumen detected a way to reverse the dilemma by making the case about something else entirely. He transforms the issue into judicial review. Thus altering the question lets him balance diverse goals, winning the game for himself and his Court. He excoriates Jefferson's administration for illegally withholding the commissions, a point scored against them. He claims the power of judicial review for his Court, big points for him. But he denies Marbury his commission, letting the Jeffersonians win the case, their consolation points. Yet by awarding them a technical win on four minor judgeships, he disarmed protest against his much bigger win over judicial review. Both sides took away something, but he and his Court took away by far the most. Marshall gives a bravura performance, worthy of one of history's greatest lawyers.

Yet for all this forensic brilliance, we should not be blinded to a certain excess of that very quality. To understand a case, the old Roman lawyers used to ask: *Cui Bono*, Whose Good? If we rivet our attention to that question, we notice the Chief Justice artfully distracting our gaze, calling our attention away from interests and power. The zeal of his advocacy casts the argument in a highly persuasive form, luring the listener onto the speaker's chosen ground, a very lawyerly failing. Instead of talking about power, Marshall talks about rights, replacing the brutal facts of power politics with an emotional appeal, a very common rhetorical device. As a result, he never openly confronts the strongest counter-arguments against judicial review, avoiding the true grounds of the controversy. These tactics may be best considered by analyzing his decision in some detail.

To turn to his precise reasoning, Marshall starts by finding Marbury and the others had an absolute right to their commissions, writing: "It is ... decidedly the opinion of the Court that, when a commission has been signed by the President, the appointment is made, and that the commission is complete when the seal of the United States has been affixed to it by the Secretary of State. ... To withhold the commission, therefore, is an act deemed by the Court not warranted by law, but violative of a vested legal right."[7]

Thus, he enjoys the pleasure of rebuking Jefferson's administration for illegality. But however wounding to their sensibilities or definite this sounds, neither had they much real cause for complaint, nor he quite so much real cause for the asserted certainty. If we read his supporting reasons, the precedents cited, the analogies drawn, the train of logic, all impressively well done. Yet at bottom and as usual, the pronouncement rests on a value judgment. If he had so desired, Marshall could have declared with equal conviction an exactly opposite conclusion, holding the appointments not made until actual, physical delivery of the commissions. It would not have been far to look for an analogy, as for example, a deed to land required delivery to take effect. Interpreting the law forces judges to pick and chose. Marshall selects a reasonable enough alternative, and so no real complaint exists. Only we need to be aware there is no ironclad logic; there is no merely "following the law." Leaps of faith must be made borne upon the wings of judicial inner conviction.

With this initial finding, one would think Marbury won his lawsuit, and he will obtain his commission. But abruptly Marshall changes course, introducing a topic that looks foreign to the facts. This tangent involves the distinction between "original jurisdiction" and "appellate jurisdiction." A grant of jurisdiction confers power on a court to hear a case; conversely, without a grant of jurisdiction a court cannot hear a case. A court with "original jurisdiction" serves as the court where a case starts out or originates. A court with "appellate jurisdiction" hears appeals from the original court. Looking back at the Constitution, we see the Supreme Court designed primarily as a court of "appellate jurisdiction," not one of "original jurisdiction." Ordinarily a lower court would hear any case first, with only appeals going to the Supreme Court.

Article III reads: "In all cases affecting Ambassadors, other public Ministers and Consuls, and those in which a State shall be a Party, the supreme Court shall have original Jurisdiction. In all other Cases ... the supreme Court shall have appellate Jurisdiction, ... with such Exceptions, and under such Regulations as the Congress shall make."

Yet recall Marbury filed his petition for mandamus first or "originally" with the Supreme Court. He did that based upon a statute passed by Congress, which authorized the Court to "issue" writs of mandamus. But Marshall will say that by passing this law Congress acted unconstitutionally. More specifically, he will rule that Congress violated the Constitution by conferring original jurisdiction on the Supreme Court, when the Constitution said the Court should have only appellate jurisdiction. Turning to his own words with added italics to stress, Marshall writes that: "[To] issue such a writ [for mandamus] to an officer for the delivery of a paper, is in effect the same as to sustain an *original action* for that paper, and, therefore seems *not to belong to appellate*, but to *original jurisdiction*. ... The authority, therefore, given to the Supreme Court, by the act establishing the judicial courts of the United States to issue writs of mandamus ... appears not to be warranted by the constitution."[8]

Once again, this may sound convincing enough, but is in no way compelled. Marshall could have ruled the other way with just as much reason. If we re-read Article III carefully, it does limit the Court's original jurisdiction to "cases affecting Ambassadors, other public Ministers and Consuls, and those in which a State shall be a Party." Marbury clearly falls outside that grant. But the Article goes on to say "with such Exceptions, and under such Regulations as the Congress shall make." Assuming, then, mandamus an original action, and a bit of a technical controversy surrounded such an assumption, could not Congress still make an exception to the general rule?

We should sense Marshall's drift. The Chief Justice is setting up the argument to reach a pre-determined conclusion, lining up the logic in the most convincing way. He is reaching toward that question of judicial review; he has determined to claim that power to declare acts of Congress unconstitutional. Each of his findings aligns with that polar resolve. He could have decided the case on the non-delivery of the commissions. Not being delivered, they are void. End of lawsuit. But he avoids that solution. Instead he rules the plaintiffs have a "vested legal right" to their commissions. Next he could have ruled Congress properly conferred jurisdiction over mandamus on the Court. Possessing jurisdiction, the Court then directs delivery of the commissions. End of lawsuit. Instead he rules the congressional grant of jurisdiction "appears not to be warranted by the Constitution." He has carefully avoided both of two perfectly rational outcomes. By so doing he has crafted an impasse, a contradiction between the right to the commissions and the Court's lack of jurisdiction. The only remedy appears to cut the Gordian knot, declaring this conflict compels him to declare the act of Congress unconstitutional and void. He has forced himself into the position of having to defend the Constitution by claiming the prerogative of judicial review for his Court.

Let us read his famous words: "It is emphatically the province and the duty of the judicial department to say what the law is. ... If two laws conflict with each other, the courts must decide on the operation of each. So if a law be in opposition to the constitution; if both the law and the constitution apply to a particular case, so that the court must decide that case conformably to the law, disregarding the constitution; or conformably to the constitution, disregarding the law; the court must determine which of these conflicting rules governs the case. ... If then the courts are to regard the constitution; and the constitution is superior to any ordinary act of the legislature, the constitution, and not such ordinary act, must govern the case to which they both apply."[9]

There it is: judicial review claimed and justified. The Chief Justice has ruled the Court possesses power to void congressional laws as unconstitutional. Almost incidentally James Madison has won the lawsuit. The law conferring original jurisdiction over mandamus being void, the case cannot be heard and is dismissed. Marbury and the others lose.

The reasoning in Marbury v Madison – Marshall's just quoted justification for judicial review looks perfectly reasonable, indeed compelling. But let us consider his reasons in the detail needed to win our informed and willing assent. Re-reading shows the argument cast in the familiar form of a syllogism, the premises leading to the conclusion. First premise: it is the duty of the courts to interpret the law. Second premise: constitutional law is superior to statutory law. Conclusion: it is then the duty of the courts to uphold the higher law of the constitution against the statutory, lower law passed by the legislature.

But does that conclusion follow from the premises as naturally as appears? Let us remember formal logic never quite works in either ethics or political science. In these realms the less rigorous criteria of informal logic must satisfy our yearning for precision. So we should not leap upon the Chief Justice over an error in formal logic; that should be expected. Yet those stricter standards do assist to detect a possible flaw. Syllogistic logic demands strict attention to the terms in the premises, and carefully scrutiny discovers a neglect of this rule. Marshall stated his first premise this way: "It is emphatically the province and the duty of the judicial department to say what the law is." While true as far as it goes, does this go far enough? Because it may well be the duty of the courts to interpret *law*, but that does not necessarily mean they should have "final" authority to interpret *constitutional law*? We will recall English judges emphatically lacked such authority, which remained with Parliament. Whether American judges should have such authority was an open question. In fact, that was the very crux of the present controversy about judicial review.

In short, Marshall's syllogism puts the problem in a plausible, but misleading form. The question was not whether the judges should have power to interpret law, including constitutional law. Of course, the answer would be yes. The question was not if constitutional law is superior to statutory law. Of course, the answer would be yes. The question was not even whether a court should give a preference to constitutional law over statutory law. Of course, again the answer would be yes. But the real question was this: Should Congress or the Court have "final" authority to determine constitutionality? The prior affirmatives simply do not add up to a further yes by a purely logical process. Rather, this final question concerns an entirely separate and greater power than all the others. It cannot, then, be inferred that since the Court possesses those lesser powers, it should also possess this ultimate power. Some additional justification is required outside this train of logic.

Marshall does offer another highly theoretical justification to buttress his initial logic. He writes: "The original and supreme will [of the people] organizes the government and assigns to the different departments their respective powers. ... The powers of the Legislature are defined and limited; and that those limits may not be mistaken or forgotten, the constitution is written. To what purpose is that limitation committed to writing, if these limits may at any time be passed by those intended to be restrained? ... It is a proposition to plain to be contested that the Constitution controls any legislative act repugnant to it, ..."[10]

Once again this sounds highly persuasive, but also once again Marshall's verbal generalship has subtly shifted the question. Instead of a frontal assault by the Court against Congress, this maneuver realigns the combatants. Marshall's imagery portrays Congress as threatening the limits written in the Constitution, while the Court rushes to defend that entrenchment. But this skews the underlying problem. It is all very well to say we want limited government, and we do. Yet to say the Court will guard the Constitution against Congress leaves out half the equation, neglecting to ask: Then who will guard the Constitution against the Court? Limited government looks as open to attack from either side, but the barricade Marshall erects faces only one way. Such a structure forgets that there are no inherently incorruptible political institutions, and in those circumstances, the best that can be done is to assure accountable institutions. Congress remains under democratic controls; in response to perceived unconstitutional laws, the people can vote the scoundrels out. But what similar restraint holds the Court accountable? None whatsoever. So in the end Marshall's formulation offers only a partial, imperfect solution.

The real question needed to be faced frankly: Should we prefer the Court to Congress as the final authority on constitutional law? This query cries out for pragmatic demonstrations grounded in historical experience. For example, if we compare monarchy to democracy, we can quickly come up with such evidence. We can consult the long record of the English kings, contrast that with the record of Parliament, and see Parliament better performs in the public interest, the mechanism of elections enforcing such a result. But we read over Marshall's opinion in vain for such empirical comparisons. Has practical experience shown judges perform better at this function than elected representatives? The Chief Justice produces not a single instance. In England, their Parliament retained the final word. Then had they disregarded basic constitutional principles? Not at all, rather under parliamentary guidance their constitution had stayed remarkably stable and served as a model to the world. Have the legislatures in the newly independent states shown a tendency to disregard the provisions of their constitutions? There is no evidence of this. What then about the actual instance in Marbury? Is Congress running roughshod over the Constitution? Conferring jurisdiction over writs of mandamus on the Supreme Court hardly seems to qualify, indeed is arguably not unconstitutional at all. We must begin to see that no actual examples are offered because none were available. And the way in which Marshall presents the argument actually evades an impressive body of empirical evidence, which suggests elected legislatures generally regard constitutional limits.

Furthermore, we have seen that "interpreting" the law, even the constitutional law, had always been a dynamic process, necessarily involving the judges in actually making law, even constitutional law. Marshall carefully seeks to eschew such a meaning for "interpret," and in a moment in later cases, we will find such a power to make constitutional law explicitly renounced. Yet already a problem appears with this renunciation. For in this very case he is making constitutional law. Article III provided that the limitation on the original jurisdiction was "with such Exceptions, and under such Regulations as the Congress shall make." So in ruling Congress could not grant the Supreme Court original jurisdiction over mandamus, his interpretation is dynamic rather than static. He is infusing the process with his own preconceptions. And we must wonder how a power which exhibits the dynamic quality of making constitutional law in the very first application is somehow to remain more limited in future use.

Marshall has carefully constructed a convincing argument to support a desired conclusion. But by so doing, he obscured vitally important aspects of the controversy. What was really at stake was this: Should Congress or the Supreme Court possess final authority to interpret the Constitution? Faced frontally and dealt with openly, this raises concerns evaded by Marshall's way of putting the question. It becomes not a matter of merely defending the Constitution, but of which institution will better perform that task. To provide the answer requires a comparison of their institutional nature, which is totally neglected.

This failure worked to conceal the fact that judicial review was a large, potentially revolutionary change from the then familiar, from the system of English jurisprudence, and carried strikingly anti-democratic implications. These implications are precisely the grounds upon which the Jeffersonians will attack the decision, as shown by a quote from Jefferson himself: "You seem ... to consider the judges as the ultimate arbiters of all constitutional questions; a very dangerous doctrine indeed, and one which would place us under the despotism of an oligarchy. ... When the legislative or executive functionaries act unconstitutionally, they are responsible to the people in their elective capacity. The exemption of the judges from that is dangerous enough."[11]

Jefferson and his partisans will go on to mount something of an attack on the federal judiciary, impeaching and removing from office one apparently insane federal judge, and impeaching but failing to remove Justice Samuel Chase, the only impeachment of a supreme court justice. But the Court will weather the storm. No sufficiently powerful opposition coalesces to overthrow the outcome of Marbury. Perhaps no one's ox had been sufficiently gored. After all, the Jeffersonians won the case. Nor were their other closely held interests sufficiently threatened in the years to come. So the power of judicial review remained on the books, although as we will see, not used. As the years passed the notion became accepted, an accustomed part of the lawyers' and judges' professional equipment. Marshall's rational was repeated: The Court stood ready to defend the will of the people as expressed in the Constitution, preventing the possible excesses of a momentary congressional majority. On the thin edge of this wedge the doctrine entered the public consciousness. There appeared no need to ask deeper questions, and any concern was further allayed by certain limitations shortly pronounced as surrounding the doctrine.

The limits of Marbury v Madison – In Marbury, Chief Justice Marshall presented a static rather than dynamic image of judicial interpretation of constitutional law. He ushered judicial review onto the stage clad in defensive armor, not armed with offensive weapons. The people having embodied their sovereign will in the fortress of a written constitution, the justices were stationed on the ramparts, secure in their carapaces of lifetime tenure, ready to repel all attacks on the document. This avoided mentioning the judges' historical role as lawmakers, portrayed them as sentries over a constitution made by the people, not an independent source of constitutional law making outside the will of the people. Acutely sensitive to counter-attacks upon judicial review as anti-democratic, this reasoning looked to reverse the table.

So important was this regarded, that in the years to come the judiciary incorporated an express legal formula, a corollary considered part of the doctrine. In a long series of cases, they repeatedly pledged never to exercise judicial review except in "clear-cut" cases, where the legislature exceeded its authority "beyond any reasonable doubt." This may be called the "original doctrine of judicial review" or the "limited doctrine of judicial review." Since almost always Congress can make a strong argument to act within the Constitution, this rule was an extremely significant limitation. It will seldom be found even all the justices concur in holding a law unconstitutional. If then the Supreme Court limited itself to overturning laws in clear-cut cases, that would leave almost all power with Congress. Judicial review would not have amounted to very much.

The judicial pronouncements about this limitation were not casual asides or isolated instances, but central to conception of the doctrine. Even before Marbury in 1803, other cases had touched on judicial review as a possibility, and already such a limitation was considered as going with the possibility. In 1796, Justice Samuel Chase of the U.S. Supreme Court itself, without determining whether the power of judicial review existed, said in a case where the issue came up: "I am free to declare, that I will never exercise it, but in a very clear case."[12] In 1800, Justice William Paterson, in the same court to the same effect, wrote that to justify declaring any law void would require "a clear and unequivocal breach of the constitution, not a doubtful and argumentative implication."[13] Justice Tyler of the General Court of Virginia in 1793 had written: "But the violation must be plain and clear, or there might be danger of the judiciary preventing the operation of laws which might produce much public good."[14]

After Marbury v Madison we can mine the soil of the cases for endless samples of this same ore. Significantly, Chief Justice Marshall himself in 1810, speaking in Fletcher v Peck: "The question, whether a law be void for its repugnancy to the constitution, is at all times of much delicacy, which ought seldom, if ever, to be decided in the affirmative, in a doubtful case. The Court, when compelled by duty to render such a judgment, would be unworthy of its station, if it were unmindful of the solemn obligation which that situation imposes. But it is not on slight implication and vague conjecture that the legislature is to be pronounced to have transcended its powers, and its acts to be considered as void. The opposition between the law and the constitution should be such that the judge feels a clear and strong conviction of their incompatibility with each other."[15]

Then in 1811, Chief Justice Tilghman of Pennsylvania: "For weighty reasons, it has been assumed as a principle in constitutional construction by the Supreme Court of the United States, by this court, and every other court of reputation in the United States, that an Act of the legislature is not to be declared void unless the violation of the constitution is so manifest as to leave no room for reasonable doubt." In 1812, Chancellor Waties of South Carolina: "The validity of the law ought not then to be questioned unless it is so obviously repugnant to the constitution that when pointed out by the judges, all men of sense and reflection in the community may perceive the repugnancy." On and on the litany sounds through the opinions. Chief Justice Shaw in 1834: "[The judges will] never declare a statute void unless the nullity and invalidity of the Act are placed, in their judgement, beyond a reasonable doubt." Justice Cowan in 1823: "Before the court will ... declare an Act of the legislature unconstitutional ... there can be no rational doubt." Chief Justice Bigelow in 1862: "It may be well to repeat the rule of exposition which has been often enunciated by this court, that where a statute has been passed with all the forms and solemnities required to give it the force of law, the presumption is in favor of its validity, and that the court will not declare it to be ... void unless its invalidity is established beyond a reasonable doubt."[16]

Last but not least, Chief Justice Remick Waite of the U.S. Supreme Court in 1878: "[T]his declaration [that an act of Congress is unconstitutional] should never be made except in a clear case. Every possible presumption is in favor of the validity of a statute, and this continues until the contrary is shown beyond a rationale doubt. One branch of the government cannot encroach on the domain of another without danger. The safety of our institutions depends in no small measure on a strict observance of this salutary rule."[17]

But this formula was no more than words on the printed page. No mechanism in the constitutional system enforced compliance. Thus, like all merely verbal proscriptions professing to limit government, it remained at the mercy of those who pronounced it. Even the sanctions of criminal law lose their force without effective law enforcement. How much less do the protestations of government officials without mechanisms of accountability.

Judicial review and the supremacy clause – A still significant source of confusion about judicial review relates to the federal nature of the union, incorporating states into a national government, while leaving them a degree of sovereignty. This leads to mixing up under a single term, "judicial review," two entirely distinct powers: first, action by the judiciary holding unconstitutional laws of coordinate branches of government, and second, action by the federal judiciary holding state laws void under the supremacy clause, either as unconstitutional or in conflict with federal statutes. This confusion needs permanent sorting out.

In strict correctness, the term "judicial review" should only refer to judges holding unconstitutional the laws of a co-equal branch of government. When the Supreme Court holds unconstitutional an act of Congress, that is judicial review properly speaking. The same goes for a state court holding unconstitutional an act of its state legislature. But it is really an entirely different animal when federal courts void an act of a state government, either as violating the U.S. Constitution or as overridden by other federal law. To make clear the distinction the later should be denominated by some term such as "action under the supremacy clause."

Of course, the "supremacy clause" in Article VI provides: "This Constitution, and the Laws of the Unites States which shall be made in Pursuance thereof; ... shall be the supreme Law of the Land." This makes the federal government the sun of the political universe, binding the states into orbit around that center.

Judicial review and action under the supremacy clause are different breeds of cat because completely different policy considerations apply. While the Court might not need to possess the first, in order for federalism to work, it has to own the second. We can imagine the Court without judicial review. The British and numerous other up-and-running constitutions lack this mechanism. But if the Court could not strike down state acts which contravene the Constitution or congressional statutes, the American federal system would lack the gravitational force which binds together the parts. The centrifugal energy within the states would propel them off into independent orbits. In addition, we just heard the judges pledge never to declare legislative acts unconstitutional except in clear-cut cases. This limitation intended to preserve the legislative primacy of Congress. But an opposite calculation operates when voiding state acts that conflict with the Constitution or congressional legislation. If the U.S. Constitution expresses the will of the people, then it appears appropriate to read that purpose expansively when applied to the states, not confined to the narrowest construction. And if congressional legislation also expresses the will of the people, a similar standard applies there. To carry through full constitutional and congressional intent, we don't want the courts ruling against them over every reasonable doubt, but giving them every reasonable doubt.

Yet these separate categories of judicial power have been continually confounded together. As a result, what should arguably be the much more extensive power, action under the supremacy clause to declare state laws void, has been constantly used to justify what should arguably be a much narrower power, judicial review to void congressional laws. In discussing the power of the Supreme Court, we need to sort this matter out once and for all. Otherwise, we risk becoming entangled by mistaking the one for the other.

From the "shot heard round the world" in 1774 to Marbury in 1803, less than thirty years pass, but in that short span, a crown prerogative transforms into a judicial power. Instead of a device for colonial control in British hands, the judiciary seizes the doctrine into their hands, pressed into service under the banner of limited government. As Justice Holmes was heard to say, "The old form receives a new content, and in time even the form modifies itself to fit the meaning which it has received."

Nor does the story end there. As we read the Court's cases over the two coming centuries, judicial review further transforms, shedding that limitation to "clear-cut" cases, and leaving behind those original restraints, assumes a highly dynamic aspect. Reinforced by the habit of use, gathering to itself interests, additional justifications provided, the institutional will-to-power forges ahead. The British mantle of power blowing away in the revolutionary wind, the American judiciary reaches out to seize a loose end. Nor once in their grasp will this fold of cloth stay the same size. Nothing in the constitutional system stops them from sewing on to the garment. So as should be expected, the power will grow.

CHAPTER 4

The Paradigm of Dred Scott

In 1857, Dred Scott shifts the paradigm for judicial review. Under the original doctrine as announced, we heard the judges repeatedly pledge never to declare a law unconstitutional except in a clear-cut case. But Dred Scott tacitly abandons this pledge. Escaping such restraint, judicial review turns from a static into much more dynamic power, freeing judges to re-make fundamental, constitutional law. This paradigm shift provides the essential methodology for the Court's present powers.

Present commentary never mentions Dred Scott without condemnation, yet the criticism fixes on the surface of the case, passing over the power shift hidden in the subtext. On the surface Dred Scott dealt with slavery, and Chief Justice Roger Brooke Taney discovers a "right to slavery" implied in the Constitution. Nowhere does his opinion acknowledgement the subtext, the power side of the case, where he suddenly disregards the earlier pronounced limits on judicial review. Yet while Taney's ruling about slavery later suffered utter rejection, the same ruling created a new paradigm for "unrestrained" judicial review never yet rejected. The substance of the case discarded, the judicial methodology remains embraced.

Dred Scott demonstrates the themes stressed in classic political analysis. Interests and the institutional will-to-power impress their outlines upon the controversy. Dred Scott was about slavery, and the interests supporting slavery speak for themselves. Ethical attitudes and legal doctrines about slavery strikingly exhibit interests in their formation. In the case itself, the tug of the will-to-power on a political institution, here the Supreme Court, stands palpably visible. Just where government officials, here judges, feel their interests and values most threatened, just when the crisis reaches a height, the temptation to expand available power fatally attracts. At that same moment, individual rights, those rights with which government should not interfere, turn out far from self-defining. Pliable to artful transformation, those rights alter from a shield to a spear, rather than defensive armor over a body of legitimate rights, an offensive weapon with which to strike at the vital rights of others. Nor can the discussion resist being forced back upon the question of institutional design: How construct political institutions to give the best possible answers to the questions raised? Throughout, the fact slavery a dead issue lends a clarity denied live controversies. No interests remaining to defend slavery, judgment may adopt the remaining consensus in comparing the performance of the political institutions.

To understand Dred Scott requires: first, a comprehension of the legal status of slavery under the Constitution, which as with so much else was ambiguous; second, a consideration of the ethical attitudes toward slavery, which as usual was strongly influenced by interests; third, a review of the national controversy about slavery, which as normal was an intense political agitation; fourth, an understanding of the way Southerners phrased their cause, which as typical was in terms of "minority rights;" and fifth, an examination of the opinion in the case, which as so often was a preconceived conclusion. This effort lets us see how Taney's ruling altered the original, more limited doctrine of judicial review, and puts us in position to compare the performance of Congress against the Court.

Slavery before the Constitution – As early as 1599, Cartwright's Case held "that England was too pure an air for a slave to breathe in," yet isolated bondage lingered in the mother country until the Abolition Act of 1833. Just as early, conditions in the far-flung Empire encouraged Negro slavery, and in America's southern colonies, the slave plantation sunk deep economic roots, which eventually entangled with every facet of that society. While their egalitarianism caused most of the Founders to oppose slavery, the inertia of interests resisted their efforts, leaving slavery diminished but in place after the Revolution.

By the Constitutional Convention in 1787, two states had adopted abolition, Massachusetts and New Hampshire. Three others had programs of gradual emancipation, Connecticut, Pennsylvania, and Rhode Island. In effect, a total of eight states qualified as non-slaveholding. In that same year, Congress under the Articles passed their famous Northwest Ordinance, prohibiting slavery in the lands later Ohio, Indiana, Illinois, Michigan, and Wisconsin. The Ordinance read: "There shall be neither Slavery nor involuntary Servitude in the said territory." In 1789, the First Congress under the Constitution re-passed this law almost verbatim.

Slavery at the Constitutional Convention – At the Constitutional Convention the foes of slavery had spoken out, but had to bend to the iron of circumstance. The slaveholding class predominated in the South, and that section would not have come into the union with emancipation the price. This intransigence forced upon the Framers a stark choice. Either practice the "art of the possible," take what progress they could get, or throw up the whole affair. They compromised rather than recede toward possible anarchy.

Once more Madison's journal records the conflict in the Convention. Madison, himself from Virginia and a slave owner, "thought it wrong to admit in the Constitution the idea that there could be property in men." Mr. Roger Sherman of Connecticut "regarded the slave trade as iniquitous." He "observed that the abolition of Slavery seemed to be going on in the U.S. & that the good sense of the several States would probably by degrees complete it." Mr. Governor Morris of Pennsylvania sounded the amen: "He never would concur in upholding domestic slavery. It was a nefarious institution. It was the curse of heaven on the States where it prevailed." Colonel George Mason, perhaps surprisingly also from Virginia, amplified these sentiments: "This infernal trade originated in the avarice of the British Merchants. The British Government constantly checked the attempts of Virginia to put a stop to it. ... Slavery discourages arts & manufactures. The poor despise labor when performed by slaves. ... Every master of slaves is born a petty tyrant. They bring the judgment of heaven on a Country. ... By an inevitable chain of causes and effects providence punishes national sins, by national calamities." Indeed, he spoke prophetic words for his state. Mason concluded he "held it essential in every point of view that the General Government should have the power to prevent the increase of slavery." To all of which Mr. John Rutledge of South Carolina gave the Southern response: "Religion & humanity had nothing to do with this question. Interest alone is the governing principle with nations. The true question at present is whether the Southern States shall or shall not be parties to the Union." Mr. Pierce Butler, also of South Carolina, remarked the "security the Southern States want is that their negroes may not be taken from them, which some gentlemen within or without doors, have a very good mind to do."[1]

Slavery and the Constitution – What, then, does the Constitution actually say about slavery? Nowhere does the word "slavery" appear. No provision guarantees a right to hold slaves as such. Only three euphemistic references touch the topic.

One of the angriest arguments at the Convention raged over reckoning slaves for apportionment in the House of Representatives. While slaves obviously lacked the vote, their Southern masters wanted them counted for purposes of congressional representation. Debate grew heated, but eventually the delegates compromised. "Representatives," Article I reads, "... shall be determined by adding to the whole Number of free Persons, ... three fifths of all other Persons." This "three-fifths compromise" turned out well for the South. In the years before the Civil War, their slaves increased their membership in the House significantly.

Another controversy concerned the African slave trade. Even most slaveholders confessed the iniquity. Result, another compromise found in Article I: "Migration or Importation of such Persons as any of the States now existing shall think proper to admit, shall not be prohibited ... prior to [1808]." Later Congress did promptly prohibit further importation of slaves on the first possible day, January 1, 1808.

Lastly comes language in Article IV, later a storm center for the fierce sectional rivalry over fugitive slave laws: "No Person held to Service or Labour in one State ... escaping into another, shall, in Consequence ... be discharged from such Service or Labor, but shall be delivered up on Claim of the Party to whom such Service or Labour may be due." This provision obviously contemplates the return of escaping slaves.

These three references make up the whole. Where, then, do these leave slavery vis a vis the Constitution? Clearly slavery exists, but do the quoted passages confer a "right" to own slaves? While such sounds strange to modern ears, accustomed to far other notions of individual rights, yet this "right" precisely describes the claim made by Southern leaders in the era before the Civil War. This supposed "right to slavery" became a foundational tenet of their legal theory. They claimed the Constitution implied a right to own property in slaves, a right they gradually came to exult as sacrosanct, the touchstone of their cause.

Even accepting such an implication plausible, yet an equally persuasive argument remains on the other hand. If the Framers intended to guarantee such a right, surely they would have done so in positive language. They were quite capable of such unequivocal self-expression. For example, Article I, Section 9 says: "No bill of attainder or ex post facto Law shall be passed." If then they meant to guarantee slavery, why not say so just as plainly? In fact, if we look ahead to 1861, the Constitution of the Confederate States employs such explicit language: "No ... law denying or impairing the right of property in negro slaves shall be passed."

Thus, sound reasons support the argument that since the Founders did not set slavery in constitutional cement, it is fair to say they left that institution in an ambiguous state, so it could later ooze or be squeezed out of the foundation. Such precisely the line Abraham Lincoln would take in his famous 1858 debates with Stephan A. Douglas in their Senate campaign: "Again; the institution of slavery is only mentioned in the

Constitution of the United States ... three times, and in [none] of these cases does the word 'slavery' or 'negro race' occur; but covert language is used each time, and for a purpose full of significance. ... and that purpose was that in our Constitution, which it was hoped and is still hoped will endure forever --- when it should be read by intelligent and patriotic men, after the institution of slavery shall have passed from among us --- there should be nothing on the face of the great charter of liberty suggesting that such a thing as negro slavery had ever existed among us. This is part of the evidence that the fathers of the government expected and intended the institution of slavery to come to an end. They expected and intended that it should be in the course of ultimate extinction. ... It is not true that our fathers, as Judge Douglas assumes, made this government part slave and part free. ... The exact truth is, that they found the institution existing among us, and they left it as they found it. But in making the government they left the institution with clear marks of disapprobation upon it. They found slavery among them and they left it among them because of the difficulty --- the absolute impossibility of its immediate removal."[2]

Then however utter certainty about "original intent" on slavery eludes, at least the matter not clear-cut, not beyond a reasonable doubt. Surely Lincoln stands for a reasonable man, in addition, one speaking for a large public opinion. Then if other reasonable men, speaking for just as large a public opinion, argue the opposite, yet the conclusion must stay something about which reasonable men disagreed, not clear-cut.

Slavery and interests – As they enter the courthouse door, such arguments put on the lawyerly robes of rational dispute, but these do not serve to hide the interests, nor frequently the mere antipathy of the litigants. The lawyers often play the role of those tailors in that tale about the emperor's new clothes, brazenly maintaining their clients dressed in raiment of supreme ethical value, woven together with invincible logic, while their cause stands shivering in naked self-interest, cloaked behind transparent rationalizations not capable to fool the innocence of a child. If such sounds too extravagant, only consider the justifications for slavery.

An apparently inescapable logic caught the slaveholders in a cleft. They claimed as their political birthright the Declaration of Independence. But if "all men are created equal," this left their practice greatly at odds with their principles. Yet such is human ingenuity that a specious pretense was not found wanting, founded too upon the highest authorities. Aristotle himself had written: "It is clear, then, that some men are by nature free, and others slaves, and that for these latter slavery is both expedient and right."[3] Those of a less classical bent quoted the Bible, translating the references to divine sanction. The racial divide furnished highly convenient theories of racial inferiority, setting a visible mark upon the brow of the natural slaves. Thus did the slaveholders come down from their dilemma, re-defining "men" into halves, abstracting Negroes from "all men," while professing to leave "are created equal" whole and untouched. By such exploits legal and political rhetoric maintains a logical tone, sufficient to satisfy the ear of an interested audience. So in 1861 at the outbreak of the Civil War, Alexander H. Stephens, vice-president of the Confederate States, proclaims in his "cornerstone" speech: "Our new government is founded upon ... its cornerstone rests upon the great truth, that the negro is not equal to the white man; that slavery --- subordination to the superior race --- is his natural and normal condition."[4]

Yet surely the lesson not that political science can rely upon either logic or the still, soft voice of conscience, overcoming interests by the force of mere rational or moral suasion. Rather interests can hold the field in the direst extremities. Over slavery a whole society formed a solid phalanx of conviction, defending an ethical position later regarded with repugnance. Even those like Jefferson, who privately lamented the wrong, could seldom bring themselves to renounce the vice. Only the rare slaveholder experienced a change of heart to the extent of manumission. Nor does the fiery oratory of Northerner abolitionists, such as William Lloyd Garrison or Wendell Phillips, do much to contradict this trend. Men may safely denounce vices denied them, but moral superiority untested in the crucible of temptation continues suspect. Present day protestations suffer from a similar lack of convincing self-sacrifice. It is easy enough to trample the Old South beneath the jackboots of moral contempt, but acquaintance with their literary remains show them a people quite as intelligent, capable, and in every way as human as ourselves. How many in 1850 would have had the intestinal fortitude to turn their backs on such a plantation as Scarlett's Tara? We must not expect such self-renunciation by the general run of mankind, but precisely the opposite.

Slavery may exhibit human capacity for rationalization to the extreme, but hardly exhibits an aberration. Throughout history and to the present day, ethical attitudes consistently demonstrate the warp of similar self-interest. A man who would construct his moral compass beyond such magnetic influence would have to go beyond the human universe, outside the pull of such gravitational attraction. No ethical norm appears entirely uninfluenced by interests.

The struggle over slavery – As Mr. Pierce Butler was heard to say in 1787 on the Convention floor: "[T]he security the Southern States want is that their negroes may not be taken from them, which some gentlemen within or without doors, have a very good mind to do." While balked at the Convention, these gentlemen did not relinquish that dangerous scheme. As the years passed, they kept bringing up the subject again and again, their righteousness hardening. For their part the slaveholders grew weary, frustrated, and increasingly intransigent. The fervor of both sides only increased over time. Working across the aisle and compromise became gradually more difficult. Finally, it was the emotional investments which became irreconcilable, overshadowing a rational assessment of interests, breaking even the consensus on union and democracy.

As mentioned, in 1787, the Confederation Congress by the Northwest Ordinance had prohibited the spread of slavery into that vast territory north of the Ohio River. Promptly in 1789, the First Congress had re-enacted that law with slight modification. At this boundary the nation paused. Then in 1803, the huge windfall of the Louisiana Purchase suddenly expanded beyond this property line, a largesse bearing the seeds of sectional discord. As the dynamic free population and economy of the North burst their bounds and headed west, they threatened to bury the South beneath an avalanche of non-slave and even anti-slave states. The Southern political elite saw their peculiar institution in danger, facing eventual extinction at the hands of a hostile majority in Congress.

In 1819, the enabling act to admit Missouri provoked a sectional crisis over slavery. A member of the House of Representatives from New York, James Tallmadge, Jr., moved an amendment, prohibiting importation of slaves into Missouri and emancipating at age twenty-five all slave children born after the date of admission. To the surprise of many, this Tallmadge Amendment sailed through the House, suggesting the emergence of an anti-slavery majority in that body. In the Senate the solid Southern phalanx blocked passage, but the height of the anger in these debates already reveals the depth of the divide. The specter of disunion looms amid threats of violence, as we hear Thomas W. Cobb of Georgia go on record, saying: "We have kindled a fire which ... seas of blood can only extinguish."[5]

Despite this verbal violence, the leadership North and South clung to the union and Congress managed a compromise, the Missouri Compromise, also called the Compromise of 1820. An enabling act admitted Missouri as a slave state, but prohibited further slavery in the Louisiana Purchase north of 36°30' latitude. This carried out west the old Mason-Dixon Line, surveyed in the 1760's between Maryland and

Pennsylvania. Thus, Congress limited the spread of slavery, the South receiving a weight in the balance.

But the eagle of manifest destiny continued to scream, and with the Mexican-American War from 1846 to 1848, the nation seized another huge chunk of real estate, later going to make up California, New Mexico, Utah, Arizona, Colorado, and Wyoming. As soon as 1849, organizing these lands sparked another crisis over slavery, replicating with more virulence the earlier crisis. John C. Calhoun of South Carolina, the leading Southern theorist, proclaimed in Congress that the North must be presented with "the alternative of dissolving the partnership or ceasing to violate our rights," meaning of course their right to own slaves. A Virginia congressman said if disunion meant war, then the fight would "be between men contending for their firesides, and the robbers who seek to despoil them of their rights, and degrade them before the world."[6] After a drawn out and wrenching clash, the congressional leadership once more managed another compromise, the Compromise of 1850. California came in as a free state, while Utah and New Mexico organized as territories without restrictions on slavery.

Yet the Compromise of 1850 failed to lay the controversy either. In 1854, the sectional rivals were back at it over Kansas and Nebraska. In 1858, William Seward, the leading candidate for the presidential nomination of the new Republican Party, would deliver his "irrepressible conflict" speech, predicting the nation would become "either entirely a slaveholding nation, or entirely a free-labor nation." In the same year Lincoln gave his House Divided Speech, saying: "A house divided against itself cannot stand."

While the slavery controversy finally erupted in the Civil War, so otherwise unprecedented in American experience, we should discern the familiar ingredients, the standard political script. On both sides, North and South, we see a gathering of interests, a marshaling of legal doctrines, an enlistment of ethical rationales, a making of emotional appeals. In such a way political factions have aligned through history and align today.

Slavery and minority rights – Throughout, Southern leaders perceived themselves in the minority, so sought out theories of minority rights, seeking to interpose these theories against their fear of the majority. It is easy to forget this today, when minority rights have come full circle, belonging to racial, ethnic, religious, and other minorities, almost any minority except that old southern white minority. But ante-bellum southern politicians, lawyers, and intellectuals broke the ground on minority rights. They were the original minority against the majority.

Along these lines the idea of "state rights" looked highly promising. These constitutional notions received articulation in the partisan warfare of the early republic and bore on their pedigree endorsement by the high names of Thomas Jefferson and James Madison. By 1798, President John Adams found his administration embroiled in a "Quasi-War" with France, a former ally which had offered us crucial aid in the Revolution. But by now the French had undergone their own, far bloodier revolution and were falling gradually back under monarchy with Napoleon. The great European geopolitical arena remorselessly pitted that nation against our former master Great Britain, opening a vortex which threatened to involve America. In attacking British commerce, French privateers inflicted serious damage on American shipping as well. Congress responded by resurrecting the defunct navy, and at Adams' orders American frigates took on the French raiders with considerable success. But Adams and Congress were Federalists, and so this undeclared war naturally excited violent denunciation from Jefferson, his lieutenant Madison, and their Republican Party. In a connected move, Congress in 1798 passed the Alien and Sedition Acts, making criminal the publication of "false, scandalous, and malicious writing" against the government. Federalist U.S. Attorneys instituted a series of prosecutions against Republican newspaper editors, who had been penning virulent philippics against Adams. Of course, the Jeffersonians denounced this law as unconstitutional, repressive, and generally iniquitous. Both sides were at each other's partisan throats, funneling legal doctrines into the fray.

Insofar as this argument concerned freedom of the press, the Jeffersonians look to have the better side. Surely the 1st Amendment contemplates free speech even in time of war. But into this context they inserted a far more dubious state rights concept, the doctrine of nullification. Under this theory, states retained power to "nullify" or void congressional acts. Never mind that the "supremacy clause" in Article VI declares: "The Constitution, and the Laws of the United States which shall be made in Pursuance thereof; ... shall be the Supreme Law of the Land;..." In the Kentucky and Virginia Resolutions of 1798 and 1799, covertly authored by Jefferson and Madison, Republican controlled legislatures professed to void the obnoxious congressional laws. Not surprisingly, Federalists denied the theory, several Federalist legislatures passing their own resolutions, formally repudiating such a power. However, no decisive confrontation developed between the federal and state governments. Jefferson unseated Adams in the election of 1800, and the Sedition Act lapsed by its own terms. The constitutional crisis passed.

But a common phenomenon in politics shows that as men and parties change places, they as conveniently change their tune. Once in office, Jefferson's administration fairly soon confronted its own foreign policy crisis. The British Navy, wielding their overwhelming supremacy, began boarding American ships, impressing seaman, and otherwise showing a lack of respect for the flag. Rather than declare war, the now Republican Congress passed the Embargo Act of 1807, designed to pressure Britain by cutting off her American trade. Except that shoe pinched both ways, especially nipping the toes of New England merchants and shippers, who were incidentally overwhelmingly Federalist in sympathy. In 1809, James Madison succeeded his chief Jefferson as president, and when the War of 1812 broke out, the British imposed a blockade, further damaging those same Northeastern, strongly Federalist mercantile interests. Looking around for a ready-made weapon, the Federalists now raised that same hue and cry of state rights, conveniently forgetting their previous condemnation of the doctrine. Massachusetts and Connecticut refused to put their militias under national control, although Article I provides: "The President shall be Commander in Chief ... of the Militia of the several States, when called into the actual service of the United States." More radical Federalists even bruited secession, the theory states could secede from the union. They called the Hartford Convention, which met in late 1814 and early 1815, apparently with such radical notions in mind, but adjourned with the passage of no more than some pale resolutions against Republican policies.

But the fire had been lit under state rights theory, which as the South fell into a minority, increasingly became a regional theme. In 1828, Congress passed a protective tariff, which favored northern manufacturers over southern agriculture. Initial concessions lowered the rates, but failed to satisfy South Carolina, which in 1832 took the next logical step, calling a convention and purporting to nullify the tariff. President Andrew Jackson, not a man to trifle with and a strong nationalist, hit back with his usual prompt decisiveness, threatening military action to enforce federal law. Congress backed him with a Force Act, and South Carolina defiantly recruited her militia. At which brink both sides blinked, working out a compromise behind the scenes. But sectional rivalry was turning up the heat under state rights theory. If still controversial, the doctrine becomes more articulate. Those dissatisfied with democratic outcomes resort more readily to its comforts. The idea is assuming the aspect of a "right" in the minds of true believers.

The leading Southern theoretician, John C. Calhoun, would develop the theory in excruciating detail. To his mind the majority poised over the minority, a constant threat to their rights. By his interpretation, the

Constitution left the states power to protect minority rights by nullification, reserving a veto over federal laws, which he referred to as a requirement for a "consensual majority." In other words, a mere majority in Congress was not enough, national laws had to command a consensus among the states. Such a conclusion appears to rest on very shaky ground, either as correctly reading the Founders' intent or the clear purpose of the Constitution. In practice, the scheme would have returned the nation to the weakness of a lose confederacy. But none of these considerations prevented Calhoun or his followers from erecting his theory into articles of faith.

But during this era, state rights enjoyed no success before the Supreme Court, whose institutional will-to-power lined up the other way. Rather the justices consistently ruled to expand "implied powers," those powers not specifically delegated in the Constitution, but reasonably implied for the federal government. To have done otherwise would have hobbled the federal enterprise at the outset, incidentally hobbling themselves, since if the federal government had little authority, neither would they. In 1819 in McCulloch v Maryland,[7] Justice Marshall's opinion upheld the congressional charter of a national bank, a highly controversial issue, and since no constitutional provision specifically spoke, a bold assertion by the Court. In 1824 in Gibbons v Ogden,[8] the "commerce clause" received expansive treatment, giving a wider sweep to congressional authority to regulate commerce. At this stage in the institutional struggle, their mutual interests made the Court and Congress allies, their common enemy the states. Only after vanquishing the states would this alliance fall apart.

Yet the boldness of both state rights theory and the Court's nationalism worked together, helping alter attitudes toward constitutional interpretation, setting the stage for Dred Scott. State rights theorists showed a readiness at bending constitutional meaning. In finding national powers implied, the justices showed a similar readiness to bend constitutional interpretation. Either way of thinking loosened constraints, taught facility in reaching longed-for conclusions. Verbal formulas that stood in the way were ripe for creative re-interpretation, and the original doctrine of judicial review, the limitation to clear-cut cases, fell exactly in that category. A barrier constructed of mere words was not likely to withstand such a storm, nor did it.

The facts in Dred Scott – Perhaps the facts of Dred Scott should begin with the man, but the sources fail to yield a definitive portrait. A short, slightly over five feet, African-American belonging to a Dr. John Emerson, Dred could not read or write, marking his X on legal documents. An article in a St. Louis newspaper the year of his famous case described him as "illiterate but not ignorant" with strong "common sense."[9] What we do know is that in 1846 he brought suit in the Missouri state courts, seeking his freedom. While a slave suing his master may sound unusual, other slaves had sought freedom down this same road to the courthouse and frequently won. Dred's claim looked to rest on strong legal grounds.

This case carried the style of Scott v Emerson, and the facts presented a straightforward story. Dr. Emerson had been dead some three years, and his widow stood as defendant. While alive, Dr. Emerson had served as an army surgeon and in transferring to military outposts took Dred along with him. These travels had carried them into the Wisconsin Territory, where the Missouri Compromise prohibited slavery. The essence of the lawsuit claimed that conveying Dred into free territory effected his legal emancipation.

What did the law say? For once the law seemed settled and clear, calling for no more than a mechanical application. This issue had come up, and the courts had decided it. As lawyers say, there were precedents, and when precedents exist, the judges are supposed to follow them. In particular, in the 1837 case of Rachel v Walker, the Missouri Supreme Court had addressed an identical set of facts.

In that earlier case a slave named Rachel had sought her freedom. The decision noted that her master, while "he was an officer of the United States army," had taken her to "Prairie du Chien ... in the Michigan Territory," just as in Dred's case, free territory under the Missouri Compromise. Judge Mathias McGirk of the Missouri Supreme Court put the question and answered it this way: "[S]hall it be said that because an officer of the army owns slaves in Virginia, that when as officer ... he is required to take command of a post in the non-slaveholding States or territories, he thereby has a right to take with him as many slaves, as will suit his interests or convenience? It surely cannot be the law; if this be true, then it is also true that the convenience or supposed convenience of the officer repeals ... the act of 1821 admitting Missouri into the Union."[10]

The court ordered Rachel freed, and the underlying legal principle was of fundamental significance to the controversy over the spread of slavery. If a slaveholder could convey slaves into free territory and still hold them in bondage, then the slaveholders carried a warrant in their pocket to obliterate all free territory. Instead, the law put an obligation over on them. Look before you leap. Understand that if you take slaves into free territory, you emancipate them by your own deed. Otherwise, the prohibition against the spread of slavery was meaningless.

In 1852 Dred Scott's case reaches that very same Missouri Supreme Court, which freed Rachel in 1837. The decision stands as a classic in the literature where judicial preconceptions control judicial outcomes. In the bare fifteen intervening years, the sectional conflict had reached fever pitch. A new pro-slavery majority of judges sits on the Missouri Supreme Court. These judges reverse the earlier rule laid down in such cases as Rachel v Walker. They held Dred Scott stayed a slave.

"Cases of this kind are not strangers in our courts. Persons have been frequently here adjudged to be entitled to their freedom, on the ground that their masters held them in slavery in territories or States in which that institution was prohibited. ... Times are not now as they were when the former decisions on this subject were made. Since then not only individuals but States have been possessed with a dark and fell spirit in relation to slavery, whose gratification is sought in the pursuit of measures, whose inevitable consequence must be the overthrown and destruction of our government. Under such circumstances it does not behoove the State of Missouri to show the least countenance to any measure which might gratify this spirit."[11]

In these words, judicial interpretation steps forward as frankly dynamic, reversing prior law, making new law, and openly acknowledging the policy considerations. Dred Scott got mangled as the machinery shifted into reverse. But while he lost, he didn't quit. Instead his lawyer filed a new case, moving from Missouri state court to federal court. This change of venue was possible only because in the interim Dred acquired a new master. Mrs. Emerson transferred title to her brother, Mr. John F.A. Sanford, a resident of New York. As Dred still resided in Missouri, this transaction created "diversity jurisdiction," which allows a citizen of one state to sue the citizen of another state in federal court. This new case carried the caption of Scott v Sandford, and yes, the official records mis-spell the defendant's name in one of the most famous cases in our legal history.

Some questions surrounding this new case will probably never be answered. Dred's suit against Mrs. Emerson looks the simple situation of a man wanting his freedom, but Scott v Sandford bears the marks of a political cause. Did the anti-slavery forces get it up as a test case? The transfer of Dred to Mrs. Emerson's brother raised some suspicions, being necessary to create the diversity jurisdiction, which allowed Dred to file his new case in federal court. Mrs. Emerson had remarried to a Dr. Calvin Chaffee of New York, who served two terms in Congress from 1855 to 1859 as a pronounced opponent of slavery. Was the transfer of Dred to Sanford a fiction to allow the new case to proceed? Sanford did not conduct the defense like a man in collusion with the plaintiff.

Historians have shifted every shred of evidence to the dregs. The fragmentary sources refuse to yield convincing proof. What can be known is that Dred's case finally reached the pinnacle at the United States Supreme Court.

Chief Justice Taney – Over the years, commentary has savagely handled Chief Justice Roger Brooke Taney, who wrote for the seven-judge majority, for his ruling in Dred Scott. But reading the extremely long opinion, one must confess the legal scholarship worthy to stand with any ever authored by the Court, revealing a first-class legal mind. The reader cannot fault him for failing to capably muster precedent or convincingly reason. If fault there be, such fault must lie elsewhere than with lawyerly skills, which suggests these not sufficient in themselves.

As Chief Justice, Taney backed his obvious professional attainments with a solid resume. Born in 1777, he was eighty years old when he authored Dred Scott, having lived long enough to become a holdover from the earlier Jacksonian era, whose allegiances go far to explain his motives. A successful lawyer, he had practiced with Francis Scott Key, best known as composer of the "Star Spangled Banner," whose sister Taney married. Rising to serve successively as Attorney General and Secretary of the Treasury in Andrew Jackson's cabinet, he became a close confidant of that president. In 1836 Jackson reciprocated his loyalty by appointing him Chief Justice to succeed the legendary John Marshall.

Where did Taney the man stand on slavery? He was from Maryland, a slave state, and in 1857 wrote a letter to a Massachusetts' clergyman much quoted against him: "Every intelligent person whose life has been passed in a slaveholding state, and who has carefully observed the character and capacity of the African race, will see that a sudden and general emancipation would be absolute ruin to the negroes, as well as to the white population."[12] Nevertheless, Taney had freed his own slaves thirty years gone by with he believed good results. In the past he had stood for eventual emancipation. But as we just heard a Missouri judge say, the times were not now as they had been. Attitudes had hardened as the crisis reached a height. It is hard to imagine any man in public life unaffected by these currents, nor was Taney.

The existing records show he had come to feel what he most treasured deeply threatened. As a Jackson man he shared his chief's passionate commitment to national union, a true patriot in that sense. Over that union loomed the imminent danger of dismemberment. And his thoughts had taken two other crucial steps, coming to believe in the Southern legal theory about a "right" to slavery and seeing the crisis as caused by the

North's wrongful aggression against Southern legal rights. Around this topic he had formed a set of fiercely held convictions.

Here were all the ingredients that call upon a man to do the right thing. If he could save the union, he must do so; if he could defend southern rights, he must do so; if he had to stretch a legal point in the process, he would do so. This psychology should be utterly familiar to those who study the history of the Court. While the issues change over time, the psychology within the judicial mind remains the same. Becoming convinced of the righteousness of a cause, the justices rule in keeping with their moral imperatives. Such is frequently lauded the very highest source of judicial conduct. So to this way of thinking we may condemn Taney's cause, but not his method. Indeed, it was he who pioneered the method right here in Dred Scott.

The ruling in Dred Scott – Turning to the opinion, in masterly legal fashion Taney proceeds to do three things: First, he extracts Negroes from the word "citizens" in the Constitution, thus ensuring they do not enjoy the fundamental rights guaranteed by that document. Second, he finds implied in the Constitution a "right to slavery," guaranteeing in perpetuity that institution across the whole nation. Third and finally, he will hold the Missouri Compromise of 1820 unconstitutional. However, since none of these conclusions clear-cut, he was forced to tacitly abandon that original, limited doctrine of judicial review, extending his reach to what previously beyond his grasp. By so doing, he establishes a new paradigm for judicial review, letting the justices interpret the Constitution upon their preconceptions, so becoming the ultimate constitutional lawmakers.

The Chief Justice disposes of his first issue this way: "The question is simply this: can a negro, whose ancestors were imported into this country and sold as slaves, become a member of the political community formed and brought into existence by the Constitution of the United States, and as such become entitled to all the rights, privileges, and immunities, guaranteed by that instrument to the citizen?"[13]

Having posed himself this question, he gives the answer: "We think they are not ... and were not intended to be included under the word 'citizens' in the Constitution, and can, therefore, claim none of the rights and privileges which that instrument provides for and secures to citizens of the United States."[14]

He reasons persuasively from a long list of legal citations, which must be recognized for what they are. While completely plausible, they are no more. Equally cogent facts and logic stood on the other side. For instance, there were many free blacks, some of whom owned slaves themselves. His argument conveniently ignores their rights, which had been frequently upheld in the courts. But at any rate, so Taney decides. Thus having abstracted blacks from the Constitution, the lawsuit should be over. If Dred not a citizen, he cannot sue in the first place. End of lawsuit. Taney says that: "Dred Scott was not a citizen of Missouri within the meaning of the Constitution of the United States, and not entitled as such to sue in its courts."[15] But not having accomplished his full purpose, he does not stop there. The Chief Justice intends to set slavery in constitutional cement for the infinite future.

Taney next writes these portentous words: "[T]he right of property in a slave is distinctly and expressly affirmed in the Constitution."[16] Again, he cites numerous precedents, tied together with impressive legal reasoning. Yet as previously discussed in some detail, the Constitution simply nowhere "distinctly and expressly affirms" slavery. Granting Taney every benefit of the doubt, his ruling can rise no higher than plausible constitutional interpretation. It cannot be accepted as clear-cut; reasonable men could and would disagree.

Even a brief reconnaissance of the main strongpoint of his argument, which rests on the 5th Amendment, shows his position far from unassailable. The 5th Amendment says no person shall be "deprived of ... property, without due process of law; nor shall private property be taken for public use, without just compensation." Taney weaves these words together with the existence of slavery, concluding the two together "distinctly and expressly" establish a constitutional right to hold slaves. But the issue was not the existence of property in slaves, rather the power to prevent the spread or abolish slavery. The 5th Amendment does not "distinctly and expressly" say that the spread of slavery cannot be prohibited. Nor does the 5th Amendment "distinctly and expressly" say that slavery cannot be abolished by the states or Congress, only requiring just compensation.

Taney next turns his guns upon the Missouri Compromise of 1820. For only the second time in the Court's history, he will hold a congressional law unconstitutional. We will recall that the Missouri Compromise forbid taking slaves north of a line on the map. Taney writes: "[I]t is the opinion of the court that the Act of Congress which prohibited a citizen from holding and owning property of this kind in the territory of the United States north of the line therein mentioned, is not warranted by the Constitution, and is therefore void; and that ... Dred Scott ... [was not] made free by being carried into this territory; even if [he] had been carried there by [his] owner with the intention of becoming a permanent resident."[17]

But what about that solemn judicial pledge never to declare laws unconstitutional except in clear-cut case beyond a reasonable doubt? Taney does not fail to claim such restraint. He writes: "It is not the province of the court to decide upon the justice or injustice, the policy or impolicy of these laws. The decision of that question belonged to the political or law-making power; ... The duty of the court is to interpret the [Constitution], with the best lights we can obtain on the subject, and to administer it as we find it, according to its true intent and meaning when it was adopted."[18]

Yet this cannot be accepted to rise above a sophism. However great his rhetorical skills, Taney cannot conceal the reality. He has made new constitutional law. In his zeal to do the right thing, he has had to leave behind the original, limited doctrine of judicial review. His conclusions are not clear-cut beyond a reasonable doubt. To impose his will forced him to seize power. He has shifted the paradigm of judicial review.

The aftermath of the case – In the outcome, the South appeared to have won. The Supreme Court found a right to slavery implied in the Constitution. Congress lacks all power to abolish or stop the spread of slavery. The entire nation is slave territory. As for the litigants in the case, Dred Scott has lost, remaining enslaved. But as a footnote, John Sanford will die some three months after the final decision. Title to Dred will transfer to a man named Tyler Blow, in whose family he had been raised, who then manumitted him. Dred died shortly thereafter in 1858 a free man.

But far from laying the controversy, historians cite Taney's opinion among the root causes of the Civil War. While inflaming Northern, anti-slavery passion to the boiling point, the ruling shut off the democratic safety valve, leaving no options except obedience or explosion. Yet the North blithely ignored the logic of their situation, went right on with democracy, ultimately electing Lincoln president, the standard bearer of the new Republican Party, all of whose aims focused around ending slavery. It was the South which then erupted into revolution, rejecting democracy for an appeal to arms.

After Dred Scott and as usual throughout the history of the Court, the winners celebrated the judicial wisdom, while the losers broadcast their wrath. The New Orleans' *Picayune* wrote of the Court as that: "August and incorruptible body, which elevated above the turmoil of parties, has so adjudged the vexed question of the times as to rebuke faction, confirm and strengthen the doubting, give the loftiest mind support to patriotism, and consolidate the Union --- be it reverently hoped --- for all time." Georgia's *Augusta Constitutionalist* trumpeted: "Southern opinion upon the subject of slavery ... is now the supreme law of the land ... and opposition to southern opinion upon this subject is now opposition to the Constitution, and morally treason against the Government." But Horace Greeley's *New York Tribune* denounced the holding as "atrocious," "wicked," and "abominable" and entitled to "just so much moral weight as ... the judgment of a majority of those congregated in any Washington bar-room." Taney was referred to as the "cunning chief" whose "collation of false statements and shallow sophistries" revealed a "detestable hypocrisy" and a "mean and skulking cowardice."[19]

Abraham Lincoln called the case "an astonisher in legal history,"[20] and it figured prominently in the 1858 Lincoln-Douglas Debates. What did Lincoln and his ilk mean to do about it? "We intend to get the decision overruled,"[21] was their position. By these words they carefully refrained from attacking the Court as an institution, stopped short of advocating institutional reform of the Court. Right then the good fight was over slavery. Men like Lincoln meant to keep all available energy focused. Not for the last time a greater cause postponed a lesser, mass appeal obscured detailed analysis, and coalition building trumped internal consistency. Opponents of slavery were not necessarily opponents of the Court. Sorting out the precise limits of judicial review required technical legal arguments, leading down an intellectual labyrinth, where the public mind might easily become confused. The issue lacked emotional appeal, unlike the visceral images of slavery. While a majority perhaps disliked slavery, start stirring in an attack on the Supreme Court, and you might scare off some of that support. The public reverenced the Constitution, had been taught to reverence the Court. Why radicalize your issue, taking on the Court as opposed to the specific case? As a matter of expediency, the foes of Dred Scott stuck with the prescription. They intended "to get the decision overruled." The opportunity was lost to address systemic, institutional issues.

After the Civil War, in 1865 and 1868, the 13th and 14th Amendments reversed the substance of Dred Scott, abolishing slavery and conferring citizenship on blacks. But the political method of Dred Scott would survive. In future, the justices would not limit themselves to voiding laws in clear-cut cases, but employ the power of judicial review dynamically.

Dred Scott and the abandonment of democracy – If we leave behind the ethical and legal guises worn by the controversialists, instead sticking with the facts of classic political analysis, we see both slavery and Dred Scott depend upon glaring violations of basic democratic precepts. Slavery disfranchised a class, denying the most fundamental democratic right, the ballot. Dred Scott transferred power from Congress to the Court, from a democratic to an aristocratic institution, denying the people's right to decide in another, but equally effective way. So much stands disclosed and open.

This same analysis reveals the institutional will-to-power, reliably operating, moving in discrete but definite steps: In 1803 in Marbury, the Court asserts the power of judicial review, at the time a dubious claim. To help that go down, they announce the doctrine as highly limited, applying only to clear-cut cases. Except that formula lacked an enforcement mechanism, amounting to no more than words on the printed page. In 1857 in Dred Scott, the Court's will-to-power breaks those verbal shackles. By tacitly interpreting away the restraint to clearcut cases, the Court creates a new, more dynamic paradigm for judicial review. By their own decree in Marbury, the justices staked their claim to judicial review, proclaiming the boundaries; by their own decree in Dred Scott, they expand the claim, extending the boundaries. No check or balance in the system prevented such judicial self-help; ultimately no device assured accountability to the people.

We should recall, too, the justification proclaimed for Marbury: That the Court would defend the people's will embodied in the Constitution, using judicial review to prevent congressional excess, protecting the minority against an out-of-control majority. But how did that theory perform in Dred Scott? The Constitution said nothing "clear-cut" about slavery, nor did Congress violate any "clear-cut" guarantee in stopping the spread of slavery. However, it must be confessed the Court did defend a minority, the slaveholding minority.

It sum, the Court did not uphold the Constitution, rather subverted constitutional process, seizing power away from the people, taking away from democracy precisely the sort of issue entrusted to that method. Nor does it seem "minorities" self-defining, sacred in and of themselves. Rather a choice remains to be made among minorities, and the Court anointed the "wrong" minority with a special status. We must notice, too, the Court took the side coinciding with its institutional will-to-power. The power of judicial review could increase only by ruling against the majority in Congress, by going with the Southern minority. Then as played out in the real world, the theory behind judicial review failed to perform as predicted, neither maintaining the Constitution nor doing a "good job" in protecting minorities.

When we come to compare institutional performance, Congress against the Court, surely the palm goes to the former. Congress offered an avenue for orderly evolution; the Court closed down the options. It was not Congress which rejected democratic processes or violated minority rights; the Court imposed judicial process and an un-appealing version of minority rights. Congress did "better" than the Court, democracy better than aristocracy.

On March 5, 1861, in his First Inaugural Address, Abraham Lincoln perhaps best sums up the implications of the Dred Scott Case: "[T]he candid citizen must confess, that if the policy of the government upon vital questions affecting the whole people is to be irrevocably fixed by decisions of the Supreme Court, the instant they are made in ordinary litigation between parties in personal actions the people will have ceased to be their own rulers, having to that extent practically resigned their government into the hands of that eminent tribunal."[22]

Public opinion may not have grasped these implications, but Lincoln had it exactly right. Dred Scott marked a change in the very form of the government. From now on "the policy of the government upon vital questions affecting the whole people" would be "irrevocably fixed by decisions of the Supreme Court." This would become evident during Reconstruction, when the justices would consolidate their new power with a further expansion.

CHAPTER 5

The Logic of Reconstruction

Reconstruction, stretching roughly from 1865 to 1877, exhibits a crucial set of conflicts between Congress and the Supreme Court, the underlying logic of interests and institutional power again decisive. A dominant majority in Congress, the Republicans, enacts a Reconstruction program to enfranchise the freed slaves and grant their civil rights, motivated not a little by partisan zeal, seeing in them a reliable block of party support. But the Supreme Court thwarts this portentous effort, interpreting away the intended rights, not failing to aggrandize judicial power in the process. By this inner logic, the Court emerges the era triumphant, institutionally enhanced, judicial supremacy confirmed and expanded, Congress defeated and lessened.

At the outset of Reconstruction another logic looked feasible. As the Civil War ended, two central problems faced the nation: First, how fit the rebel states back in the union? Second, how fit the freed slaves into society? These presented novel questions, not addressed in the Constitution, uniquely and for the first time raised. Yet really the Founders contemplated exactly such unexpected events, which past experience taught them to expect. Unable to predict the exact shape of the future, yet they predicted the best way to proceed into that uncertain future, also upon past experience. With the Constitution they set up a democracy. Then as the unforeseen arrived, you went forward through that method. The logic was simple and straightforward. That institution was supposed to churn out the best answers. Nor with the benefit of hindsight, did they err in reliance on democratic process, that guidance system navigating well. Congress set a course for equality and individual rights. Only the Founders' foresight failed to forestall tinkering with the system itself. The innovation of judicial supremacy threw off the gyrocompass, steering the ship of state away from equality and rights, veering toward the rocks of segregation. The aristocratic element in the constitution overcame the democratic element, radically altering course.

Present historical scholarship generally regards Reconstruction from still another perspective, viewing racism as the cause for the failures, racism as causing black disenfranchisement and loss of civil rights. Thus, once again the standard approach prefers an ideological explanation, neglecting institutional influences. In this familiar re-telling, Reconstruction becomes a morality tale about racism, prejudice motivating the white majority, causing discrimination against the black minority. Indeed, this story now serves as the classic exemplification of majority oppression of a minority. But however widespread the racism, this version cannot entirely cover the facts. Congressional Reconstruction guaranteed blacks the franchise and their civil rights. Such a program enacted by Congress must be taken to express the will of the majority. Then how can majority racism account for the ultimately negative outcomes? Some other factor or factors must have intervened, frustrating the will of the people.

Considering the essential role they play, we might think to look at the Court's personnel to find such an explanation, perhaps expecting to find a partisan divide between the justices and Congress, which the Republicans controlled during Reconstruction. But that expectation disappoints. In the cases of this era, thirteen justices participated.[1] This number includes a single holdover from the Taney Court, Justice Nathan Clifford, a New Englander with Southern sympathies, also the only justice appointed by a Democratic president, James Buchanan in 1858, and who lingered as late as 1881. Republican presidents appointed all the rest; all were Republicans; all held anti-slavery views before the Civil War; all resided in the North with two exceptions. Justice William Burnham Woods made his career as an Ohio lawyer, but after the War moved to Alabama, which hardly converts him to a southern sympathizer. Justice John Marshall Harlan came from the border state of Kentucky and had actually been a slaveholder, but stayed loyal to the Union, served in the Union army, and as a justice generally sided with congressional Republicans, voting for the freedmen's rights.

How can such biographies explain the Court's hostility to Northern and Republican policies during Reconstruction? Why did Republicans in Congress take one course, but Republicans on the Court an opposite course? But the social fact of institutional interests reconciles these inconsistencies. In Congress, Republicans acted to maintain their power by befriending the freedmen; on the Court, Republican justices acted to increase their power by ruling against the freedmen. The institutional will-to-power operated reliably, overriding partisan allegiance.

Stubbornly sticking with classic political analysis brings clarity to the era. At the most fundamental level, the defeat of Reconstruction rested upon a rejection of democratic principles, not just by the Court, but across the board. Democracy enacted congressional Reconstruction, giving the vote and their civil rights to the freedmen. But a minority, southerners and their northern partners, stubbornly resisted this course, which threatened their interests. Impelled by the judicial will-to-power, the Court intervened on behalf of this minority, overruling Congress, opening the way for black disenfranchisement and segregation. Aristocratic methodology replaced democratic processes, benefiting the minority whose interests coincided with the interests of the Court.

The politics of Reconstruction – The earthquake of the Civil War rent the national tectonic plate, leaving behind a giant fissure between North and South. The Union remained inside the constitutional boundary, the former Confederacy outside. Reconstruction required re-attaching the displaced landmass. But another fault line divided the political parties, the familiar Democrats and Republicans. Re-unification threatened to shift their constituencies like an aftershock. During Reconstruction these two features of political geology collide, running one-way North and South, another way Democrat and Republican.

In the North, Republicans rightly claimed credit for total victory. But as usual in American wars, the party-out-of power, this time the Democrats, had fought a stubborn political guerilla war on the home front, attacking every war measure or failure. Early in the 1864 election, these tactics looked likely to deliver them an electoral victory, only the fall of Atlanta in September turning the tide, saving Lincoln and his ticket barely in the nick of time. By the skin of their teeth the Republicans survived to achieve their supreme war aim, the preservation of the Union, the abolition of slavery coming as a necessary adjunct. In the aftermath their prestige soared, while the Democrats crashed with the collapse of their dire predictions. In April 1865, Republican leaders savored a rare moment of euphoria over Lee's surrendered at Appomattox. A brief month later in May, they stood on the reviewing stand in Washington for a ritual triumph, the Grand Review of the Armies, hardened Union veterans parading past in thousands, one of the great armies in military annals. Pride of accomplishment must have swelled their bosoms. Nor were these deeds trivial or ephemeral. Peeking around the corner of history, what would America have become without their feat of arms and will? As a country divided against itself, neither national half could have developed in fullness. Except even as they exalted in the present, the political ground began to move beneath their feet, a tremor the more prescient all along sensed coming. In the long run their great cause of union carried a negative corollary for them, which endangered their ascendency and put in peril a peace on their terms.

They could not doubt the defeated South, whose capacity and

persistence in the war would carry over to the peace, the terrible cost of their lost cause only reinforcing the emotional commitment. In this respect southerners differed little from many conquered peoples, whose resentments often persist for centuries. Cultures appear far more eager to treasure a grievance than learn a lesson. So as the warfare of armies gave way again to the strife of the parties, the order of battle would not re-align. Confederate veterans would not suddenly recruit the Republican Party. No, the nation might re-unite, but southerners would re-unite with the Democrats, not the hated Republicans. Yes, the South would rise again, re-deployed in the ranks of the Democratic Party, possibly tipping the balance of power.

Only what about the new freedmen? About four million ex-slaves stepped forward to assume some greater role. In a population of thirty-one million, they represented a large and distinct group, sure to coalesce around their interests, for their friends and against their foes. They looked as unlikely as the Confederates to forgive and forget, the psychology of hurt feelings the same, although resting on firmer ground. In these people Republicans saw a potential counterweight in the balance, a dilution of Democratic strength.

As eager as 1861 showed southerners to leave home, in 1865 they were as ready to get back in the house. Conceding the abolition of slavery, why shouldn't they take up their rights of occupancy just the same? They would just hold new elections, send new senators and representatives to the Capitol, and resume their former abode. In fact, by refusing to let them depart, hadn't the North insisted they return? Or if a state couldn't secede, they had never left. Either view forced them once more into the government. Of course, this sudden alacrity involved strong prudential motives. It made a great deal more sense to re-seat yourselves at the national council board, taking part in the deliberations, rather than stand shivering in your estranged relatives' anteroom, awaiting unpleasant pronouncements. And under this rosy scenario, southerners would shortly arrive on the doorstep in greater numbers. We will recall the "three-fifths" compromise, where slaves counted three-fifths for apportioning the House. Now the freed slaves counted a whole, growing the South's proportionate share. With the ex-slaves still disenfranchised, that gain went to the ex-slaveholders. All of which neatly hoisted Republicans with their own petard. The very same men who populated the Confederate Congress would take seats in the Senate and House of the United States, and there would be more of them. Attaching to the Democrats, they would re-form a block, united in opposition, able to impact if not dictate policy. They would not soon vote to enfranchise the freedmen, but what might they not vote to do?

It is hardly imaginable Republicans granted the force of such arguments. If possession nine-tenths of the law, they were the tenant in possession of Congress. Article I provides that: "Each House shall be the Judge of the Elections, Returns and Qualifications of its own Members." They rejected the new members sent in by the South. Next they meant to use their legislative power, setting some preconditions for re-admission. In their view, legal technicalities were either beside the point or in their favor. Whether the Confederate States never left or forcibly re-united made no difference. In either event, Congress could pass laws and propose constitutional amendments. By this authority they meant to guarantee the freedmen's rights, most importantly the franchise. Their prudential motives stand out as clearly as the ex-Confederates. If they did the right thing by the freedmen, their interests drove them to it. They needed those potential allies; they needed their votes. Whatever their missteps, this basic political calculation underlies all they did during Reconstruction.

Congressional Reconstruction – Traditionally after civil wars reconciliation waits on retribution, and vengeance operates in tandem with policy, the first step a bloodbath, the second step designed to put the losers at some permanent disadvantage. But despite cries for such a settling of scores, the congressional program for Reconstruction varied widely from this tradition. No fresh effusion of blood came after the ceasefire, and the Confederate states fairly quickly came back into the union under the same terms as everyone else.

Of course, the laws already made treason a capital crime, and southerners had violated those laws en masse, most notably their political leadership and cadre of famous generals, many of whom had compounded their felony by breaking oaths earlier given to the U.S. government or army. Yet only one misfortunate soul suffered on the scaffold, Captain Henry Wirz, commandant of the notorious Andersonville Prison Camp. Jefferson Davis languished three unpleasant years in confinement, but was never brought to trial and lived out his days in comfort, unrepentant to the end. General Robert E. Lee and most others never spent a day in captivity. An attempt was made to exclude them from office, but this operated only to an extent and for a time. Unlike Davis, most former Confederates quickly managed to re-take their stations in the national life. Even such a notable as the Confederate Vice-President, Alexander H. Stephens, went on to serve in the U.S. House and as Governor of Georgia. His irrepressibility was the norm.

Yet the South did suffer through a period divided into military districts, army generals ruling like proconsuls. Many of the familiar re-enactments of Reconstruction portray this phase. Such highly colored versions as *Birth of a Nation* became the stuff of Southern legend, depicting whites deprived of their rights, insulted, and resorting to the clandestine violence of the Klan to win back their honor and "redeem" their region. More recently, revisionists have largely had their way, condemning Southern racism, indeed usually condemning Northern racism in the same breath, blaming both for the rise of segregation. Yet at the time congressional Republicans fought long and hard for the freedmen.

This commitment reflects in the permanent congressional Reconstruction program, designed to last into the foreseeable future. This effort raised three great pillars of constitutional law, the Reconstruction Amendments, and added a civil rights act for good measure. In 1865 the 13th Amendment abolished slavery; in 1868 the 14th Amendment guaranteed the freedmen their civil rights; in 1870 the 15th Amendment granted them the franchise. Because of their scope, the Reconstruction Amendments have sometimes been called the "Second American Constitution." Finally, the Civil Rights Act of 1875 prohibited segregation. When the temporary expedients of military occupation receded, these legal structures were intended to stay in place, permanently fixing the political landscape.

Whatever the errors of the military phase, these Reconstruction laws describe the over-arching, long-term congressional program. The wisdom, moderation, and determination should be easily seen. Everything flows from and through democratic principles and methods. The reasoning applies the Founder's logic, carries forward by extending the principles of "equality," "unalienable rights," and "consent of the governed." Give the freedmen the vote and their other rights. Let the situation evolve from there; let democracy work; let everyone find their own level. If such a program shows wisdom and moderation, Congress was wise and moderate. If constitutional amendments show determination, Congress was determined.

But it was not to be. As shortly became evident, all this vast legislative effort would go for naught, rendered an unfulfilled promise written on the face of the Constitution for three-quarters of a century. Through a remarkable process of constitutional interpretation, the Supreme Court would turn these laws inside out, reversing the intended effect. Instead of guaranteeing black enfranchisement and civil rights, the exact opposite would be allowed.

What is perhaps surprising, the "majority" and democracy continue to take the blame, not the Court. In the name of their rights, a minority rejects the congressional program for Reconstruction. Using their new powers under judicial review, the Supreme Court upholds this minority. Yet today we hear these Court decisions repeatedly referred to as "majoritarian." By the methods of judicial supremacy, blacks endure disenfranchisement and denial of their rights, a route contrary to democratic principles, reversing democratic outcomes. Yet institutional performance is ignored in the re-telling, reversing the moral of the tale as well. Since blacks end up segregated, democracy must have failed, the majority must have oppressed the minority. So mis-assigning the blame, this version condemns the people and democracy, while absolving the Court. So misunderstanding the object lesson, this view wants to repeat a failed strategy, enforcing minority rights through judicial supremacy instead of adhering to democracy.

The intent of the 14th Amendment – The congressional program for Reconstruction began with the 13th Amendment, which abolished slavery. Ratified in 1865, the operative language reads: "Neither slavery nor involuntary servitude ... shall exist within the United States." Thus, Congress reversed Dred Scott, overturning Justice Taney's ruling the Constitution guaranteed a "right" to slaves. If that meaning had ever been in, it was now out. More than that, the Constitution now expressly forbade slavery.

Even the South accepts this end to slavery, but in 1865 military Reconstruction was not yet in full force. The ex-Confederates still control those state legislatures, and they began to fight a legal rearguard action. They began enacting so-called "Black Codes." These laws contemplated replacing slavery with a sort of peonage, relegating blacks into a second-class status. The Mississippi Vagrant Law of 1865 serves as a typical: "If any freedman, free negro, or mulatto shall refuse to pay any tax levied ... it shall be prima facie evidence of vagrancy, and it shall be the duty of the sheriff to arrest ... such person ... and proceed at once to hire for the shortest time such delinquent tax-payer to any one who will pay the said tax." The Alabama effort along these lines declared a "stubborn or refractory servant" or "servants who loiter away their time" as "vagrants," punishable by a fined of $50 and in default of payment "hired out" for "six months."[2] The tendency of such legislation is obvious.

But the Republicans in Congress could pass legislation, too, with a purpose just as obvious. They had no intention to put up with the chicanery of Black Codes, which cheated both them and the freedmen, rendering each incapable of assisting the other. They had heard enough about state rights before the war and in no mood for the same song, second verse. If Southern legislatures could deny black rights by state law, that left ex-slaves to the tender mercies of their former masters, not really free except in name. Republicans in Congress could not lend them a hand up, nor reduced to second-class citizens, could they return the favor. Rather than accept that, Republicans determined to interdict recalcitrance at the source, once and for all. Not only would they pass a law, they would amend the Constitution. In 1866 they brought forward a bill to guarantee the freedmen their full panoply of civil rights. When ratified in 1870, this law became the 14th Amendment. An examination of the sources leaves no doubt of the intent.

The very first sentence of the 14th Amendment is that: "All persons born or naturalized in the United States ... are citizens of the United States and of the State wherein they reside." In these words we still hear the reverberations of Dred Scott, where Chief Justice Taney ruled Negroes non-citizens, putting them outside constitutional protections. Well, if someone wanted to argue that abolition did not confer citizenship, this made it perfectly clear, and they would have to find another argument.

However, the next sentence of the 14th Amendment contains the most famous and significant language: "No state shall make or enforce any law which shall abridge the privileges or immunities of citizens ... nor shall any State deprive any person of life, liberty, or property, without due process of law; nor deny to any person ... the equal protection of the laws."

As usual with constitutional language, this sounds impressive, appealing emotionally. But we have to ask: What exactly does it mean?

The Amendment starts by enjoining that "[n]o state shall abridge the privileges or immunities of citizens." Referred to as the "privileges and immunities clause," what did these words intend in the real world? That question defers for the future those two other great clauses, "due process of law" and "equal protection of the law." In the passage of time, these last two far eclipse the career of the former. But at the outset, the "privileges and immunities" looked of equal dignity, holding out an immediate promise of rights to the freedmen.

This conclusion becomes evident by reading the congressional debates, preserved in the *Congressional Globe*. Customarily the member introducing a bill expounds the purpose, and on May 23, 1866, Senator J.M. Howard of Michigan rises to perform that office, speaking on behalf of the proposal which became the 14th Amendment. He addresses specifically and extensively the "privileges and immunities clause."

The Founding Fathers had used that term "privileges and immunities of citizens" in the Constitution, where Article IV, Section 2 says: "The Citizens of each State shall be entitled to all Privileges and Immunities of

Citizens in the several States." In an 1823 case, Corfield v Coryell, Supreme Court Justice Bushrod Washington, incidentally a nephew of George Washington, had provided a further definition, writing: "[W]hat are the privileges and immunities of citizens in the several States? We feel no hesitation in confining these expressions to those privileges and immunities which are in their nature fundamental ... What these fundamental principles are it would, perhaps, be more tedious than difficult to enumerate. They may, however, be all comprehended under the following heads: liberty, with the right to acquire and possess property of every kind, and to pursue and obtain happiness and safety."[3]

Justice Washington obviously gives a sweeping definition, leaving us asking: What right would not fit under this roomy umbrella? In his speech, Senator Howard quotes in full Justice Washington's words, emphatically adopting these as his own, saying: "Such is the character of the privileges and immunities spoken of in ... the Constitution."[4]

Yet Senator Howard does not stop there, instead reaching out to expressly include the Bill of Rights. He continues: "To these privileges and immunities, whatever they may be --- for they are not and cannot be fully defined in their full entire extent and precise nature --- to these should be added the personal rights guaranteed and secured by the [Bill of Rights] of the Constitution; such as freedom of speech and of the press ... the right to be exempt from unreasonable searches and seizures ... and [the] right to be tried by an impartial jury."[5]

Senator Howard has now told what he intends "privileges and immunities" to signify in the 14th Amendment. These words cover Justice Washington's definition plus the Bill of Rights. Like the justice, the senator evidently means a generous, open-handed, inclusive reach, encompassing every "fundamental right," incorporating too the Bill of Rights. In the essence of caution, he refuses to give a precise list, fearing to leave something out. What more could he do to bring before the country a very broad range of protected rights?

But we recall the Constitution already contains a privileges and immunities clause, already contains the Bill of Rights. Why then does the country need the 14th Amendment? If the people already possess all these rights, why bother to re-state them in a new constitutional amendment?

The answer was that these rights restrained only the federal government, not the state governments. Over the years the courts had uniformly upheld this understanding. Senator Howard makes that very point: "Now, sir, here is a mass of privileges, immunities, and rights, ... and it is a fact well worthy of attention that the course of decision of our courts and the present settled doctrine is, that all these immunities, privileges, rights, thus guaranteed by the Constitution or recognized by it, are secured to the citizen solely as a citizen of the United States ... They do not operate in the slightest degree as a restraint or prohibition upon State legislation. States are not affected by them."[6]

Senator Howard has reached the pivot in his speech. After broadly defining privileges and immunities, he has told us these rights bind only the federal government, not the states. Next he will turn and tell us the very purpose of the 14th Amendment is to change that settled legal doctrine, to make all these privileges and immunities binding on the states, to place all those rights under federal protection. This essential comprehension expresses the dynamic intent of the Amendment, and it cannot be too much stressed.

Let us read what he says, adding italics to stress the crucial meaning: "The great object of the ... amendment is, therefore, *to restrain the power of the States and compel them at all times to respect these great fundamental guarantees.*"[7]

Congressional intent, then, in proposing the 14th Amendment was to guarantee the "privileges and immunities" of the freed slave, which is to say all their civil rights. When we understand the background of the controversy and Republican motivation, there can really be no doubt of this reading.

Gutting the privileges and immunities clause – In 1873, a bare few years after Senator Howard spoke with such clarity, the Supreme Court hands down the Slaughter-House Cases. The pun proved irresistible to commentators, who have repeatedly remarked that the case "gutted" the privileges and immunities clause. Instead of guaranteeing the freedman's civil rights, that purpose suffers a virtual repealer. Congressional intent becomes an unfulfilled promise, a dead letter on the face of the Constitution. In the wider world, the process of judicial interpretation changes the course of history.

These Slaughter-House cases come out of Louisiana, do not directly concern blacks at all, but critically concern the privileges and immunities clause. At issue is the constitutionality of a Louisiana statute. In 1869 their legislature created a corporate monopoly over the slaughter-houses in New Orleans, centralizing and regulating that noxious trade, a measure justified with some reason by public health concerns. But the common law inherited from England arguably forbids governmental grants of monopoly. Numerous butchers felt their livelihood threatened and filed suit, claiming a violation of their "privileges and immunities" under the 14th Amendment.

The case presents a straightforward legal issue: Does or does not the "privileges and immunities clause" of the 14th Amendment forbid such monopolies? In turn this issue presents a classic exercise in constitutional interpretation. Nothing in the Amendment mentions monopolies; looking back at Senator Howard's speech, nothing mentioned monopolies. Does such neglect mean the rule against monopolies outside the privileges and immunities clause? That is, did Congress intend to prevent such state grants of monopoly? Not necessarily. Legislators cannot cover every eventuality in debate. Senator Howard carefully left considerable wiggle room in his definition, understanding new and unforeseen circumstances always arise.

As has been said, where the law contains such gaps, their legitimate and essential function requires the courts to interpret the law, giving the answers. However, when judges go further, over-writing clear meaning, substituting their preferred meaning, this as clearly raises significant questions. It is one thing to interpret law; it is still another to ignore the manifest purpose of legislation. For courts to do the later disregards that rule conceding legislative primacy, replacing legislative process with judicial law making. Of course, in speaking about the 14th Amendment, we are speaking about constitutional rather than statutory law, yet similar considerations apply. Where, as with the "privileges and immunities" clause, the legislature makes clear the intent of a constitutional amendment, an intent later ratified by the people, serious concerns arise if courts do more than fill in gaps, if they go so far as to cancel the obvious intent, reading in their own intent. Yet in the Slaughter-House Cases this is precisely what happens.

Mr. Justice Samuel Freeman Miller delivers the opinion for the Court. To define privileges and immunities, he begins by re-quoting that same language Senator Howard quoted from Justice Bushrod Washington: "[W]hat are the privileges and immunities of citizens in the several States? We feel no hesitation in confining these expressions to those privileges and immunities which are in their nature fundamental ... What these fundamental principles are it would, perhaps, be more tedious than difficult to enumerate. They may, however, be all comprehended under the following heads: liberty, with the right to acquire and possess property of every kind, and to pursue and obtain happiness and safety."[8]

Precisely at this point in his speech Senator Howard had pivoted, telling us: "The great object of the first section of the amendment is, therefore, to restrain the power of the States and compel them at all times to respect these great fundamental guarantees."

But at this identical, critical pivot point, Justice Miller leaps precisely the opposite way, as shown by the added italics: "The description [of fundamental rights by Justice Washington], when taken to include others not named, but which are of the same general character, embraces nearly every civil right for the establishment and protection of which organized government is instituted ... They are ... rights belonging to an individual as a citizen of a state. ... *They are left to the state governments for security and protection, and not by this article placed under the special care of the Federal government.*"[9]

The contrast between the Senator's intent and the Justice's ruling could not be more glaring. The startling result is this: Justice Miller has adopted that very broad definition of "privileges and immunities," including "nearly every civil right for the establishment and protection of which organized government is instituted." Next he has said these rights "are left to the state governments for security and protection." So in effect, he negates federal protection for virtually every right the clause intended to protect. "They are left to the state governments for security and protection, and not by this article placed under the special care of the Federal government."

What is left of the privileges and immunities clause of the 14th Amendment? The answer is almost nothing. Justice Miller seems to have felt some such criticism might be made. He writes: "But lest it be said that no such privileges and immunities are to be found if those we have considered are excluded, we venture to suggest some which owe their existence to the Federal government ... One of these is ... the right of the citizen of this great country ... to come to the seat of government to assert any claim he may have upon that government ... He has the right of free access to its seaports ... Another privilege of a citizen ... is to demand the care and protection of the Federal government over life, liberty and property when on the high seas."[10]

In other words, the privileges and immunities clause guarantees no more than the travel to Washington City and the national seaports, as well as protection on the high seas. Not surprisingly then, in the case about the New Orleans's slaughter-houses, the Court upholds the monopoly. Any common law right against monopoly falls outside such a tight definition of privileges and immunities. But other, wider implications stood out as immediately obvious.

Justice Miller acknowledges elsewhere in the opinion that "lying at the foundation" of the 14th Amendment, the "pervading purpose" is "the freedom of the slave race, the security and firm establishment of that freedom, and the protection of the newly made freedmen and citizens from the oppression of those who had formerly exercised unlimited dominion over him."[11] If such a purpose lay at the foundation, then he had just sapped away all the solid matter in that foundation, leaving behind empty air. He gutted the privileges and immunities clause as a guarantee for the freedmen's civil rights. Indeed, such would be the result in the real world. The privileges and immunities clause became a dead letter.

At the same time he demonstrates the dynamic doctrine of judicial supremacy. All notions of deference to congressional intent disappear, all deference to the intent of constitutional amendments. The original doctrine of judicial review is completely reversed, going in the opposite direction. No longer limited to voiding congressional laws in "clear-cut" cases, the justices feel free to interpret away the "clear-cut" meaning of the Constitution itself, simply reading in their own meanings. In effect, the Court now possesses the power to amend that document, imposing the justices' own preconceptions.

The intent of the 15th Amendment – To democratic theory the franchise stands as the most fundamental right, the only real power to the people, the source, the defense of all their other rights. The experience of all history confirms the theory. While on the other hand, projects to deny or dilute the franchise, either to cut out foes or rope in friends, stand as a constant temptation to political factions. Such endeavors are very much with us to this day, as witness the gerrymander or disputes about voter registration and identification. But during Reconstruction this problem presented in acute form, the enfranchisement of the freedmen being the essential issue of that era.

The 13th Amendment had freed the slaves; the 14th Amendment had conferred citizenship and their civil rights. But neither Amendment explicitly granted the vote. In 1869, the Republicans, with their firm majority in Congress, moved to foreclose any doubt with another constitutional amendment. Senator William M. Stewart of Nevada well summed up their sentiments, speaking on January 28, 1869, at the start of the debate: "It must be done. It is the only measure that will really abolish slavery. It is the only guarantee against peon laws and against oppression. It is that guarantee which was not put in the Constitution of the United States originally, the guarantee that each man shall have a right to protect his own liberty. ... Let it be made the immutable law of the land; let it be fixed; and then we shall have peace. Until then there is no peace. ... I want a vote."[12]

In 1870, the states ratified the 15th Amendment, providing that: "The right of citizens of the United States to vote shall not be denied or abridged by the United States or by any State on account of race, color, or previous condition of servitude." And further, "The Congress shall have the power to enforce this article by appropriate legislation."

Congress quite promptly passed the Enforcement Act of 1870, designed to enforce the right: "[A]ny ... officer of election, whose duty it is or shall be to receive, count, certify, register, report, or give effect to the vote of [a] citizen, who shall wrongfully refuse or omit to receive, count, certify, register, report, or give effect to the vote of such citizen ... shall ... be guilty of a misdemeanor."[13]

Interpreting away the franchise – But once again a minority would appeal to the Court against the majority. And once again the justices would interpret away congressional intent, beginning with U.S. v Reese in 1876.

The facts of this case present an uncomplicated picture. Two men named Reese and Fouchee stand in the dock accused. While serving as inspectors in a Kentucky municipal election, they refused to receive or count the vote of one William Garner, "a citizen of the United States of African descent." The U.S. Attorney secures an indictment and prosecutes them under the Enforcement Act. The jury convicts them.

But when the appeal reaches the Supreme Court, we learn again about legal logic backed by judicial power. Chief Justice Morrison Remick Waite writes the opinion, beginning: "The Fifteenth Amendment does not confer the right of suffrage upon anyone. It prevents the States, or the United States, however, from giving preference in this particular, to one citizen of the United States over another, on account of race, color or previous condition of servitude."[14]

This phrasing sounds confusing at best. Reading carefully, he says: "The Fifteenth Amendment does not confer the right of suffrage upon anyone." But didn't the 15th Amendment say "the right of citizens to vote shall not be denied or abridged on account of race, color, or previous condition of servitude?" Then what can Justice Waite mean by saying that the Amendment "does not confer the right of suffrage upon anyone?" What can he mean by going on to say that it only "prevents giving preference on account of race, color, or previous condition of servitude." Isn't that a distinction without a difference?

Chief Justice Waite is engaging in a subtle, all-important verbal quibble. Does the 15th Amendment protect the right of blacks to vote? Or can you interpret it to mean something less? How about this alternative: The 15th Amendment *only* protects blacks against discrimination in voting *based upon race*, the unspoken corollary being they are *not* protected against discrimination *on some other basis*? Justice Waite just chose that second option. Carried out to the logical conclusion, his reasoning will lead to astonishing and momentous consequences.

But before following to that end, what can it matter in the immediate case? The facts disclose a denial based on race, Reese and Fouchee having refused to count the vote of Garner, "a citizen of African descent." Where's the problem then? Except Justice Waite's first hyper-technical distinction carefully sets up another, equally technical distinction.

We must recall the defendants not charged with violating the 15th Amendment, rather with violating the Enforcement Act. The Amendment grants the right to vote, but doesn't itself make denying the vote a crime. Rather the Enforcement Act makes denying the vote a crime. Indeed, the Constitution enacts no crimes; Congress passes criminal statutes. However, it can only do so under power delegated by the Constitution. In this dichotomy lies a crucial distinction upon which Justice Waite means to play.

He next writes: "The Amendment has invested the citizens of the United States with a new constitutional right. ... That right is exemption from discrimination in the exercise of the elective franchise on account of race, color or previous condition of servitude. ... This leads us to inquire whether the Act now under consideration is appropriate legislation for that purpose."[15]

He is maneuvering to attack the constitutionality of the Enforcement Act. First, he limited the 15th Amendment to racial discrimination. Put another way, he declared the Amendment does not protect the right to vote, instead only protecting the right to vote against racial discrimination. Now he has asked: Is the Enforcement Act "appropriate legislation" for that more narrowly defined purpose? Obviously he is setting up a negative answer. He will next say that the Enforcement Act protects against *more* than racial discrimination. Therefore, he will conclude the Act overbroad, not "appropriate legislation" as authorized by the Amendment, and so unconstitutional and void.

What about that? To re-read the Enforcement Act: "[A]ny officer of election whose duty it is ... [t]o count ... the vote of [a] citizen who shall wrongfully refuse ... [t]o count ... the vote of such citizen ... shall ... be guilty of a misdemeanor."

Since the 15th Amendment outlaws racial discrimination in voting, the Enforcement Act might seem "appropriate legislation" to punish such a wrongful refusal. But in a remarkable instance of judicial tunnel vision, Justice Waite refuses to see the Amendment and the Act at the same time and fit them together into an intelligible pattern. Instead he rules it was not enough for Congress merely to say: *refused to count a vote*. Instead Congress should have said: refused to count a vote *because of race*. Since Congress neglected the extra verbiage, the Enforcement Act is overbroad, not appropriate legislation, and hence unconstitutional.

Chief Justice Waite brings down the ax of judicial review on the neck of the unfortunate Enforcement Act, decapitating it, with these words: "It is only when the wrongful refusal [to receive a vote] at such an election is because of race ... that Congress can interfere, and provide for its punishment. ... We feel compelled to say that, in our opinion, the language of the [Enforcement Act] does not confine [its] operation to unlawful discrimination on account of race."[16]

What was the result in the wider, real world? Not only did Chief Justice Waite throw out the Enforcement Act of 1870. That was a heavy blow in itself. But carry out his reasoning, and where does the logic arrive? If the 15th Amendment only prevents racial discrimination in voting, that does not prevent discrimination on an alternative basis, provided someone clever enough to think one up. So you can cut off voting rights by inventing such devices as literacy tests, property qualifications, or whether a man's grandfather could vote. Re-label discrimination another way, and reach the same end by another means. That is the deliberate teaching of Reese.

It is not too much to say that the Court has turned upside down and pulled inside out the 15th Amendment. Down South laws appeared on the statute books like: "He [the elector] shall be able to read and write, and shall demonstrate his ability to so do when he applies for registration ... If he is not able to read and write ... then he shall be entitled to register and vote if he shall ... be the bona fide owner of property assessed ... at the valuation of not less than three hundred dollars ... No male person who was on January 1st, 1867 ... entitled to vote ... and no son or grandson of any such person ... shall be denied the right to register and vote in this State by reason of his failure to possess the educational or property qualifications prescribed."[17]

This "grandfather plan" accomplished exactly the scheme proposed in Reese. Since few blacks could read and most owned little property, those provisions eliminated them. As none voted prior to 1867, nor were sons or grandsons of such persons, that provision benefited them not at all. Thus, the law excluded blacks from the franchise for reasons supposedly unrelated to race. A Negro might still be a Negro by any other name, but as long as the law used that other name, it was legal to discriminate against him.

Was this the reform Congress and the people intended by the 15th Amendment? It is impossible to believe. How did blacks end up disenfranchised down South after Reconstruction? Who gutted the promise in the 15th Amendment? Anyone who reads the Reese Case can see the justices wielding the bloody knife. It is incomprehensible they did not understand exactly what they were doing.

While if we remember the original doctrine of judicial review, it is only too obvious how far the power has come. In the Slaughter-House

Cases, the justices felt free to read their own meaning into the Constitution. Now in this Reese Case, they first read their own meaning into the Constitution, then use that meaning to declare a congressional law unconstitutional. Any limitation to "clear-cut" cases utterly disappears. Deference to Congress becomes a chimera, as does even deference to the will of the people. Filling up the new paradigm for judicial review, the Court ascends in the power gradient.

The Civil Rights Act of 1875 – It surprises many to learn that as long ago as 1875 Congress enacted an anti-segregation law, the Civil Rights Act of 1875. Often over-looked or forgotten, this law fits badly in the standard version of Reconstruction, which depicts the era as implacably racist. Nor does the Act's judicial fate comport well with the image of the Court as defending minority rights. But both the law and its fate line up perfectly with the logic of Reconstruction, Congress and the Court reaching contrary outcomes, the judicial will-to-power predominant.

The Civil Rights Act of 1875 read: "That all persons within the jurisdiction of the United States shall be entitled to the full and equal enjoyment of the accommodations, advantages, facilities and privileges of inns, public conveyances on land or water, theaters and other places of public amusement; subject only to the conditions ... applicable alike to citizens of every race and color, regardless of any previous condition of servitude."[18] Violations carried a fine of up to $500.00, a pretty stiff sum in those days, and injured individuals could also sue for damages.

Obviously, the Act prohibits segregation in places of public accommodation, resort, and transportation. But after what we have seen so far, we may already begin to wonder: How is the Court going to say the Act violates the Constitution?

Now the 13th Amendment had said: "Neither slavery nor involuntary servitude ... shall exist within the United States." The 14th Amendment had said: "All persons born or naturalized in the United States ... are citizens of the United States and of the State wherein they reside." And: "No state shall make or enforce any law which shall abridge the privileges or immunities of citizens ... nor shall any State deprive any person of life, liberty, or property, without due process of law; nor deny to any person ... the equal protection of the laws." Both Amendments further said: "Congress shall have the power to enforce this article by appropriate legislation."

Those who pushed through the Civil Rights Act had argued it was "appropriate legislation" under either Amendment, part and parcel of abolishing slavery, defining citizenship, assuring the privileges and immunities of citizens, due process, and equal protection. In this same vein, they argued that far from invading any constitutional rights, the Act made effectual those rights, preventing invidious discrimination. But opponents answered from another, already familiar direction, interposing concepts of limited government and personal freedom. They argued that the Act improperly intruded government in people's lives. At bottom this a non-trivial argument and still very much with us. Although as applied to race relations it later became anathema, we see an earlier version of the "zone of privacy" theory, which now deployed around an entirely different set of rights, such as abortion and untrammeled sexual conduct. But we should recognize the reasoning, which still goes to strictly limit the government, leaving wide individual freedom.

But coming back to the Civil Rights Act itself, we see playing out what has now become the conventional script. In the first act the democratic characters perform. Congress debates and passes the Civil Rights Act of 1875. The majority has spoken their lines, concluding their part. But the play is far from over, the climatic scene yet to be acted. The aristocratic characters now take center stage. Under judicial supremacy, the Court plays the leading role and utters the final words in the drama. In 1883, the Court delivered that speech with the Civil Rights Cases.

The Civil Rights Cases – The factual issues, what happened, are all uncontroverted and show violations of the Civil Rights Act. The defendants "Stanley and Nichols ... [denied] to persons of color the accommodations and privileges of an inn or hotel." The defendant "Ryan ... [refused] a colored person a seat in the dress circle of Maguire's theater in San Francisco." The defendant "Singleton ... [denied] to another person, whose color is not stated, the full enjoyment of the accommodations of a theater known as the Grand Opera House in New York." The "case of Robinson and his wife against the Memphis and Charleston R.R. Company was ... [for] the refusal by the conductor ... to allow the wife to ride in the ladies' car for the reason ... that she was a person of African descent."[19]

All of which make several things clear. Widespread resistance exists to the Act, indicating widespread racism in the society. Nevertheless, blacks demonstrate a willingness to stand up for themselves and litigate their rights. Moreover, they have enjoyed at least some success, winning verdicts. Then despite the racism, this shows a degree of opposition to segregation and support for the Act.

Justice Joseph P. Bradley delivers the opinion for the Court. He begins by rejecting the 13th Amendment abolition of slavery as a source of congressional power. "[I]t is assumed," he writes, "that the power vested in Congress to enforce the [13th Amendment] by appropriate legislation, clothes Congress with power to pass all laws necessary and proper for abolishing all badges of slavery and incidents of slavery in the United States."[20] He demolishes this position in few words: "[W]e are forced to the conclusion that such an act of refusal [of accommodation] has nothing to do with slavery or involuntary servitude."[21] So Congress cannot constitutionally prohibit such discrimination under the 13th Amendment.

Turning to the 14th Amendment, Justice Bradley as quickly disposes of that by drawing a distinction easily seen by the superimposed italics: "The ... 14th Amendment ... declares that '*No State* shall make or enforce any law which shall abridge the privileges or immunities of citizens' ... *It is state action of a particular character that is prohibited. Individual invasion of individual rights is not the subject-matter of the Amendment.*"[22]

In this way he severely narrows the 14th Amendment. If "no state" may do any of these things, that fails to cover individuals or organizations. Insofar as the Act attempts to prohibit individuals or organizations from discrimination, he rules the provisions unconstitutional and void, exceeding the authority delegated to Congress. Individuals and organizations possess a right to refuse accommodations; Congress cannot interfere. And since the states run no hotels, theaters, or railroad cars, the practical effect negates the entire Act.

Except we might ask, what about, for example, the "commerce clause," which says Congress shall have the power "to regulate commerce among the several states," or the well-recognized right to travel about the country, not specifically mentioned in Constitution, but repeatedly reaffirmed by the Court. Then why doesn't Congress have authority to regulate commerce or travel by regulating hotels and railroads or steamboats? So with just as much logic Justice Bradley could have concluded the Congress had the necessary power.

It is no matter. The Supreme Court had a purpose, and the majority of justices reached the conclusion they intended to reach. Only Justice John Marshall Harlan dissented, saying: "The opinion in these cases proceeds, it seems to me, upon grounds entirely too narrow and artificial. I cannot resist the conclusion that the substance and spirit of the recent Amendments of the Constitution have been sacrificed to a subtle and ingenious verbal criticism. 'It is not the words of the law but the internal sense of it that makes the law; the letter of the law is its body; the sense and reason of the law its soul.' Constitutional provisions adopted in the interest of liberty, and for the purpose of securing, through national legislation, if need be, rights inhering in a state of freedom, and belonging to American citizenship, have been so construed as to defeat the ends the people desired to accomplish, which they attempted to accomplish, and they supposed they had accomplished by changes in their fundamental law."[23]

Harlan found ample authority in the 13th Amendment abolition of slavery. He wrote: "That there are burdens and disabilities which constitute badges of slavery and servitude, and that the power to enforce by appropriate legislation the 13th Amendment may be exerted by legislation of a direct ... character, for the eradication, not simply of the institution, but of its badges and incidents, are propositions which ought to be deemed indisputable."[24]

Taken in conjunction with the earlier Slaughter-House Cases and Reese Case, what had the Supreme Court wrought with these Civil Rights Cases? In the Slaughter-House Cases the justices defined down the privileges and immunities of citizens to almost nothing. In Reese they defined away black enfranchisement to almost nothing. Now they have defined discrimination to almost nothing. What is left of the key Reconstruction laws? The answer is almost nothing.

Which institution did better during Reconstruction, Congress or the Court? Did Congress violate the Constitution? Did the Court protect the Constitution? Did Congress violate minority rights? Did the Court protect minority rights? Look back at the controversies:

In 1865, the 13th Amendment abolishes slavery, reversing the Court's effort in Dred Scott to write slavery into the Constitution for all time. In 1868, the 14th Amendment guarantees the privileges and immunities of citizens, due process of law, and equal protection of the law. But in 1873 with Slaughter-House Cases, the Court guts that intent. In 1870, the 15th Amendment grants the franchise to the freedmen, Congress also passing the Enforcement Act to enforce that right. But in 1876 with the Reese Case, the Court declares the Enforcement Act unconstitutional. Instead, the justices blaze a trail to black disenfranchisement, as long as a false racial neutrality covers the deed. Finally in 1875, Congress enacts the Civil Rights Act to prohibit segregation. But in the 1883 Civil Rights Cases, the Court declares the Act unconstitutional, allowing private individuals and organizations to discrimination after all.

Tabulating the score: Congress did not violate the Constitution; the Court interpreted away the purpose of the Reconstruction Amendments. Congress did not violate the minority's rights; the Court protected one minority at the expense of another, rather than leaving both equal. On every item Congress reached one outcome and the Court reached a contrary outcome. Congress lost every time; the Court won every time. Democracy was defeated; aristocratic methodology won.

In every case the Court ruled in keeping with its institutional will-to-power, every case increasing judicial power. After Marbury in 1803, the judiciary had pledged themselves to judicial restraint, promising never to declare an act of Congress unconstitutional except in a clear-cut case. In 1857 in Dred Scott, they forgot that restraint. Now during Reconstruction, judicial review becomes utterly dynamic. The justices feel free to interpret away the clear intent of constitutional amendments. Under the banner of judicial supremacy, the Court's power ascends to still greater heights.

CHAPTER 6

The Invention of Substantive Due Process

Industrialization will witness another series of institutional clashes much like those over Reconstruction. Congress and the states respond to industrialization by passing new laws, the progressive reforms, which aimed to remedy the accompanying ills. But the Court will repeatedly throw out these laws. Any restraint to "clear-cut" cases long gone, the Court will go on to invent "substantive due process," a doctrine which adds even more power to judicial review. Under this new doctrine the judges can declare unconstitutional laws they deem "unreasonable," and since nothing precisely defines "reasonable," this power turns them into a sort of "super-legislature," able to substitute their opinion for the legislature's opinion. Once again they will decisively intervene, once again acquiring more institutional power in the process.

The force of industrialization – Industrialization trod hard on the heels of Reconstruction, vying for attention, the speed and impact uniquely upsetting. Going all-out, America re-structured from an agricultural to an industrial economy. But it was a phenomenon not a plan. As this new dawn prophets did not fail to proclaim from the rooftops, some haling the light, others bewailing the darkness. Both were right, both were wrong. Driven by human forces, but driven by forces beyond human control, industrialization left everyone scrambling to catch up, not least government and the law.

Beneath an avalanche of statistical data, life changed forever. Before the Civil War, Americans lived down on the farm; by 1890 over half worked in factories. Rural scenes made up the ante-bellum landscape; by the turn of the century, eighty-eight cities had doubled in size. Where before muddy and rutted roads had meandered to local markets, in a few decades 100,000 miles of railroad track riveted together a continental marketplace. Farmers grew record crops almost every year, but the value of manufactured goods exceeded commodities. America grew from an adolescent economy into a vigorous young economic giant, knocking off Great Britain as king of the industrial heap in coal, iron, and steel production.

In a lot of ways, the human spirit took off on a marvelous adventure. Technological marvels might personify the age, as gaslight gave way to electricity, the steam engine to the dynamo. These breakthroughs unyoked mankind from behind the plow, leaving behind dependence on that age-old, backbreaking livelihood, leaving behind, too, subservience to an inconstant and often grudging Mother Nature, finally out-thinking her immemorial dictates. A prior unimaginable plentitude descended on the land, an abundance of essentials, a wealth of luxuries that soon became essentials. Industrialization released a liquid flow of money, power, and prestige, and opportunity auditioned across the social spectrum, opening a career to talents, beckoning with rapid upward mobility. It was much less where a man started in life, but what he could make of himself.

Yet Mark Twain and others labeled this era the Gilded Age, the surface shine concealing an often leaden reality. The shift to industrialization mangled a lot of people in the gears. Sometimes you could hardly tell if the people were running the factories or the factories running the people. Captains of industry reveled in the command of veritable armies of production, but service in the ranks wasn't as pleasant. The relentless lockstep of the assembly line could work you to death in a mindless servitude. The factory broke the ties between master and man that had subsisted in the old craft workshops, elevating the owners to mighty and impersonal capitalists, the workers declining to almost interchangeable parts themselves. Efficient managers treated wages and working conditions like any other raw material, cutting to the bone. In the boardroom the directors contemplated with quite satisfaction the upward graph of corporate profits; down on the factory floor men, women, and children toiled around the clock for starvation wages. The contrasts were stark and often bleak. If anyone faltered, fresh recruits stood ready to step into the ranks, over 12,000,000 emigrants entering the country from 1880 to 1910.

Nor did the winners and losers neglect to originate ethical theories to justify their success or excuse their failure. The creed of social Darwinism served for the winners, applying the survival of the fittest to human society. Under the logic, those at the top of the economic food chain were the superior human adaptations, those at bottom the less fit. The well-remember words of Herbert Spencer, a leading exponent whose book *Social Statics* came out in 1851, distills the flavor: "We have unmistakable proof that throughout all past time, there has been a ceaseless devouring of the weak by the strong ... [S]houlderings aside of the weak by the strong ... are the decrees of a large, farseeing benevolence."[1] If this smacks of the industrialists as the carnivores and the public as the hoofed beasts, at the other end of the spectrum we find socialism rising, such radicals as Karl Marx condemning capitalism utterly, demanding a root and branch upheaval, a revolution waged through whatever violence and terror.

The progressive movement – But the formal American response, that is, the laws passed, avoided the extremes, although favorably inclined to laissez-faire capitalism. Economic ambition had fueled Americans from the beginning, the very reason many came, much of the motivation behind the Revolution and the Constitution. Not surprisingly, then, the culture evidenced a strong preference for wide-open markets, as well as a settled hostility to government regulation of business. These outlooks deeply ingrained the attitudes and the laws, where they lodged strongly defended by force of habit, not to mention powerful moneyed interests. Nonetheless, the "progressive movement" made considerable headway, pushing for reforms such as outlawing monopoly, empowering unions, and regulating working conditions. Following this impulse, Congress and the state legislatures did not reject free enterprise whole, rather showing a preference to ameliorate the ills of industrialization piecemeal.

But the Supreme Court performs very differently from Congress and the state legislatures, serving as the inveterate foe to the progressive reforms. The justices will hobble the law against monopolies, rein in unions, and hamstring regulation of factory conditions.

Today the standard explanation views the Court as gripped by "conservatism." But why would that be? Why would the justices exhibit more conservatism in this era than over any similar span? We might speculate "conservatives" controlled the country, electing presidents and Congresses while elevating fellow travelers to the bench. But progressivism strongly influenced Congress and the administrations of several presidents. The undeniable proof is the many progressive laws passed by Congress and signed by the president. We might speculate the Court inherently "conservative," justices coming from the ranks of vested interests. Except we have seen such a model justice as John Marshall lead the charge to change from the front. We have seen such a "conservative" justice as Roger Taney remain quite pliable into advanced old age, as long as the pliability served his ends. In the not too distant future, we will see the Court leading a "judicial revolution," serving as the *avant-garde*. So in the end, how account for this steady run of anti-progressive rulings during industrialization?

Yet a consistency exists between the Court in this era and the previous eras, a consistency that will carry forward to future eras. During industrialization the Court consistently rules so as to confirm and increase its own power, governing in line with the institutional will-to-power. Turning to examine the cases, that steadiness of course becomes evident.

The rise of the trusts – Monopolies are nothing new. By the late Middle Ages, John D. Rockefeller's spiritual ancestors had already figured out the formula. Corner a market and name your price. And the public had already eaten enough bread so priced to learn the profit margin stuck in their throats. By 1516, Sir Thomas More, that renowned "man for all seasons" and Chancellor of England, who so unfortunately lost his head in the matrimonial and religious quarrels of Henry VIII's reign, has been claimed to have gone on record with the first remembered used of the word monopoly. His *Utopia* advised: "Suffer not thies ryche men to bye vp all, to ingrosse and forstalle, and with theyr monoplye to kepe the market alone as please them."[2]

During industrialization, this old problem emerged again in a new context and virulent form. Economies of scale and mass production favored huge firms. But their size sometimes let them crush all competitors, say by underselling them until they broke, and then what began as efficiency in production could immediately become efficiency in profits. At the same time trade linked into huge nationwide networks, and if a firm could seize on a pressure point, they could likewise name their own price for turning on and off the spigot. Such temptations proved irresistible to the era's great capitalists.

Nobody had ever seen anything quite like the gargantuan "trusts" these lures called forth: Rockefeller's Standard Oil, Carnegie's U.S. Steel, the Southern Pacific Octopus in railroads, the Sugar Trust, the Whiskey Ring, the Big Four in meatpacking, the list goes on. The shrewdness, tenacity, and sheer wealth of the men who forged these mega-firms adds not a little to the legend of all-out American capitalism. Their very dynamism compelled them toward monopoly, a dominant trait the passion to stand triumphant upon a stricken economic field, all rivals bankrupt at their feet. On one hand, here was creative destruction hurled on a gigantic canvas, driving technology and business methods to dizzying heights, generating amazing production and stupendous wealth. On the other hand, it was "a tight-fisted hand at the grindstone ... squeezing, wrenching, grasping, scraping, clutching, covetous."

The Sherman Anti-Trust Act – Increasingly, the latter description better fit the spectacle. If this was the survival of the fittest, perhaps it was time to think about revising the laws of the economic jungle. In

1889 at the opening of the Fifty-first Congress, Senator John Sherman of Ohio filed a piece of legislation that proposed to do just that and carried his name to posterity. Filed as Senate Bill No. 1, the formal title read: "A bill to declare unlawful trusts and combinations in restraint of trade and production."[3] After passing through the congressional furnace, this bill came out the form still the basic American law on monopoly. As often with statutes, it is commonly referred to by the name of the initial sponsor, being known as the Sherman Anti-Trust Act.

Senator Sherman, brother of the Civil War general, had piled up an impressive public career himself. After entering Congress in 1855, he stayed in uninterrupted office the next forty-three years, finally stepping down as Secretary of State in 1898 during the Spanish-American War. Sherman served as Senator from Ohio for thirty-two of those years, all that time a member and often chair of the influential Finance Committee, in between spending four years as Secretary of the Treasury in the cabinet of President Rutherford B. Hayes. This portrait delineates a seasoned and respected legislator, particularly concerned with issues of economics and finance. What did he mean by introducing this bill?

In the debates on the Senate floor Sherman told the country what he meant, saying that: "[Certain capitalists] are not satisfied with partnerships and corporations competing with each other, and have invented a new form of combination commonly called 'trusts,' that seek to avoid competition by combining the controlling corporations, partnerships, and individuals engaged in the same business, and placing the power and property of the combination under the government of a few individuals, and often under the control of a single man ... The sole object of such a combination is to make competition impossible. It can control the market, raise or lower prices as will best promote its selfish interests, reduce prices in a particular locality and break down competition, and advance prices at will where competition does not exist ... Such a combination is far more dangerous than any heretofore invented, and when it embraces the great body of all corporations engaged in a particular industry in all the states of the Union, it tends to advance the price to the consumer of any article produced."[4]

In his peroration Senator Sherman draws an analogy against monopoly from the political sphere: "If the concentrated powers of this combination are entrusted to a single man, it is a kingly prerogative, inconsistent with our form of government; ... If we will not endure a king as a political power, we should not endure a king over the production, transportation, and sale of any of the necessities of life. ... [W]e should not submit to an autocrat of trade, with power to prevent competition and to fix the price of any commodity."[5]

Thus, Senator Sherman has perceived what will later come to be called a "market failure." The free-market had become self-defeating, the competition in the "market" cancelling out the "free." In response he proposes a legal reform to outlaw monopoly, restoring and defending the free-market.

But what about the Constitution and our rights? Does Senator Sherman's new law exceed the powers delegated Congress by the Constitution? He does not neglect to address these concerns: "I believe this bill is clearly within the power conferred expressly upon Congress to regulate commerce with foreign nations and among the several States ... Can it be with this vast power (over commerce) Congress cannot protect the people from combinations in restraint of trade ... ? It may 'regulate commerce;' can it not protect commerce, nullify contracts that restrain commerce, turn it from its natural course, increase the price of articles, and therefore diminish the amount of commerce?"[6] He is referring to Article I, Section 8, the "commerce clause," which reads: "The Congress shall have Power ... [t]o regulate Commerce with foreign Nations, and among the several States."

After referral, the Judiciary Committee hammered out a final draft, Senator George F. Edmunds of Vermont, the committee chair, writing most of the version reported out. In this form the bill sailed through by a near unanimous vote of 52 to 1. After some wrangling, the House passed by a margin of 200 to 42. On July 2, 1890, President Benjamin Harrison signed the bill into law.[7] The numbers supporting passage and the president's signature give evidence of a resounding consensus.

The Act declares that: "Every contract, combination in the form of trust or otherwise, or conspiracy, in restraint of trade or commerce among the several States, or with foreign nations, is hereby declared illegal ... Every person who shall monopolize, or attempt to monopolize any part of the trade or commerce among the several States, or with foreign countries, shall be guilty of a misdemeanor."[8]

The E.C. Knight doctrine – It was time for the third shoe to drop: Congress having passed the law, the president having signed the law, it was time to hear from the Court. By now such has become the accepted routine. And this is the very next case in the lexicon, U.S. v E.C. Knight, decided in 1895. Again the Court will employ the same techniques developed during Reconstruction, again ostensibly in defense of limited government and personal freedom, but again really no more than taking sides, again the side replacing congressional with judicial outcomes, again the side coincident with the judicial will-to-power. By these methods, as Chief Justice Charles Evans Hughes will later incautiously remark: "The Constitution is what the judges say it is."[9]

Before looking at this case, let us return for a moment to listen in the Senate, where Senator Sherman had gone on in his speech to say: "I might state the case of all the combinations which now control the transportation and sale of nearly all the leading productions of the country ... such as the cotton trust, the whiskey trust, *the sugar refiners' trust*, the copper trust, the salt trust, and many others ... They are all combinations of corporations and individuals ... with power to ... absolutely control the supply of the article which they produce, and with the uniform design to prevent competition."[10] Also we hear from Senator Edmunds that: "I am in favor of ... breaking up of great monopolies, which get hold of the whole or some parts of a particular business in the country, and are enabled therefore to command everybody, laborer, consumer, producer, and everybody else, as *the Sugar Trust* and the Oil Trust."[11]

E.C. Knight concerns that very same sugar trust highlighted by the added italics. The entity in question, American Sugar Company, while castigated on the Senate floor, produced and sold about 65% of the nation's sugar. But apparently passage of the Act gave the directors no pause whatsoever. By 1892 they had arranged to buy up four Pennsylvania corporations (E.C. Knight, Franklin, Spreckels, and Delaware), which produced and sold another 33% of the total sugar, leaving nobody out of the ring except little ole Revere up in Boston, with a minuscule 2% share. With 98% control, American Sugar would have effected a corner on refined sugar in the United States.

Except the administration of President Grover Cleveland sued under the Sherman Act to prevent the combination. American Sugar's scheme looked to fit the outlawed behavior like hand in glove. If 98% wasn't "restraint of trade" and "monopoly," what was? Both Sherman and Edmunds had held up the sugar trust as a prime example with only 65% control. Obviously the purpose of the Act aimed at precisely such engrossing conglomerates.

But when the case reaches the Supreme Court, the justices hold the congressional purpose unconstitutional, not authorized by the "commerce clause," exceeding the power delegated Congress. Writing the opinion, Chief Justice Melvin Weston Fuller draws a distinction between "manufacture" and "commerce," holds Congress cannot regulate "manufacture," only "commerce," and finds American Sugar engages in "manufacture," not "commerce." Therefore, he exercises judicial review to prevent Congress from interfering with the monopoly.

Justice Fuller writes: "The argument is that the power to control the manufacture of refined sugar is a monopoly over a necessary of life, to the enjoyment of which by a large population of the United States interstate commerce is indispensable, and that, therefore, the general government in the exercise of the power to regulate commerce may repress such monopoly."[12]

Indeed, this is the argument we heard from Senator Sherman, deducing from the "commerce clause" congressional authority to regulate monopolies. To repeat the operative words from Article I, Section 8: "The Congress shall have Power ... To regulate Commerce ... among the several States ... ."

However, Justice Fuller has only stated that position to reject it: "Doubtless the power to control the manufacture of a given thing involves in a certain sense the control of its disposition, but this is a secondary and not the primary sense; and although the exercise of that power may result in bringing the operation of commerce into play, it does not control it, and affects it only incidentally and indirectly. Commerce succeeds manufacture and is not a part of it."[13]

In the next and final step in his logic, since "manufacture" isn't "commerce," Congress cannot regulate the company under the "commerce clause."

Making every concession to Justice Fuller, how can such a conclusion rise above a leap in logic dictated by an agenda? True, close to hand lay those old arguments about limited government, personal freedom, and state rights. And by this time laissez faire was in its heyday, crying hands-off, let the free-market go where it would. These notions lent a gloss. Supporters could claim the Court turned back an unwarranted governmental intrusion. Yet an air of unreality suffuses the opinion for two reasons: In the first place, to say a company which "manufactures" 98% of the refined sugar, selling that sugar in every state in the nation, somehow isn't engaged in "commerce" crams the real world into an artificial verbal straitjacket. In the second place, it was only too evident the Constitution said nothing at all about monopoly, either pro or con.

Really the question was entirely novel, un-provided for by the Constitution. True, the Founders did favor free-markets; they did favor limited government; they did favor personal freedom; they did reserve rights to the states. Yet they also delegated Congress power to regulate interstate commerce, and despite the venerable antiquity of monopoly, the Constitution spoke not at all about the topic. This silence reflects that in their economic day and agrarian circumstances, the issue looked of purely local concern. They could not foresee industrialization, let alone the rise of monopoly under industrial conditions, which spread such schemes nationally, eluding state regulation.

It will thus be seen Justice Fuller was in pursuit of his own agenda, not defending the Founder's "original intent." Limited government, personal freedom, state rights, monopoly, in their day none of those ideas covered these new sort of industrial monopolies, which were unforeseen. If anything, the stronger argument appears on the other side. Since they delegated Congress power over interstate commerce, that power would apply now that monopoly had come to affect interstate commerce.

To turn and think about this case in terms of institutional power, we must see a striking transformation in judicial review. The limitation to "clear-cut" cases disappears entirely. Nothing about E. C. Knight is clear. Restraint gone, deference to Congress forgotten, the justices read their own meaning into the Constitution, dropping in and out their purpose. They have proceeded from strength to strength, as one notion became customary, further extending the custom.

Redirecting statutory intent – During industrialization, the cases over unions illustrate another aspect of judicial supremacy. We recall that English jurisprudence gave primacy to parliamentary statutes, a principle binding their judges beneath legislative intent. American jurisprudence inherited this principle, still widely pronounced, set forth in elaborate legal formulas. The Court is supposed to interpret a statute to bring about the purpose Congress intended. But just as no effective mechanism enforces the limits on judicial review, nothing enforces legislative primacy either. So just as the Constitution has come to mean whatever the judges say it does, congressional statutes have also come to mean whatever the judges say they do.

In the exemplification, unions suffered a series of defeats before the Court. Having found a way to avoid applying the Sherman Anti-Trust Act against an intended target, the sugar trust, next these very same justices find a way to turn the Act against a wholly unintended target, the labor unions. Not for the last time the Court co-opts a congressional program, utterly changing the purpose.

William Howard Taft, chief justice from 1921 to 1930, let slip a comment with respect to labor: "That faction we have to hit every little while."[14] And Taft and his fellow justices were as good as his word. In these cases a settled preconception lurks behind the judicial mask, attitudes similar to Herbert Spencer's theory about "the decrees of a large, farseeing benevolence" assuring a "ceaseless devouring of the weak by the strong." The justices regarded unions as upsetting this natural order, an outlook that might strike as rather an odd thought process. On the one hand, they view huge corporations as the economic survival of the fittest. While on the other hand, they view unions as upsetting the Darwinian scheme. But why does a business corporation stand for a superior adaptation rather than a labor union? If the test is the just the biggest lion, why not throw the raw meat out in the yard between capital and labor, check back in the morning, and see which one is left alive? Why prefer one carnivore over the other in that kind of fight?

But more than that, the Court ignored a real problem. The factories demanded human servitors in the millions, and profit driven corporations treated wages, hours, and working conditions like nothing more than a cost of doing business. Right then the demographics made labor cheap, immigrants flowing into the country. This gave management the whip hand with notorious results, child labor, sweatshops, starvation wages, inhumane hours, hazardous workplaces, and so on. Rather than accept that fate the workers tried to fight back by organizing unions. But they ran up against a stiff resistance, the core naturally corporate interests. This opposition fought many a successful rearguard action in the legislative halls, but if all else failed, found a reliable ally of last resort in the Court.

In 1908, the Danbury Hatters Case was the cutting edge in this litigation. While in E.C. Knight the justices had found the Sherman Act could not stop the sugar trust, in Danbury Hatters they found the Act could stop a labor union. Unable to prevent monopoly, Congress suddenly learned they had meant to prevent unionization. Officially styled Loewe v Lawlor, the lawsuit starts out life in the federal district court in Connecticut.

Located in Danbury, Connecticut, the plaintiff Deitrich Loewe and his partners own "a factory for the making of hats, for sale by them in the various states of the union" and "employing more than two hundred and thirty (230) persons in making and annually selling hats of a value exceeding four hundred ($400,000) dollars."[15] A much smaller operation than the sugar trust, yet just like American Sugar, Loewe's hat company engages in "manufacture" rather than "commerce," as narrowly and artificially defined in E.C. Knight. Even if the hat company had made 98% of the hats in America, the federal government could not touch them under the Knight doctrine. Only this time the case involves a union, a distinction that will make all the difference. The United Hatters of North America are trying to organize the factory. Loewe files suit against union agent Martin Lowler and union members, seeking an injunction against the union activity as well as money damages, alleging a violation of the Sherman Act.

We recall the Sherman Act outlaws "restraints of trade." The hat company claims a union strike and boycott constitute a restraint of trade. Except how can the Sherman Act apply? In the first place, the Act was about trusts, not unions. In the second place, clearly the hat company engages only in manufacture rather than commerce. If nothing the company does touches commerce, then nothing the union does in relation to the company can touch commerce either. Under E.C. Knight both the business and the union remain outside the reach of the Sherman Act.

The local federal district judge in Connecticut dismisses the case on precisely those grounds. "It is not perceived," he wrote, "that the Supreme Court has as yet so broadened the interpretation of the Sherman Act that it will fit such an order of facts as this complaint presents."[16]

Loewe appeals on to the Supreme Court, and what the justices couldn't bring themselves to do against a trust, they persuade themselves to do against a union. Chief Justice Melville Weston Fuller, the very same who authored E.C. Knight, writes the opinion. He begins by reasoning that the Sherman Act provides; "every contract, combination, or conspiracy in restraint of trade was illegal. The records of Congress show that several efforts were made to exempt, by legislation, organizations of farmers and laborers from the act, and that all these efforts failed, so that the act remained as we have it before us."[17] Therefore, the Sherman Anti-Trust Act does indeed apply to unions.

Can this be correct? When we heard Senator Sherman introduce his bill, he referred the evil to certain capitalists who "not satisfied with competing with each other ... have invented a new form of combination commonly called 'trusts,' that seek to avoid competition." Then what did his reform have to do with unions? The answer appears absolutely nothing. But when Sherman laid his bill before the Senate, it sparked extensive debate, and this issue came up. Every Senator who spoke except one opposed including unions, and a motion carried to specifically exclude unions from the act. At this point the bill went to committee for final drafting. The version referred back to the floor dropped the specific reference excluding unions. Did this omission mean the committee intended to include unions or merely that the drafters thought unions excluded without need for specific reference?

Today almost all the scholarship agrees with one eminent commentator who concluded: "On the basis of the congressional debates ... it is believed that no valid evidence can be found in the records of the legislative proceedings that Congress intended the Anti-Trust Act to apply to labor organizations."[18] After all, it is the Sherman *Anti-Trust* Act, not the Sherman Anti-Union Act. Yet this omission gave Justice Fuller his toehold to scale the rock face. But he could not have performed that feat without real determination. Put in the context of the other cases over unions, obviously this resolve comes from a preconceived resolve "to hit that faction every little while."

Really this attitude becomes obvious in the case itself. The discussion cannot forget E.C. Knight. In that case the Court had ruled the company engaged only in "manufacture not commerce" and could not be regulated under the "commerce clause." Then as long as the hatters' union deals with a company engaged only in "manufacture not trade," isn't the union in the same posture as the sugar trust? If the federal government cannot regulate the one, it cannot regulate the other.

Justice Miller deals with that cavil in classic judicial fashion. "We do not pause," he writes, "to comment on cases such as E.C. Knight ... in which the undisputed facts showed that the purpose of the agreement was not to obstruct or restraint interstate commerce."[19] And so much for that.

The Supreme Court wanted to help out the trusts in E.C. Knight, and so it did. The Court wanted to hit the unions "every little while" in Danbury Hatters, and so it did. In both cases the real explanation lay in the justices' unspoken attitudes, not in the publicly expressed rationale. Following the trajectory of the judges' decisions right on up to the New Deal proves this thesis. These cases reveal a consistent pattern of bias in favor of business and against unions.

In terms of institutional power, we see in the Danbury Hatters Case an unrestrained process of statutory interpretation. Just as the justices had come to over-ride clear constitutional meaning, now they come to over-ride clear statutory intent. A statute designed to outlaw monopoly is incongruously pressed into service to attack unions. The rule of legislative primacy amounts to nothing as against the judicial will-to-power. Under judicial supremacy the justices not only control the Constitution, they control the statutory law as well.

Judicial rejection of legislative control – However as regards statutory law, Congress looks to have a countervailing check. If they disagree with a judicial interpretation, they can re-pass a statute in altered or more specific form, making their intent absolutely clear. But as the cases on unions go on to show, this remedy turns out largely theoretical, since nothing prevents the Court from simply persisting. Having superimposed their purpose on the first version, they can interpret away the revision as well.

Working primarily through injunctions, the judiciary had pushed on a campaign against the unions. An injunction is nothing more than an order from a judge ordering someone to do or not to do something. And the federal judges hedged unions so thick with these injunctions the movement could hardly operate. Turning to Congress for relief, the unions won passage of the Clayton Act, specifically to limit injunctions in labor disputes. Only the justices refused to comply with the obvious intent, again enforcing their own intent.

Injunctions in labor disputes worked this way. If a union tried to organize or strike, the corporate lawyer went to the local federal court, filed a petition for an injunction, and asked the judge for an order prohibiting the union activity. This procedure bypasses our usual picture of an adversarial hearing with lawyers and witnesses for both sides. The lawyer simply presented the judge with a sworn affidavit setting forth the company side of the facts. The judge had discretion to put an injunction into immediate effect. Only some weeks or months down the road did the union have a chance to contest the matter. Meanwhile, they had to obey the injunction. Even after a full-blown hearing, federal judges tended to keep these orders in effect. That was the judge's decision without any right to jury trial. Violating the injunctive was contempt of court, punishable by fine or imprisonment.

Federal judges routinely followed this formula and granted sweeping injunctions, which basically disqualified the unions from playing the game, forbidding everything from organizing to strikes. But these injunctions weren't in the Constitution, but rested on statutory law. For example, in Danbury Hatters the petition for injunction relied on that strange interpretation of the Sherman Act. And so the unions saw hope in asking Congress for a remedy. Under judicial supremacy, when the Court interprets the Constitution, that's it, Congress has no further say. But Congress can still change the statutory law. In 1914, the unions persuaded Congress to pass the Clayton Act, a law hailed by Samuel Gompers, head of the American Federation of Labor, as labor's "Magna Charta."[20]

Section 20 provided: "That no restraining order or injunction shall be granted by any court of the United States ... in any case between and employer and employees ... involving, or growing out of, a dispute concerning terms and conditions of employment, unless necessary to prevent irreparable injury to property ... And no such restraining order or injunction shall prohibit any person ... from peacefully persuading any [other] person to work or abstain from working; or from ceasing to patronize or employ any person to such dispute, or from recommending, advising, or persuading others by peaceful and lawful means to do so."[21]

Obviously this act intended to stop injunctions against peaceful union activity. In other words, Congress disagreed with the Court's interpretation of such statutes as the Sherman Act, disagreed with the judicially developed policy of anti-union injunctions, and so passed a new statute to make absolutely clear not to use the prior statutes for those purposes. But the Supreme Court still had the last word and proved unwilling to submit itself to the congressional will.

This becomes evident in the 1921 Duplex Printing v Deering Case, which started out in the federal district court in New York. Located in Battle Creek, Michigan, Duplex Printing Company manufactures printing presses, the big kind that weigh from 10,000 to 100,000 pounds, and sells these throughout the U.S. The company employs about 200 machinists, 50 office personnel, some traveling salesmen, and a road force of expert machinists to supervise installation at the customer location. In 1913, the International Association of Machinists, a union some 60,000 strong, calls a strike at the Duplex plant in Michigan, basically seeking an eight-hour day, a union wage scale, and a closed shop. The strike has absolutely no effect, except some fourteen union members leave Duplex's employment.

But the union doesn't give up, initiating a secondary boycott, particularly in New York City, a prime market for Duplex presses. A secondary boycott persuades or pressures third parties to boycott a recalcitrant company. For example, picketers pass out leaflets to the public, urging them not to buy newspapers printed on Deering presses, or the union asks the teamsters not to haul paper to newspapers using Deering presses. Obviously, the tactic endeavors to apply pressure from the outside to the inside, bringing a company to heel.

In response Duplex sues for an injunction against the secondary boycott. But at this first level of the court system, the federal district judge turns them down, basing his decision on the Clayton Act. He writes: "Under section 20 of the Clayton Act, I cannot grant a restraining order or injunction ... unless it is necessary to prevent irreparable injury to property ... No such restraining order or injunction is permitted which shall prohibit any person ... from ceasing to perform work or labor, or recommending, advising, or persuading others by peaceful and lawful means to do so."[22]

This judge just tracks the statutory language quoted above as his guide. Finding no proof the union went beyond "peaceful and lawful means," he denies the injunction. When Duplex appeals to the next level, the federal circuit court of appeals, there a three-judge panel affirms the first judge. The judge writing the opinion says: "that the designed, announced, and widely known purpose of section 20 ... was to legalize the secondary boycott ... ."[23]

Duplex appeals on up to the Supreme Court, where Justice Mahlon Pitney writes the opinion, beginning: "Section 20 must be given full effect according to its terms as an expression of the purpose of Congress."[24] Thus, he professes to regard the rule of legislative primacy. But then he writes: "Full and fair effect will be given to every word if [the operation of section 20] be confined --- as the natural meaning of the words confines it --- to those who are proximally and substantially concerned as parties to the actual dispute respecting the terms or conditions off their employment."[25]

What can this sentence mean? Justice Pitney is weaving a web to entangle the section 20 prohibition against injunctions. It will stand on the books, but amount to almost nothing. He encompasses this ruin by confining section 20 to those "proximally and substantially concerned as parties to the actual dispute." In plain English, he limits the application to those fourteen members of the union employed by Duplex, totally to the exclusion of the other 60,000 members of the machinists' union. The congressional interdict on injunctions covers only those fourteen employees. The federal courts can go ahead and issue injunctions just like always against the other 60,000.

Pitney rules the lower judges erred because: "[They] appear to have entertained the view that ... section 20 operated to permit members of the Machinists' Union elsewhere --- some 60,000 in number ... to make that dispute their own, and proceed to instigate sympathetic strikes, picketing, and boycotting against employers wholly unconnected with [the Duplex] factory ... [except] in the course of purchasing its products in the ordinary course of interstate commerce."[26]

But he rules this was wrong. The Clayton Act meant only the immediate employees of a given company. A union as a whole could not "make that dispute their own." Yet surely it was Justice Pitney who was wrong. The sources clearly establish congressional intent. As the Court of Appeals had said: "[T]he designed, announced, and widely known purpose of section 20 ... was to legalize the secondary boycott." The Supreme Court had again interpreted away congressional intent.

The dramatic impact of Duplex Printing should be evident. The fourteen machinists employed by the company possess zero clout. If they cannot unite to act with the whole 60,000 man union, they're a lost patrol in an army whose command and control has been annihilated. The same applies to every labor dispute across the United States. The labor movement has been cut into segments incapable of effective cooperation. The injunction still rides high. Forget what Congress intended by the Clayton Act.

Duplex Printing inaugurated another decade of broad injunctions and broken strikes. Nor would it be the last time the Court refused to regard congressional efforts to limit judicial power. Since the Court always has the last word, it is easy enough say: No, Congress didn't really mean that. Of course, Congress might repeat itself again, only again to be told that is not what it meant. But as a practical matter, the press of business and the partisan divide come to the Court's rescue, preventing such congressional insistence, allowing the Court's final word to stand.

The judicial invention of substantive due process – The narrative reaches the high watermark of the famous or infamous case of Lochner v New York, decided in 1905. Scholars always cite this case when talking about the genesis of the equally famous or infamous doctrine of "substantive due process." By creating this doctrine, the justices adroitly redefine an old legal concept, using the by now familiar technique of judicial self-help to further expand judicial power. They will then use this new authority to turn back a host of progressive reforms.

However muckraking journalists heightened the negative, such efforts as Sinclair Lewis' still read 1906 novel *The Jungle* drew upon ample evidence, attesting to real ills associated with industrialization. This list included such items as starvation wages, long hours, child labor, dangerous factories, and defective, unsanitary, or unsafe products. All of which led to calls for government regulation. It was another approach to the same industrial ailments which called up the union movement. Under the basic theory behind unions, organized workers could bargain as a group, winning a fair contract. This other reform traveled an alternative route to the same destination. By organizing as voters, they would win laws to regulate employment and factory conditions.

Lochner v New York, as said decided in 1905, involved exactly such a regulation. In 1895, the New York legislature passed a Bakeshop Act, setting a limit on hours of employment, providing "no employee shall be required, or permitted, to work in a ... bakery ... more than sixty hours in any one week."[27] To our familiarity with a 40-hour workweek, perhaps this looks a not more than moderate reform.

In 1902 one Joseph Lochner, owner of a small bakery in Utica, gets indicted for exceeding that number, the charge being that he "violated [the Bakeshop Act] ... in that he wrongfully and unlawfully required and permitted an employee working for him to work more than sixty hours in one week."[28] The truth of this allegation was never an issue, and Lochner suffers conviction in the trial court, which levies a fine of $50.00. Now begins the rather lengthy appeal process. Lochner appeals to the Appellate Division of the New York Supreme Court, which affirms the lower court. He next appeals to the New York Court of Appeals, which affirms again. As a state prosecution, everything so far has taken place in the New York state courts, where Lochner has now lost to the highest available level. But a litigant who loses all the way to the top in a state court system has one last forlorn hope. An appeal always remains to the U.S. Supreme Court. A determined man, Lochner takes that appeal.

And as sometimes happens, that final card turns up the ace of trumps. The Supreme Court reverses the conviction, holding the Bake Shop Act violated Lochner's constitutional rights. In other words, the Court declares the Act unconstitutional. Since the law is void, Lochner cannot be found guilty for violating it. In reaching this outcome the Court deploys the new doctrine of substantive due process. To understand that doctrine requires an analysis of the case in some detail, which also shows the wider significance.

Justice Rufus Wheeler Peckham writes for a five-man majority. Here is the heart of his opinion: "The [Bakeshop Law] necessarily interferes with the right of contract between the employer and employees, concerning the number of hours in which the later may labor in the bakery of the employer. *The general right to make a contract in relation to his business is part of the liberty of the individual protected by the 14th Amendment* ... Under that provision no state can deprive any person of life, liberty, or property without due process of law. The right to purchase or to sell labor is part of the liberty protected by this Amendment."[29]

Reading carefully with particular attention to the words to which the italics have been added for emphasis, we see Justice Peckham asserts three connected propositions: First, a "right to contract" exists between employers and employees; *second, this right is protected by the "due process" clause of the 14th Amendment*; and third, the New York legislature violated that right by limiting the hours of work. The logic relies on the familiar from of a syllogism with the first two propositions leading to the last, the conclusion.

What about all that? And in the first place, it is perhaps surprising to see our old friend the 14th Amendment suddenly pop up in this context. If we recall, that Amendment, when ratified back in 1868, had meant to assure black equality, a hope blighted by the Court. But now Justice Peckham has found the "due process" clause of that Amendment guarantees a right to contract, prohibiting a law that limits work to sixty hours a week. What does an amendment to protect black rights have to do with hours of employment?

Let us return again to the 14th Amendment, re-reading in full the operative language: "No State shall make or enforce any law which shall abridge the privileges or immunities of citizens ... nor shall any State deprive any person of life, liberty, or property, without due process of law; nor deny to any person ... the equal protection of the laws."

Throughout Reconstruction, the Supreme Court had treated those words like a problem child. In the 1873 Slaughter-House Cases, the justices held the "privileges and immunities" of citizens amounted to almost nothing, gutting the intent to secure basic civil rights for blacks. In the 1883 Civil Rights Cases, the justices held nothing in the

Amendment authorized Congress to protect blacks against discrimination by individuals or any private entity. After all this one couldn't be blamed for regarding the 14th as nothing more than a gutted hulk rotting in the wake of judicial review. But now suddenly in 1905, the 14th Amendment does stand for something after all. It prevents a state from interfering with contracts between employer and employee, in particular disallowing any limit on the hours of work. How can this be?

Let us search once more through Justice Peckham's words: *"The general right to make a contract in relation to his business is part of the liberty of the individual protected by the 14th Amendment* ... Under that provision no state can deprive any person of life, liberty, or property without due process of law. The right to purchase or to sell labor is part of the liberty protected by the Amendment."

On the surface his logic flows naturally to an appealing conclusion. Surely there is a "right to contract;" surely there is a right to "due process of law." These sound like good things, and he affirms our possession of them, assuring us one comes from the other, that: "The right to purchase or to sell labor is part of the liberty protected by the Amendment." Yet we might want to ask: Exactly how did a "right to contract" come to be included under the term "due process of law?" And how exactly does a right to contract prevent a regulation on hours of work? What are the intervening steps, the supporting precedents, the train of deductions? Did all of this simply arrive out of thin air?

And we will find that phrase "due process of law" goes way back in Anglo-American legal history, so far back that it started out another phrase altogether. As long ago as the thirteenth century, Magna Charta[30] used the term "law of the land" to mean roughly the same thing. In a 1354 statute[31] from the reign of Edward III appears the formula "due process" of law. That renowned authority Lord Coke, whose years are 1552 to 1634, stated in his *Institutes* that "by the law of the land" was meant "by the due course and process of the law."[32] Hundreds of years later and prior to 1789, several state constitutions still retained the "law of the land" form. The Constitution itself employs the phrase "due process of law" two separate times, in the 5th Amendment ratified in 1791 and in the 14th Amendment ratified in 1868.

So what constitutes "due process of law?" A term with such a long pedigree must have acquired a precise definition. But not at all, rather exactly the opposite. Due process of law serves as one of those legal portmanteau phrases in which all sorts of meanings can be conveniently crammed. An imprecise science like the law simply cannot afford to lock all its definitions away in rigid meanings. As life constantly unfolds, the judicial system faces new and unexpected combinations of circumstances. Our legal tools have to remain flexible enough to mold a response to ever changing legal questions. Due process of law is a broad legal concept adapted to this function.

Nevertheless, some contours existed. In 1856 in Murray's Case, the Supreme Court had a go at an outline, while still leaving plenty of leeway. Equating "due process" and "law of the land," the Court indicated two sources for elucidating the concept: First, due process was that procedure required by the specific provisions of the Constitution, such as the right to jury trial or a lawyer. Second, due process was "those settled usages and modes of proceeding existing in the common and statute law of England, before the emigration of our ancestors, and which are shown not to have been unsuited to their civil and political condition by having been acted on by them after their settlement of this country."33 Perhaps that may not look too helpful, but a careful winnowing will reveal some useful observations.

Crucial for our discussion, due process of law originally referred to "procedural law" as opposed to "substantive law." In the technical language of the law, substantive law is the substance of the law, while procedural law is the procedure by which the substance of the law is enforced. To take an instance, the law making murder a crime is a substantive law. By contrast a jury trial is a procedure by which to enforce the law against murder. So since the procedure to enforce the law takes place before the courts, we should see due process of law refers to procedure in those courts, not the substance of the law as passed by the legislature. Although an exception exists when the legislature passes a law affecting court procedures, which contributes to a degree of confusion in separating out the concepts.

In the hundreds of years of Anglo-American legal experience, numerous court procedures had come to be regarded as "due process of law." We are justly proud and jealous to guard the fairness of these procedures. The Founders incorporated many of the most fundamental in the Constitution. For an instance, the 6th Amendment guarantees the right to speedy and public trial, as well as the right to an impartial jury. While not written in the Constitution, numerous other rights existed so fundamental as to qualify. If we will remember Bushell's Case, that right of jurors to their verdict, uncompelled by any outside authority, would make the grade. All such rights constitute important procedural guarantees. But no all-inclusive list is written down anywhere of the rights which qualify as such due process.

An interesting proof comes from one of the Founding Fathers, showing the original meaning of due process limited the concept to procedure in the courts. Speaking in the New York Assembly on

February 6, 1787, taking part in a debate on the New York Constitution, Alexander Hamilton is recorded thus: "The words 'due process' have a precise technical import, and are only applicable to the process and proceedings of the courts of justice; they can never be referred to the acts of a legislature."[34]

Then if we return with this background to Justice Peckham's opinion, we see his conclusion does not correctly flow from his premises. Once more to quote with emphasis added to help disclose the flaw: "The general right to make a contract in relation to his business is part of the liberty of the individual protected by the 14th Amendment ... Under that provision no state can deprive any person of life, liberty, or property *without due process of law. The right to purchase or to sell labor is part of the liberty protected by this Amendment.*"

No, it cannot be, because *due process of law* refers to procedure in the courts, not the substance of the law passed by the legislature. There may very well be a right to contract, covering a right to purchase or sell labor. But it cannot come from the due process clause of the 14th Amendment, because that clause relates to another subject entirely, to the procedure in courts.

Justice Peckham has deliberately confused two legal concepts. The due process clause secured "procedural due process," that is, guaranteed certain accepted procedural safeguards in the courts. The due process clause had nothing to do with the substantive law, the body of the law as opposed to the procedure. But Justice Peckham pretends to find the substantive law included in and protected by the due process clause. Mixing these two concepts creates the doctrine of "substantive due process."

Since the Constitution guarantees certain judicial procedures, he pretends those guarantees cover the substantive law passed by the legislature as well. Standing on this faulty premise he takes another giant stride. He weighs the Bakeshop Act against his own social and economic values and finds the law impermissibly shifts the balance, then declares it unconstitutional. We must see that the net effect merely substitutes his judicial will for the legislative will. No more precise standards guide the interpretation.

The wider significance of substantive due process as expounded in Lochner should become immediately evident. If due process now means something more than procedural due process in the courts, if due process now means substantive due process, then precisely what constitutes substantive due process? Procedural due process was vague enough, but where are the limits of substantive due process? And the answer will turn out no more exact than "reasonableness." As any particular statute comes up for review, the judges deem the law reasonable or not, thumbs up or thumbs down, life as constitutional or death as unconstitutional. Such convenient facility will empower them to reach any result they want, able to enforce their preconceptions and call that due process. It has been said this new power reconstituted the Court into a sort of "super-legislative body," able to substitute their judgment for the legislative judgment.

Lest it be thought this pitches it too strong, perhaps we may call upon the authority of the *Oxford Companion to the Supreme Court*, a useful sourcebook generally somewhat laudatory toward the Court, which describes the shift from procedural to substantive due process this way: "Due process was originally thought of only as a guarantee that laws would be enforced through correct judicial procedure, but the concept changed drastically in the late nineteenth century. Under a theory called 'substantive due process' courts assumed the power to examine the content of legislation ... ."[35]

Lochner v New York didn't go off without some resounding dissents on the Court itself. Justice John Marshall Harlan, writing for himself and two others, would have upheld the limitation to a sixty-hour workweek as a proper regulation enacted for health purposes. Justice Oliver Wendell Holmes, Jr., than whom none could turn a neater phrase, weighed in with a fourth dissent: "This case is decided upon an economic theory which a large part of the country does not entertain. ... The 14th Amendment does not enact Mr. Herbert Spencer's Social Statics. ... I think that the word 'liberty,' in the 14th Amendment, is perverted when it is held to prevent the natural outcome of a dominant opinion, unless it can be said that a rational and fair man necessarily would admit that the statute proposed would infringe fundamental principles as they have been understood by the traditions of our people and our law."[36]

But the majority of the Court kept resolutely down the same path. In 1918 in the Hammer v Dagenhart Case,[37] they struck down a federal law limiting child labor. When Congress sought to get around their objections by enacting a slightly re-tooled version, they threw that out in 1922 with Bailey v Drexel Furniture Co.[38] In 1923, Adkins v Children's Hospital[39] overturned a minimum wage law for women. Back in 1908, the Employee Liability Cases[40] had already voided an early workers' compensation law. Moving on from employment law to the regulation of product quality, in 1924 the Jay Burns Baking Case[41] held unconstitutional an attempt to standardize weights for loaves of bread. The Weaver v Palmer Brothers Case[42] of 1926 held the same regarding a law on the quality of bedding material.

These cases stifled progressive reforms across the entire nation. When the Supreme Court turns down a child labor law in one state, similar laws in all fifty states go down like a row of falling dominoes. And the underlying judicial attitude spreads a chill beyond the facts of the case. As people catch on the justices don't like unions or do like business, that understanding shapes the possibilities. If a pressure group sees the courts leaning their way, why not litigate and give the judges a chance to prove it? On the other hand, why make the effort to push through laws the judges will regard with disfavor?

But the progressives didn't give up. They kept endeavoring. If the Supreme Court blocked one passageway, the reformers often stubbornly tried to punch a shaft to the light by another route. It wouldn't give a complete picture to say the justices stopped all progress. The front was too wide and too deep.

Unexpected itself, industrialization altered the economic and social fabric in utterly unforeseen ways, offering much but threatening much. Congress got the message loud and clear, since the members had their ears to the ground, listening for their electorate. And Congress responded, trying to sort out the good from the bad. In some ways they helped along industrialization, such as giving land grants to the railroads, an enormous governmental subsidy. But other laws sought to ameliorate the ills, preventing monopoly, giving unions a place in the scheme of things, regulating working conditions and products.

By contrast the Court rigidly resisted, yet stayed quite flexible in inventing ways to resist. The justices creatively interpreted the Constitution and statutes, coming up with remarkable meanings. They finally went so far as to invent an entirely novel doctrine, substantive due process. But whether rigid or creative, they always served their own cause, always promoted the judicial will-to-power. Then how can we fail to see the institutional influences at work? Congress performed as should have been predicted, attracted by the members' interests. The Court also performed as should have been predicted, attracted by the institutional will-to-power.

Amidst the wreckage of this industrial litigation, the Court stood triumphant. They had confirmed and enhanced judicial supremacy. From 1803 in Marbury to 1905 in Lochner, the Court had traveled a considerable distance. Judicial review had begun as a doubtful power, fenced about with careful barriers. The justices were supposed to defer to Congress, only declaring laws unconstitutional in clear-cut cases beyond a reasonable doubt. But by now they have come so far as to declare laws they deem "unreasonable" void, a standard lacking any clear-cut edges. By their own decisions the justices had constantly transferred power to themselves. The Court's ascent to power has been relentless and successful.

CHAPTER 7

The Enactment of Segregation

As industrialization powered up, Reconstruction lost steam, finally going in reverse. Crucial to the loss of inertia, using the same sort of judicial re-design as blocked progressive reforms, the Court finishes shutting down congressional Reconstruction, and re-routing the project, opened the legal track to segregation. At this work the latest judicial technology, that machinery of unrestrained judicial review, moved constitutional mountains. Congressional Reconstruction had erected a whole structure of black rights on the bedrock of the franchise. But eating away that constitutional granite, the Court interpreted away the meaning, leaving blacks suspended over a chasm, no solid rights under foot. Next the justices invented another, entirely novel legal doctrine, "separate but equal," bridging across to legalized segregation. Congress gave blacks a ticket to ride the train to democracy, but the Court punched their tickets for an alternate line, which carried to the desolate way station of segregation.

The march toward segregation – All took a number of years and a number of cases to unfold. In the last decades of the nineteenth century, a strict racial separation gradually closed down, especially in the South, yet the enactment of segregation was not foreordained. The historian C. Vann Woodward, still the leading authority on the era, later wrote: "It was a time of experiment, testing, and uncertainty --- quite different from the time of repression and rigid uniformity that was to come toward the end of the century. Alternatives were still open and real choices had to be made."[1] Most significantly, the alternatives turned on the choice between democracy and a rejection of democracy.

The national majority had already made a choice, both ratifying constitutional amendments and passing congressional legislation, the oft-mentioned 13th, 14th, and 15th Amendments and Civil Rights Act of 1875. Their professed beliefs, their habits of thought, their habitual ways of doing business, their interests, their mere antipathies, all worked together. The logic of an open political marketplace carried them along.

As a commodity, the freedmen's votes counted for the same value as any other votes. Republicans showed eager to bid for this support and wrap up a package deal. They would do the right thing by the black man, add votes to their ranks, strike another blow over the lingering resentments from the late war, and beat the Democrats again, all at once. Being in the ascendant, they passed their Reconstruction program. Blacks got the vote and civil rights. They were brought inside the democratic system.

Nor did these underlying incentives change, so reversing this course did not come easy. The Court's cases record a stubborn fight. In every case, this political re-alignment fought hard to carry through their policies as laid down in congressional Reconstruction. But what they won in the democratic arena, they as constantly lost in the judicial forum. Nor did they take defeat tamely. As previously seen, in 1883, the Court had canceled out the Civil Rights Act, writing void over that promise with the Civil Rights Cases. But eighteen states passed state civil rights acts much like the federal one.[2] When shortly the narrative comes to the penultimate case, Plessy v Ferguson, handed down in 1896, where the Court enacts the penultimate doctrine of segregation, "separate but equal," the justices hardly heard universal applause. Much of the Northern press derided the decision, while not even all the organs of Southern opinion re-sounded with acclaim. In New York City, eight out of nine newspapers criticized the Court. Prominent among the detractors stood out church periodicals, such as those of the Methodist Church, the Catholic *Globe* and *Donahoe's Magazine*, the *United Presbyterian* of Pittsburgh, journals of the Methodist Episcopal Church, North, as well as editors among Congregationalists, Unitarians, and Free Baptists. The General Assembly of the southern Presbyterian Church and the official publication of the Methodist Episcopal Church, South, ventured reservations.[3] This evidence shows "separate but equal" hardly arrived on the scene an accepted normative doctrine.

As formal Reconstruction wound down, federal troops left the South, and a wide variety of practice described race relations. Those days lacked much in the way of statistical studies, but the anecdotal evidence shows a situation in flux. An oft-quoted passage comes from black Boston lawyer T. McCants Stewart, who doubled as correspondent for the New York *Freeman*, a black newspaper. In 1885, Stewart took a trip home to his native South Carolina, reporting back by a series of letters. "On leaving Washington, D.C., I put a chip on my shoulder and inwardly dared any man to knock it off." But traveling by railroad he found: "Along the Atlantic seaboard from Canada to the Gulf of Mexico --- through Delaware, Maryland, Virginia, the Carolinas, Georgia, and into Florida, all the old slave States with enormous Negro populations ... a first-class ticket is good in a first-class coach." Nobody picked a fight, and he concluded the series: "For the life of [me], I can't 'raise a row' in these letters. Things seem (remember I write seem) to move along smoothly as in New York or Boston ... If you should ask me 'watchman, tell us of the night,' ... I would say, 'The morning light is breaking.'"[4]

But the social, economic, and political patterns of the old South exerted an inertia the other way. Being used to exploiting a monopoly, rather than competing in an open market, their customs resisted an inclusive democracy. If the South had bet the limit with secession and the Civil War, wiped out by that wild gamble, they still showed willing to play an aggressive hand, looking to recoup their losses. Nor did they regard the rules any more than in the past. Just like they ignored the constitutional rules against rebellion, now they sought to ignore the constitutional rules about black voting and rights. As the opening ploy, they bid to take back their state legislatures, and when they won control, leveraged those winnings, driving blacks out of the game, passing laws to disenfranchise and segregate them. In this way, they practiced a sort of civil disobedience long before Gandhi or Martin Luther King, Jr., state lawmakers daring the punishment by breaking the constitutional laws. But they also practiced another, very uncivil sort of disobedience, the intimidation of the Klan and lynch mobs, not to mention social and economic coercion. Yet could all this have been enough, if the courts had merely upheld the rule of law, enforcing the Reconstruction Amendments? However bold their bluff, they were playing a losing hand under the rules of a democratic game, where a man with a ballot never goes bankrupt, since he can always ante up for the next round, and sooner or later holds some cards, sooner or later shares a pot.

But Southern lawyers were past masters at playing the legal game as well. They knew how to claim their "rights." American lawyers had honed this national pastime to a sharp edge, with which they spent their profession lives trying to cut each other's throats. Yet Southern lawyers enjoyed a certain prominence in the field, going all the way back to Virginia's own Patrick Henry, who fought the ratification of the Constitution almost to a standstill, claiming a federal government threatened the people's "liberty." In the ante-bellum period, John C. Calhoun had expounded the same line, somewhat modified to fit the South's peculiar needs at the time, claiming the "rights" of the Southern, slaveholding minority against the fear of a dominant Northern majority. In the Dred Scott Case, they had won a signal victory, persuading the Court to find a "right" to slavery in the Constitution. The South's current legal talent proved not inferior to their illustrious forebears.

Ready to hand stood the long-standing American preoccupation with limited government and guarantees for minority and individual rights. These lent support for two similarly long-standing and connected arguments about how to construe the Constitution: first, that all delegations of government power should be narrowly construed, second, that all guarantees for minority and individual rights should be broadly construed. The logic went that to limit government you should disfavor governmental authority, while that to guarantee rights you should favor minorities and individuals. Such attitudes and arguments underlay much of what went before, would underlay much of what went after.

Yet still this was not enough. The Southern legal team had to move a lot of constitutional weight. The old-fashioned legal machinery could not have done so much work. The original doctrine of judicial review could raise no more than a small dam, doing no more than block unconstitutional laws in "clear-cut" cases. They had a much bigger job on hand, so needed a much less limited legal technology. They wanted to tear down huge constitutional monuments, the Reconstruction Amendments, whose meaning clearly chiseled on their face. Over the rubble they wanted to erect a towering structure, whose meaning not written in the Constitution, a system of segregation. But these astute and determined gentlemen did not despair before such feats of legal engineering. After all, it was only words. The industrial age showed you could build railroads, bridges, and skyscrapers with steam and steel, but you can build castles in the air with words. And they already had some experience, already had laid the groundwork. They were the very ones who had re-designed the paradigm on judicial review with Dred Scott. Now they meant to follow up on that success. They just needed to release the potential horsepower in unrestrained judicial supremacy.

And they needed just one more thing. They needed to persuade the Court. Fortunately for them, their will-to-power aligned with the judicial will-to-power. They wanted to regain their social, economic, and political power, letting them exploit their old monopoly over blacks. The Court wanted to gain more power, letting them exploit a greater monopoly over the Constitution. The ambitions of each offered an opportunity to the ambitions of the other. If the justices signed off on the Reconstruction Amendments, they signed off on the existing balance of power, leaving blacks part of the balance, leaving Congress dominant in the balance. While the justices could not sign off on segregation except by taking greater power for the Court. If not their better stars, yet their powers aligned.

The centrality of disenfranchisement – The enactment of segregation had to start with disenfranchisement. In 1870, the 15th Amendment had said: "The right of citizens of the United States to vote shall not be denied or abridged by the United States or by any State on account of race, color, or previous condition of servitude." These words had appeared to put in the most fundamental law, the Constitution, the most fundamental right, the vote. These words had appeared to put all other black rights under the protection of that overriding right. These words had appeared to put any attack upon black rights to fight a losing battle. Americans understood how democracy worked, and that if blacks had the vote, they had the where-with-all to defend their other rights, as well as their other interests.

The psychology of American electioneering has not changed, despite the changing fashions in political correctness, as well illustrated by a piece from the pen of David Ross Locke, one of the famous humorists of the day, who wrote under the pseudonym Petroleum V. (for Vesuvius) Nasby. This particular offering appeared in 1869 at the time the controversy raging over ratification of the 15th Amendment. Covering the physiognomy of his alter ego with burnt cork, the author transforms him into a Negro minister. On a mission to raise money for his church, this false reverend visits an Indiana county, where a hundred or so black residents are the potential swing votes. Reverend Nasby goes to see the Democratic candidate for Sheriff and reports his reception: "I WUZ NOT KICKT! On the contrary quite the reverse. The gushin candidate kindly, blandly and winningly begged me to be seated; he askt me, with tears uv interest gushin from his eye, ez to the prospex uv our Zion; ..." Although previously denouncing "nigger emigration," the candidate now took a different line. "The admirishen I feel for the Afrikins --- the respec I hev for thermany qualities uv head and heart make me say in the language uv the inspired writer, 'The more the merrier.'" Handing over a donation to Nasby's church, the candidate concludes: "And next fall, after the Amendment is ratified, and your people git the rites which wus allus theirn, I trust yoo will remember at the polls them wich hev stood yoor friends, uv whom I am wich."[5]

The very roughness carries conviction. Americans understood. Politics not only makes strange bedfellows, but many a marriage of political convenience. When ardent for votes, a candidate will court without regard for color. In fact, Reverend Nasby's story calls to mind the late-in-life conversions of some modern, very non-fictional segregationists, say Alabama Governor George Wallace or South Carolina Senator Strom Thurmond, who in need of votes, learned to woe across the color line. But if in 1869 the country had wanted more elevated language, they might have visited the Senate gallery and heard Senator William M. Steward of Nevada, speaking on the floor to urge passage of the 15th Amendment, as recorded in the *Congressional Globe*: "[The] ballot is the mainspring; the ballot is power; the ballot is the dispenser of office."[6] From the editorial pages to the halls of Congress and everywhere in between, Americans understood.

Legal schemes for disenfranchisement – The 15th Amendment looked as clear as the psychology. Except already back in 1876, a prior chapter visited the Reese Case. To recall, that case ruled unconstitutional the Enforcement Act of 1870, a law punishing election officials who denied blacks their votes. In the opinion, the Court had discovered a subtle distinction. The justices held the Amendment only protected blacks against disenfranchisement based on race, not for other reasons, and since the Enforcement Act not specifically confined to race, they found the law overbroad, exceeding congressional authority, and hence unconstitutional. More than that, the implications carried far beyond the opinion. If the 15th Amendment only prohibited disenfranchisement based upon race, why not find other reasons?

In the coming years, the southern wing of the Democratic Party seized with avidity on this broad hint. Blacks made up the backbone of the Republican Party in the South. If you could fillet them out, the party would collapse in the region. Democratic controlled legislatures began passing the sort of voting laws suggested by Reese. Ostensibly racially neutral, yet these laws had the obvious purpose and effect to disenfranchise blacks.

In 1898, the case of Williams v Mississippi brought these efforts to the Supreme Court. The Williams of the caption, one Henry Williams, had been indicted and convicted of murder in Mississippi, but the appeal dealt not at all with the gruesome facts of the crime. Rather his lawyers attacked the fairness of the trial, which amounted to an attack on the Mississippi law disenfranchising blacks. As usual, the complexity requires unwrapping several layers.

Williams, a black man, had been indicted by an all-white grand jury and convicted by an all-white trial jury. For those not versed in the complexities of criminal procedure, a grand jury indicts or charges with a crime, while a trial jury, also called a petite jury, actually tries the case and returns the verdict of guilty or not guilty. A grand jury amounts to just that, a grand or larger jury, often consisting of more than twelve persons. They determine whether probable cause exists that the suspect committed a crime, and if so, hand down an indictment charging him. Next the trial or petit jury, a smaller jury traditionally of twelve persons, hears the evidence at the actual trial. They decide whether the defendant guilty beyond a reasonable doubt.

Why were Mississippi juries all white? This question goes to the language of the 1890 Constitution of Mississippi, which set forth qualifications for voters this way: "Every male inhabitant ... except idiots, insane persons, and Indians not taxed ... and whoever has never been convicted of bribery, burglary, theft, arson, obtaining money or goods under false pretenses, perjury, forgery, embezzlement, or bigamy, and who has paid ... all taxes which may have been legally required of him."

It also required: "[E]very elector shall, in addition to the foregoing qualifications, be able to read any section of the Constitution of this state; or he shall be able to understand the same when read to him, or give a reasonable interpretation thereof." Next the law provided for officials called "managers of the election." This language read: "Prior to every election the commissioners of election shall appoint three persons for each election district to be managers of the election ... *The managers ... shall be judges of the qualifications of electors.*"[7] The superimposed italics direct out attention to the key, operative element.

As required by Reece, the face of this law looks race neutral, never mentioning blacks by name. But the provisions vested wide discretion in the "managers of the election" to *"be judges of the qualifications of"* a voter. And as a matter of fact, they were exercising that discretion to purge all blacks from the voter rolls. For example, they determined whether a prospective voter could "read any section of the Constitution of this state; or ... understand the same when read to him, or give a reasonable interpretation thereof." Those with the wrong skin hue almost never passed such tests. And also of course, since jurors drawn from the voter rolls, this voting law explains why no blacks served on either the grand or petit jury in Williams' case.

But the Supreme Court did not have much trouble with it, the justices signing off on the Mississippi plan without a single dissenter. Mr. Justice Joseph McKenna writes this unanimous opinion, his rationale as follows: "The question presented is, Are the provisions of the Constitution of the state of Mississippi and the laws enacted to enforce the same repugnant to the 14th Amendment of the Constitution of the United States? ... It has been uniformly held that the Constitution of the United States, as amended, forbids ... discriminations by the general government, or by the states, against any citizen because of race; but it has also been held ... that such denial must be the result of the Constitution or laws of the state, not the administration of them. ... The Constitution of Mississippi and its statutes ... do not on their face discriminate between the races."[8]

Sorting through this language, we see that Justice McKenna starts by merely tracking the rationale in Reese, saying: "The Constitution of

Mississippi and its statutes ... do not on their face discriminate between the races." In other words, you can discriminate against blacks by any other name. But then he takes another crucial step, extending the logic of Reese, going even further. We see that when he says: "such denial must be the result of the Constitution or laws of the state, *not the administration of them.*" In other words, as long as a state enacts voting laws which "do not on their face discriminate," a state can enact voting laws which permit discrimination in "the administration of them."

Surely such an outcome seems backwards. If the Constitution prohibits racial discrimination in voting, that should direct an administration of the law which enforces enfranchisement, rather than permitting an administration which allows disenfranchisement. Of course, it really depends on what you want to accomplish. And what did the Court mean to accomplish here? The answer must be the justices pre-determined to allow black disenfranchisement. As long as the Southern states were clever enough not to openly state their purpose to disenfranchise, they could get away with a system administered so as to discriminate. Such was the unspoken, but plainly operative principle of interpretation, lurking behind the facade of objectivity.

As for Henry Williams' fate, the Supreme Court certainly gave him no help. And he may have been guilty as sin. Only setting aside voting rights, looking at the implications for criminal procedure, the case should raise some concerns. In America, juries traditionally serve as integral to the democratic system. Juries strongly tend to keep the criminal law from excessive severity, strongly tend to keep the prosecutorial zeal from going too far. In the last analysis, both the legislators and the prosecutors know they have to get it past a jury. If un-persuaded, the jurors can simply refuse to go along, for whatever reason. Sometimes called "jury nullification" this potential check goes all the way back to 1670 and England, where as earlier seen, Bushell's Case held jurors had to answer to no one for their verdict. So to exclude an entire race from the jury box takes that check out of their hands. When the South bound up this exclusion with a racial caste system, they were enlisting the criminal justice system as a part of the apparatus to maintain caste lines. In short, it was a situation in the administration of criminal justice ripe for repressive official misconduct.

But to return to disenfranchisement, without a doubt the 15th Amendment meant to prevent that. But the Supreme Court made a choice to permit it. This choice was not compelled by an objective analysis of the law. Rather the judges deliberately adopted a policy to frustrate the clear-cut purpose of the Constitution.

Reese and Williams combined with other cases, turning the 15th

Amendment inside out. Rather than interpreting the language to guarantee black votes, they interpreted the language to allow black enfranchisement. But the language compelled no such conclusion. Read the promise of the words: "The right of citizens of the United States to vote shall not be denied or abridged by the United States or any State on account of race, color, or previous condition of servitude." How did that promise translate into black disenfranchisement in the last decade of the nineteenth century? By no literal translation, by no translation true to the spirit, but a translation determined to take all the truth and poetry out in pursuit of earthly interests. Who doubts the judges knew exactly what they meant to accomplish with these cases? They meant to allow the disenfranchisement of blacks. And what did they accomplish? They opened the way for laws which by the turn of the century had disenfranchised blacks in the South. For example, in 1896 there were still 130,334 blacks registered to vote in Louisiana. By 1904 the number had shrunk to a mere 1,342. The same story is told across the South, but it was a close thing. To call again on Professor Woodward's authority, he observed: "In spite of the ultimate success of disenfranchisement, the movement met with stout resistance and succeeded in some states by narrow margins or the use of fraud."9 In such a close run race, who doubts how crucial the intervention of the Court on the side of disenfranchisement?

Yet let us not forget, the Court did defend a version of limited government, a version of minority and individual rights. They narrowly construed the powers delegated to Congress by the Reconstruction Amendments. They broadly construed the minority and individual rights of the segregationists. Nor let us forget that by so doing, they rejected the majority outcomes reflected in the Reconstruction Amendments. They protected a minority against the majority. Such is the theory and practice of judicial supremacy.

Dynamic constitutional interpretation – By another series of cases, culminating in 1896 with Plessy v Ferguson, the Court enacts the doctrine of "separate but equal," in effect, legalizing segregation. These finishing touches complete the ruin of congressional Reconstruction, while confirming another advance for judicial power. The Court rejects the congressional purpose for the Reconstruction Amendments and Civil Rights Act of 1875. But in doing so, the justices not merely use judicial review as a negative power, not merely voiding law as unconstitutional. Rather, they use judicial review as a positive, dynamic power, interpreting away the clear meaning of constitutional provisions, then interpreting in a diametrically opposite meaning. The meaning changes from black enfranchisement and civil rights, instead becoming segregation. By this further reach, judicial review escapes entirely from the limits of the original doctrine, where the Court could void laws only in "clear-cut" cases of unconstitutionality. Instead, not only can the justices void a law as unconstitutional, they can create constitutional law. By these methods, on the demolished rubble of the Reconstruction laws, the Court will build a system of legal segregation.

Earlier steps toward segregation – Several of the legal steps toward segregation had already taken place. We will recall that the 1875 Civil Rights Act had actually intended to prevent segregation, reading: "That all persons ... shall be entitled to the full and equal enjoyment of the accommodations, advantages, facilities and privileges of inns, public conveyances on land or water, theaters and other places of public amusement." But we will also recall that with the 1883 Civil Rights Cases, the Court held this law unconstitutional as applied to individual, including corporate bodies.

Importantly, let us remember the Court's exact reasoning, which relied on the "doctrine of delegated powers," Under that doctrine, Congress cannot pass a law unless the power to do so delegated in the Constitution. As discussed, one view has always called for a narrow interpretation of any delegation, arguing narrow limits on governmental power better protect liberty. The Court took this view in the Civil Rights Cases. Congress had claimed a proper delegation of power. In passing the Civil Rights Act, they pointed either to the 13th and 14th Amendments. The 13th Amendment prohibited slavery. The argument went that segregation a badge of slavery, and so Congress could outlaw segregation as part of outlawing slavery. The 14th Amendment guaranteed the freedmen's civil rights. The argument went that segregation denied those civil rights, and so Congress could outlaw segregation to protect them.

But in the Civil Rights Cases, the Court rejected both arguments. In his opinion Justice Bradley wrote: "We are forced to the conclusion that such an act of refusal [of accommodation] has nothing to do with slavery or involuntary servitude." So the 13th Amendment failed to delegate to Congress the needed authority. As for the 14th Amendment, the Court concluded that operated only against *state* as distinguished from *individual* action. Justice Bradley wrote: "It is state action of a particular character that is prohibited." Therefore, the 14th Amendment failed to delegate to Congress the needed authority to outlaw segregation caused by *individual* as opposed to *state* action.

However dubious this reasoning, the conclusion at least seems to say *states* could not segregate by law. Justice Bradley had written: "It is *state action* of a particular character that is prohibited." Therefore, logically state laws to segregate could be prohibited, and in fact, remained prohibited under the 1875 Civil Rights Act. Then at a minimum a state could not pass a law directing segregation. Such a deduction appears compelled. But as already amply demonstrated, logic alone stands a weak barrier to the judicial will, and the justices will shortly will away this barrier.

Laws prohibiting segregation – Another early step toward legal segregation came in 1878 with Hall v De'Cuir. This case originated in Louisiana and involved a law to prohibit segregation in public transportation. Promulgated during Reconstruction, Article 13 of the Louisiana Constitution had provided: "All persons shall enjoy equal rights and privileges upon any conveyance of a public character." In 1869 and in keeping, the Louisiana General Assembly enacted a statute which provided: "All persons engaged within this State, in the business of common carriers of passengers, shall have the right to refuse to admit any person to their railroad cars, streetcars, steamboats ... or other vehicles ... Provided, [they] make no discrimination on account of race or color; ... For a violation ... of this Act, the party injured shall have a right of action to recover damage."[10]

This law clearly shows how the fundamental right of black enfranchisement served as a robust protection for blacks' other rights. In 1869, blacks voted in Louisiana and sat in that state's legislature. Their enfranchisement explains the law. They had the power to erect barriers against segregation.

Under the facts of the case itself, one Josephine De'Cuir, described as "a person of color," books passage on the Governor Allen, a steamboat regularly carrying passengers between New Orleans, Louisiana, and Vicksburg, Mississippi. Ms. De'Cuir boards in New Orleans for the Hermitage, an upriver landing within the state of Louisiana. The owner and master of the boat, one John G. Benson, refuses the lady "accommodations, because of her color, in the cabin specially set apart for white persons."[11] She sues under the Louisiana law and wins $1,000 in damages, a hefty sum in those days. On appeal to the Supreme Court, the case receives the caption of Hall v De'Cuir, since in the interim Benson dies and his daughter, Eliza Jane Hall, as administratrix of the estate, stands in for him, a routine procedure when a party dies in the course of the litigation.

Chief Justice Morrison Remick Waite delivers the opinion for the Court. He will hold the Louisiana anti-segregation statute unconstitutional and void. His reasoning begins this way: "There can be no doubt but that exclusive power has been conferred upon Congress in respect to the regulation of commerce among the several states."[12] His reference goes to the "commerce clause" found in Article I, Section 8 of the U.S. Constitution, which reads: "The Congress shall have Power ... To regulate Commerce with foreign Nations, and among the several States."

From this premise Chief Justice Waite moves to his conclusion. He writes: "[W]e think it may safely be said that state legislation which seeks to impose a direct burden upon interstate commerce, or to interfere directly with its freedom, does encroach upon the exclusive power of Congress. The statute now under consideration, in our opinion, occupies that position."[13]

To translate this lawyerly language, the "commerce clause" confers power on Congress to regulate interstate commerce; the Louisiana anti-segregation statute "burdens, interferes, or encroaches upon the exclusive power of Congress" to regulate interstate commerce; therefore, he declares the Louisiana statute unconstitutional and void.

But we might already notice a problem. Recall Ms. De'Cuir booked passage between two landings inside Louisiana, traveling *intrastate*, going only from New Orleans to the Hermitage. Then how does her trip involve *interstate* commerce, travel between states? By the same token, Louisiana only purported to regulate transportation within her own borders. Then how does such a law burden, interfere, or encroach upon *interstate commerce*, travel between states? But Waite solves this difficulty in few words: "While it purports only to control the carrier while engaged within the State, it must necessarily influence his conduct to some extent in the management of his business throughout the entire voyage. ... A passenger in the cabin set apart for the use of whites without the State must, when the boat comes within, share the accommodations of that cabin with such colored persons as may come on board afterwards."[14]

Now such seems fair enough on the surface, since we can imagine state regulations on commerce which could seriously disrupt travel between states. Yet we might suspect the logic somewhat result driven, since this Louisiana anti-segregation statute hardly looks to rise to that level. To say the law might "influence [a carrier's] conduct to some extent in the management of his business through the entire voyage" hardly looks so strong a supposition as to compel a conclusion. But if we doubted the hidden hand of preconception, we might recall an almost incredible contradiction. We might recall how we already saw the Court decide the Civil Rights Cases in 1883, compared to how we just saw the

Court decide this De'Cuir Case in 1878.

In 1878 in De'Cuir, the Court held Congress had the right to regulate interstate commerce and Louisiana impermissibly interfered. As a result, they voided the Louisiana law requiring equal accommodations on steamboats. But if Congress had the power to regulate interstate commerce about accommodations on steamboats, Congress had already exercised this delegation with the passage of the 1875 Civil Rights Act, which we have seen said: "That all persons ... shall be entitled to the full enjoyment of accommodations, advantages, facilities, and privileges of ... public conveyances on land and water, ..." Thus, Congress had mandated equal accommodations, and the Louisiana statute was right in line with the congressional mandate. So how could the Louisiana law burden, interfere, or encroach upon a congressional policy that it completely followed? But in 1878 while deciding De'Cuir, the Court conveniently forgets the 1875 Civil Rights Act. More than that, when in 1883 it came to deciding the Civil Rights Cases, the Court conveniently forgets De'Cuir. If Congress had the power under the "commerce clause" to regulate such things as accommodations on steamboats, then the Civil Rights Act so regulating accommodations was not unconstitutional, but the Court held it was unconstitutional, as exceeding the powers delegated to Congress.

Laws mandating segregation – But at any rate, so the law stood until 1890, when the Court would take the next step with Louisville, New Orleans and Texas Railway Company v Mississippi. At first this case seems on all fours with De'Cuir. The lawyers say a case is on all fours when they mean identical in all material respects. And these two cases present mirror images of each other. In 1869, Louisiana had passed a law regulating accommodations on steamboats. In 1888, Mississippi would pass a law regulating accommodations on trains. All Mississippi did was reverse the image. While Louisiana had forbidden segregation, Mississippi required segregation. But what's good for the gander is good for the goose. If Louisiana law violated the "commerce clause," how could the Mississippi law not violate the same clause?

This Mississippi statute read: "That all railroads carrying passengers in this State ... shall provide equal, but separate, accommodation for the white and colored races, by providing two or more passenger cars for each passenger train, or by dividing the passenger cars by a partition so as to secure separate accommodations."[15]

Once again, we should notice the crucial role of enfranchisement in the process. Louisiana passed their anti-segregation law when blacks voted and sat in their legislature. Then why did Mississippi pass the opposite, pass a segregation law? Clearly because by now the South largely "redeemed," blacks mainly disenfranchised. Without that fundamental right, they could no longer protect their other rights, no longer defend themselves against segregation.

As for the facts of the case, this railroad operated between Memphis, Tennessee, and New Orleans, Louisiana, and for whatever reason, probably related to the costs, neglected to comply with the sovereign will of the State of Mississippi as expressed in the quoted statute. The Mississippi authorities promptly indicted and convicted the corporation, a conviction upheld on appeal by the Supreme Court of Mississippi. The railroad took that final appeal to the U.S. Supreme Court.

It looked like De'Cuir was what the lawyers call the controlling case. De'Cuir was precedent right on point, and the Court is supposed to follow prior decisions that already determine an issue. But Justice Brewer writing for the Court found a distinction: "In this case, the Supreme Court of Mississippi held that the Statute applied solely to commerce within the State; ... If it be a matter wholly respecting commerce within a state, and not interfering with commerce between the States, then obviously there is no violation of the commerce clause of the Federal Constitution."[16]

In other words, since Mississippi said it only meant to regulate commerce only within that state, the Supreme Court took them at their word. But this railroad ran across state lines just as surely as the steamboat in De'Cuir. So what had happened to those concerns expressed in De'Cuir that: "While it purports only to control the carrier while engaged within the State, it must necessarily influence his conduct to some extent in the management of his business throughout the entire voyage." Why did the same logic not apply to the railroad?

Both De'Cuir and the Mississippi case are clearly outcome driven, reaching preconceived conclusions. Both set the stage for Plessy v Ferguson in 1896.

The judicial enactment of separate but equal – As the South "redeemed" from Reconstruction in the last quarter of the nineteenth century, the region's laws underwent a sea change. Instead of the equality engineered by congressional Reconstruction, their laws came to engineer inequality, in other words, enacting segregation. But since the Reconstruction Amendment wrote equality in the Constitution, and since under the "supremacy clause" the Constitution "the supreme law of the land," how did this redesign succeed? And the answer is that only because the Supreme Court offered crucial aid to the segregationist. The justices interpreted away the Reconstruction Amendments, finally interpreting in the doctrine of "separate but equal." In 1896, the case of Plessy v Ferguson culminated the process.

Once again, the case comes out of a state fertile in constitutional litigation, Louisiana. As witnessed, back in 1869 with blacks enfranchised, the Louisiana legislature had passed a law against segregation in public transportation. But just as we saw Mississippi redeemed, Louisiana shortly also redeemed, which is to say, just as blacks gradually disenfranchised in the one state, they were gradually disenfranchised in the other. And just as in 1888, the redeemed Mississippi legislature passed a law mandating segregation in transportation, so in 1890, the redeemed Louisiana General Assembly passed a Separate Car Law, which read: "[A]ll railway companies carrying passengers in their coaches in this State shall provide equal but separate accommodations for the white and colored races, by providing two or more coaches for each passenger train, or by dividing the passenger coaches by a partition so as to secure separate accommodations."[17]

This law gave rise to the case of Plessy v Ferguson. Since black disenfranchisement not yet complete in Louisiana, some eighteen black representatives still sat in the Louisiana General Assembly. They voted nay in a block. Louis A. Martinet, a "person of color," attorney, physician, and founder of the New Orleans *Crusader*, editorialized against the measure in the pages of his newspaper, urging a court fight: "We'll make a case, a test case, and bring it before the Federal Courts."[18] On September 1, 1891, New Orleans's blacks formed the Citizens' Committee to Test the Constitutionality of the Separate Car Law. After raising some $3,000 for legal fees, Martinet contacted A.W. Tourgee, a New York lawyer and a leading white publicist for Negro rights, who signed on as lead counsel without fee. In New Orleans a noted criminal lawyer, James C. Walker, took the brief as local counsel. It only remained to set up a test case.

On June 1, 1891, a thirty-four-year named Homer A. Plessy purchased a ticket on the East Louisiana Railway, a line operating totally inside the state, for the trip from New Orleans to Covington. According to the records, Plessy an "octoroon," which amounts to one-eighth, and "the mixture of colored blood [was] not discernible." And apparently the railroad cooperated in setting up this lawsuit. Probably for purely economic reasons, the corporation disliked the burden of separate cars. At any rate, when Plessy insisted on boarding a coach reserved for whites, he suffered arrest for violating the Separate Car Law.

Plessy's lawyers defended against the charge by attacking the constitutionality of the law. But the state judge hearing the case, Judge

John H. Ferguson, upheld the statute. Plessy's lawyers then moved to federal court, filing what is known as a writ of prohibition against Judge Ferguson. The technicalities of the procedure are not important. But we see the case made up. In the Supreme Court, the caption read Homer A. Plessy v John H. Ferguson, the judge who ruled against him in the state court.

Before inspecting the decision, an initial question occurs. Why would Plessy and the rest go to the trouble? Hadn't the Court already spoken on this issue? We have already witnessed the justices approving a Mississippi law requiring separate cars in the Louisville Railroad Case. And yes, they had approved separate cars, but no, they had not addressed the grounds Plessy's lawyers intended to raise. The Louisville Case merely dealt with whether separate cars interfered with the right of Congress to control commerce. In the New Orleans' Case the argument shifted to far more fundamental things. One more time Plessy's lawyers intended to try to persuade the Supreme Court to enforce the 13th and 14th Amendments. They claimed segregation violated the abolition of slavery by fixing a badge of servitude upon the Negro; they claimed segregation violated the privileges and immunities of citizens, due process of law, and equal protection of the law.

Justice Henry Billings Brown wrote the opinion for the Court in Plessy v Ferguson. First, he disposes of the position separate facilities impose a badge of servitude upon blacks in violation of the 13th Amendment: "That it does not conflict with the 13th Amendment, which abolished slavery ... is too clear for argument. ... A statute which implies merely a legal distinction between the white and colored races --- a distinction which is founded in the color of the two races, and which must always exist as long as white men are distinguished from the other race by color --- has no tendency to destroy the legal equality of the two races."[19]

Next in the way stands the 14th Amendment guarantee of privileges and immunities, due process of law, and equal protection of the law. Justice Brown gets over that uneven ground this way: "The object of the [14th] amendment was undoubtedly to enforce the absolute equality of the two races before the law, but in the nature of things it could not have been intended to abolish distinctions based upon color, or to enforce social, as distinguished for political, equality, or a commingling of the two races upon terms unsatisfactory to either. Laws permitting, or even requiring their separation in places where they are likely to be brought into contact do not necessarily imply the inferiority of either race to the other."[20]

Harlan's dissent – With this utterance the U.S. Supreme Court anoints the doctrine of separate but equal. And there is really no need to break down this logic, since Justice John Marshall Harlan filed a lone dissent in Plessy, performing that service for us. A Kentuckian and once a slaveholder himself, Harlan looked through the form to the reality. In some of the most memorable words ever written by a Supreme Court Justice, he wrote: "It is... to be regretted that this high tribunal, the final expositor of the fundamental law of the land, has reached the conclusion that it is competent for a state to regulate the enjoyment by citizens of their civil rights solely upon the basis of race.

"... The present decision ... will encourage the belief that it is possible, by means of state enactments, to defeat the beneficent purposes which the people of the Unites States had in view when they adopted the recent amendments of the Constitution, by one of which the blacks of this country were made citizens ... and whose privileges and immunities, as citizens, the states are forbidden to abridge. ... The destinies of the two races in this country are indissolubly linked together, and the interests of both require that the common government of all shall not permit the seeds of race hate to be planted under the sanction of law. What can more certainly arouse race hate, what more certainly create and perpetuate a feeling of distrust between these races, than state enactments which in fact proceed on the ground that colored citizens are so inferior and degraded that they cannot be allowed to sit in public coaches occupied by white citizens? That, as all will admit, is the real meaning of such legislation as was enacted in Louisiana.

"The arbitrary separation of citizens, on the basis of race, while they are on a public highway, is a badge of servitude wholly inconsistent with the civil freedom and the equality before the law established by the Constitution. It cannot be justified upon any legal grounds.

" ... We boast the freedom enjoyed by our people above all other peoples. But it is difficult to reconcile that boast with a state of the law which, practically, puts the brand of servitude and degradation upon a large class of our fellow citizens, our equals before the law. The thin disguise of 'equal' accommodations for passengers in railroad coaches will not mislead anyone, or atone for the wrong this day done.

"I am of the opinion that the statute of Louisiana is inconsistent with the personal liberty of citizens, white and black, in that state, and hostile to both the spirit and the letter of the Constitution of the United States. If laws of like character should be enacted in the several states of the Union, the effect would be in the highest degree mischievous. Slavery as an institution tolerated by law would, it is true, have disappeared from our country, but there would remain a power in the states, by sinister legislation, to interfere with the full enjoyment of the blessings of freedom; to regulate civil rights, common to all citizens, upon the basis of race; and to place in a condition of legal inferiority a large body of American citizens, new constituting a part of the political community, called the people of the United States, for whom and by whom, through representatives, our government is administered. Such a system is inconsistent with the guarantee given by the Constitution to each state of a republican form of government."[21]

The least dangerous branch – And it came to pass as Justice Harlan had foretold. But let us not forget, Plessy accomplished something else as well. The case strongly re-affirmed that greater judicial power, not just to interpret the Constitution, not just to fill in gray areas, but to interpret away clear intent, create entirely fresh constitutional doctrine. In this last respect, Plessy reminds of the cases over industrialization such as Lochner, where the Court invented the doctrine of substantive due process, letting them void as unconstitutional laws they deemed "unreasonable." In a quite similar way with Plessy, the Court invented another new doctrine, "separate but equal," enacting segregation into the Constitution. In this way, Plessy strikingly confirmed such judicial power. The Court could not only impose a negative, voiding congressional laws. Now they possessed a positive power, able to make new constitutional law.

Let us pause to think about this power side of the cases, how the enactment of segregation fits with the Court's ascent to power. Back at the very outset, when outlining the Court's institutional nature, certain inherent limitations appeared to weaken the judiciary. No one more pithily summed up these appearances than Alexander Hamilton, writing in the *Federalist No. 78*, the very number that argued so persuasively for judicial review, later providing the rationale used to such effect by Chief Justice Marshall in Marbury. To Hamilton these indwelling restraints served as another justification to trust the Court, making the judiciary "the least dangerous branch." He had written:

"Whoever attentively considers the different departments of power must perceive, that in a government in which they are separated from each other, the judiciary, from the nature of its functions, will always be the least dangerous to the political rights of the constitution; because it will be least in capacity to annoy or injure them. ... The judiciary ... has no influence over either the sword or the purse, no direction either of the strength or wealth of the society, and can take no active resolution whatsoever. It may truly be said to have neither Force nor Will, but merely judgment; and must ultimately depend upon the aid of the executive even for the efficacy of its judgments.

"This simple view of the matter suggests several important consequences. It proves incontestably that the judiciary is beyond comparison the weakest of the three departments of power, that it can never attack with success either of the other two; and that all possible care is requisite to enable it to defend itself against their attacks. It equally proves, that though individual oppression may now and then proceed from the courts of justice, the general liberty of the people can never be endangered from that quarter... ."

All of which goes to show how much easier the historian's task than the task of the historical prognosticator, how much easier to tell what went before than foretell what will come after. Hamilton's vivid language accurately conveys the relative weakness of judges as he knew them, but even his acute perceptive failed to anticipate the unexpected consequences. Judicial review thrust a novel feature into an already shifting constitutional landscape. It looked a good idea to have a written constitution, setting limits on government once and for all; it looked a good idea to require a super-majority for amendments, putting the fundamental law above the reach of a bare or transient majority; it looked a good idea to have judicial review, enforcing this constitutional rule of law through an independent judiciary. But all these good ideas worked together over time, producing an unanticipated result, reminding once again about the severely pragmatic nature of political science, where appealing but untested reforms so often come to grief.

Hamilton had said: "[the judicial branch] can never attack with success the other two." Yet we have seen the judiciary attack with success both progressive reforms and congressional Reconstruction. He had said: "the judiciary has "no active resolution whatsoever," that "[i]t may truly be said to have neither Force nor Will, but merely judgment." Yet we have see the Court active in resolution, not merely sitting in judgment, but showing both Force and Will, inventing substantive due process and enacting segregation. He had said: "the general liberty of the people can never be endangered from that quarter." Yet we have seen the liberty of a whole class of citizens more than endangered, destroyed, blacks disenfranchised and deprived of their civil rights. More than that, we have seen the liberty of the people to govern themselves destroyed, democracy destroyed, the public will repeatedly destroyed by the will of the un-elected justices.

Putting all the cases together, the Court had gradually surmounted those initial weaknesses, which Hamilton thought inherent in the very institutional nature. The Court had transformed itself by no more than the power to re-define the words in the Constitution. Someone once remarked "that if a man were permitted to make all the ballads of a nation he need not care who should make the laws." But the lawyers will settle for the power to re-define the words. Thus they make their living. And that is exactly how we have seen the justices on the Supreme Court making a very good living.

The abandonment of democracy – What caused segregation? Quite simply, an abandonment of democracy, and the Supreme Court crucially assisted at the deed. Yet today we routinely hear democracy condemned for causing segregation, and the Court regarded as the trusted guardian against a repeat of such an event. What turned around the story?

In this accepted telling, the underlying cause for segregation ascribed to "racism." The majority whites united in racism, united in active hostility or at least passive indifference to black rights. Ergo, the dominant, white majority united in enacting segregation. Further, such illustrates the "democratic contradiction," a classic example of a democratic majority oppressing a minority. Ergo, the country needs a weight in the balance against the majority. The Supreme Court provides that counter-weight, protecting the rights of the minority as set forth in the Constitution.

Without much effort, the starting point for this logic easily proved, since the racial prejudice, hostility, and indifference easily shown. Back at the time, numberless speechmakers and writers made racism their theme, and innumerable instances of actual behavior evidenced the attitudes. Yet the train of thought neglects a crucial fact. Since however whites united in racism, the record also convincingly shows them not united as a majority. Rather whites divided among themselves, most prominently along party lines, and in pursuit of the partisan divide, showed willing to work across the racial divide. How else explain the Reconstruction Amendments? The Republican Party reached across the color line, seeking support for the party line. In fact, during Reconstruction, a lot of Southern whites so forgot their prejudice as to travel in the freedmen's company toward electoral victory. So even Southern Democrats might have forgiven their skin color, if they could have forgiven their party. Then while racism undoubtedly contributed to segregation, such hardly seems the efficient cause, the *sin qua non*, the without which nothing. As long as blacks enfranchised, they found white friends, if only friends of convenience. They became bereft of such friendships only when bereft of ballots.

Nor does segregation well illustrate the "democratic contradiction," the democratic majority oppressing a minority After all, the democratic majority enacted the Reconstruction Amendments. Nor did the democratic Congress enact segregation. Not even Southern legislatures enacted segregation, until democracy driven from their chambers. Democracy did not contradict itself, as long as the inner logic allowed to work. Democracy did not fail the black minority, as long as blacks part of the system. Democracy did not fail, but was forcibly left behind. Such seems to show not so much the democratic contradiction, as never to abandon democracy.

As for the Court, how well did the justices perform as trusted guardians? They utterly failed to guard the clear meaning of the Constitution; they utterly failed to guard democracy; they utterly failed to guard black rights. Instead, they joined with an artful minority to reason all away. Of course, they did defend a version of minority rights, but by so doing, showed no inherent capacity to defend the right version. What inspires our trust?

Then let the story not get turned around. History is the laboratory of political science, being almost nothing except a record of failed experiments, often willfully misdirected, often conducted at terrible human cost. Surely segregation just such a failed experiment, coming at just such a price. We cannot afford to misinterpret the experiment, misread the objective data.

As a legal doctrine, segregation exemplifies a remark by the English historian A.F. Pollard: "There is, however, no end to the paradoxes for which liberty has been the excuse or justification."[22] In keeping, the segregationists argued directly from political maxims fundamental to liberty, concepts of limited government and minority and individual rights. Yet their ingenuity altered "liberty" into an "excuse and justification" for a rigid caste system, for segregation, a paradox in the face of proclaimed equality. Once again, the human capacity for rationalization proved incredibly pliant, capable of contorting "rights" into astonishing shapes, all at the behest of interests.

What are the lessons for political science? Surely that men can bend the noblest words to serve their basest interests. Surely that if given the power over the words, no merely verbal doctrine can stand in their way for long. No proclamation of the rights of man, no bill of rights, no constitution can hold them back. Words alone cannot hold the field against interests united with power.

Then what the problem for political science? Surely to reverse the flow. Surely to unite the nobler words with sufficient power to resist the basest interests.

The American experiment with judicial supremacy offered a solution to just this problem. First, put the noble words in a constitution. Second, put lifetime judges to guard that constitution. Being above partisanship, such judges would carry out their role above partisan interests. But during segregation, how well did that theory work in practice? The noble words were clearly written in the Constitution. The lifetime judges were guards over the Constitution. But being above partisan interests failed to put the judges above all interests. They still had their own interests, their professional interests, their interests in power and place. And over segregation, their interests failed to coincide with the noble words in the Constitution. So they interpreted the words away. They did just like anybody else with the power to bend the words to serve their ends.

Democratic theory goes about the problem quite otherwise. Democracy unites the power of the people with the words, trusting them to sort out and uphold the nobler words. How well does that theory work in practice? Over segregation, democracy looks to have done a great deal better than judicial supremacy.

But predominate power united with interests again prevailed. The predominate power and interests of the Court again prevailed. The justices had the final word. In 1896 with Plessy v Ferguson, they spoke that dolorous word. The Court enacted segregation into the Constitution.

CHAPTER 8

An Institutional Defeat

By the Roaring Twenties, the Supreme Court had never been more powerful. But beginning in 1929, America fell into the Great Depression, and economic crisis has a way of reversing political fortunes. In the next presidential cycle, 1932, the Republicans, dominant since the Civil War, not only lost the election, but their ascendency. Nor did the Court escape the fallout, even their lifetime offices not sufficient shelter. Within a short decade by 1938, the Court would suffer a grievous institutional defeat, shearing away much acquired power.

The conflict over economic control – By the end of World War I, the earlier agrarian economy had become a modern, complex, industrial economy. Already the justices have been seen thrusting themselves against the gears of this machinery. Inventing substantive due process, they had rejected progressive reforms aimed at industrial conditions; narrowly construing the commerce clause, they had restricted the law against monopolies. Overall, they had laid down strict limits on governmental regulation or economic management. But however well adapted to pre-industrial times, these judicial policies became increasingly ill-adapted in the changing economic times. The Great Depression accelerated this growing gap, judicial theory separating ever farther from economic reality. While before the Great Depression a serious inconvenience, during that crisis judicial interference proved a crippling obstacle.

By the nature of the thing, the Court's hand lay like a dead weight on the economic levers, braking innovation and adjustment. When the Court opened the legal floodgates to segregation, the state legislatures could pour through, carrying out the purpose, passing the laws to segregate. But the Court's economic policy operated wholly through a negative, halting federal or state action. The Court stopped government efforts to remedy industrial conditions, stopped government regulation almost entirely. The justices exemplified top-down managerial style with a vengeance, rigidly imposing inaction from above.

Today it looks evident that judicial talents fit badly with economic governance. Today national fiscal and monetary policies are accepted macro-economic tools and neither lend themselves to judicial management. Today business regulation is accepted, nor can the justices hope to provide such detailed regulations or day-to-day administration. The consensus now regards these functions as the preserve of Congress and the bureaucracy. But at the time the justices refused to give up the power. Even in the face of the stark demands made by the Great Depression, the Court refused to accede. But for once their will-to-power betrayed them too far, bringing on a memorable encounter with the presidency.

When the new president, Franklin Roosevelt, responded to the crisis with his New Deal, the Court obstinately declared all these new laws unconstitutional. More than frustrated by their intransigence, Roosevelt saw his own power and success assailed. Either accept judicial destruction of the New Deal or find another option. But there was no other option. The Court had thoroughly boxed him in, leaving the only live choice to turn on his judicial tormentors. After some hesitation, he took that resolution, well understanding the risks. In the public mind, an aura of myth surrounds the Court, the justice's guardians of the Constitution, much like the Levites camped around the Arc of the Covenant. Powerful interests supported the Court, not least the lawyer lobby, surely the most influential lobby in America. Attacking the Court opened Roosevelt to easy calumny, his many enemies waiting to pounce. He could feel it coming, knew what they would say: Roosevelt wants to be a dictator; Roosevelt is destroying the Constitution. But in the end, he simply saw no alternative except his own failure and defeat. Some of his advisors suggested a constitutional amendment to rein in the Court. But as a past master of political maneuver, he took the leap a more immediate way. He threatened the Court with institutional reform through congressional action, his "court-packing" plan. At the same time, he opened a publicity campaign, forcibly reminding the justices of a weakness in their armor, their lack of agility in the arena of mass appeal.

Roosevelt did not win four presidential elections through any lack of political canniness. As this startling clarion call summoned them to mortal combat, the justices awoke from their dogmatic slumbers. The peril of their strategic misalignment dawned in their minds. They found themselves entrenched behind a judicial Maginot Line, rendered obsolete by the march of economic events, out flanked by a presidential blitzkrieg. Prudence appeared the better part of valor. Reluctantly but with precipitation, they beat a hasty, somewhat undignified retreat, yet not entirely disorderly. They abandoned on the field the trophies of many a legendary triumph, leaving behind substantive due process, likewise leaving behind a narrow reading of the commerce clause. Yet by surrendering these doctrines to their foe, they mitigated the disaster, ceding ideological provinces, but keeping their heartland intact, lifetime tenure and judicial review still secure in their rear. With these resources in reserve, their institutional army could recruit new strengths. Already by the end of the era, the prospect for a counter-offensive glimmered on the Court's horizon.

The crisis of the Great Depression – Fixing blame for the Great Depression continues a lively indoor sport, since the lessons claim present applicability. Back then people pointed partisan fingers, and they still point fingers. But while that blame game goes on, no one doubts the predictable effect upon the political system. In the American polity, hard times forecast heavy weather for the party-in-power, who take the blame, no excuses accepted.

No doubt either the economic vital signs collapsed. Black Thursday, October 24, 1929, began the panic on Wall Street. For three long years, the blood pressure of that storied market steadily declined. Main Street fared no better. Across the country 5,000 banks broke, wiping out 9,000,000 savings accounts. Unemployment climbed to near 13,000,000, one out of every four. The GNP dropped a huge third. In human terms, the photojournalists recorded the scenes, numbed crowds outside the stock exchange, depositors forlorn in front of closed banks, breadlines and soup kitchens. Squatter towns sprang up on the city fringes, the Hoovervilles. At least a million, perhaps two million, wandered around the country in search of work, adventure, or a sense of movement. Mother Nature herself seemed to join in the downward spiral, as the topsoil of Oklahoma and Kansas blew away in the Dust Bowl. The Okies loaded in their jalopies and clogged the roads to California. Rather than Wagons West, it was a migration of despair. The American dream looked closed for business.

In 1932, the voters acted upon the predictable political equation, turning out Republican Herbert Hoover, electing Democrat Franklin D. Roosevelt as well as a solidly Democratic Congress. The people wanted something done. But if nobody quite yet agrees on the causes, back then nobody quite agreed on the solutions either. Nor in his campaign did Roosevelt offer much in the way of specifics. In such favorable circumstances he kept the onus on the incumbent, expressing the alternative as a bold new vision, set forth in broad generalities, making the widest possible appeal. But he certainly promised change, saying: "The country needs and, unless I mistake its temper, the country demands bold, persistent experimentation."[1] In his speech accepting the nomination, he coined the phrase that stuck to the era: "I pledge you, I pledge myself to a new deal for the American people."[2]

But campaign rhetoric gives way to responsibility and governance as marriage succeeds to wooing. What did the Roosevelt's prenuptial promises mean in practice? In cards a new deal reshuffles the deck, but who gets the better cards problematic. Such precisely describes much of the New Deal, many programs calculated gambles that might or might not pay off. But a deal also has a meaning like a business deal, and a new deal suggests renegotiating the contract. Such better describes the permanent effects of the New Deal, which re-negotiated the social contract, especially the economic clauses. New Deal legislation reflects these twin meanings. Some of the laws were frankly experimental, endeavoring to kick-start the economic engine, although the cylinders never caught with a steady roar until World War II. Side by side, other laws carried out many progressive reforms with more thrown in for good measure. These laws remedied industrial conditions, gave unions a bigger role, provided unemployment insurance and worker's compensation, enacted social security. Together all these steps, sometimes partially taken, sometimes taken in confusion, strode a long way down a turning in the road. From the welter of the New Deal emerged the welfare state, like it or not, good or bad, looking inevitable and necessary.

From an institutional standpoint, then, the democratic institutions gave a rapid response. Congress and the presidency turn over, and both frantically seek to solve the crisis of the Great Depression. Their rapid response led to more basic and permanent responses. Only national, government management and regulation could deal with the modern, industrialized economy. Congress and the president recognized this changed reality, moved to such a system, and the inertia carried on to the welfare state. While the efficacy of that rapid response remains controversial, their more basic and permanent responses remains a matter of fact. Today no one seriously suggests the national government not manage and regulate the economy and revoking the welfare state out of the question. But nothing happened smoothly.

While for their institutional part, the Supreme Court resisted every step of the way. The interests of Congress and the presidency compelled them to change, but the Court's interests lined up against change. Once again the institutions clashed over power.

The National Industrial Recovery Act – The National Industrial Recovery Act (NIRA) served as the keystone in the New Deal arch.

Roosevelt took office March 4, 1933, and by June 16, was signing this major piece of legislation. The speed reflects the urgency. The crisis demanded action, and the president and Congress took action. As the title suggests, this law aimed at industrial recovery, and as the provisions will show, the program a new departure. But neither haste nor newness generally characterize the best legislation, which matures better upon due consideration, evolves better by gradual increments. Perhaps mindful of such concerns, Congress time-limited the Act, requiring renewal after two years.

Several trains of thought coalesced in the NIRA plan. Roosevelt's advisors, his brain trust, viewed industrialization as causing "overproduction" and "underconsumption," leading to a "lack of balance" in the marketplace. On the one hand, they saw factories churning out ever-higher levels of goods, say cars, radios, refrigerators, but on the other hand, they thought wages had failed to keep pace. A corollary placed some of the blame on "technological unemployment," better technology letting fewer workers turn out more goods, reducing the number of workers. In net effect, they thought a greater quantity of goods chasing a falling price, as rising production bid for ever fewer cash-strapped consumers, causing prices to exhibit instability, if not collapse. They also perceived "predatory competitive practices" as contributing, cutthroat competitors debasing products and underselling costs, desperate for market share, frantic to survive in the short term. Then as the brain trust put together a solution, they needed to cool off the production side, running the assembly line at a more regulated speed, while they needed to heat up the consumer side, getting more money into the hands of more workers. As they phrased this last, the economy required "an increase in mass purchasing power," the overall goal being expressed as to "balance production and consumption."

Accepting these premises, government needed to manage and regulate the industrial sector. And for government to manage and regulate, government needed a bureaucracy. Section I of the NIRA set forth their purposes with a broad declaration: "[T]he policy of Congress [is to promote] ... the organization of industry ... to increase the consumption of industrial and agricultural products by increasing purchasing power ... and otherwise to rehabilitate industry ... ." Section 2 authorized the president to set up the bureaucracy to do just that: "To effectuate the policy of this [act], the President is hereby authorized to establish such agencies ... as he may find necessary." As for the details of the program, Section 3 said: "[T]he President may approve a code or codes of fair competition for [each] trade or industry."[3]

FDR immediately created by executive order the National Recovery

Administration (NRA), an enormous administrative agency. Thus brought into being, the NRA energetically set about promulgating "codes of fair competition," administrative regulations with the force of law. These regulations deployed a toolbox of novel tactics. Production quotas sought to stop "overproduction." Price controls sought to promote market stability, combining with rules on standardized quality to halt "predatory competitive practices." Wage and hour rules sought to combat "underconsumption." Maximum work hours put more people to work, forcing companies to replace one worker on a twelve-hour shift with one-and-a-half workers on an eight-hour day. Minimum wage laid an income floor under this larger workforce. Together these appeared to add up to more consumers with more money to spend, stimulating "an increase in mass purchasing power." By such devises the brain trusters sought to achieve their overall goal of "balance" in the marketplace. In an impressive effort, within less than two years, the agency enacted some 546 such codes and 185 supplemental codes, covering every industry from the 3,500,000 workers under the retail trade code to 45 workers in the animal soft hair trade. By May, 1935, about 95 percent of all industrial workers had been brought within an NRA code, some 23,000,000 workers in all.[4]

But in a nation known to worship the free-market like a religion, such a program more than smacked of heresy, moving toward government regulation, a good way toward centralized planning and control, perhaps even toward socialism. So the orthodox hurled their anathemas. But leaving ideology aside, did the NIRA pass the acid test? Did it work? And the economy did pick up, but then staggered again, falling into a mini-depression within the longer depression. Roosevelt's critics blame his flawed doctrine, damning his lack of faith in free-markets, condemning his misapplication of a profane dogma. They may be right or wrong. Fortunately, such a debate falls outside the present requirements, which concern institutional performance, the Court versus Congress and the presidency.

Speaking at the signing ceremony for the bill, Roosevelt had said: "History probably will record the National Industrial Recovery Act as the most important and far-reaching legislation ever enacted by the American Congress. It represents a supreme effort to stabilize for all time the many factors which make for the prosperity of the nation and the preservation of American standards. Its goal is the assurance of a reasonable profit to industry and living wages for labor, with the elimination of the piratical methods and practices which have not only harassed honest business but contributed to the ills of labor."[5]

Perhaps he overstated his case. Yet who can doubt he wanted this law to succeed? He had laid his bet. He has kept his promise of "bold experimentation." But within two short years the Supreme Court would void the Act, ruling that Congress and the president had acted unconstitutionally. When in the midst of a crisis as profound as the Great Depression, the elected Congress passes such a law and the elected president signs such a law, the president announcing the event as "the most important and far-reaching legislation ever enacted," and in less than two years the unelected justices throw the whole thing out, it is certainly a phenomenon in the life of any government professing to call itself a democracy.

Schechter Poultry, the sick chicken case – Judicial hostility toward the New Deal appeared a given. The Court had already held unconstitutional many progressive reforms which went not as far as Roosevelt's programs. Their lawyers' briefcases crammed with these precedents, the loyal opposition put the lost election behind them and turned toward the courthouse, seeking that now familiar change of venue with alacrity and understandable optimism. By 1935, some 389 cases against New Deal laws pended in the courts. But might the Great Depression have altered the judicial mind-set? Perhaps with all that had happened, the time had come to temporize, working out a judicial accommodation with the forces of reform. Initially, the justices seemed to signal some such wavering. In 1934, the Court let some New Deal like laws slip through the portal. The Home Building and Loan Association Case[6] approved a Minnesota statute that extended relief to farmers against mortgage foreclosures. Nebbia v New York[7] approved a statute setting milk prices. But slowly, then abruptly, the judicial gate banged shut.

In 1935, the Hot Oil Case[8] invalidated a part of the NIRA, a provision that regulated the oil industry. The Railroad Retirement Case[9] voided the Railroad Pension Act. Finally, on another black day, May 27, 1935, this time Black Monday, the justices rolled out the guillotine of judicial review and officially began the massacre of New Deal legislation. In three cases handed down that day, they warmed up by killing off a federal mortgage act in aid of bankrupt farmers and presidential authority over independent agencies. Then most stunning of all, in Schechter Poultry v U.S., the justices executed the National Industrial Recovery Act. But really they went much farther, signing a judicial death warrant for the whole New Deal.

Media coverage of the day nicknamed Schechter Poultry "the sick chicken case." The facts implicated the Live Poultry Code, one of those more than 500 codes of "fair competition" promulgated by the NRA, this one covering the poultry market in New York City. The largest such market in the U.S., the lines of supply ran back and forth across state lines. About 96% of the chickens came from out-of-state, 75% of shipments off-loading at the New York Central Railroad terminal in Manhattan, the rest at four New Jersey terminals. Schechter Poultry itself operated a slaughterhouse in Brooklyn, purchasing live at the West Washington Market in New York City, the railway terminals, or sometimes from commission men in Philadelphia. After trucking to Schechter's slaughterhouse, the unfortunate chickens suffered their fate, being re-sold to retail poultry dealers and butchers inside the state.

Into this marketplace the Live Poultry Code inserted a New Deal style regulatory scheme. Under the NRA procedure, a "trade association" could ask the agency to promulgate a code. In the New York region, some 350 wholesale firms, 150 retail shops, and 21 commission agents came forward with such a request. They made up about 90% of the local industry, supplying the metroplex with poultry from 41 states, employing about 1,610 people, and transacting an annual business of $90,000,000. After notice and hearing, the Administrator of the NRA duly recommended a code. His accompanying report noted employment in the industry down 40% and claimed the code would boost workers about 19% and wages about 20%. Accepting this recommendation, the president signed an executive order putting the code into effect.

The law made code violations a misdemeanor, which brings the story back to Schechter Poultry. The authorities shortly charged and convicted that company with numerous violations: one count for selling an unfit, hence "sick chicken" to a butcher; ten counts for selling by the chicken rather than the coop; two counts for selling chickens not inspected or approved; two counts for selling to unlicensed dealers; two counts for violating wage and hour rules; two counts for failing to report or making false reports; and one count for conspiring to do all this.

Is there a problem here? On sober consideration, a problem should appear. When parsing the law, we should have noticed an awful lot of blank space. It contained a broad mandate, go forth and save the industrial sector; it vested the president with power to set up an administrative agency; it vested the agency with power to promulgate regulations with the binding force of law. That was pretty much it. A law creating a program and agency with so few congressional guidelines should be of some concern.

Under the separation of powers, the legislative branch passes the laws and the executive branch carries out the laws. But what happens when Congress passes a law conferring power on the president to create an agency, an agency which can make regulations, which regulations have the force of law? In effect, such a congressional law passes law making over to the executive branch, which in effect, violates the separation of powers.

Here enters a conundrum that continues to bedevil. Bureaucracy serves as a necessity to modern government. But Congress lacks the time or expertise to set forth all the bureaucratic details. Then also of necessity, Congress must delegate much to bureaucracy, leaving much for them to fill up with their regulations, letting them in effect make laws. As a practical matter, there is no getting around this situation, and the solution, more or less a matter of degree, more or less observed, requires Congress to pass the initial laws setting up any agency with sufficient specificity, limiting the bureaucracy to a mandate, holding them to definite guidelines. If properly done, such safeguards leave legislative primacy with Congress, the bureaucracy no more than agents of the congressional will, accountable to carry out the congressional program.

In Schechter, the Supreme Court uses these legitimate concerns to call down the New Deal. Chief Justice Charles Evans Hughes writes the opinion, saying: "[T]he discretion of the President in approving or prescribing codes, and thus enacting laws for the government of trade and industry throughout the country, is virtually unfettered. We think that the code-making authority thus conferred is an unconstitutional delegation of legislative power."[10]

He looks absolutely right. In fact, this ruling stands a rare exercise, judicial review as originally conceived. The Court upheld a clear-cut constitutional meaning, standing up for a fundamental principle, the separation of powers. In hurried response to economic crisis, Congress had ventured into largely untested legal waters, the then shallow sea of administrative law, which governs the creation and operation of administrative agencies. In the coming years the shoals of this region would become increasingly well mapped. But the New Deal stands at the headlands of these voyages of exploration, ushering in extensive, long-term reliance on administrative agencies, leading to the present golden age of bureaucracy, now the fourth branch. In the haste and confusion of those early times, Congress neglected what later became a recognized and primary rule of administrative law. In creating any agency, the legislature must set forth the mandate and guidelines with sufficient specificity.

Then let the argument go thus far with the Court. Except Chief Justice Hughes fails to stop there, a curiosity being why not. Under a fundamental rule of judicial economy, if a judge can dispose of a case on one reason, he does not go on to talk about other reasons not needed to make the ruling. To do so may involve several dire consequences. He may wander off into territory not properly developed in the case, saying something not fully considered from all sides; he may cover too much ground, saying something which later fences him in; he may go off on a roving commission, saying something which carries him far afield. Such is the well-known rule, which largely on account of the last temptation, the Court much honors in the breach. The justices may have decided a case, but when an ulterior motive exists, when they long to assert control over a larger political controversy, they find it convenient to keep on talking. Chief Justice Hughes gives in to this peril in Schechter.

His next words most troubled Roosevelt and his New Dealers. Because the chief justice next rules that Congress cannot regulate businesses such as Schechter period. He accomplishes this purpose by returning to that old, narrow definition of the commerce clause, whether phrased as a distinction between *intrastate* and *interstate* commerce or between *manufacture* and *commerce,* all amounting to the same thing. Recall first encountering this doctrine back in 1895 in the E.C. Knight Case, where although the sugar trust manufactured 98% of the nation's sugar, yet the Court held Congress could not regulate the monopoly. The justices said the company engaged only "manufacture" not in "commerce," so Congress lacked power to regulate them under the commerce clause. Now suddenly the law recoils to E.C. Knight.

Justice Hughes writes: "Much is made of the fact that almost all the poultry coming to New York is sent there from other States. But ... [w]hen defendants had made their purchases ... at the railroad terminals serving the city, or elsewhere, the poultry was trucked to their slaughterhouses in Brooklyn for local disposition. The interstate transactions in relation to that poultry then ended. ... The undisputed facts thus afford no warrant for the argument that the poultry handled by the defendants at their slaughterhouse markets was in a 'current' or 'flow' of interstate commerce and was thus subject to congressional regulation."[11]

From this rationale fell cascading consequences, ever steeper and wider to the bottom. First, Schechter Poultry wins the case. Congress having violated the company's right against regulation, the Court reverses the convictions. Second, the NRA more than loses the case, going out of existence. Congress having exceeded their authority under the commerce clause, the Court puts the agency out of existence as unconstitutional. Third, Congress and the presidency lose even more, their entire effort to manage and regulate industry voided as unconstitutional. The codes of more than 500 industries, covering 23,000,000 jobs are nullified. The attempt to balance production with consumption, balancing the market, the wage and hour provisions, the whole plan to stabilize industry, all vanish in the same moment. Fourth, they faced the prospect of even greater loses, since the rest of the New Deal survived only under sentence of imminent demise. If the New York poultry market not in the "current or flow" of "interstate commerce," then neither was almost anything else. If that made the NIRA unconstitutional, that made virtually the whole New Deal unconstitutional.

The Agricultural Adjustment Administration – If the NIRA was the king of New Deal programs, the AAA was the twin king. AAA stood for Agricultural Adjustment Act and created an agency meant to do just that, to "adjust" and "administer" agriculture. While the National Recovery Administration attempted to revive industry, his brother agency, the Agricultural Adjustment Agency, was supposed to revive agriculture. Contrasting with the Court's view, this twin-headed approach saw the economy as a linked system, industry and agriculture moving together. Conceiving if one fell down, it pulled down the other, and if you lifted up one, it lifted up the other, these two monarchs among agencies were intended to mutually assist each other.

In the 1930s, some 6,000,000 farms grew the food, but this vast agricultural army had advanced in confusion to calamity. Ironically, the productivity of American farmers had reversed the age-old tale of scarcity and famine, raining down a plague of plenty. Overproduction had pilled up vast agricultural surpluses, reducing market price below subsistence levels for farmers, who became victims of their own success. As the bankruptcy lawyers say, the farmers were "underwater," and as they went down the suction pulled others into the vortex. Without money, the farmers quit buying manufactured goods, idling factories and factory workers. Railroad shipments to and from farmers fell, hurting the railroads. Then with farmers unable to make their mortgage payments, the banks foreclosed, but by now with cash and confidence in short supply, no one bid market value at the sheriff's sale. Failing to recoup their loan value, the rural banks gradually sank under the uncollectible paper. As these outlying banks failed, their collapse embarrassed their big city correspondent banks. The bottom seemed nowhere in sight.

In response, Roosevelt's brain trust came up with another radical departure from laissez-faire economics, and in 1933, Congress rammed through the Agricultural Adjustment Act in just fifty-seven days. The key proposal looked counter-intuitive. The AAA would pay farmers not to grow crops, raising the money to pay them with an excise tax on food processors. This strange-looking reversal of market incentives hoped to set off a chain reaction running the other way. If farmers planted less acreage, they would grow fewer crops. If farmers grew fewer crops, the surplus would fall. If the surplus fell, prices would go up. These higher prices plus the government subsidies would put more money in farmers' pockets. If they had more money, they would again buy manufactured goods. If they bought more goods, the factories would fire up and hire workers, putting more money in the hands of city folks. If city folks had more money, they would buy more agricultural products, supporting farm prices, incidentally paying the extra cost of that excise tax on food processors, which would inevitably be passed on to them. If farmers again prospered, they would again pay their mortgages, and banks would rebound. The polarity of the market would reverse, going from negative to positive.

Roosevelt himself summed up the underlying theory this way: "We need to give 50 million people who live directly or indirectly upon agriculture a price for their products in excess of the cost of production. That will give them the buying power to start your mills and mines to work, to supply their needs. They cannot buy your goods because they cannot get a fair price for their products. You are poor because they are poor. ... A restored agriculture ... will provide a market for your products. That is the key to national economic restoration."[12]

He also confessed the experimental status of the AAA, saying: "I tell you frankly that it is a new and untrod path, but I tell you with equal frankness that an unprecedented condition calls for the trial of new means to rescue agriculture. If a fair administrative trial of it is made and it does not produce the hoped-for results, I shall be the first to acknowledge it and advise you."[13]

Did this bold experiment work? In 1933, the year the AAA began, farm income went up 24%, in the next two years 15% and 16%. The government subsidies counted heavily toward these gains, in 1933 more than one-fourth, in 1934 more than two-thirds, and in 1935 more than half.[14] Overproduction also slowed, but in 1933 and 1934, severe droughts may have done more to erase the agricultural excess. As for priming the industrial pump, did the extra income in farmers' hands at least promote a trickle? In the AAA's second annual report, their statisticians attempted an answer, making a study of industrial shipments from sixteen Northeast states to ten Southeast agricultural states. Waybills from the four biggest railroads reflected a 75.1% increase in items principally for farmers, 57.6% in domestic and personal items, 43.2% in items for industry and commerce, and 31.3% in items used generally in industry, farms, and homes. In addition, new car registrations in the same ten agricultural states climbed 157% in 1933 and 238% in 1934.[15]

These figures sound impressive. But we can be sure a program paying farmers not to grow crops, in essence paying people not to work, did not escape censure on that ground alone. The AAA seemed almost un-American, replacing hard work with a government handout. This could not escape criticism, nor did it. But once again this dispute fortunately falls outside our purposes. In our story line, what matters is the Court's judgment on the AAA.

The Court's judgment – In the 1936 Butler Case, the Court handed down that judgment, finding the AAA unconstitutional. They did so by playing another variation on that familiar theme, the dichotomy previously titled "intrastate not interstate, manufacture not commerce," now re-titled "local not national" and "reserved to the states not delegated to the federal government." While before we heard this distinction played over the commerce clause, now we hear a version scored for the taxing power. But however phrased or orchestrated, the judicial music stays the same. If the Constitution was an orchestra of powers, the Court was the conductor, and the justices were not going to pass the baton to Congress.

Justice Owen Josephus Roberts writes the opinion in Butler, beginning with that time-honored claim about judicial deference to Congress: "There should be no misunderstanding as to the function of this court ... It is sometimes said that the court assumes a power to overrule or control the action of the people's representatives. This is a misconception. ... When an act of Congress is appropriately challenged in the courts as not conforming to the constitutional mandate the judicial branch of the Government has only one duty --- to lay the article of the Constitution which is invoked beside the statute which is challenged and to decide whether the later squares with the former."[16]

Such a description hardly fits how the Court has gone about business so far. Yet if Justice Roberts makes that claim, let us watch him "lay" the Constitution "beside" the Agriculture Adjustment Act and "decide whether the later squares with the former." Let us see if his practice conforms to his principles.

As said, the AAA planned to cool down overproduction by paying farmers to let land lay fallow, raising the funds from an excise tax on food processors. The Butler in the caption of the Butler Case served as receiver for such a food processor, Hoosick Mill Corporation. He filed suit, challenging the tax as unconstitutional.

Article I, Section 8 delegates to Congress the power to tax: "The Congress shall have Power To lay and collect Taxes, Duties, Imposts and

Excises, to pay the Debts, and provide for the common Defense and General Welfare of the United States." Then does the excise tax exceed the delegated power to tax? To follow Justice Roberts' suggested method, we "lay the article of the Constitution ... beside the statute ... to decide whether the later squares with the former." To focus on the operative words from Article I: "Congress shall have Power To Lay and collect Taxes ... for the ... General Welfare." Laying this article beside the statute, doesn't the tax "provide for the general welfare?" If so, "the later squares with the former," and how can we say the tax not constitutional?

Yet a real difficulty lurks. The Constitution constantly expresses generalities, the present language being a perfect instance. If Congress can tax for the "general welfare," where would the taxing power end? Without more specific guidelines, Congress could dispatch a tax on almost any errand. But in a government of "limited powers," some limit must exist, even on so broad a power as the general welfare. Only where draw the line? And who draws that line? It is ingenuous to maintain the Constitution itself contains or can utter its own answers.

Actually this controversy over the taxing power goes back to the Founding, which Justice Roberts well knows, as he briefly recaps that history, writing: "The Congress is expressly empowered to lay taxes to provide for the general welfare. ... Since the foundation of the nation sharp differences of opinion have persisted as to the true interpretation of the phrase [to provide for the general welfare.] Madison asserted that it amounted to no more than a reference to the other powers enumerated ... Hamilton, on the other hand, maintained the clause confers a power separate and distinct from those later enumerated ... and Congress consequently has a substantive power to tax and appropriate, limited only by the requirement that it shall be exercised to provide for the general welfare of the United States. ... Mr. Justice Story, in his Commentaries, espouses the Hamiltonian position."[17]

The Justice Story referenced is Joseph Story of Massachusetts, who served on the U.S. Supreme Court from 1811 to 1845, and whose famous *Commentaries on the Constitution*, which first appeared in 1833, have been justly influential through the years.

So there exists a broad and a narrow view of the taxing power. Madison held Congress could levy a tax only in aid of some other "power enumerated." Hamilton held Congress could also tax in aid of the "general welfare," whatever that might be, a view supported by Story. Having laid out the alternatives, perhaps surprisingly Justice Roberts selects the more expansive reading. "Study of all these," he writes, "leads us to conclude that the reading advocated by Mr. Justice Story is correct."[18]

But then Justice Roberts goes on: "[T]he adoption of the broader construction leaves the power to spend subject to limitations."[19] In support he refers again to Justice Story: "A power to lay taxes for the common defense and general welfare of the United States is not in common sense a general power. It is limited to those objects. It cannot constitutionally transcend them. ... [Story] makes it clear that the power of taxation and appropriation extend only to matters of national as distinguished from local welfare."[20]

He is transitioning his argument. Having "adopted" the "broader construction" of the taxing power, he now says that power remains "subject to limitations." Further, he says Story "makes clear" the power "extends" only to "national as distinguished from local" matters. We should easily catch his drift, which lines up with that prior distinction between *interstate* and *intrastate* commerce in Schechter, which dealt with the commerce clause, defining it narrowly. Butler deals with the taxing power, and Justice Roberts is heading toward confining that narrowly, too, using the same distinction between *interstate* and *intrastate*, now phrased as *national* and *local*.

But where in the Constitution will he find such limits, such a line between national and local matters? To do so he brings in another part of the Constitution altogether, the 10th Amendment, the last article in the Bill of Rights, which reads: "The powers not delegated to the United States by the Constitution ... are reserved to the States."

He will put the taxing power under the 10th Amendment, finding the first held down by the second. Here is how he does it: "We are not now required to ascertain the scope of the phrase 'general welfare of the United States' or to determine whether an appropriation in aid of agriculture falls within it. Wholly apart from that question, another principle embedded in our Constitution prohibits the enforcement of the Agricultural Adjustment Act. The act invades the reserved rights of the states. It is a statutory plan to regulate and control agricultural production, a matter beyond the powers delegated to the federal government."[21]

Thus, the AAA is unconstitutional as a violation of "the reserved rights of the states," as found in the 10th Amendment.

Did Justice Roberts keep his word? Did he "lay" the 10th Amendment "beside" the AAA to see "whether the later squares with the former?" No, that describes his method not at all. The 10th Amendment does not say "regulation and control of agricultural production" are "powers not delegated" to the federal government, but "reserved to the States." Those are Justice Roberts' constructs, not the words of the Constitution. Then perhaps Justice Roberts demonstrates this implied intent, quoting from the constitutional debates, the ratifying conventions, or other sources? He cites none. Perhaps a long line of judicial decisions supports him? But again, he cites none. Instead he relies upon his own unaided reasoning as follows: "[P]owers not granted are prohibited. None to regulate agricultural production is given, and therefore legislation by Congress for that purpose is forbidden."[22] So Justice Roberts did not keep his word. Rather he has done what the justices have been witnessed to do over and over. He has manipulated the words to reach his own preferred conclusion.

Thus, the AAA was held unconstitutional. And there were other immediate and very real costs for this decision. The treasury had to refund some $200,000,000 in taxes already collected under the AAA program. This put a significant strain on an already groaning federal budget.

The larger result – In the larger picture, where did the Butler Case leave the Country? Already with Schechter, the Court had prevented national management and regulation under the commerce clause. Now the Court has prevented any such attempt under the taxing power either. The second of the two major New Deal programs is dead on arrival. The rest of the smaller fry looked bound for glory by the same short drop. By now some 1,700 cases pended in the courts against New Deal laws. As the Court kept processing these indictments, they kept up the promised massacre. Prominent among the victims, the 1936 Carter Coal Case[23] held unconstitutional the Bituminous Coal Conservation Act of 1935, thus holding the vital coal industry a local rather than national matter. The Court appeared determined to continue unabated to the end of the proscription.

Putting this run of cases against the New Deal together with the earlier run of cases against the progressive reforms, and what do we see? The New Deal cases said the Constitution prohibits Congress from managing or regulating the economy. The earlier progressive cases said the Constitution prohibited the states from regulating the economy. The effect was a whipsaw. First the federal government cannot regulate, all the economic pieces being local, reserved to the states. Then the states cannot regulate, national constitutional rights protecting all the economic pieces, preventing state laws. Perhaps the words of one legal commentator best sum up the resulting situation: "What we face now, at numerous critical points, is the question, not how government functions shall be shared, but whether in substance, we shall govern at all."[24]

Roosevelt's court-packing plan – While the Supreme Court shredded his New Deal, Roosevelt was preoccupied in another political arena. However unpopular his programs with the justices, the 1936 presidential election showed him highly popular with the electorate, who carried him back to office with a landslide 60.8% of the vote, in the Electoral College a stunning 523 to a mere 8. But despite this resounding mandate, he realized his second term loomed under almost certain failure. All he might propose stayed doomed before the Court, leaving him pilot of the ship of state, but forbidden to put a hand on the rudder. Unable to steer, he must stand on the burning quarterdeck, hoping the wind and current drifted him to safe harbor. If he would rather resume his own destiny, the time had come to make his resolution and stand by his guns, somehow fighting free of the Court's meddling with his command.

On February 5th, 1937, he fired off a first shot, signaling hostilities with a message to Congress, asking them to add one new justice to the Supreme Court for every member over the age of seventy. So carefully had he guarded the secret, the crack of this cannon took many of his closest advisors and allies by surprise.

The Constitution says justices serve life terms, but omits to set the number on the Court. In fact, the number has varied over the years. The original Judiciary Act of 1789 established the Court with only six members. Since then the figure fell as low as five in 1801, rising as high as ten in 1863. The size stabilized at nine with the Judiciary Act of 1869. Also in 1869, as part of a voluntary retirement bill for federal judges, an identical proposal to add justices actually passed the House, being deleted in the Senate. The Attorney General made a similar recommendation for lower federal judges in 1913, 1914, 1915, and 1916.

Yet none of these precedents really lent support to Roosevelt's sudden move. No president before proposed enlarging the Court to dilute a hostile majority. All the ups and down in size, all the talk about judicial retirement, nothing related to any such scheme. Seeking to lessen the novelty and mute the impact, Roosevelt brought to bear all his rhetorical and political adroitness. In his congressional message, he stuck to a claim the Court over worked. "The simple fact," he wrote, "is that today a new need for legislative action arises because the personnel of the Federal judiciary is insufficient to meet the business before them."

Perhaps with tongue visibly in cheek he went on: "A part of the problem of obtaining a sufficient number of judges to dispose of cases is the capacity of the judges themselves. This brings forward the question of aged or infirm judges --- a subject of delicacy and yet one which requires frank discussion. ... Modern complexities call also for a constant infusion of new blood in the courts. ... A lowered mental or physical vigor leads men to avoid an examination of complicated and changed conditions. Little by little, new facts become blurred through old glasses fitted, as it were, for the needs of another generation; older men, assuming that the scene is the same as it was in the past, cease to explore or inquire into the present or the future."[25]

Probably with this excuse Roosevelt hoped to do no more than buy some time, entering the thin edge of a less radical idea, preparing the public mind for the thicker wedge of a more radical idea. Yet this pretext was quickly cast aside, as it had to be. After a brief pause for the notion to grow more familiar, Roosevelt rolled out the heavy artillery and delivered a formal broadside. In a radio address March 9, 1937, he took his case to the people, taking on the Supreme Court as they had never been taken on before, certainly not from the White House. His words bear quoting at some length:

"Tonight, sitting at my desk at the White House, I make my first radio report to the people in my second term of office.

"I am reminded of that evening in March, four years ago, when I made my first radio report to you. We were in the midst of the ... crisis. ...

"In 1933 you and I knew that we must never let our economic system get completely out of joint again --- that we could not afford to take the risk of another great depression.

"We also became convinced that the only way to avoid a repetition of those dark days was to have a government with power to prevent and to cure the abuses and the inequalities which had thrown that system out of joint. ...

"National laws are needed to complete that program. Individual or local or state effort alone cannot protect us ...

"The Courts, however, have cast doubt on the ability of the elected Congress to protect us against catastrophe by meeting squarely our modern social and economic conditions. ...

"Last Thursday I described the American form of Government as a three horse team provided by the Constitution to the American people so that their field might be plowed. The three horses are, of course, the three branches of government --- the Congress, the Executive, and the Courts. Two of the horses are pulling in unison today; the third is not. ...

"It is the American people themselves who are in the driver's seat. It is the American people themselves who want the furrow plowed. It is the American people themselves who expect the third horse to pull in unison with the other two. ...

" ... in 1803 ... [t]he Court claimed the power to declare [an act passed by Congress] unconstitutional. ... But a little later the Court itself admitted that it was an extraordinary power ... and ... laid down this limitation upon it: 'It is but a decent respect due to the wisdom, the integrity and the patriotism of the Legislative body, by which any law is passed, to presume in favor of its validity until its violation of the Constitution is proved beyond all reasonable doubt.'

"[S]ince the rise of the modern movement for social and economic progress through legislation, the Court has more and more often and more and more boldly asserted a power to veto laws passed by the Congress and State Legislatures in complete disregard of this original limitation.

"In the last four years the sound rule of giving statutes the benefit of all reasonable doubt has been cast aside. The Court has been acting not as a judicial body, but as a policy-making body. ...

"That is not only my accusation. It is the accusation of most distinguished Justices of the present Supreme Court." Here FDR ran over a quick review of cases invalidating New Deal laws, quoting some of the dissenters. "In the face of these dissenting opinions, there is no basis for the claim made by some members of the Court that something in the Constitution has compelled them regretfully to thwart the will of the people. ...

"The Court in addition to the proper use of its judicial functions has improperly set itself up as a third House of the Congress --- as a super-legislature, as one of the Justices has called it --- reading into the Constitution words and implications which are not there, and which were never intended to be there. ...

"Those opposing this [proposed] plan have sought to arouse prejudice and fear by crying that I am seeking to 'pack' the Supreme Court ... Let me answer this question with a bluntness that will end all honest misunderstanding of my purposes. If by that phrase 'packing the court' it is charged that I wish to place on the bench spineless puppets who would disregard the law and would decide specific cases as I wished them to be decided, I make this answer --- that no President fit for his office would appoint, and no Senate of honorable men fit for their office would confirm, that kind of appointees to the Supreme Court.

"But if by that phrase the charge is made that I would appoint and the Senate would confirm Justices worthy to sit beside present members of the Court who understand those modern conditions --- that I will appoint Justices who will not undertake to override the judgement of the Congress on legislative policy --- that I will appoint Justices who will act as Justices and not as legislators --- if the appointment of such Justices can be called 'packing the Courts,' then I say that I and with me the vast majority of the American people favor doing just that thing --- now."[26]

By this address Roosevelt arraigned the Court before another court, the court of public opinion, where the justices badly adapted to compete. They could not give a speech in return, being forced to let their cases speak for themselves. But that testimony told against them. Roosevelt's every rhetorical stroke hit home, charged with those most telling of rhetorical devices, truth and reality. The Court had "more and more often and more and more boldly asserted a power to veto laws;" the Court had "been acting ... as a policy-making body;" the Court had been acting "as a super-legislature, reading into the Constitution words and implications which were not there, and which were never intended to be there." Moreover, by so acting the Court was blocking the need for national management of a modern economy, a need made ever more evident by the Depression.

The switch in time which saved nine – Roosevelt's court-packing plan, an assault on a political institution of mythic dignity in the public mind, an institution backed by so many potent interests, moreover, an assault made by a political figure with so many virulent foes, could not but summon a storm of protest. The thunder and lightning sounded swift and fierce, inside and outside Congress, nor has the din quite died away. Some who most admire Roosevelt, least admire this episode. But the president convinced his core audience. Reluctantly but in short order, the justices gave him what he had to have. They got out of his way. By so doing they finally assented to national management of a modern economy. But of vast importance to them, they managed to preserve intact the true sources of their power, incidentally saving the number nine on the Court. Some anonymous wit dubbed this sudden reversal of form "the switch in time that saved nine," a catchphrase which stuck.

The rout began with four cases handed down March 19, 1937, so-called White Monday, and ended with Roosevelt master of the field, although not entirely unmauled himself. But besides saving nine, this advance to the rear saved the Court's most essential powers, which lived to fight again another day.

Leaving behind substantive due process – Only a year ago in the 1936 Tipaldo Case,[27] the Court had voided a New York minimum wage law for women. Now a short nine months later in West Coast Hotel Hotel v Parrish, Justice Owen Josephus Roberts, he of Butler Case fame, switches sides, making up a new five-man majority. The case deals with a minimum wage law for women in Washington state and no real difference exists between the previously invalidated New York law and this Washington law. Yet this time around, the Court reaches an exactly opposite ruling.

We will recall that in 1905, the Lochner Case helped invent "substantive due process," which let the Court void laws as "unreasonable." But now on White Monday in 1937, West Coast Hotel begins to abandon this doctrine. Comparing the language of the two cases, we detect no more than a subtle change in emphasis, which belies the huge change in judicial attitude, the extent becoming evident only with the outcome. West Coast Hotel involves an underlying power shift, one of those transfers so frequently concealed beneath the Court's formal language. But this time the power moves away from the Court, returning to Congress.

Lochner had invalidated a law limiting work to a 60-hour a week. Writing the opinion, Justice Rufus Wheeler Peckham said: "The general right to make a contract in relation to his business is part of the liberty of the individual protected by the 14th Amendment." He held a law limiting hours of work "necessarily interferes with the right of contract between the employer and employees, concerning the number of hours in which the later may labor."

Now in West Coast Hotel, Chief Justice Charles Evans Hughes writes the opinion, saying this: "The Constitution does not speak of freedom of contract. It speaks of liberty and prohibits the deprivation of liberty ... In prohibiting that deprivation the Constitution does not recognize an absolute and uncontrollable liberty. ... But the liberty safe-guarded is a liberty in a social organization which requires the protection of law against the evils which menace the health, safety, morals, and welfare of the people. ... This essential limitation of liberty in general governs freedom of contract in particular."[28]

The difference no more than adds a context. In Lochner, Justice Peckham elevates the "right to contract," leaving out any context, not mentioning any other rights that might limit that right. But Justice Hughes carefully remembers the context, saying the right to contract not "absolute and uncontrollable," rather safeguarding "a liberty in a social organization," which requires other laws to protect "the health, safety, morals, and welfare of the people." Justice Hughes brings a great deal more into the field of vision, items deliberately obscured by Justice Peckham.

Yet the larger import comes not from this legal re-formulation, but from the spirit displayed in the application. In this next step, Chief Justice Hughes upholds the Washington minimum wage law for women, reversing the law. This outcome strongly signaled a major shift in attitude, away from the right of contract, toward restricting that right through other rights. In terms of institutional power, this signaled another major shift, away from judicial control, toward legislative control. If the right to contract had lost the Court's backing, this opened the way for Congress to pass other laws limiting that right. By implication, all those progressive reforms on wages, hours, and industrial conditions could creep back onto the statute books, too, as indeed would shortly happen. The Court had abdicated reign over this realm of the law, rather Congress may now regulate almost to any extent.

The retreat on White Monday paused not yet for breath. The Virginia Railway Case[29] upheld the collective bargaining provisions of the Railway Labor Act, a clear step toward judicial acceptance of a more union friendly policy. The Sonzinsky Case[30] upheld a broad sweep for congressional taxing power. Finally, Wright v Vinton Branch Mountain Trust Bank,[31] upheld the revised Frazier-Lempke Act, allowing a bankrupt farmer to reorganize his loan payments, an act revised because in 1935 an earlier version had been struck down in Louisville Bank v Radford.[32]

Leaving behind a narrow reading of the commerce clause – In less than a month, on April 12, 1937, the Court's drums beat a further dramatic withdrawal. On that day, five cases sweepingly affirmed the National Labor Relations Act of 1935, also known as the Wagner Act. Pulling up stakes, the justices abandoned their former claim to the commerce clause, turning over a gold mine from which Congress would shortly extract a wealth of authority. Whereas before they had construed most economic activity as intrastate commerce, outside congressional regulation, in future they found most interstate commerce, subject to regulation. Before it was over, congressional power under the commerce clause could intervene almost anywhere.

By the National Labor Relations Act, passed July 15, 1935, Congress again took up cudgels on behalf of labor. As discussed, they had previously done so only to suffer continual rebuff before the Court. But once more they endeavored into the breach, seeking to give labor a secure place in the legal scheme of things. Section 7 of the Act bluntly read: "Employees shall have the right to self-organize, to form, join, or assist labor organizations, to bargain collectively through representatives of their own choosing, and to engage in concerted activities, for the purpose of collective bargaining or other mutual aid or protection."

Once more Congress relied upon the commerce clause for authority. Section 1 set forth the rationale: "The denial by employers of the right of employees to organize and the refusal by employers to accept the procedure of collective bargaining led to strikes and other forms of industrial strife or unrest, which have the intent or the necessary effect of burdening or obstructing commerce. ... It is hereby declared to be the policy of the United States to eliminate the causes of certain substantial obstructions to the free flow of commerce ... by encouraging the practice and procedure of collective bargaining and by protecting the exercise by workers of full freedom of association, self-organization, and designation of representatives of their own choosing, for the purpose of negotiating the terms and conditions of their employment or other mutual aid and protection."[33]

In a series of cases affirming the NLRA, the Court now finally accepted such a broad reading of the commerce clause, permitting congressional regulation down to the minutest details. The cases descend in size, beginning with the National Labor Relations Board v Jones & Laughlin Steel Corporation, the defendant a huge, national, industrial entity, and going down the scale to a small business of the local sort.

In Jones & Laughlin, Chief Justice Charles Evans Hughes again crafted the opinion, writing; "The fundamental principle is that the power to regulate commerce is the power to enact 'all appropriate legislation' for its 'protection or advancement' .... Although activities may be intrastate in character when separately considered, if they have such a close and substantial relation to interstate commerce that their control is essential or appropriate to protect that commerce from burdens and obstructions, Congress cannot be denied the power to exercise such control."[34]

The definition of "interstate commerce" changes abruptly and forever. From that day to this, if "activities" have "a close and substantial relation to interstate commerce" and cause "burdens and obstructions," Congress can regulate under the commerce clause. And it only need be added as immediately became clear, that a "burden," or an "obstruction," required no more than a touch. In future this horse would run with reins loose on its neck.

Perhaps in 1942, Wickard v Filburn reached the outer extreme. That case held the federal government could prevent a farmer from growing wheat for personal consumption. Justice Jackson reasoned: "But even if [a farmer's] activity be local and though it may not be regarded as commerce, it may still, whatever its nature, be reached by Congress if it exerts a substantial economic impact on interstate commerce."[35] If this activity fits that description, what more need be said? Thus construed, the commerce power has since permitted congressional and bureaucratic regulation to almost any desired degree.

Coming to compare performance during the Great Depression, the Court against Congress and the presidency, surely the democratic institutions did "better." They deployed a rapid response to the economic ills, seeking to discover a cure, whereas the aristocratic institution displayed a much higher pain threshold, ignoring messages from the lower limbs of the body politic. The justices only relented when their own feet were held to the fire.

Yet in one instance the Court gave a rare display, using judicial review as originally conceived. When in their haste over the NIRA, Congress abdicated legislative functions to the president, the justices turned back this error. Their ruling rested on clear-cut grounds, the separation of power, a fundamental constitutional principle. It may be wondered how vital this service, since it appears doubtful Congress would routinely give away excessive authority, being usually quite jealous of its power, preferring to keep the president on a short leash. Nor does it appear constitutional systems lacking judicial review have generally succumbed to the chief executive by this route, the legislatives not willingly succumbing in such a way. It rather appears that principle of administrative law, which requires specificity and accountability in the creation of bureaucracy, learnable from sources other than judicial teaching. Nevertheless, for once the Court performed as predicted by the theory, defending the Constitution against a congressional excess.

But the different performances should have been predictable, since each actor was following a script dictated by separate interests. Needing their votes, Congress and the president played together to the public. Wanting to keep power, the justices stubbornly occupied stage front and center, a spot they had come to claim by right, reserved for the star in the national drama, a vantage from which they had grown accustomed to deliver the climatic lines, bringing down the curtain to applause. But this time the other actors rudely elbowed them in the ribs, threatening to eject them altogether. Finally they stepped to the wings to avoid a worse indignity.

What it all amounted to was this: The Court had suffered a grievous institutional defeat, but managed to limit the damage. The justices sacrificed two highly pliable servants, losing their services. The doctrine of substantive due process and a narrow reading of the commerce clause, these went the way of all flesh, reluctantly consigned by their masters in the service of a greater good.

So much for what was lost, but the Court did not lose lifetime tenure or judicial review. The institutional tree could now grow new doctrines to replace those gone. The gales winds of the Great Depression blew off some branches, but the taproot still sank deep in rich soil. The interests of the lawyers and the judiciary stayed green in the trunk, a living force, driving the sap upward toward the light, toward power and business, regenerating the monarch of the forest.

Footnote Four – Scholars generally see the germ of the Court's rebirth to power in the Carolene Products Case of 1938, buried in Footnote Number Four, "the most famous footnote in constitutional history." The justices will shortly bring this notion above ground, plant and nurture the seed, and grow a fabulous crop. By such careful tillage, they will restore the prosperity of their region, re-establishing the Court's power and prestige.

The case itself looks innocuous, concerning the Filled Milk Act. For whatever reasons good or bad, Congress had by this Act prohibited the interstate shipment of skim milk made with any fat or oil other than milk fat. Carolene Products concocted a skim milk called Milnut with coconut oil. The company sued, claiming the law "unreasonable." But by now the "reasonableness" test of substantive due process is long gone. Approval of far-reaching economic regulations has become routine. Justice Harlin Fiske Stone, in writing the opinion, states that "the existence of facts supporting the legislative judgement is to be presumed."[36] No more second guessing Congress. Result, another rubber-stamp on a New Deal program. Carolene loses and the Act is upheld.

But then Justice Stone cannot resist tacking on a footnote, the famous Footnote Four. Having let fall deference to Congress in such all-embracing terms, he has second thoughts and wants to qualify his language a bit. He has kept up the retreat before the New Deal, but cannot quite bring himself to burn all his bridges as he marches away. As a prudent commander, the justice knows the fortunes of war may change. He may want to attack over this same ground some day. How can he leave structures intact behind him, which may help him maneuver to victory in some new campaign? In the small print and legal-speak of his footnote, Stone carefully selected certain ideas for preservation from the general ruin. In retrospect it almost looks like he laid out a program.

Having just said in the opinion that "the existence of facts supporting the legislative judgement is to be presumed," Stone then drops down in the footnote and qualifies that statement. He says: "There may be narrower scope for operation of the presumption of constitutionality when legislation appears on its face to be within a specific prohibition of the Constitution, such as those of the [Bill of Rights.]"

He goes on: "It is unnecessary to consider now whether legislation which restricts those political processes which can ordinarily be expected to bring about repeal of undesirable legislation, is to be subjected to more exacting judicial scrutiny ... Nor need we inquire whether similar considerations enter into the review of statutes directed at a particular religion ... or national ... or racial minorities ... whether prejudice against discrete and insular minorities may be a special condition, which tends seriously to curtail the operation of those political processes ordinarily to be relied upon to protect minorities, and which may call for a correspondingly more searching judicial inquiry."

What is all this about? In the opinion itself, he has said laws have a "presumption of constitutionality." Such a presumption amounts to a return to that original doctrine of judicial review, renewing the pledge to void laws only in a clear-cut case. But in the footnote he says "there may be a narrower scope for the operation of the presumption of constitutionality" in certain cases, suggesting such cases may be "subjected to more exacting judicial scrutiny." In other words, in those cases the Court may not return to the original, more limited doctrine of judicial review.

Well, then, if the clear-cut standard may not apply, what standard might apply? He mentions "more exacting judicial scrutiny." What does that mean? Well, we should be able to see that phrase, which sounds like judicial watchfulness, rather amounts to judicial discretion. If the Court not bound by clear-cut, then what formula binds the Court? And the answer is no clear guidelines at all. Escaping any precise limits, the Court can go back to doing just as in the past. It will be back to the paradigm of Dred Scott, back to unconstrained constitutional interpretation, back to inventing doctrines like substantive due process, in short, back to rule by judicial will and preference.

The delights of such power had been too sweet. Justice Stone could not bring himself to renounce them forever. Perhaps sometime in the future the justices could taste such pleasures again. Well then, when might that be? What sorts of cases offered such a chance? Let us consider his list: first, the Bill of Rights, such things as freedom of speech, freedom of religion, and so forth; second, "legislation which restricts those political processes which can ordinarily be expected to bring about repeal of undesirable legislation," a complicated way of saying the democratic process itself, such things as the franchise or legislative apportionment; and third "statutes directed at a particular religion ... or national ... or racial minorities," shorthand for such things as individual rights and civil rights. Not only important rights, these stretch across a vast expanse.

Everyone knows the outcome. The Court would shortly take up Justice Stone's suggestion. The justices would step forward as defenders of the Bill of Rights, democratic processes, and religious, national, and racial minorities. In so doing they also took up his second suggestion as well, as such defender shedding any restraint to clear-cut cases.

But surely these are worthy rights, so this a worthy project. Except we have already seen the Court defending a worthy set of rights, the right to property, the right to contract, freedom of association, limited government. But so far the Court has not done a particularly worthy job, not nearly as good as Congress. Then why would the Court now to do a better job with this new set of rights, better than Congress? Not because the institutional nature of either has changed, since that stayed the same. Nor should we fail to notice the Court once again empowering itself. By picking up this new set of rights, shouldering these fresh causes, the justices felt free to shrug off another burden, that restraint finally forced on them over the first set of rights. So once again the judicial will-to-power coincides with the course down which the Court goes. Indeed, if the Supreme Court was to remain supremely important, there was no other avenue open. The institution could subside, merely deciding routine lawsuits, following where Congress led. Or it could find fresh justifications, re-energizing judicial power, once more taking command.

Like a monarch who sacrifices his ministers to the popular fury over costly and failed policies, the Court offered up substantive due process and a narrow reading of the commerce clause. By surrendering the agents of his will, the monarch avoids personal responsibility and maintains all the substance of his prerogative. So too, by giving up on these agents of their authority, the justices evaded institutional responsibility and retained the substance of their power. The monarch is now ready to appoint new men to carry on his same old government. The Court is now seeking new theories to carry on, the nominations already suggested. Once these replacements are installed, the justices will again resume their sway.

CHAPTER 9

The Moral of Brown

The present moral authority of the Supreme Court flows directly from Brown v Board of Education in 1954. But while praise deserved, the lesson mis-learned. Brown finally declared segregation unconstitutional. The Court rightly claims credit. But the moral of the story shows not a conversion experience, rather confirms a settled character. Once more in Brown, the justices attract down the axis of their institutional will-to-power. Only the political earth had rotated a half turn, and that gravitational force pulled the other way. While before they could only acquire power by enacting segregation, now they could only acquire power by rejecting segregation. The institutional nature stayed fixed, but the political stars realigned in the heavens. In following its star, the Court set a new course. Brown veered around, and the applause has not yet died. But the enthusiasm goes beyond the case, endowing the Court with supreme moral authority.

Segregation in education – Brown fits as the most prominent piece in the Footnote Four strategy. We recall Justice Stone had suggested that: "There may be narrower scope for operation of the presumption of constitutionality ... [in] the review of statutes directed at a particular ... *racial minorities.*" And in light of the Court's past record, this implied concern for "racial minorities" is strikingly original, a bolt out of the judicial blue. In 1896 with Plessy v Ferguson, the Court itself had created separate but equal, and in succeeding years, had given not a "narrower scope" to segregation, but an ever-widening scope, toward ever-greater discrimination.

In 1899 in Cumming v Board of Education, they had specifically extended the doctrine to schools, while signaling something more, an attitude which would come to infuse the future application. In Cumming, the justices manifested a selective myopia, seeing separate clearly, but unable to focus on equal. Nothing in the opinion acknowledges this bias in the judicial vision, yet no one could fail to see the partiality. Under this informal technique of interpretation, "separate" continued to pass judicial scrutiny, while "equal" fell out of sight.

This case comes out of Georgia, when three plaintiffs, "citizens of Georgia and persons of color,"[1] J.W. Cumming, James S. Harper, and John C. Ladeveze, sue two defendants, the County Board of Education of Richmond County, Georgia, and Charles S. Bohler, the tax collector. The allegations read that: "[F]or many years continuously prior thereto, the board maintained a system of high schools in Richmond county in which the colored school population had the same educational advantages as the white school population, but on July 10th, 1897, it withdrew from and denied the colored school population any participation in the educational facilities of a high-school system in the county."[2] Further, they "had children attending the colored high school then existing, but who were now debarred from participating in the benefits of a public high-school education though petitioners were being taxed therefor."[3]

From a present-day perspective, when public schools blanket the nation, these Richmond County schools look an odd patchwork. In 1897, public education had a long way to go, especially down South. Richmond County had no public high school for white males, who attended Richmond Academy for Boys, tuition $15 per year for county residents and $40 for nonresidents. White females did attend a public high school, the Tubman High School, located in a building donated by a Mrs. Emily H. Tubman, but though a public school, the girls had to pay the same tuition as the boys. Complicating this picture, in 1876 the "board deemed it wise to give its assistance"[4] to the Hephzibah High School, run by the Hephzibah Baptist Association. Students at Hephzibah School also paid tuition of $15. Finally, blacks attended Ware High School, established in 1880, tuition $10.

The Board admitted closing the black high school, but cited extenuating circumstances, blaming a financial shortfall. In June 1897, the Board had appointed a special committee on the status of the schools. "[T]he colored patrons [of Ware High School] were called before the committee and were heard ... with every respect and consideration."[5] The committee recommended converting Ware into a primary school. This was "[b]ecause four hundred or more of negro children were being turned away from the primary grades unable to be provided with seats or teachers; because the same means and same building which was used to teach sixty high-school pupils would accommodate two hundred [primary] pupils."[6] The committee noted three other private high schools in the area accepted black students, the tuition no greater than Ware. The committee also claimed Tubman High School had to continue a girl's school, since Mrs. Tubman's grant of the property reverted if not so used.

Subsequently, the full board adopted these measures. "[T]he petitioners were heard and their request fully considered."[7] But the Board thought that: "[I]t would be unwise and unconscionable to keep up a high school for sixty pupils and turn away three hundred little negroes who are asking to be taught their alphabet and to read and write. No part of the funds ... appropriated to the education of the negro race has been taken from them."[8]

Nothing in the record disproves the expressed motives, yet the timing might excite suspicion. In 1880 toward the end of Reconstruction, the board establishes a high school for blacks, but now in 1897 as the South "redeemed," the funding dries up. Nevertheless, budgetary constraints being all too familiar and accepting the board's version for the sake of discussion, why not educate more black children at the primary level as opposed to fewer at the secondary level? Only even seen in this best light, does the separation measure equal? No, whites receive public funding for their high schools, but not blacks. Blindfolded justice with her balance beam could not weigh these separate shares as equal.

The Georgia state judge who initially heard the case so concluded and entered an order restraining the board "from using any funds ... for educational purposes in said county for the support, maintenance, or operation of any white high school in said county until said board shall provide or establish equal facilities in high school education ... for such colored children ... in said county as may desire a high-school education."[9]

In other words, that judge insisted on compliance with the "equal" in separate but equal. But on appeal the Georgia Supreme Court reversed, ruling that the Board could: "... in their discretion ... without a violation of the law or any constitution, devote a portion of the taxes collected for school purposes to the support of this high school for white girls and to assist a county denominational high school for boys. In our opinion, it is impractical to distribute taxes equally."[10]

Of course, we are never quite told why such a distribution "impractical." But up at the U.S. Supreme Court, this same reasoning passed constitutional muster. In an opinion by Justice Harlan, hard to reconcile with his great dissent in Plessy, he writes: "Under the circumstances disclosed, we cannot say that this action of the state court was, within the meaning of the Fourteenth Amendment, a denial by the state ... of the equal protection of the laws or of any privileges belonging to them as citizens of the United States."[11]

In effect, these words marginalize the half of "separate but equal," leaving "separate" whole, but edging around "equal." Harlan did carefully note the record failed to establish the Board acted "with any desire or purpose ... to discriminate against any of the colored school children of the county on account of their race."[12] This reservation suggested if you could show a direct intent to discriminate, it might be different. Yet "equal" was not a bright line; it had begun to waver. Future cases would quickly erase the chalk marks on this playing field altogether, and the umpiring became ever more biased. Legally segregated schools often operated grossly unequal and inadequate facilities.

Legally segregated schools – But while equal receded into vagueness, separate sharpened. The Berea College Case of 1908 well illustrates how far things went. Rather than wanting racial separation, little Berea College wanted black students. Founded in 1854 in the Kentucky mountains, their charter began: "God hath made of one blood all nations that dwell upon the face of the earth."[13] In keeping with this precept, the 1904 enrollment consisted of 753 whites and 174 blacks. But in that same year, Kentucky passed a law making such a racially mixed student body illegal, providing: "That it shall be unlawful for any person, corporation or association of persons to maintain or operate any college, school or institution where persons of the white and negro races are both received as pupils for instruction."[14]

Berea refuses to comply and ends up fined $1,000, and when their appeal reaches the Supreme Court, the justices pass the Kentucky law through their constitutional portal. Not to rehash, but briefly recap, we see how far the law has come, moved by the process of judicial interpretation. The Reconstruction Amendments intended to guarantee black civil rights, but step-by-step the Court has interpreted away that intent. In the 1883 Civil Rights Case, the justices said no more than individuals and organization had a right to discriminate, but still said a state could not discriminate. But by now it has come about not only can a state discriminate, but individuals and organizations can be compelled to discriminate. Our rights protect discrimination, but those same rights did not protect so much as voluntary non-discrimination. Plessy had stood against "a commingling of the two races upon terms unsatisfactory to either," but Berea stood against a commingling on terms satisfactory to both.

In these years, the Court put the finishing touches on the enactment of segregation. Separate became increasingly rigid, while equal became increasingly disregarded. But just as the Court's economic policy grew more ill adapted during industrialization, this racial policy grew gradually more misaligned, not fitting changing social and political realities. However, the justices would not need a Franklin Roosevelt to drive them out of segregation. Their institutional interests would entice them to make that switch so long delayed in time.

The political realignment – Brown cannot be understood in isolation, but as part of a continuum, both in the Court's life and the national life. By the end of World War II, much had changed, not least the political calculations surrounding race. By this time, blacks had grown much stronger, a pent up force awaiting release. In the political marketplace reformers promoted black civil rights as an ethical product, alert political entrepreneurs grasped their potential as consumers, and other interest groups longed to tap into their under-developed resources. In the same timeframe, the Court was seeking new outlets, business to replace the doctrines closed by the New Deal, and the old partnership with the segregationists had grown moribund, all the profits exploited and spent. Idealists, trendsetters, and dealmakers began to put this two-and-two together, black needs and the Court's needs. Wherever their thoughts began, they always came up against the Court, which under judicial supremacy owned the national franchise on segregation and legally blocked any creative restructuring. But what if they could persuade the justices to switch product-lines, re-aligning their consumer base? All this required was to sell them on the profitability of a simple concept: Just as they had recently canceled their ban on economic regulation, why not cancel their ban on black participation? While the Court experienced the first as a painful contraction, make them see the second as opportunity knocking. Keeping blacks down had become an obsolete and unsustainable policy, widely condemned as hypocritical, a taint on the name of American democracy, and threatened to explode with revolutionary fervor. Then rather than defending an out-of-date doctrine, as they had done during the New Deal, let them take the lead in re-designing and modernizing the doctrine. If they struck off the bonds of black disability, that group would immediately arise and go into coalition with other interest groups, who were eager to receive them, forming a powerful political conglomerate. All these related firms would then buy shares in this new judicial offering, raising the value of the Court's stock. Recapitalized by this fresh infusion of political support, the justices would re-take the moral high ground, re-affirm the vitality of judicial supremacy, and re-assume leadership over the government and nation. It was a brilliant strategy, welding together ethical justifications, group interests, and the judicial will-to-power, all moving together with impressive inertia.

Crucially, by the 1950s, blacks brought a great deal more to the bargaining table, making them more capable partners, which served as essential to their eventual success. Over this stretch of time, they had acquired education, skills, property, and experience. More and more blacks had won to fame and fortune. They counted for more as a group. In many states they voted, their leaders heard in the inner council, their interests gaining influence. However disregarded in practice, separate but equal still guaranteed them a formal equality. These ingredients made up a familiar political script: a rising group, a legal order to their disadvantage, yet constitutional formulas with which to work. This set of circumstances might remind of the English middle class before the Glorious Revolution of 1688, which used the power of their growing wealth to re-order the constitution. It might remind of the American colonists before 1776, who used the power of their greater independence to win their complete independence. It might even remind of the segregationists, who having lost their slaveholding power, used the remnants to win an alternative. In all these instances, existing power was essential to the further development. In their turn, blacks now possessed significant power.

Not their least strength was a call for simple justice, which constantly gained conviction. Political causes always require ethical justifications, which are never wanting, although more or less persuasive. In making the Glorious Revolution, the English middle class claimed a right to property, a right to enjoy the fruit of their labors, untaxed except by their consent through Parliament. In the American Revolution, the colonists claimed a similar right, "no taxation without representation." The segregationists claimed rights that sprang from these same theories, limited government and freedom of association. Now blacks claimed "equality," appealing with direct immediacy to that proclamation in the Declaration of Independence: "all men are created equal." The power of these arguments could no longer be denied.

During the New Deal, blacks had turned Lincoln's portrait to the wall and migrated from the Republican to the Democratic Party, leaving a party of failed hope, turning to a party with a new hope. Thwarted in their earlier efforts to forge a common front with blacks, Republicans had come to rely on other allies. In their years of dominance before the Great Depression, they gravitated to normalcy and business as usual as success bred satisfaction with the status quo. While in uniting his New Deal coalition, the "New" Democratic Party, Roosevelt reached out to those discontented with that status quo, social progressives, labor, immigrant and ethnic groups, and also blacks. In this big tent, politics did make strange bedfellows, since a strong wing of the Democratic Party continued the solid South, solidly Democratic, solidly segregationist. Yet within the party blacks found firm new friends, strong elements willing to assist them, much for the same reasons Republicans tried during Reconstruction, counting on their support in return. Nor was this entirely a partisan divide, as parts of the Republican Party continued to favor black rights, either through ethical or ideological commitment or perhaps wishing to re-recruit black support.

As for the Court, after the institutional defeat at Roosevelt's hands, its power languished. In the pre-war years, the justices spent their time no more glamorously than taking a back seat to Congress. Their control over economic policy went into abeyance, never to revive, and they had renounced substantive due process. It was like Othello with his occupation gone. The Supreme Court was no longer running the show. But gradually their disastrous turn in front of the lights during the New Deal faded in memory. They still had their lifetime offices and judicial review; powerful interests still longed for their support. And there was still the prescient suggestion of Justice Stone in Footnote Four: "There may be narrower scope for operation of the presumption of constitutionality when legislation appears on its face to be within a specific prohibition of the Constitution, such as those of the [Bill of Rights.] ... It is unnecessary to consider now whether ... similar considerations enter into the review of statutes directed at a particular religion ... or national ... or *racial minorities*."

Those who watch the Court with the same care a courtier bestows on his sovereign's countenance picked up this hint, including the possibly changing mood about "racial minorities." They could see that "separate but equal" no longer advanced the Court's power, also see abrogating that policy would begin an advance in a new direction. During Reconstruction, imposing segregation had transferred power from Congress to the Court, but Congress had long ago bowed to the judicial will, accepting segregation as constitutional. Congress had labored to raise the mountain of the Reconstruction laws; the Court had ordered the mountain leveled. That work had been done, leaving nothing further for the Court to command. Except once you enforce obedience to a task, what shows more dominance than to compel the task undone? Having ordered the dirt hauled away, order the dirt hauled back. Congress having finally acquiesced in separate but equal, now reject their acquiescence. To command desegregation would be once more to command. The astute court watchers perceived these dynamics and understood the significance of the shift. Rejecting segregation now lined up with the judicial will-to-power. They had only to couch their arguments so as to persuade the Court the time had come to seize the power.

A gathering of forces signaled that strong reserves, probably a majority, would rally behind such a move by the Court. By the 1950's the party platforms of both major parties opposed racial discrimination. Between 1938 and 1954, Congress passed some civil rights legislation. In 1941 and 1948, executive orders had prohibited discrimination in defense industries and racial segregation in the armed forces. More blacks gradually won appointment and election to office at all levels, federal, state, and local. By the mid-1950's, every major church in America condemned racial discrimination and intolerance. Hundreds of tax supported municipal and semiofficial agencies worked to promote racial peace and friendship. The executive branch would support the decision in Brown, as did the American Jewish Congress, the American Federation of Teachers, the Congress of Industrial Organizations, and the American Veterans Committee, each of who filed amicus curiae, "friend of the court" briefs in favor of overruling Plessy.

And to give credit where credit is due, through these years the Supreme Court itself somewhat narrowed separate but equal. Starting in 1938 with Missouri ex rel. Gaines[15] the judges required black admission to graduate and professional schools. In the 1950 Henderson Case,[16] the U.S. government joined with black plaintiffs to persuade the judges to hold segregation in dining cars on interstate railroads unconstitutional.

All of this set the stage for Brown v Board of Education in 1954. By reversing segregation, the Court would perform an inestimable service, which under judicial supremacy had to wait upon their performance. But however late in coming, Brown finally lived up to that pledge of "equality" in the Declaration of Independence. Without the Court's adherence, no real progress could occur, and the Court at last adhered. More than that, Brown worked like a catalyst, releasing black hopes, ambitions, and indeed frustrations, which now claimed the highest constitutional ground as well as demanded the fullest participation in the democratic process. But Brown was also the most prominent piece in realizing the Footnote Four program, restoring the Court's lost power. In fact, the eventual power gain would far surpass anything perceived by Justice Stone in Footnote Four, even exceed anything perceived by any of the justices when they signed on to Brown.

The facts in Brown – Handed down May 17, 1954, Brown v Board of Education finally reversed "separate but equal," holding segregation in education unconstitutional. But Brown really refers to a set of cases. First comes what legal scholars call Brown I, which itself consisted of four joined cases. Second comes a companion case handed down the same day, Bolling v Sharpe. Then in 1955 would come Brown II, dealing with how to desegregate. Together these decisions made up a remarkable package, which when unwrapped immediately present a splendid gift, the end of legal segregation. But as so often with the Court's munificence, further unwrapping reveals a further aggrandizement of judicial power.

Brown I joined four cases for a single decision. Listed first in the caption, so lending a name to posterity, comes Brown v Board of Education of Topeka, Shawnee County, Kansas. A border state, Kansas law allowed but did not mandate segregation, leaving the matter a local option. Topeka segregated the elementary grades, although not beyond. The plaintiffs sued in federal court on behalf of all black children of elementary school age. That lower court "found that segregation in public education had a detrimental effect upon Negro children, but denied relief on the ground the Negro and white schools were substantially equal."[17] Thus, those judges reluctantly accepted the authority of Plessy, while openly questioning the fairness.

The next two cases come out of South Carolina and Virginia respectively, charter members of the Old Confederacy, where the laws mandated segregation. These were Briggs v Elliott and Davis v County School Board. The plaintiffs again brought suit in the federal courts, which upheld the separation, but found "that the Negro schools were inferior to the white schools"[18] and ordered the inequality remedied. Thus, again the lower judges followed Plessy, but displayed a new willingness to enforce "equal."

The fourth and last case comes out of Delaware, Gebhart v Belton, where the laws also mandated segregation. This time the plaintiffs brought suit in the state courts, which ordered "immediate admission to school previously attended only by white children, on the ground that the Negro schools were inferior."[19] Once again those judges comply with Plessy, but turn the doctrine against itself, using "equal" to cancel "separate."

All these lower court opinions, as well as the willingness to bring the cases, showed a growing hostility to segregation. But none of those lesser judges quite felt up to the task of declaring Plessy unconstitutional, a reluctance they would not likely have exhibited toward mere legislation. It is one thing to void congressional or state laws, a practice by now habitual with judges at all levels. It is another to hold the Supreme Court itself has been wrong, a feat seldom performed on the lower rungs of the judicial ladder. Due regard for the judicial pecking order demands all judges defer within the hierarchy, while any judge can peck a legislature. But if the Supreme Court longed to strike a blow, their humbler brethren had loudly signaled a willingness to second them.

Chief Justice Warren's ruling – Chief Justice Earl Warren writes for the Court, an unusually brief, unanimous opinion. And surely Brown is the greatest case ever handed down by the U.S. Supreme Court, greatest in principle, greatest in effect. We search in vain for another outcome of equal stature. Yet this deserved esteem comes from the ruling against segregation, and the case has a seldom-mentioned underside, as usual the power side. The ruling against segregation gives voice to those proclamations in the Declaration of Independence of equality, inalienable rights, and consent of the governed. By finally forcing through those promises for blacks, Brown's public face brought about real good in the real world. But the other face, the power side, lingers in the shadows. Let us look at the lineaments of both these visages.

In writing the opinion, Warren displays a mastery of judicial, indeed of political skills worthy the greatest jurists in Anglo-American tradition, right up there with John Marshall himself. The statesmanship and courage have seldom been matched in a public document. Yet just as a close reading of Justice Marshall discovered certain lawyerly failings, a close reading of Justice Warren cannot fail to notice related traits, much for the same reasons. These professional weaknesses do not touch the heart of the case, where the rejection of segregation is eloquently justified, simply expressed, clearly reasoned. But just as Marbury was fundamentally about the Court's power, Brown implicates that same power, and just as Marshall obscured this underlying theme, Warren shows a similar concern. With customary judicial reticence, nowhere does he explicitly mention judicial power, while consolidating and increasing that very power. Paired with this silence, he muffles the sound of the Court's past cases, muting almost entirely the jarring noise of their essential complicity in segregation. But then at last and suddenly, he succinctly rules segregation inherently unequal. The conviction carried by this ruling lifts Brown to deserved heights.

Brown had been argued in the spring, 1953 term of the Court, and set over for reargument to the fall term. Warren begins his opinion this way: "Reargument was largely devoted to the circumstances surrounding the adoption of the Fourteenth Amendment in 1868. ... This discussion and our own investigation convince us that, although these sources cast some light, it is not enough to resolve the problem with which we are faced. At best, they are inconclusive. The most avid proponents of the post-War Amendment undoubtedly intended them to remove all legal distinctions among 'all persons born or naturalized in the United States.' Their opponents, just as certainly, were antagonistic both to the letter and the spirits of the Amendments and wished them to have the most limited effect."[20]

Now this is nothing but the truth, but is it the whole truth? Beyond a reasonable doubt, the Reconstruction Amendments and the 1875 Civil

Rights Act meant to enfranchise blacks and guarantee their other rights, prohibiting segregation on public conveyances and in public places. Why not say that? Instead he limits inquiry to "the circumstances surrounding the adoption of the Fourteenth Amendment in 1868," asks if these help "to resolve the problem with which we are faced," but finds these sources "at best inconclusive," musing "avid proponents intended to remove all legal distinctions" and "opponents wished the most limited effect." With this quick glance over his shoulder at the past, Warren narrows the field of vision, employing a typical rhetorical device, carefully omitting and as carefully including. For what has he just done with this innocuous looking historical survey? He has multitasked to achieve a pair of never explicitly expressed goals: He has maintained the fiction the Court interprets rather than re-makes the Constitution, incidentally assuming the power to do both totally normal; and he has evaded the Court's responsibility for segregation, incidentally leaving that guilt on Congress.

For when did it start to matter what Congress had meant by the 14th Amendment? The Court had never before shown the least concern to enforce that purpose, rather interpreting it away. Yet Warren's words imply the Court is seeking after congressional intent. You would think if they felt free to impose separate but equal in 1896, they would feel free to impose the opposite in 1954. If the Court had the one power, surely it has the other. But Warren eschews such a frank approach to judicial power, avoids an open acknowledgement that Court can simply re-make constitutional law at will, although that exactly sums up what he will shortly do. At the same time, he conveys the impression Congress did not quite know what it intended with the 14th Amendment, failed to act with sufficient clarity and forcefulness. Then wasn't Congress to blame for the subsequent debacle, not the Court?

Next Warren goes on: "An additional reason for the inconclusive nature of the Amendment's history, with respect to segregated schools, is the status of public education at that time. In the South, the movement toward free common schools, supported by general taxation, had not yet taken hold. ... Even in the North, the conditions of public education did not approximate those existing today. ... As a consequence, it is not surprising that there should be so little history of the Fourteenth Amendment relating to its intended effect on public education."[21]

Well again, this is true enough, but off on a tangent, not mentioning the Court's part. What about such cases as Cumming v Georgia or Berea College? The justices had explicitly extended "separate but equal" to the schools, approving rigidly separate while winking at equal. But once again, he leaves the Court firmly outside the line of sight, escaping the taint.

But then Warren does finally mention his Court, saying: "In the first cases in this Court construing the Fourteenth Amendment, decided shortly after its adoption, the Court interpreted it as proscribing all state imposed discrimination against the Negro race."[22] Well of course, the Court may have mouthed such platitudes, but that wasn't the operative language. In support he cites two cases in a footnote, one being the 1873 Slaughter-House Cases. Now we visited this case in some detail, and while the opinion formally nodded to "proscribing all state imposed discrimination against the Negro race," the effective ruling stood for an exactly opposite proposition. That case gutted the protection for black rights intended by the "privileges and immunities clause." Why does he neglect to mention this real outcome? Once again, the Chief Justice declines institutional responsibility.

Finally, he must mention Plessy, and here is how he does it: "The doctrine of 'separate but equal' did not make its appearance in this Court until 1896 in the case of Plessy v Ferguson, involving not education but transportation."[23] We should see how artfully worded this muted reference. He says: "made its appearance in this Court." This phrasing shuts out entirely the harshness of the judicial machinery, the wrenching logic by which the Court imposed "separate but equal" on an unwilling Constitution. And he says Plessy "involve[ed] not education but transportation." But Plessy involved everything across the board. Not just the seats on a New Orleans' streetcar, but every seat in the nation. By this careful presentation, Warren neatly avoids the Court's institutional complicity. We are left to conclude segregation "appeared" from somewhere, forgetting Congress tried to prevent it.

But at last the statesmanship and courage appear. Warren asks and answers the fundamental question: "Does segregation of children in public schools solely on the basis of race ... deprive the children of the minority group of equal educational opportunities? We believe it does."[24]

To supply his rationale, Warren quotes from the lower federal court in the Wichita case: "Segregation of white and colored children in public schools has a detrimental effect upon the colored children. The impact is greater when it has the sanction of law; for the policy of separating the races is usually interpreted as denoting the inferiority of the negro group."[25]

In summation, he concludes: "Separate educational facilities are inherently unequal. Therefore, we hold that the plaintiffs ... are, by reason of the segregation complained of, deprived of the equal protection of the laws guaranteed by the Fourteenth Amendment."[26] As for past sins, he writes: "Any language in Plessy v Ferguson contrary to this finding is rejected."[27] While hardly a mea culpa, so succinctly is Plessy finally overruled, having stood on the books from 1896 to 1954, exactly fifty-eight long years.

The legal rationale for Brown – What about this rationale? His logic rests on those familiar clauses from the 14th Amendment: "No State ... shall abridge the privileges or immunities of citizens ... nor shall any State deprive any person of life, liberty, or property, without due process of law; nor deny to any person ... the equal protection of the laws."

Long ago and now inconveniently, the Court had destroyed the "privileges and immunities" clause. The original intent looks a natural fit, which we will recall meant to "embrace nearly every civil right for the establishment and protection of which organized government is instituted." Unfortunately, in those 1873 Slaughter-House Cases, the justices had interpreted that purpose away, leaving the words a guarantee of almost nothing, an unfulfilled promise on the face of the Constitution. Now they want to resurrect the spirit of the clause, except they had buried the body so deep and it had been dead so long, an exhumation would have raised too much of a stench.

Instead and conveniently, Warren is able to rely on the "equal protection" clause, words never entirely ignored. Plessy allowed "separate," but required "equal." While later cases largely disregarded the second half of this formula, yet that neglect depended upon an attitude displayed in the application, coming from an informal rule of construction, never officially recognized. Being undead in theory although on life-support in practice, Warren could breathe fresh life back into "equal protection," reviving the clause. He can simply find that: "Separate educational facilities are inherently unequal."

In part this finding rests on the evidence from sociology, some studies being mentioned in a footnote, prominently Kenneth Clark's *Effect of Prejudice and Discrimination on Personality Development*. But the real conviction comes from common sense and what everyone knew. Not only were "segregated educational facilities inherent unequal," segregation as a whole was "inherently equal." Nor could it be made equal. Segregated schools operated often grossly inadequate facilities. But segregation as a whole operated a caste system, by its very nature thrusting blacks into a second-class category.

Everything lines up, and the rationale is compelling. The 14th Amendment says: "No State ... shall ... deny to any person ... the equal protection of the laws." Segregated schools violated both the letter and the spirit of the clause. The Amendment meant to assure black equality.

Now at last, the Court was enforcing that equality. More than that, the whole spirit of the Declaration of Independence and the Constitution affirms equality. Now at last, the Court was enforcing that spirit.

The power side of Brown – But let us not neglect to ask about the power. Has the power moved? Indeed it has. Warren has taken up that proffer in Footnote Four about "racial minorities," coming to the defense of blacks. By so doing he has re-affirmed judicial supremacy in no uncertain terms. Nor can we fail to notice how far this power has come. Under the original doctrine of judicial review, the Court stood as guardian over the will of the people as expressed in the Constitution, ready to void as unconstitutional any clear-cut violations. But back in 1896 in Plessy, the justices had destroyed clear-cut constitutional meaning, imposing their own opposite meaning with "separate but equal." Now in 1954, they have destroyed the clear-cut meaning they themselves previously imposed. In the process they have consolidated and further aggrandized their power. They have re-asserted the absolute primacy of the Supreme Court as supreme lawgiver to the nation. The Court can make, un-make, and remake the Constitution.

Substantive due process again – The four cases in Brown I left some unfinished business, which the Court handled in a companion case the same day, Bolling v Sharpe. The District of Columbia also segregated the schools, but the federal authorities control that local government, not a state, an anomaly that escaped the logic of Brown, forcing the Court to find another logic. They used the occasion to engineer the return of "substantive due process," reinstating in favor that so recently disgraced doctrine, revitalizing another judicial power.

Article II vests Congress with power "[t]o exercise exclusive Legislation" over the District of Columbia. However, those schools were not segregated by congressional law, rather the local authorities had exercised their considerable discretion to segregate them. Plaintiffs black children brought suit in the local federal court, which dismissed their complaint, and they appealed to the Supreme Court.

Surely if the states cannot segregate, the District of Columbia cannot segregate either. Except such straightforward common sense ran up against a quandary. Looking back at the 14th Amendment, we remember it says: "*No State* ... shall ... deny to any person ... the equal protection of the laws." Then reading those words literally, the provision applies against the *states*, but not the *federal government*. So the rationale in Brown I, which relied solely on this "equal protection clause," extended not at all to the federal authorities over the D.C. schools. Such an outcome certainly seems a paradox. A state cannot, but the federal government can segregate. How get around this unacceptable conclusion?

For all their pledges to eschew the doctrine, the justices had not forgotten the conveniences of "substantive due process." Of course, we previously saw the Court invent that doctrine. The "due process clause" of the 14th Amendment guaranteed fair procedures before the courts, but they had begun to apply the clause against the substantive law passed by the legislature, letting them declare laws unconstitutional they deemed "unreasonable." And this same "due process clause" actually appears twice in the Constitution. Once as repeatedly seen, in the 14th Amendment, but also in the 5th Amendment, which reads: "No person shall be ... deprived of life, liberty, or property, without due process of law." As part of the Bill of Rights, the 5th Amendment undoubtedly binds the federal government.

Chief Justice Warren turns to these words in the 5th Amendment and rules: "In view of our decision that the Constitution prohibits the states from maintaining racially segregated public schools, it would be unthinkable that the same Constitution would impose a lesser duty on the Federal Government. We hold that racial segregation in the public schools of the District of Columbia is *a denial of due process of law guaranteed by the Fifth Amendment* to the Constitution."[28]

Well, he is absolutely right that "it would be unthinkable." So all have applauded his ruling, but not his rationale. Since how can "racial segregation" be a "denial of due process of law?" Due process relates to procedure in the courts, and racial segregation is not a procedure in the courts, but a substantive law. After a few short years in exile, this disgraced doctrine is restored to favor. Having been rushed to the rescue of desegregation, will it not be rushed to the rescue again, whenever the justices next feel an urgent need? Indeed it will, as we shall see.

The judicial power of doing equity – In deciding Brown I, the Court reserved on the remedy, that is, exactly how to desegregate, putting this question over to the next term for further argument. We begin to conceive a cause for such hesitation by contemplating the revolutionary nature of the case, which not only reverses segregation, but permanently alters the traditional role of a judge. The first is easily seen, the second necessarily implied. In 1896 in Plessy, the Court could act through merely interposing a negative, interpreting away congressional action, thus letting the states segregate. But now in 1954, the Court is not only interposing a negative, but directing action, ordering the states to desegregate. Moreover, such an order will require some sort of ongoing judicial supervision. In Plessy, they could just open the constitutional gate and get out of the way, letting the states out of the corral, but to carry out Brown they would have to boss a cattle drive, prodding the states all the way up the trail to the railhead. Taking on such a job had both allure and hazard. It is one thing to write an elegant opinion in the cloistered quiet of your chambers; it is another to come down out of the ivory tower and ramrod that opinion through the wilderness of the real world. It was the difference between formulating policy papers and implementing the policies. Now really for the first time the judges were assuming both such authority and such burdens. Despite their sure-handedness in handling legal doctrine and handing down legal judgment, the justices must have felt a degree of unease at this prospect. Brown announced a legal doctrine in their traditional way, but threatened to entangle them in far from traditional activities, efforts more like executive functions. While quite willing to issue commands, they were not quite sure about the potential downside in taking such direct command.

As policy, desegregation carried them into an uncharted territory of tendentious complexity. They well knew the reception awaiting as Brown stepped off the train, all the way from a welcome greeting to reluctant acknowledgement and intransigent rudeness. They as well knew the challenges presented by the size of desegregation, which must rapidly spread across the country, extend to thousands of schools, affect millions of children, impact as many communities, upset established practices, interfere with countless local and state authorities. They could not fail to perceive themselves entering the perilous precincts of two highly volatile topics, people's concern for their children and their touchiness over taxation. It would later be said that the Court had reconstituted itself into a sort of national school board, and no politics are more tendentious than the politics of school boards, precisely for these two reasons, the emotions invested and the finances.

Putting the case over to the next docket bought some time, letting the issues ripen, the options develop, but finally the day of decision had to come. Handed down May 31, 1955, Brown II would be another very short, unanimous opinion crafted by Chief Justice Warren. Here is the essence: "In fashioning and effectuating the [remedies], the courts will be guided by equitable principles. Traditionally, equity has been characterized by a practical flexibility in shaping its remedies ... . These cases call for the exercise of these traditional attributes of equity power." Further: [T]he cases are remanded ... to take such proceedings and enter such orders and decrees consistent with this opinion as are necessary and proper to admit to public schools on a racially nondiscriminatory basis with all deliberate speed the parties to these cases."[29]

Reading carefully, we see Warren's political astuteness. He does not get too far out in front of his support. His words sound confident, the conclusion obvious. Yet really he says as little as possible, and seems not to say that much. And while cautiously stepping around the vastness of desegregation, he is as cautiously stepping toward a similar vastness of judicial power. He doesn't quite want his audience to peer down into the depths of the first, nor quite look up at the heights he suggests for the second. As so often, enforcing judicial will requires increasing judicial power. To advance on desegregation compels him to a corresponding advance in judicial power. Not that he perceived the full development these two would reach in tandem, desegregation and judicial power mutually reinforcing, going ever farther. In time-honored judicial fashion the evolution will happen incrementally, judicial power gradually increasing.

As for desegregation, he does not really define that term, a crucial neglect. He sends back, remands to the lower courts, all the cases, telling those judges to "enter such orders ... as are necessary and proper to admit to public schools *on a racially nondiscriminatory basis* ... the parties to these cases." Before long the superficial clarity of this command will turn our almost an evasion, lacking the necessary specificity, a classic example of passing responsibility down the line. As this controversy unfolds, to say "a racially nondiscriminatory basis" proves one of those generalities so difficult to apply in detail.

As for the assertion of judicial power, he is as resolutely vague, saying: "In fashioning and effectuating the [remedies], the courts *will be guided by equitable principles.* Traditionally, equity has been characterized by a practical flexibility in shaping its remedies .... These cases call for the exercise of these traditional attributes of equity power." What exactly does "will be guided by equitable principles" signify?

For those not versed in the technical language of the law, the implications require a grasp of the distinction between an "equitable remedy" and a "legal remedy." An "equitable remedy" is an order from the court to do or not do something, in other words, an order commanding behavior. In contradistinction, a "legal remedy" is money damages, a monetary judgment. Traditionally, courts could order an equitable remedy only if the legal remedy of money damages was "inadequate."

In the classic illustration, A trespasses on B's land and cuts down some trees. The landowner seeks a "legal remedy" by suing the trespasser for money damages. The money damages make the landowner whole and so are "adequate." But say A moves onto B's land and refuses to leave, cuts down some trees, builds a log cabin, and starts farming. In those circumstances, the landowner seeks an "equitable remedy" by asking for an order of the court forcing the trespasser to vacate the premises. Nor will the policy of the law let the trespasser get away with just paying money damages, rather the law vests the landowner with a right to occupy his land himself. Money damages are labeled an "inadequate" remedy, and the courts will order the trespasser off the land. Otherwise one man could just move into another man's house and change the locks, saying sue me. But filing a lawsuit for money damages would leave the homeowner out in the cold, not made whole. It might take months or years to win a verdict. Then how collect the money? At the extreme, such a situation would render the ownership of real property highly tenuous, rewarding acts of violent dispossession, leaving the remedy largely an illusion.

As should easily be seen, in numerous other situations money damages are inadequate, and the courts need to turn to "equitable remedies," entering orders that direct behavior. And obviously this rule exactly fits the remedies required to desegregate. Blacks want their right to equal admission to the schools. Paying money damages would not achieve that end, but are "inadequate." They want their right to an ongoing, quality education. Again paying money would not attain the goals. So Warren is saying the courts need to order equitable remedies, finding a way to make the injured parties whole, which will require directing behavior.

Also traditionally, these equitable remedies must retain extreme flexibility, adaptable to solve all the multifarious messes people construct for themselves. A standard text reads: "[A]n equity court ... adapts its relief and molds its decrees to satisfy the requirements of the case ... The court has such plenary power, since its purpose is the accomplishment of justice amid all the vicissitudes and intricacies of life. It is said that equity has always preserved the elements of flexibility and expansiveness so that new remedies may be invented or old ones modified to meet the requirements of every case ... In other words, the plastic remedies of equity are molded to the needs of justice ... and the flexibility of equitable jurisdiction permits innovation in remedies to meet all varieties of circumstances which may arise in any case. Moreover, the fact there is no precedent for the precise relief sought is no consequence."[30]

We must begin to see such enormously broad language confers on judges as enormously broad powers. Plainly the courts need such authority, but where does that authority end? Equity "preserves flexibility and expansiveness;" equity "invents new remedies or modifies old ones;" to equity "the fact there is no precedent is no consequence;" in equity "the plastic remedies are molded to the needs of justice." Where, then, find the limits of equity, except in the judges' sense of justice?

The judicial power of class actions – We begin to conceive the potential for judicial power in Brown II, but have not yet conceived the full potential. To reach that requires putting the power of equity together with another changing judicial power, the "class action." Recalling all the cases up to Brown in 1954, we also recall those cases stayed between discreet plaintiffs and defendants. In 1803 in Marbury v Madison, Marbury and three others sued James Madison, the Secretary of State. In 1896 in Plessy v Ferguson, the parties were only two, Homer Plessy and Judge John Howard Ferguson, the state judge who had upheld the Separate Car Law. We might even call to mind Lincoln's reference to the Dred Scott Case in his 1861 First Inaugural Address: "[I]f the policy of the government upon vital questions affecting the whole people is to be irrevocably fixed by decisions of the Supreme Court, the instant they are made *in ordinary litigation between parties in personal actions*, the people will have ceased to be their own rulers, having to that extent practically resigned their government into the hands of that eminent tribunal." While all these older cases affected a great many people in their application, yet distinct individuals came forward to sue on their own behalf. The lawsuits remained "ordinary litigation between parties in personal actions."

But Brown brings to prominence the legal device called a "class action," a technique that has been around a long time, but suddenly assumes a new prominence. Discreet individuals still come forward to sue, but not just on their own behalf. Rather the plaintiffs file suit on behalf of a "class" including "all others similarly situated." In the lead case in Brown, the plaintiffs sued on behalf of all the thousands of black children in Wichita. And from Brown forward this routine use of such class actions will radically extend the reach of judicial power. To speak of "ordinary litigation between parties in private actions" becomes a misnomer. Instead we need to recognize the appearance of a new type of lawsuit, extraordinary litigation between huge political constituencies in national political controversies.

Combining equity with class actions – Putting "equitable remedies" with the "class action," the combination amounts to the invention of a political method of immense consequence. In effect, the lawyers and judges have engineered a change of venue, removing national political controversies from the democratic agenda, bringing them as cases before the courts. Judges no longer just hand down opinions, ruling between discreet plaintiffs and defendants. Instead, judges can actually run the controversies, handing down rulings that control millions of litigants, the cases going on for years, new rulings handed down as required, the judges able not only to direct the litigants, but assuming control of legislative programs and executive agencies. And the lawyers no long represent distinct individuals, but vast political constituencies. Indeed, as a practical matter the lawyers constitute themselves as the leaders of these constituencies. They originate and control the litigation. Moreover, since in effect they are assisting the judges to further power by bringing the cases, in many instances they become the judge's right hand man, cooperating with him in molding the outcome. It need only be added that in these sorts of cases the remuneration usually comes out of the public coffers, and the judges have shown a willingness to richly reward the lawyers from that over-flowing source of funds. It will be seen that this legal invention meets all the criteria that appeal so strongly to the professional mind. The courts acquire more power and prestige; the lawyers acquire more business, more money, and more prestige.

If we think about the actual practice contemplated by Brown, we see how it will work. Say the judge orders that "plaintiffs negro children" have a right to attend a particular school. If the local school superintendent, or the governor for that matter, stands in the schoolhouse door and blocks their entry, then the judge orders the police to remove the offending official. If the school board fails to implement a policy in compliance with the judge's desegregation order, he will enter another order directing them to promulgate a suitable policy. Over the years he will enter such future orders as necessary to assure continued and complete compliance. All of this is simple enough, but where does it stop? If the schoolhouse attended by whites is not big enough to hold all the blacks too, why not order the school board to build a new facility? If whites and blacks live in separate neighborhoods, why not order a school built between the neighborhoods? If the neighbors are too far apart for that, one in suburbia and one in the inner city, why not bus the children to mix up the races? Why not order new and better schools built across the metropolitan area, magnet schools to attract the races together? If the tax rates fail to provide enough money for these improvements, why not order taxes raised?

Where does this new power for the judges end? It appears the implications of Justice Warren's innocent enough sounding directive contain an almost limitless potential. To read again what Warren wrote in Brown II: "These cases call for the exercise of these traditional attributes of equity power." Now traditionally "the plastic remedies of equity are molded to the needs of justice." So when this directive is combined with the proliferation of the class action, the word "traditional" appears a little out of context. Warren is suggesting a radically new role for the courts. He has seized vast new power for the federal judiciary. Rather than deciding cases between individuals, the judges will be able to run social programs across the whole nation for decades.

By 1992 more than 500 desegregation cases were pending in the federal courts, some for more than 30 years. And this only suggests the potential in the realm of desegregation. Applied across the board to every legal issue in America, the wider picture begins to emerge. Why should not the federal courts make sure all the vast state and federal bureaucracies run according to "due process" or "equal protection?" Never mind how the legislature or the executive intended an agency to operate. If the judges disagree with the social policies of the elected branches, they can just order their own views implemented under the guise of due process and equal protection. For example, why shouldn't the judges run the prisons, mental health care system, and so on?

The power had begun to move, once more toward the judiciary, once more by their familiar method of self-help. In the three brief sentences quoted from Brown II, Chief Justice Warren encapsulated a scheme that would rapidly develop, undoubtedly past anything he had consciously in mind. He was feeling his way. But just as we saw Chief Justice Taney do a hundred years before, Warren has conceived a moral certainty. Just as in 1857 Taney's conviction suffused Dred Scott, Warren's suffuses Brown. Surely Warren has the better cause, but the psychology is the same. Just as Taney had to expand his power to enforce his view, now Warren has to expand his power to enforce his view. And just as the paradigm of Dred Scott would further evolve, pushed on by the judicial will-to-power, so should we expect Warren's new model to evolve, pushed on by the same judicial interests. Nor will it be long to wait. Quickly in the succeeding years the Court will promulgate a new model judicial supremacy, more potent yet.

Coming to compare the institutional performance, there is not much to compare. The Court has acted, but not Congress. Brown did not hold a congressional statute unconstitutional, but reversed Plessy, overruling prior judge-made constitutional law. The Court earns high marks, but Congress no deduction. Then what is the moral of Brown for our tale of government?

As repeatedly told in the standard version, segregation serves as the prime exemplar of the democratic contradiction, democracy causing minority oppression, while Brown illustrates the benefits of judicial supremacy, the Court rescuing the nation from the failures of democracy. Just enough truth resides in this account to pass smoothly over a lawyer's tongue, yet this narrative picks and chooses among the facts and puts together a plausible argument by cleverly shifting emphasis and responsibility. The jury of public opinion needs to keep in mind the completeness of the historical evidence, recall the proper sequence of events, remember the institutional records.

During Reconstruction, Congress had built a constitutional wall around black rights, formidable in height and thickness, founded on black enfranchisement. But the segregationists began undermining that foundation, disenfranchising blacks, and rather than defend the wall, the Court unbarred the gates from inside. Although neither strong enough alone, together the segregationists and the Court were able to overthrow Congress and occupied the citadel of the Constitution. Imposing their constitutional settlement, they ruled jointly and amicably for over fifty years, sharing the pleasures of power. As the strong right hand, the Court enforced segregation, while the segregationists backed the Court, rendering the regime impregnable.

But now the hinge of events and relationships swings the other way. The old alliance with the segregations has come to circumscribe rather than empower the Court, and new allies have beckoned to re-align, releasing power another direction. These proffers ripened, and the justices abruptly turned on their former collaborators. Using the same tactics invented to enact segregation, they proclaim Brown, ending segregation, driving their discarded friends back out of the Constitution, simply by re-interpreting the meaning. Free at last, the long-beleaguered citizenry rushes into the streets, rallying behind the judicial chivalry. Completing the rout, the congressional militia will shortly enact the 1964 Civil Rights and 1965 Voting Rights Act, re-erecting the original Reconstruction walls, finally built on a firm basis since finally supported by the Court.

With victory won, the populace throngs to garland their knightly deliverers, the justices, but their euphoria might do well to pause before passing an act of oblivion, not entirely to forget the recent past, not entirely to forget present motives. More prudent counsel might suggest to demand hostages from the Court, some guarantee of future loyalty. For once the judicial will-to-power has lined up with democracy, locking shields in a solid phalanx around the Constitution, but such a coincidence of interests has been a rare occurrence so far. Nothing binds the justices to the popular cause; experience proves them devoted to their own cause. In leading this counter-revolution, they renounced not their high status, but re-affirmed their pre-eminence in a revised order. Gratitude may go too far in accepting their continued pretensions.

Nor should we forget that in Brown the Court had to begin by reversing itself, and under judicial supremacy only the Court could reverse itself. Thus, if the justices saved us, they saved us from themselves, and only they could save us. If this is freedom, it is an odd sort of freedom, more like traditional notions of servitude. Subjects wait upon masters, not masters upon subjects; masters make choices for subjects, not subjects for masters. Judicial supremacy compels a sequence where the Court is the master and the people the subjects. Over segregation the Court waited not upon the people, but the people upon the Court; the people made not their own choices, the Court made the choices for them. Neither responsive nor accountable, the Court reigns over, above, and beyond the public will. However appreciative for a favor at last conferred, should a proud and free people continue to bend their neck to this judicial yoke?

Segregation violated fundamental democratic principles, which would suggest duty consists in defense of democracy. Was it not democracy that labored and brought forth congressional Reconstruction, enfranchising blacks, guaranteeing their rights? Was it not the Court whose power served essential to defeat this program, instead enacting segregation? Then hurling the segregationists out may feel like triumph, but leaves half the enemy in possession, the justices manning their fortress, commanding all the avenues in and out of the Constitution. Then why should the Court now march arm-in-arm with democracy to an amicable future? If the judicial interest varied so far from the public interest in this past, why will this interest not vary in this future? If the elected Congress performed well in that past, why will Congress not perform well in that future? Rather than trusting the justices as guardians, would the people not do better to re-man the guard in person, enforcing their will through Congress?

CHAPTER 10

The New Model Judicial Supremacy

Brown created a new model judicial supremacy. Under this new model the Court re-interprets a few words in the Constitution, usually "due process" or "equal protection," re-casting a policy choice as a constitutional commandment, thus replacing congressional or executive authority under the Constitution with judicial authority over the Constitution. Then with equitable remedies and class actions, the judiciary directly carries out their own policy choices, running what amount to legislative and executive programs. In a further refinement, they take over bureaucratic agencies, re-directing these to serve their same ends. By these new modeled methods, the Court comes not only freely to re-make the Constitution, but as freely takes on legislative and executive functions, further ascending in power.

Judicial power over policy – Following a now familiar pattern, this side of Brown, the power side, unfolds in the next series of cases. Long ago in 1857 with Dred Scott, Justice Taney had shifted the paradigm for judicial review, and the Reconstruction cases had developed the full potential. Now in 1955 with Brown II, Justice Warren suggests a new model judicial supremacy, and the desegregation cases will develop the full potential. Ideologically these cases look utterly unrelated, the earlier line supporting slavery and enacting segregation, the later affirming racial equality. Yet on the power side, the lineage descends like the deeds of a noble house, an aristocracy of the robe rather than the sword, but relentless as feudal lords in seeking domain. Bequeathed by Justice Marshall a narrow fiefdom of judicial review, Justice Taney raised this heritage to share in the highest councils of state, and Justice Warren further enhanced their estate to dominate much of the council. Taney fought clear of the tight borders confining judicial review, overrunning the boundary confining them to "clear-cut" cases. During Reconstruction, his judicial heirs realized the full potential, not only interpreting away clear constitutional meaning, but substituting their own constitutional meaning, not only interpreting away the freemen's rights, but substituting their own doctrine of "separate but equal." In 1955 with Brown II, Warren makes a further suggestion: Why not use class actions and equitable remedies? During desegregation, the Court realizes the full potential. First, they interpret away the congressional program for school desegregation, substituting their own judicial program. Next, using class actions and equitable remedies, they directly carry out their program. By this descent, judicial review to void laws again expands, acquiring judicial power to command legislative and executive acts.

As a matter of practice, the Court comes not only to make, but carry out policy. Initially, what the Constitution did not command or forbid stayed a "policy choice," left up to ordinary political processes, that is, largely left to Congress. The original, limited doctrine of judicial review carefully preserved this distinction. The Court could not void congressional laws except in clear-cut cases, and the Constitution said not much clear-cut, so most live questions stayed policy choices, which Congress could answer. But such judicial restraint was no more than words on the printed page, enforced by no effective mechanism of accountability. So like the good lawyers they were, the justices eventually talked their way around the words. Now no longer limited to clear-cut cases, their verbal adroitness also let them rephrase almost any policy choice as a constitutional question, which their Court could answer and answer finally. Thus, the Constitution said nothing clear-cut about slavery, leaving a policy choice, a question for Congress or the states, but the Court rephrased that policy choice as a constitutional question, then pronounced final judgment in favor of slavery. Thus, the Reconstruction Amendments made a policy choice at the constitutional level, guaranteeing the freedmen's rights, but the Court went so far as to reverse constitutional policy, substituting their own judicial policy, enacting segregation. In 1955 with Brown II, Justice Warren makes his further suggestion: Why not directly carry out their policy choices with class actions and equitable remedies? Thus, the Court will rephrase the policy choices about school desegregation as constitutional questions, answer those questions with their own policy choices, phrased as constitutional commands, and then go on to directly carry out their policies. Such full power over policy and implementation sums up the new model judicial supremacy.

The politics of school desegregation – School desegregation would be the cutting edge, yet for the ten years after Brown, the Court paused. In 1955, Brown II commanded the lower courts "to admit to public schools on a racially nondiscriminatory basis with all deliberate speed." This sounded like a clarion call, only as the local federal judges sallied forth to do legal battle, they found the stricken field shrouded in the fog of combat. Go forth and end segregation resonated as a moral commandment, but lacked the necessary specificity as rules of engagement. During this interregnum, the justices issued no clarifying orders, letting the situation on the ground develop.

In those same ten years after Brown, school desegregation made gains, but appeared to stall out. Only 142 out of 27,000 school districts had been desegregated through federal court orders. Initially, voluntary compliance made more headway. In 1954, seventeen states and the District of Columbia had legally segregated schools, four others with local option; one year later, only eight states stayed segregated. Yet by 1966, about half the schools in Southern and border states still evidenced patterns of segregation and across the eleven states of the Old Confederacy, 97.5% continued in all black schools, in Alabama, Mississippi, and Louisiana more than 99%.[1] Such statistics looked like foot-dragging, in some cases downright "intransigent resistance."

In this same timeframe, the civil rights movement took off in earnest, spurred on not a little by the hopes Brown ignited. Blacks flexed their slowly acquired political muscle, gave evidence of a new assertiveness, and called upon still stronger allies. The news filled with bus boycotts, sit-ins, freedom marches, and civil disobedience. Dr. Martin Luther King, Jr., stepped forward as a persuasive and respected leader of the cause. With the obliging assistance of Bull Connor and other intransigent racists, they succeeded in dramatizing the repressiveness of the segregationist order, delivered almost by live feed on the nightly news, an early illustration of the impact of that technology. As events would show, public opinion swung behind them.

The political factions fought over this changing terrain, appealing for recruits, assailing each other with countervailing lines of persuasion. Their warfare drew in Congress, which with the 1964 Civil Rights Act tried to negotiate an end to hostilities. But the congressional treaty only laid the preconditions for a resumption of fighting on the judicial front, signaling the strategic moment when the Court could re-enter the conflict with maximum safety and maximum gain. When the political wars poise in the balance, the Court sits perfectly placed, able to tip the balance-of-power, able to do so on their terms, able do so with small fear of successful counter-attack. Whichever side they take, sufficient support breaks a united front forming against them. Alert to this moment, the justices wheeled their big battalions into line, joining the ranks in step with their judicial interests, but masking their movements, advancing by increments. By these tactics outflanking Congress, the Court re-took the commanding heights lost by their New Deal defeats and carried on to still greater elevations of power.

Desegregation or integration – After all, what amounted to "desegregation in education?" Almost immediately the cases drew a distinction between de jure versus de facto segregation, which set terms to the argument, but turned out to lack hard edges. All the cases joined in Brown had dealt with "de jure" or "legal" segregation, where the law ordered separate schools. By contrast, "de facto" amounted to segregation "in fact," caused by racially separate communities and neighborhoods. The first described a set of laws, the second demographic patterns. Yet segregation by law had often caused segregation in fact, and so a remedy for the one seemed to imply some remedy for the other. But in the end, "desegregation in education" fell between these two stools, starting out firmly seated against "de jure" segregation, but never able to take as firm a seat against "de facto" segregation.

The Court had remanded the four cases in Brown, sending them back to the lower courts for suitable remedies. One had come out of South Carolina, Briggs v Elliot. In 1955 in this remanded case, a three-judge panel handed down an opinion that proved highly influential. They summed up their comprehension of Brown this way: "[T]he Supreme Court ... has not decided that the states must mix persons of different races in the schools ... What it has decided, and all that it has decided, is that a state may not deny to any person on account of race the right to attend any school that it maintains. ... The Constitution, in other words, does not require integration. It merely forbids discrimination. It does not forbid such segregation as occurs as the result of voluntary action. It merely forbids the use of governmental power to enforce segregation."[2]

Under this reading, Brown canceled the laws that ordered segregation, but did not require "integration," that is, "racial mixing in the schools." Then basically, children should attend schools where they lived, the neighborhood schools. And such a reading certainly grasped the easier handle. If a law ordered segregated schools, simply strike the offending language from the statute books, and Brown drew a heavy stroke of the judicial pen across those very pages, which now stood mute and fading, testament to a bygone era. Yet those dead words haunted the living present, their effects lingering. Blacks often lived racially separate not through "voluntary action," but through force of past laws, say restrictive covenants in deeds against sale to their race. Blacks often attended separate schools through force of those same laws, which say located schools to assure the separation. Cancelling out these laws failed to cancel out these lingering effects.

From this start, many civil rights activists took an advanced position. Brown said, "admit to public schools on a racially nondiscriminatory basis." They started with a series of ever widening propositions: First, almost all racial separation evidenced past legal segregation. Second, segregation depended not just upon written law, but upon custom and usage enforced with all the rigor of law. Third, segregation evidenced a pervasive and underlying "racism." They concluded that desegregation demanded a root and branch remedy, uprooting not only the laws, but the custom and usage, and a thoroughgoing eradication of all "racism." As their working formula, any racial separation in schools raised a strong presumption of improper motivation, and only racially mixing in the schools could overcome the presumption. As practical matter, they advocated such things as gerrymandered school districts, and more controversially, massive busing. Finally, they reversed the meaning pronounced by the judges in Briggs v Elliot. They read Brown not only to "forbid discrimination," but to "require integration," that is, "mixing persons of different races in the schools." Desegregation by law must be measured by desegregation in fact.

Yet this reasoning never rallied the same support as Brown's ringing renunciation of legal segregation. The 1896 Plessy doctrine of "separate but equal" has never commanded an overwhelming consensus, being initially opposed by the majority and never able to suppress the lingering resentment and resistance. In 1954, Brown trampled out the vintage where those grapes of wrath were stored, but the public proved hardly willing to drain this proffered cup of racial mixing to the lees. The ardent toasts for segregationists to drink a bitter taste heard the applause die, as others at this banquet grasped they had to drink right along with them. Vainly the toastmasters protested the beverage good for you, only sour to those concealing racism in their hearts. They never persuaded the public willingly to swallow the draught.

Culture, class, and racism – Rather, most preferred old wine in old bottles, a brand which advertised under the label "neighborhood schools," a term much cried up. Traditionally and naturally enough, children went to school near their homes, and uprooting that relationship touched more than one nerve. People wanted their children physically close, in schools just down the street, part of the community, where parents knew the local actors and had a voice, usually through elected school boards. That tradition tied into another American tradition, people being accustomed to conduct their affairs locally, quick to resent interference from higher ups, as quick to reflect their resentment at the ballot box. Sheltering under these arrangements, culture and class strongly marked neighborhood schools, and culture and class stubbornly defend their turf. Cultural groups naturally live together, as witness the renowned ethnic neighborhoods in American cities. At some past time, living together gave rise to culture in the first place, bonds running deep and lasting long, reacting strongly against dilution. Classes as naturally congregate, all the way from the slums to the wealthy enclaves, and all look askance at intruders. The call for "neighborhood schools" drew strength from all these sources and rested upon highly esteemed values, people's attachment to their culture, neighborhood, and community, the freedom to live their own lives, making their own choices.

The experience of Irish-Americans conveniently illustrates the history, tenacity, and intensity of these influences. In the 1830s, the Irish began arriving in large numbers, greeted with a degree of hostility, as usual with such mass cultural encounters. But not so much race as religion marked this collision, the earlier settlers Protestant, the Irish uniformly Catholic. In the resulting push and shove, the rooted cultures pushed against these intruders, but the Irish shoved right back, elbowing their way in, rubbing off some of their outer Irish, yet keeping a core identity, especially their Catholicism. The Irish were fighting in adversity for their culture, an endeavor looked back upon with sympathy. So for example, they resisted amalgamation with Protestants in the public schools, preferring Catholic parochial schools. By the 1950s, they had won their way, economically and socially prosperous, yet still fighting, only now for hard-won class gains as well as their culture. So for example, just as in the last half of the nineteenth century they resisted going to school with Protestants, in the last half of the twentieth they resisted going to school with blacks. One of the ugliest episodes over school desegregation will erupt in Boston, the Irish furiously against a busing plan ordered by the local federal judge, Judge Arthur W. Garrity, Jr. Nor did their stubbornness fail them anymore on this latter occasion. In 1970, some 62,000 whites attended the Boston public schools, 64% of the total. By 1992 after two decades of Judge Garrity's busing order, whites were down to 11,000, only 18% of the total in a city 58% white. In 1973, the average black child went to a school 24% white, by 1993, only 17% white. Judge Garrity had spared no effort, as shown by the fact that in 1991, one out of every twelve Boston education dollars went for busing.[3] But while the people couldn't vote him out, they voted against him with their feet and their money, moving away or paying for private schools.

Other hyphenated Americans could tell more or less the same story of a struggle up, German-Americans, Italian-Americans, Jewish-

Americans, and so forth. The "melting pot" poured out a uniquely American mix, but not a fully amalgamated one. Even less easily did these European-Americans blend with those other hyphenated Americans, the African-Americans, who were quite a bit more alien by race, history, and culture. Moreover, since these last had been kept down, class stratification added another layer to the social off standing. We need only imagine an upper middle class suburb with a superior school and our imagination as immediately pictures a white suburb and school. This better school was a purposeful accomplishment, part of the community status. The higher property values marked a class boundary line, prices partially maintained by the school, which helped attract the affluent, sustaining demand. Residents saw the better school as part of their success, essential to passing that success on to the next generation. Then busing their children to a much inferior, black, inner-city school, while busing black children in return, expropriated and re-distributed some of their economic and social capital. Even among those who supported the end of segregation, few volunteered for such self-sacrifice in the cause.

Such resistance opened whites to the charge of racism, nor could they entirely refute the accusation. In the first place, many had earlier convicted themselves out of their own mouths. Even such as later publicly foreswore lingered under the suspicion of inner reservations. Others sought to interpose a more technical defense, arguing "racism" should mean formal theories of racial inferiority, and they disclaimed such theories. Yet in common usage, racism denoted as well "racial prejudice," a negative response to another race. And what white culture could escape this attaint? Culture comes from living together, the races start out living apart, and so usually race marks cultural lines. And cultures exhibit mutual antipathies, often quite intense. As a result, generally whites will demonstrate some negative response toward blacks, since as generally they come from different cultures. Some whites plead for a further distinction, urging cultural self-preference not necessarily the same as racial prejudice. Perhaps they raised a plausible ground upon which to rest a defense, or perhaps two faults so closely resembling allow of no acquittal. Certainly, in the arguments over desegregation, their foes seldom granted this plea as legitimate. But guilty or not of the crime, whites persisted in the conduct, not welcoming blacks with open arms.

Meanwhile of course, blacks exhibited the same behavior. They had little problem riding the bus to better schools in white suburbs, thereby ousting their cultural rivals and hoping to move up in class. Yet they passionately felt the justice of their cause. After slavery, after segregation, after so much, they were in no mood for further pettifogging, quibbling, evasion, or delay. The great constitutional principle said "all men are created equal." Act upon that principle, act now, act decisively. Whatever their present demands, their past wrongs justified a settling of scores in their favor. If such just demands asked some sacrifice from others, justice demanded the sacrifice.

Later some would argue all this talk drifted somewhat, obscuring the initial and real concern, which started out and stayed an equal and quality education for blacks. Such an aim looked at least something more than going to school with whites nor did blacks need to go to school with whites to attain that aim. This line of argument urged moving away from measurement of desegregation by racial mixing, toward measurement by standards of educational quality. But a counter-argument went that racially separate schools could never equal out, since the dominant whites would game the system to win the bigger share. Another line of counter-argument held integration served essential educational purposes, early breaking down racial stereotypes, building friendships and paths of cooperation, teaching people to live together.

Then what should amount to "desegregation in education?" Was it enough to end legal segregation, send children to school where they lived, and let things shake out? Or did the races need mixing in the schools? What about educational quality? The answers did not appear self-evident. Nor did the Constitution respond with self-evident answers. So some government institution would have to give the answers. Such a process is compelled. So the first, underlying question was not which answer, but which institution. And so as usual, Congress and Court would conflict over which had the power, as well as returning very different replies.

The Civil Rights Act of 1964 – By declaring segregation unconstitutional, Brown took the muzzle off Congress. Under judicial supremacy, when the Court utters the final word, they render Congress mute. Back in 1896 with Plessy v Ferguson, the justices had enacted "separate but equal," ruling segregation constitutional. Ever since, Congress had lacked power to overturn that ruling. But at long last the Court had reversed itself, releasing Congress again to legislate. They responded with the 1964 Civil Rights Act and 1965 Voting Rights Act, which assaulted segregation on all fronts, enfranchising blacks and outlawing discrimination.

Undoubtedly, these congressional laws showed majority support for Brown's end to segregation. Since their passage beat down a last-ditch filibuster in the Senate, that majority looks quite solid. Yet which version of Brown did this majority endorse? With respect to desegregation in education, they sided with the lesser extreme.

The 1964 Civil Rights Act laid out the congressional program for school desegregation. Labeled "Desegregation of Public Education," Title IV, Section 401 read: "'Desegregation' means the assignment of students to public schools and within such schools without regard to their race, color, religion, or national origin, but 'desegregation' shall not mean the assignment of students to public schools in order to overcome racial imbalance."[4]

Of major significance to later discussion, Section 407 went on: "... nothing herein shall empower any official or court of the United States to issue any order seeking to achieve a racial balance in any school by requiring the transportation of pupils or students from one school to another or one school district to another in order to achieve such racial balance, ..."[5]

What was the legislative intent? Careful reading shows the language as carefully crafted, making policy choices, while definitively closing an option. Congress clearly sided against segregated schools, but just as clearly sided with neighborhood schools, just as clearly against busing. The three positive commands combine to compel these conclusions. First, assign students "without regard to their race;" second, do not assign students "to overcome racial imbalance;" and third, do not "[transport] students from one school to another or one school district to another in order to achieve racial balance." No method of school assignment meets these three criteria except geographic attendance zones, children going to school in the neighborhoods where they live. Busing is definitively foreclosed.

The debates in the *Congressional Record* support this interpretation. A speech by Senator Hubert Humphrey of Minnesota, a leading proponent and floor manager in the Senate, makes the point: "Desegregation does not mean that there must be intermingling of races in all school districts. It means only that they may not be prevented from intermingling or going to school together because of race or color."[6] As for busing, Humphrey specifically stated that section 407: "[S]hould serve to soothe fears that [the law] might be read to empower the Federal Government to order the busing of children around a city in order to achieve a certain racial balance or mix in schools."[7]

Next Congress turned to enforcement. Labeled "Nondiscrimination in Federally Assisted Programs," Title VI read: "No person in the United States shall, on the ground of race, color, or national origin, be excluded from participation in, be denied the benefits of, or be subjected to discrimination under any program or activity receiving Federal financial assistance."[8] Behind this language lurked an increasingly familiar and highly effect device, the threat to cut off federal funds. As they say, show me the money, and Congress could show the money. Or in that cynical variant of the Golden Rule, he who has the gold makes the rules. Congress had the gold and was going to make the rules. In fiscal 1964, the federal government doled out $176,000,000 in school funding to the seventeen states legally segregated at the time of Brown. The 1965 Elementary and Secondary Education Act made available another more than half billion dollars to those same states. For the South as a whole, federal educational funding quadrupled between the 1963-64 and 1971-72 school years, going from $2.7 billion to $14.7 billion.[9] These sums made up a mighty tempting carrot and an awfully big stick. Take the money and play their desegregation game, or the feds would take their money and go home.

In the next crucial move, the Act charged the bureaucracy to carrying out the program, giving them authority to cut off funds. These marching orders put the bureaucratic inertia behind school desegregation. However enthusiastic the NAACP Legal Defense Fund or civil rights lawyers, they had not gotten very far with their lawsuits. A 1966 White House Conference reported: "It was the Congressional purpose, in Title VI of the Civil Rights Act of 1964, to remove school desegregation efforts from the courts, where they had bogged down for more than a decade. Unless the power of the Federal purse is more effectively utilized, resistance to national policy will continue and, in fact, will be reinforced."[10] This attack of the bureaucrats would prove irresistible, like setting on an omnipresent, omnivorous swarm of ants to devour the carcass of the old segregationist order.

Thus, Congress answered the contentious issue of school desegregation, an answer too little or too much, good or bad, depending upon preconceptions and values. As so typical, Congress took a middling, compromising course, not satisfactory to either extreme, straddling the fence of a working majority. The segregationists resisted period; ardent civil rights activists wanted a great deal more. Congress came down for a law the majority of members could support, indeed as said, quite a solid majority, two-thirds being needed to overcome the Senate filibuster. Unless Congress badly misread their constituents, this law reflected public opinion as a whole, the will of the majority prevailing.

But Congress and the majority would not long prevail. Rather, once again the Court would prevail. The Court would side with the minority, rejecting the congressional program as constitutionally insufficient, rejecting neighborhood schools, rejecting the limit against busing.

Instead, the Court promulgated its own program, which would measure desegregation by racial mixing and require massive busing. In a further step, they would seize control over the bureaucratic program to cut off funds, shouldering aside congressional or presidential control, running that program themselves. In this way and once again, the Court would successfully assert power over Congress and the presidency, indeed over the people.

The bureaucracy intervenes – In 1968, Green v County School Board took the initial step, re-interpreting policy choices as constitutional commandments, thus replacing congressional control over policy with the Court's control over the Constitution. But as so often, the justices moved with circumspection. In Green, they never specifically held unconstitutional the 1964 Civil Rights Act, rather indirectly held the law constitutionally insufficient. And as so often, the power moves not on the face of the opinion, but through the implication, putting two and two together. First, the justices carefully refrain from basing their ruling on the Civil Rights Act, instead relying on their own prior cases. Second, they approve the bureaucratic regulations promulgated by the Department of Health, Education, and Welfare (HEW), which measured school desegregation by racial mixing, percentages unreachable except by massive busing. For those able to decipher this double legal-speak, the handwriting stood on the wall. The justices had no purpose to be governed by Congress, but would themselves govern. In place of the congressional program for school desegregation, they would substitute their judicial program. They would enjoy power over school desegregation, not Congress.

Understanding the import of Green begins with HEW's administrative regulations. As seen, the Civil Rights Act provided for cutting off federal funding to force desegregation, assigning HEW such authority. Following routine agency procedures, HEW next passed a set of administrative regulations, setting forth their congressional mandate into specific guidelines. Such a two-step legislative process characterizes administrative law, the initial, congressional statute always more or less general, the administrative regulations filling up the details. HEW's 1965 regulations closely tracked congressional intent, stressing geographic attendance zones and freedom of choice. In essential part these read: "A school system will be eligible for Federal financial assistance by submitting a desegregation plan providing for the assignment ... of pupils ... on the basis of: 1) Geographic attendance areas ... 2) Freedom of choice ... or 3) A combination of geographic attendance areas and freedom of choice."[11]

Almost immediately, the lower federal courts seemed to signal an acceptance of the agency guidelines as properly defining school desegregation. In the 1965 Denison Case, Judge John R. Brown wrote: "These executive standards, perhaps long overdue, are welcome."[12] This case came out of the Fifth Circuit, the court with jurisdiction in six states of the lower South.

But in 1966 and for whatever reason, HEW promulgated a revised set of regulations, which differed radically from the earlier, 1965 version. The new version provided that, "The single most substantial indication as to whether a free-choice plan is working ... is the extent to which Negro or other minority group students have, in fact, transferred from segregated schools."[13] So as one commentator has observed, "Hence, under the 1966 Guidelines, the test of the validity of a freedom-of-choice plan was whether it actually produced racial integration in the schools."[14] In other words, there was really no more freedom-of-choice. Ending legal segregation would no longer be enough, rather, the agency meant to require integration, that is, racial mixing. Nor was there any way to achieve this goal except by massive busing. So in other words, the agency meant to ignore the congressional restrictions against busing in the 1964 Civil Rights Act.

This administrative re-writing of a congressional law excited something of a firestorm in Congress. Some members vividly recalled those pledges against busing made in the debates, pointed to those strictures against busing so evidently written into the Act. A North Carolina representative filed an amendment negating HEW's requirement of racial balance. One from Florida said: "[T]he guidelines are beyond the law. They are outside the law. They are a law unto themselves."[15] But others in Congress sat quite content while the agency went this extra mile, winning by agency ruling what they had lost through the legislative process. This internal congressional division prevented formation of an effective front against the agency action.

These facts present another constitutional problem, more and more significant as bureaucracy grows ever larger, assigned ever-wider tasks, ever-wider discretion. How keep the bureaucrats faithful to their congressional mandate, the servant rather the master of Congress? We will recall how this issue presented back in 1935 with the Schechter Case. By the National Industrial Recovery Act, Congress had conferred almost unlimited authority on the president, letting him create an agency by executive order, an agency with almost unlimited authority to pass regulations having the force of law. In effect, Congress had abdicated law making to the presidency and the agency, leaving no congressional check in place. But such unrestrained delegation of legislative power violated the separation of powers. In the Schechter Case, the Court had quite rightly called down Congress, insisting on adherence to a fundamental rule: In passing a statute to create an agency, Congress must do so with sufficient specificity, keeping the agency within a mandate.

Now thirty years later, the same problem presents in another aspect. Congress having stated the mandate with sufficient specificity, yet the bureaucracy ignores the mandate. What remedy exists? Of course, Congress and the president retain controls, ways to call down the bureaucrats. Congress can pass new laws, enforcing the congressional will; the president can issue executive orders, enforcing the presidential will. Yet what if Congress and the presidency lack the will, as appears here? No ready answer offers. But enter still another aspect of the problem, an opening for the Court. Under judicial supremacy they have final say over the Constitution, and so they can assert final control over the bureaucracy, simply by re-defining any issue as constitutional. By this technique, the Court can shoulder aside congressional or presidential management of the bureaucracy, instead imposing judicial management.

Court ordered integration – The new, 1965 HEW regulations offered the Court just such an opportunity, which brings the discussion back to the Green Case. Justice William Joseph Brennan, Jr., writes the opinion, beginning with the facts: "New Kent County is a rural county in Eastern Virginia. About one-half the population of some 4,500 are Negroes. There is no residential segregation in the county; ... The school system has only two schools, the New Kent school on the east side of the county and the George W. Watkins school on the west side. .... the school system serves approximately 1,300 pupils, of which 740 are Negro and 550 are White. ... There are no attendance zones. Each school serves the entire county. ... 21 school buses --- 11 serving the Watkins school and 10 serving the New Kent school --- travel overlapping routes throughout the county to transport pupils to and from the two schools."[16]

So Green presents a classic instance of segregation by law, not segregation in fact. The races live jumbled together, not separate. But whites attend New Kent, blacks Watkins. After filing of the lawsuit and in an effort to stay eligible for federal funds, the school board adopts a freedom of choice desegregation plan. Given the option, 35 blacks enroll at the previously all white school in 1965, 111 in 1966, and 115 in 1967. No whites enroll at the black school.

This fact situation clearly violates the 1964 Civil Rights Act, whose provisions cut both ways. To recall the wording: "'Desegregation' means the assignment of students to public schools and within such schools without regard to their race," and further, no "transportation ... [of]

students ... to achieve racial balance." Then where the races live intermixed, but bused to separate schools, this must violate one or the other of these provisions, either assigning with regard to race or busing to achieve racial balance. While generally thought of as a device of desegregation, surely "no busing" cuts both ways, not allowing busing as a device for continued segregation. Then to follow congressional intent, just cut New Kent County down the middle. Assign students to school where they live and end segregation.

But in delivering the opinion, Justice Brennan does not deign to mention the Civil Rights Act. Instead, he cites Brown II. Rather than analyze congressional intent, he analyzes judicial intent, saying: "It is of course true that for the time immediately after Brown II the concern was with making an initial break in a long-established pattern of excluding Negro children from schools attended by white children. ... Under Brown II that immediate goal was only the first step, however. The transition to a unitary, nonracial system of public education was and is the ultimate end to be brought about. ... School boards ... operating state-compelled dual systems were nevertheless clearly charged with the affirmative duty to take whatever steps might be necessary to convert to a unitary system in which racial discrimination would be eliminated root and branch."[17]

Reading carefully, we discover the remedies required by Brown have evolved in the judicial mind, however vaguely. While earlier "the concern was with making an initial break in a long-established pattern," yet "that immediate goal was only the first step." Now that goal has moved, becoming "transition to a unitary, nonracial system of public education," where "racial discrimination would be eliminated root and branch."

Well, but what exactly qualifies as "a unitary, nonracial system?" What qualifies as "elimination of racial discrimination root and branch?" Of tremendous significant, Brennan mentions HEW's newly promulgated regulations in a footnote, adopting these by implication.

Now we know by fitting together the pieces. On its face, Green dealt with a clear violation of the 1964 Civil Rights Act. Justice Brennan could quite rightly have used the Act to strike down that scheme, thus implementing the congressional program for school desegregation. But he pointedly refuses to do so, which would have conferred judicial approval upon the congressional program. Instead he bases the decision solely upon the Court's prior cases, approving the HEW regulations as in line. In this roundabout way he tacitly holds the Civil Rights Act constitutionally insufficient, voiding the preference for neighborhood schools and the prohibition on massive busing. Rather than the congressional law, he adopts the bureaucratic regulations, which reverse the congressional law.

The Court and bureaucracy won, Congress lost. Beneath this surface, the power moved, the justices taking a decisive step, developing the potential for power in Brown, moving toward the new model judicial supremacy. By re-interpreting policy choices over school desegregation as constitutional commandments, they replaced congressional control over policy with judicial control over the Constitution. A judicial program replaces the congressional program. Next they would further develop the new model, using class actions and equitable remedies to directly carry out their policy and program.

Court ordered busing – In 1971, the Court takes this next decisive step with Swann v Charlotte-Mecklenburg Board of Education. First, they re-interpret that oft-repeated phrase "equal protection of the laws" to command racial mixing as the measure for school desegregation and massive busing as a remedy. Next, they use a class action and equitable remedies to carry out their commandments. The class action covers tens of thousands across a metropolitan area; the equitable remedies let the local federal judge directly run the controversy.

Chief Justice Warren Earl Burger writes the opinion, beginning with the facts: "The Charlotte-Mecklenburg school system, the 43d largest in the Nation, encompasses the city of Charlotte and surrounding Mecklenburg County, North Carolina. The area is large --- 550 square miles, spanning roughly 22 miles east-west and 36 miles north-south. During the 1968-1969 school year the system served more than 84,000 pupils in 107 schools. Approximately 71% of the pupils were found to be white and 29% Negro. As of June 1969 there were approximately 24,000 Negro students in the system, of whom 21,000 attended schools within the city of Charlotte. Two-thirds of those 21,000 --- approximately 14,000 Negro students --- attended 21 schools which were either totally Negro or more than 99% Negro."[18]

Underlying these figures, the school system serves as a classic example of segregation in fact, no longer segregated by law. Across this 550 square mile metroplex, blacks and whites live racially apart, the vast majority of blacks in the city of Charlotte, the vast majority of whites in the suburbs of Mecklenburg County. Legal segregation being long gone with Brown, yet the schools reflect these demographics.

What remedy offers under the 1964 Civil Rights Act? Congress said assign students "without regard to their race," do not assign students "to overcome racial imbalance," and do not "[transport] students from one school to another or one school district to another in order to achieve racial balance." Within these guidelines, the school board submitted a plan going about as far as you could go, actually severely gerrymandered to racially mix. They drew high school districts "typically shaped like wedges of a pie, extending outward from the center of the city to the suburban and rural areas of the county."[19] These slices apportioned ten high schools with a student body 17% to 36% black, although just 2% in the eleventh, Independence H.S. In twenty junior highs, blacks ranged from 0% to 38%, one school still 90%. At the elementary level, more than half stayed in nine schools 86% to 100% black, about half the whites in schools 86% to 100% white.

The local federal judge, Judge James B. McMillan, appointed an expert, Dr. John Finger, to come up with a more thoroughgoing alternative. This "Finger Plan," as it became known, "required that an additional 300 Negro students be transported from the Negro residential area of the city to the nearly all-white Independence High School." For the junior highs, the Finger Plan set up nine "satellite" zones. "Under the satellite plan, inner-city Negro students were assigned by attendance zones to nine outlying predominantly white junior high schools, thereby substantially desegregating every junior high school in the system."

As for elementary schools: "[T]he Finger plan does as much by rezoning school attendance lines as can reasonably be accomplished. However, unlike the board plan, it does not stop there. It goes further and desegregates all the elementary schools by the technique of grouping two or three outlying schools with one black inner city school; by transporting black students from grades one through four to outlying white schools; and by transporting white students from the fifth and sixth grades from the outlying white schools to the inner city black school."[20]

Obviously, the Finger Plan violated the ban in the Act against "transporting students from one school to another or one school district to another in order to achieve racial balance." Nothing daunted, Judge McMillan ordered the plan anyway. On appeal, the Supreme Court affirmed their lower judge and made three things absolutely clear: One, desegregation meant whatever the Court said it meant, never mind what Congress said in the Civil Rights Act. Two, the Court would require racial mixing as the measure of desegregation, disregarding the congressional preference for neighborhood schools. Three, the Court had no intention of regarding the congressional restraint against massive busing.

To deal with the last issue first, Berger begins by quoting from the Civil Rights Act: "[N]othing herein shall empower any ... court ... to issue any order seeking to achieve a racial balance in any school by requiring the transportation of pupils ... from one school district to another in order to achieve ... racial balance." But he simply uses the time-honored technique of interpreting around, saying: "On their face the sections quoted purport only to insure that the provisions ... of the Civil Rights Act of 1964 will not be read as granting new powers. The proviso ... is in terms designed to foreclose any interpretation of the Act as expanding the existing powers of federal courts to enforce the Equal Protection Clause. There is no suggestion of an intention to restrict those powers or withdraw from courts their historic equitable remedial powers."[21]

If ever a lawyerly evasion figured prominently in a case, this reasoning appears to qualify. Burger says: "On their face the sections quoted purport only to insure that the provisions ... of the Civil Rights Act of 1964 will not be read as granting new powers." But clearly Congress meant to prevent court ordered busing altogether, not merely concerned the Act "not be read as granting new powers." He next says: "There is no suggestion of an intention to restrict those powers or withdraw from courts their historic equitable remedial powers." But if those "historic equitable remedial powers" included busing, clearly Congress meant to restrict or withdraw those very powers.

By negotiating this obstacle, the Chief Justice avoids a more fundament issue, that being the constitutional power of Congress to check his Court. In setting up the judicial branch, Article III provides: "[T]he Supreme Court shall have appellate Jurisdiction ... with such Exceptions, and under such Regulations as the Congress may by law have directed." Then at least theoretically, Congress can make "exceptions" and "regulations" to that "jurisdiction," including a restriction or withdrawal of jurisdiction, say to order busing. Such constitutional power would give Congress a significant check upon the Court. But we should not expect the justices to look favorably upon any such attempt, nor did they. If Congress had so endeavored, the Court simply ignored them.

Nor does the Chief Justice show any more regard for the rest of the 1964 Civil Rights Act. He writes: "The basis of our decision must be the prohibition of the Fourteenth Amendment that no State shall 'deny to any person within its jurisdiction the equal protection of the laws.'"[22] In other words, the Civil Rights Act and congressional intent are irrelevant. Rather, those five words from the Constitution form the basis for all decision, "equal protection of the laws." And of course, the Court will decide what those words mean for school desegregation.

Going on, Justice Berger makes it perfectly clear "equal protection" requires racial mixing as the measure of school desegregation. Judge McMillan had directed "efforts should be made to reach a 71-29 ratio in the various schools." Berger approves such a percentage formula, saying:

"From that starting point the District Court proceeded to frame a decree that was within its discretionary powers, as an equitable remedy for the particular circumstances."[23]

He also approves gerrymandered and even noncontiguous attendance zones: "The maps submitted in these cases graphically demonstrate that one of the principal tools employed by school planners and the courts to break up the dual school system has been a frank --- and sometimes a drastic --- gerrymandering of school districts and attendance zones. ... More often than not, these zones are neither compact nor contiguous; indeed they may be on opposite ends of the city. As an interim corrective measure, this cannot be said to be beyond the broad remedial powers of a court."[24]

Finally, he specifically approves massive busing: "Thus the remedial techniques [of busing] used in the District Court's order were within that court's power to provide equitable relief."[25]

Once again, Congress proposed, but the Supreme Court disposed. Congress passed a program to end segregation, but wrote in limits, favored neighborhood schools, prohibited busing. But the Court refused to regard those limits. Instead, they re-interpret that phrase in the Constitution: "equal protection of the laws." They concluded those five words rendered the Civil Rights Act of 1964 constitutionally insufficient; they concluded the Constitution commanded racial mixing and busing to desegregate the schools. Thus, having replaced the congressional program with their own judicial program, next they used a class action and equitable remedies directly to carry out their program.

The extent of class actions – The new model quickly further expanded, as two well-known cases illustrate. In 1974, Milliken v Bradley stretched the size of class actions; in 1977, the Kansas City Case stretched equitable remedies as far. Before it was over, the judiciary could reach almost anywhere and do almost anything.

To begin with Milliken, this case comes out of Detroit, a city with a comparatively good civil rights record. As long ago as 1867, Michigan prohibited discrimination in her schools, and the Detroit school board had been pro-active in pursuit of desegregation. By affirmative action hiring from 1960 to 1970, they increased black teachers from 23.2% to 42.1% and black administrators from 4.5% to 37.8%, once holding open 240 teacher vacancies, rejecting white applicants until qualified blacks applied. But in 1970, the Detroit board finally outran their electoral support by promulgating a busing plan. The unpopularity excited the Michigan legislature to intervene, which in July enacted a law abrogating the busing plan, substituting a policy of open enrollment with priority to residential proximity. Detroit voters also initiated a recall, and in August 1970, recalled four members of the school board.[26]

At this point, the Detroit NAACP engineered the now familiar change of venue, filing a class action in federal court. Initially, they named as plaintiffs "all school children in the City of Detroit."[27] Such a class roped in a citywide constituency, but failed to account for "white flight." After World War II, whites across America had begun moving to the suburbs, while blacks had begun moving to the cities. Detroit exemplified the trend, leaving few white children inside the city. Later realizing this lack, the lawyers came up with a creative solution. They moved to expand the size of the class, looping in huge chunks of suburbia.

The local federal judge, Judge Stephen Roth, obliged. He entered an order adding in 85 school districts in three counties around Detroit. This class size joined half the population of Michigan in the lawsuit, over 4,000,000 people, some 1,000,000 school age children. The land area covered almost 2,000 square miles, as big as Delaware, half bigger than Rhode Island, ten times bigger than the District of Columbia. However, Judge Roth later pared down somewhat, leaving 54 school districts with 780,000 students. Still his final plan called for busing more than 300,000.[28] Only by such dimensions could he obtain enough white children, the necessary material for busing into inner city Detroit, breaking up the effect of black and white residential patterns.

Such a size surpassed prior class actions by an order of magnitude, and as it turned out, Judge Roth had momentarily gone a bit too far for the Supreme Court, which called a pause, if not a halt. In a narrow five to four opinion, Chief Justice Warren Berger wrote for the majority, saying: "The record before us ... contains evidence of de jure segregated conditions only in the Detroit schools; ... With no showing of significant violation by the 53 outlying school districts and no evidence of any interdistrict violation or effect, the [lower] court went beyond the original theory of the case ... and mandated a metropolitan area remedy. ... To approve the remedy ordered by the court would impose on the outlying districts, not shown to have committed any constitutional violation, a wholly impermissible remedy."[29]

Examining his words in detail, it is hard to conclude this ruling rests on any rationale except expediency. The Chief Justice says: "The record before us ... contains evidence of de jure segregated conditions only in the Detroit schools." Yet to recall, the Court imposed no such burden in the Charlotte-Mecklenburg case, made no requirement to show de jure segregation in the suburbs as well as the city. Then why approve the plan in Charlotte-Mecklenburg, but not Detroit? The only real difference appears scale. Judge Roth's proposal was simply too big, too fraught with problems, too highly unpopular.

At any rate, many perceived Milliken to rein in the grandiosity of future busing schemes, but not really. The careful wording left plenty of room for a federal judge determined to take the bit between his teeth. All he had to do was find a "significant violation" by the suburban schools or an "interdistrict effect," thus justifying his plan. So no one should express surprise if Judge Roth's vision for metropolitan-wide busing went into effect elsewhere, which in fact happened in Wilmington, Delaware, Louisville, Kentucky, and Indianapolis, Indiana. In fact as will be seen, even a nation-size class would later win approval.

The extent of equitable remedies – Meanwhile, what Judge Roth was doing for the size of class actions, Judge Russell Clark was doing for the size of equitable remedies with the Kansas City Case. This litigation began in 1977, and at the outset, demonstrates an interesting phenomenon. The Kansas City, Missouri, School District (KCMSD), together with the children of two members of that school board, filed suit against the state of Missouri and other defendants. In other words, the school district sued itself to desegregate. While the Judge Clark later "realigned" the school district as a party defendant, throughout KCMSD "pursued a friendly adversary relationship" with the plaintiffs and against the state.

As the litigation progressed, this feature explained itself. The school district "proposed ever more expensive capital improvements with the agreement of the plaintiffs" and devised "a variation of the magnet school concept." Magnet schools seek to desegregate by offering incentives, special programs to attract nonminority students. KCMSD open-handedly proposed "to make a magnet of the district as a whole," with "every senior high school, every middle school, and approximately one-half of the elementary schools"[30] becoming magnet schools.

Judge Clark obliged. "Finding that construction of new schools would result in more 'attractive' facilities than renovation of existing ones, [he] approved new construction at a cost ranging from $61.80 per square foot to $95.70 per square foot as distinct from renovation at $45.00 per square foot." His capital improvements went on to include "a 2000-square-foot planetarium; greenhouses and vivariums; a 25-acre farm with an air-conditioned meeting room for 104 people; a Model United Nations wired for language translation; broadcast capable radio and television studios with an editing and animation lab; a temperature controlled art gallery; movie editing and screening rooms; a 3,500-square-foot dust-free diesel mechanics room; ... swimming pools; and numerous other facilities."[31]

But a legal roadblock stood in the way. These projects carried a price tag in excess of half a billion dollars, far exceeding the school district's budget. More than that, the Missouri Constitution and state law restricted property taxes, and under these limits, the school district could never raise the money. But in another creative response, Judge Clark simply abrogated the laws which limited taxation and himself levied the taxes to pay for the programs. Under his assessment property taxes doubled.

On appeal, the Supreme Court left Judge Clark's desegregation plan in effect, but said he went too far raising taxes. Instead of raising taxes himself, they said he should have simply ordered the school board to raise them. Justice Byron White wrote: "The District Court believed that it had no alternative to imposing a tax increase. But there was an alternative, ... it could have authorized or required KCMSD to levy property taxes at a rate adequate to fund the desegregation remedy and could have enjoined the operation of state laws that would have prevented KCMSD form exercising this power." Justice White assured: "The differences between the two approaches is more than a matter of form."[32] But perhaps taxpayers might be pardoned for not seeing the distinction in this difference. In either event, they paid the higher tax. Nor was this a gentle burden. By 1995, the cost had reached $1.3 billion over and above the normal school budget, an extra $36,111 for each of the district's 36,000 students.[33]

But beyond the cost, under equitable remedies what power had the judiciary not come to possess? In the Anglo-American legal tradition, no power belonged more exclusively to the legislature than the power of the purse. In England, parliamentary control over taxation served as the essential cause behind the English Civil War, and the triumph of Parliament over the crown established nothing more fundamental than such parliamentary control. The same central contest featured in the American Revolution, whose great slogan summed up the principle: "No taxation without representation." But now called an equitable remedy, the unelected judiciary acquires a power to tax.

The bureaucratic synergy – Starting up in 1970 and running for twenty years, the Adams Case demonstrates a fully developed new model judicial supremacy. The federal judge handling the case, Judge John H. Pratt, bases his decision upon prior judicial re-interpretations of the Constitution, which as seen replaced the congressional program for school desegregation with a judicial program. Using a class action, he controls a nationwide controversy; using equitable remedies, he directly carries out the judicial program. In the final refinement, he takes over and runs a huge bureaucratic agency, supplanting congressional or presidential management with judicial management. All the pieces in place, the new model displays in a plentitude of judicial power.

Already the cases show the judiciary and bureaucracy often in synergy. In Green, the Court sided with HEW against Congress, approving HEW's regulations on school desegregation, which disregarded the 1964 Civil Rights Act, substituting an agency and judicial program for the congressional program. In the Kansas City Case, the school board sued itself to desegregate, and again the judiciary sided with the bureaucracy, the judge and the school district running in tandem, overriding Missouri state law. The Adams Case further exemplifies such a bureaucratic and judicial embrace. But while both parties come willingly to this union, the terms hardly amount to a modern marriage of gender equality, rather the old-fashioned patriarchal type, the bureaucratic bride pledging to honor and obey the judicial groom, so eager to escape the household of her legislative and executive parents, she eagerly pays the price of legal tutelage to a judicial husband.

In the twentieth century, the bureaucracy has vastly proliferated and become a thoroughgoing civil service system. The virtues of civil service include merit hiring and promotion of government employees, while terminating them only for cause. But corresponding vices neglect the prefix "merit" before hiring and promotion, while the suffix "for cause" turns termination into a near impossible task. Civil servants come to occupy virtual sinecures. Thus insulated from accountability, they gather in their growing enclaves, doing a great deal of useful work, but breeding the familiar "bureaucratic cultures." Seldom failing to rationalize their motives as the very best, they as seldom fail to rationalize more funding, staff, and authority for their agencies. In short, the bureaucracy displays an institutional will-to-power.

And who stands in their way? Usually the legislature and chief executive, whose accountability to the public imposes restraints. Mindful of the unpopularity of a bureaucratic scheme, they rein in the scheme; mindful of the unpopularity of taxes, they rein in bureaucratic budgets. Thus frustrated, being sued may come upon the bureaucrats as a blessing in disguise. Let someone sue their agency; let the judge rule against their agency; let the judge take over and run their agency. They merely exchange one master for another, likely escaping servitude to a narrow-minded and miserly legislative and executive. Instead, their title deeds are transferred to a more enlightened and bountiful judicial possessor. Being unelected, the judge need neither worry about the unpopularity of his measures or the unpopularity of the costs. Here is a man with the where-with-all to gratify the desires of his servants as well as himself, a man with a bottomless purse, and the more money they spend, the richer it makes him, since all expenses come out of someone else's pocket, redounding to his ultimate credit. Their ideas for human improvement will likely appeal to him as well, since as their pleasure grows in doing good, his pleasure will grow to the same extent. To see the vistas opened before the bureaucratic mind, we have only to recall the judge's bounty to the school board in the Kansas City Case. While from the judge's point of view, no longer need he keep lonely vigil in his chambers, writing dry legal opinions. He becomes the center of the action. By taking over an agency, he surrounds himself with a host of bureaucratic minions, who rush to do his will. Nor should we forget the court's lawyerly retainers, who assist by filing the lawsuit, their reward more business and richer fees. What can these three not accomplish together? Jilting the legislative and executive, the bureaucracy, judiciary, and lawyers form a more perfect union, replacing a clash of interests with an harmonious *ménage a trois*.

The facts behind the Adams Case – The Adams Case serves as the classic illustration. Filed in 1970, this case generated out of discontent with the 1968 election, which elevated Richard Nixon to the presidency. As reflected in the 1964 Civil Rights Act, the majority had already shown their preference for neighborhood schools and no busing, but we recall that back in 1966, HEW had promulgated its new set of regulations, replacing this congressional program with racial mixing and busing. In his campaign, Nixon played upon the public disaffection with this policy change, tacitly promising to "cool off" desegregation. Of course, his critics charged this "Southern strategy" an offer of aid and comfort to the segregationists, nor should we suppose him unmindful of such an appeal. Yet his camp denied the accusation, claiming a commitment to desegregation, but a concern over heavy-handed bureaucratic enforcement, which they argued damaging to educational quality. At any rate, Nixon took his win as a mandate and made a serious effort to tug school desegregation back toward the congressional program, using his power as chief executive to rein in the bureaucracy.

The presidency had two tools ready at hand. Recall the 1964 Civil Rights Act allowed federal funding cut offs, entrusting that authority to HEW and also authorized the Attorney General to file lawsuits compelling compliance. The president appointed the heads of both agencies. Nixon picked Robert Finch as Secretary of HEW and John Mitchell as Attorney General. Their marching orders directed them to assert their control over the agencies and re-align the school desegregation program.

In a March 10, 1969 interview, Finch signaled the shift. Carefully professing a continued commitment to school desegregation, he claimed to have "cut off funds to the first five school districts in the South, and gave them 60 days to see if they could not bring themselves into compliance." But he went on: "We have found in a number of these school desegregation cases --- particularly in the South --- where the federal compliance agents said in effect: 'We're here to bring about integration, and we're not concerned about education.'" He suggested: "[T]o threaten to cut off funds --- which might mean closing some schools --- results in good teachers leaving and in the creation of private schools." He stressed: "I intend to put education first." Finally, Finch indicated the goal would move away from "arbitrary percentages" of black to white.[34]

On July 3, 1969, Finch and Attorney General Mitchell issued a formal statement: "This administration is unequivocally committed to the goal of finally ending racial discrimination in schools, steadily and speedily, in accordance with the law of the land." All school districts had to propose a plan for full compliance by the 1969-70 school year. Yet they wanted "[t]o minimize the number of cases in which it becomes necessary to employ the particular remedy of a cutoff of federal funds, recognizing the burden of the cutoff falls nearly always on those the Act was intended to help; the children of the poor and the black." Lastly, they claimed their intent was "[t]o ensure to the greatest extent possible, that educational quality is maintained while desegregation is achieved and bureaucratic disruption of the educational process is avoided."[35]

Many heard this language as no more than buzzwords for continued segregation, and among these ranked a strong bureaucratic contingent, who saw their oversight of school desegregation threatened from above, their hard-won program of racial mixing and busing in jeopardy. Over at HEW disaffection surfaced within the Office of Civil Rights (OCR), where the director, Leon Panetta, differed with the re-alignment and resigned. On the day his successor was announced, 125 members of the staff (more than one-third the total) expressed their "bitter disappointment"[36] in a letter to the president. Over at Justice, 65 of the 100 lawyers in the Civil Rights Division signed a petition declaring the administration's action "inconsistent with clearly defined legal mandates."[37]

But this presidential initiative faced more than bureaucratic dissent, contravening a more powerful foe, the federal judiciary, who had already signed off on the bureaucratic program school for desegregation. The executive interference with the bureaucracy meddled with their judicial control as well. The moment had struck for the third member of this triumvirate, the public interest lawyers, to file their lawsuit. A reliable source advises they worked "covertly with disaffected HEW bureaucrats."[38] In 1970, their collaboration became the Adams Case, filed in the Federal District Court for Washington, D.C., putting the matter into the hands of Federal District Judge Pratt. The complaint alleged a failure to enforce the 1964 Civil Rights Act, alleging HEW not processing complaints or cutting off funds fast enough in furtherance of school desegregation.

The doctrine of executive discretion – Now traditional legal doctrine carefully preserved the president a wide discretion. Unless a law specifically commands the performance of an act, the executive branch retains discretion as to how or whether to perform the act. Legal terminology designates an act not specifically commanded a "discretionary act." However, if the law does specifically command an act, the executive must perform it. Legal terminology designates an act so specifically commanded a mere "ministerial duty." Under this long-accepted legal theory, a court cannot order the executive branch to perform a "discretionary act," since for a judge to compel the executive would replace executive discretion with judicial discretion, violating the separation of powers. On the other hand, a court can order the executive to perform a mere "ministerial duty," since if a judge could not compel the executive to perform a clear-cut obligation imposed by law, the executive would be above the law. Obviously, this two-edged distinction serves as fundamental both to the separation of powers and the concept of a government of laws not men.

To illustrate with a legal precedent, we can go all the way back to 1803, citing Marbury v Madison itself. To recap the facts in that famous case, James Marbury sued James Madison, the Secretary of State, demanding delivery of his commission as a federal justice-of-the-peace. President John Adams had signed the commission, but Madison, the incoming Secretary of State in Jefferson's new cabinet, found the commission lying on his desk and refused delivery. Marbury's lawyers claimed delivery of the commission not a *discretionary act*, but a mere *ministerial duty*, not a discretionary power conferred on the executive, but a duty compelled by law. They argued that while the president possessed discretion to appoint, mere delivery of the commission a duty owed the appointee.

In his opinion, Chief Justice John Marshall summed up the well-accepted doctrine: "The province of the Court is solely to decide on the rights of individuals, *not to inquire how the Executive or Executive officers perform duties in which they have a discretion.* Questions, in their nature political or which are, by the Constitution and laws, submitted to the Executive, can never be made in this court." And, "It is scarcely necessary for the Court to disclaim all pretensions to such a jurisdiction. An extravagance so absurd and excessive could not have been entertained for a moment."[39]

Thus, executive "discretion" existed unless the "rights of individuals" interposed. But what exactly gave rise to the "right of an individual" which cut off executive discretion? Marshall goes on to summarize the settled rule: "[T]he President is invested with certain important political powers, in the exercise of which he is to use his own discretion, and is accountable only to his country in his political character, and to his own conscience. ... But when the legislature proceeds to impose on [an executive] officer other duties; when he is directed peremptorily to perform certain acts; when the rights of individuals are dependent on the performance of those acts; he is so far the officer of the law; is amenable to the laws for his conduct; and he cannot at his discretion sport away the vested rights of others."[40]

In other words, presidential discretion ends where the legislature "imposes" a clear "duty to perform certain acts," which creates "vested rights" in individuals. To illustrate with a modern instance, say an individual reaches retirement age under the Social Security program. That individual possesses a vested right to draw the retirement, the law imposing a clear duty upon the executive to a pay the benefits. No discretion remains with the executive branch, sending the check a mere ministerial duty.

The Adams Case – So much for long-accepted doctrine of executive discretion, and we immediately discern the plaintiffs in Adams stand in precisely the same place as the plaintiffs in Marbury. They want the executive compelled to act. To focus on the key element, they want the executive compelled to cut off funds to school districts. Well then, does the statute in question confer discretion on the president or compel him to cut off funds? That becomes the essential inquiry.

To answer that question, we must look at the precise words of Title VI, and we find: "Compliance ... *may be* effected ... by the termination of ... assistance."[41] Those two words with the emphasis added say it all. To say *may be* is not the same as to say *shall*. If Congress had intended that the president *must* terminate funds, they would have written "shall" in place of "may." A funding cut off was a discretionary act of the executive. A funding cut off was not a mere ministerial duty which a court could compel the executive to perform.

In 1803, Chief Justice Marshall had said: "It is scarcely necessary for the court to disclaim all pretensions to such a jurisdiction. An extravagance, so absurd and excessive, could not have been entertained for a moment." Yet Judge Pratt holds the executive branch has delayed too long. He orders HEW to "within 60 days ...communicate with each of the 85 districts listed ... putting them on notice to rebut or explain the substantial racial disproportion in one or more of the district's schools." As to another 42 school districts, he gave HEW 60 days "to commence enforcement proceedings by administrative notice of hearing, or to utilize any other means authorized by law."[42]

The Circuit Court of Appeals unanimously affirmed Pratt's order. As to the unique nature of such interference with presidential discretion, the circuit judges blandly observed: "The terms of Title VI are not so broad as to preclude judicial review."[43] Eh voila, there you have it once more. So simply is "may" converted into "shall." So easily was executive discretion transformed into judicial command.

The duration of litigation – The Adams Case went on for twenty years, spreading horizontally as well as vertically. Judge Pratt's initial order covered only 85 named school districts; in 1975, he expanded the order to all seventeen border and Southern states; in 1977, another order extended nationwide. Meanwhile, other litigants piled on, sometimes quarreling among themselves over the allocation of resources. In 1974, the Women's Equity League (WEAL) joined, followed shortly by the National Federation of the Blind (NFB), next by Mexican-American groups.

In 1990, Adams was finally dismissed, having run its course, but the precedent stayed on the books, the finishing touch to new model judicial supremacy. All the elements were up and running. The judiciary can re-interpret the Constitution, replacing legislative and executive discretion with their constitutional commands. Using class actions and equitable remedies, they can directly carry out their commands. They can manage bureaucratic agencies. In future they will use these same methods to take over and run such things as prisons and mental health care. What can they not take over and run?

Comparing institutional performance – Comparing institutional performance, much remains in the eye of the beholder, but not all. No historical consensus yet emerging, the point of view decisively alters the perspective, warping judgment as to which institution did better, Congress or the Court. Yet from any point of view, certain facts focus. We see Congress expressing the will of the majority, the Court siding with a minority. We see both institutions gravitating along their interests, judicial interests winning out. Looking back across time, we see how far the Court has come. From any vantage, we see the new model judicial supremacy.

Undoubtedly, the 1964 Civil Rights Act expressed the will of the majority about school desegregation. Congress listens for their audience, playing for the loudest applause, delighting in ovation. Unless they very much misheard, the public put their hands together for ending legal segregation, made a noise for neighborhood schools, but hissed busing. Congress got the message loud and clear, passed a law to desegregate the schools, keep neighborhood schools, and not bus. In so doing, Congress reliably operated on their interests, the will-to-stay-in-power by getting re-elected. Congress performed as predicted.

Just as undoubtedly, the Court sided with a minority, ordering school desegregation by racial mixing through massive busing. But did the Court perform as predicted? Did they defend the Constitution? Not really. The 14th Amendment said "equal protection of the laws," which prohibited legal segregation, but nothing in the Constitution ordered racial mixing and busing. If anything, when the Constitution does not otherwise command or forbid, the Constitution still commands democratic process. Constitutional silence leaves Congress free to speak, expressing the will of the people. No principle is more fundamental. But the Court did not defend this fundamental constitutional right to self-government, instead replacing democratic process with judicial process.

Well then, did the Court defend "minority rights?" As seen, they defended no minority rights clearly expressed in the Constitution. Nor does the 1964 Civil Rights Act seem a law passed by an out-of-control majority, the traditional image called up to justify defending minority rights. Rather than trampling on black rights, the majority vindicated those rights. The Act still stands as the legislative bedrock under black equality. Nor do neighborhood schools and no busing seem continued segregation, rather a program for school desegregation, arguably adequate or not enough, depending upon the point of view. It seems, then, as if the majority themselves defended minority rights, and that the Court only defended another, more extreme version, perhaps preferable, but not self-evidently so.

Yet seen from another angle, the Court did unequivocally perform as should have been predicted. Every step of the way, they performed in keeping with their judicial will-to-power. By replacing the congressional program with their own program, they seized power over school desegregation. With far-flung class actions and far-reaching equitable remedies, they directly carried out their power. By taking over and running a bureaucratic agency, they exerted further power. Then if minority rights mean the version conferring maximum power on the judiciary, the Court defended minority rights so defined, and such performance should have been predictable.

Looking back over time, we see how far the Court has come. The arrow on the power graph moves up with but a single stagger down. First, they claim the power of judicial review. Second, they abrogate the original limits on that power. Third, they expand that power to re-interpret the Constitution. Fourth, they invent the further power of substantive due process, letting them act as a sort of super-legislature. But fifth, they suffer an institutional defeat, being forced to renounce substantive due process. Yet sixth, they reclaim their lost power to serve newer causes, the Footnote Four Agenda. And finally sixth, they acquire power to directly carry out what amount to legislative and executive functions. The Court turns into not only a super-legislature, but a super-executive. They not only make, but carry out policy. The Court re-ascends in power by remodeling judicial supremacy.

CHAPTER 11

Religion

Already in 1947 with the Everson Case, the Court had turned to another item on the Footnote Four agenda, that mention of "statutes directed at a particular religion." From this indirect reference, beginning with this case, the Court began erecting a new "wall of separation," directed at changing the existing relationship between church and state. To understand the change requires no more than to understand the original intent about religion, then to understand how the Court changed that original intent. To understand the politics driving the changes requires no more than understanding the influence of the usual interests and institutions. But to understand the ultimate complexity quite likely goes beyond our understanding, since the influence of religion so complex.

The original intent on religion – Understanding the original intent on religion must begin with the Constitution itself, where Article VI says: "[N]o religious Test shall ever be required as a Qualification to an Office or public Trust under the United States." But more famously, when ratified in 1791, the 1st Amendment added the "establishment clause" and the "free exercise clause," saying: "Congress shall make no law respecting an establishment of religion, or prohibiting the free exercise thereof."

What did these "religious clauses" mean at the time? We read three distinct prohibitions. First, "no religious test" for "office" looks clear enough on its face. Second, "Congress shall make no law respecting an establishment of religion" seems clear enough, too, except what amounts to an "establishment of religion?" But we quickly recall English law "established" an official church, the Church of England, and as quickly that many Americans descended from the dissenters and nonconformists, who greatly resented those laws. It would appear, then, as if this "establishment clause" meant to prevent Congress from setting up such a national church. Third, the "Congress shall make no law ... prohibiting the free exercise thereof." This "free exercise clause" appears to assure those same dissenters and nonconformists from congressional laws against the free exercise of their religion. And in fact, the original intent was just as it appears, a meaning amply attested by the Founders' words and practice.

English law had established the Church of England as the exclusive national church. The monarch headed the church and appointed the bishops; the Act of Uniformity (1662) prescribed the public prayers, the sacraments, and other rites; the Corporation Act (1661) and various Test Acts made membership a qualification for civil or military office; the Conventicle Act (1664) closed other churches; however, the Toleration Act (1689) later allowed most Protestant churches; last but not least, the Church Rates taxed land to support the church.

The Constitution prevented Congress from passing such laws, and precision requires noticing this prohibition applied *only* to Congress, that is, *not* the states. Both the specific language and the history of the 1st Amendment confirm the studied significance. Initially as written, the Constitution merely forbids the old English "religious tests" for public office, that language in Article VI. But during the controversy over ratification, opponents attacked the omission of a bill of rights, including the lack of further religious guarantees. Supporters responded such superfluous, since nothing delegated the federal government a power over religion. James Madison himself took this stance, when in the Virginia ratifying convention he replied: "There is not a shadow of right in the general government to interfere with religion. Its least interference with it would be a most flagrant usurpation."[1] Yet to mollify their critics, they pledged to add a bill of rights, which became an important item in the very First Congress. Madison served in the House and drafted these proposals. The debates show a clear intent to limit application of the religious clauses to "Congress," not in any way limiting the states.

Madison introduced his draft Bill of Rights on June 8, 1789, and his proposals touching religion read this way: "The civil rights of none shall be abridged on account of religious belief or worship, nor shall any national religion be established, nor shall the full and equal rights of conscience by in any manner, or on any pretext, infringed." And, "No state shall violate the equal rights of conscience."[2] After referral to committee, these proposals were reported out in a somewhat amended form: "[N]o religion shall be established by law, nor shall the equal rights of conscience be infringed."[3]

But in the debates that followed, some expressed concerns that the language might be construed to infringe state rights, since some states still "established by law" a religion. To make clear that the language applied only to the national government, a motion was made to change the language to "Congress shall make no laws touching religion, or infringing the rights of conscience."4 The motion carried and the 1st Amendment emerged from the vicissitudes of the legislative process in the form we have: "*Congress* shall make no law respecting an establishment of religion, or prohibiting the free exercise thereof." Obviously, the alteration to "Congress" expressed a purposeful legislative intent. The limitation applied *only against* the *national Congress, not the state legislatures*.

Over many years, the Supreme Court itself so interpreted the 1st Amendment. In the 1845 Permoli Case, Justice John Catron wrote: "The Constitution makes no provision for protecting the citizens of the respective States in their religious liberties; this is left to the State constitutions and laws; nor is there any inhibition imposed by the Constitution of the United States in this respect on the States."5

Actual practice confirms this original intent. All the states embodied some guarantees for religious freedom in their constitutions, but nothing in the U.S. Constitution so compelled them. While little remembered, back in 1791 when the 1st Amendment ratified, seven of the fourteen states actually maintained religious establishments, and several others favored Christianity in various ways. Four states (Rhode Island, New Jersey, Pennsylvania, and Delaware) never had established churches, and three had abolished theirs by the time of the Constitution. By 1833, all the states disestablished their churches, Massachusetts being the last.[6] But if a state could establish a church, the 1st Amendment restricted them not at all.

Recognition and aid of Christianity – Nor did the 1st Amendment prevent all recognition of Christianity by the federal government, even a degree of aid or assistance. The very next day after the House passed the 1st Amendment, Representative Elias Boudinot of New Jersey proposed a resolution that the president issue a Thanksgiving Day proclamation, saying he "could not think of letting the session pass over without an opportunity to all the citizens of the United States of joining with one voice, in returning to Almighty God their sincere thanks for the many blessings he had poured down upon them."7 This resolution carried and within two weeks President Washington issued just such a proclamation: "Now, therefore, I do recommend and assign Thursday, the 26th of November next, to be devoted by the people of these States to the service of that great and glorious Being who is the beneficent author of all the good that was, that is, or that will be."8

In the same way, other presidents have appealed to the Almighty in their messages; prayers continue to open each congressional session; the Supreme Court still begins each session with the clerk intoning: "God save the United States and this Honorable Court;" oaths taken in court refer to God; the Pledge of Allegiance refers to "one nation under God;" the national motto is "In God We Trust;" and Thanksgiving and Christmas remain holidays. Moreover, in 1789, that same First Congress re-passed the famous Northwest Ordinance, and among the provisions we find this language: "Religion, morality, and knowledge, being necessary to good government and the happiness of mankind, schools and the means of education shall be ever encouraged."[9] In this vein, Congress throughout the eighteenth and nineteenth centuries appropriated tax money time and again for Indian education carried on by religious organizations. Usually cited as typical is Jefferson's treaty with the Kaskaskia Indians, which provided for the tribe's Roman Catholic priest and church.

Perhaps Justice Joseph Story best sums up the initial understanding. Previously consulted in these pages, Story served on the Supreme Court from 1811 to 1845, simultaneously held down a professorship at the Harvard Law School, and in his spare time wrote a comprehensive treatise on the Constitution, widely-accepted as authoritative, his *Commentaries on the Constitution of the United States*. Story had this to say: "Probably at the time of the adoption of the Constitution, and [of the 1st Amendment], the general if not universal sentiment in America was, that Christianity ought to receive encouragement from the State so far as it was not incompatible with the private rights of conscience and the freedom of religious worship. An attempt to level all religions, and to make it a matter of state policy to hold in utter indifference, would have created universal disapprobation, if not universal indignation. ... The real object ... was not to countenance, much less to advance, Mahometanism, or Judaism, or infidelity, by prostrating Christianity; but to exclude all rivalry between Christian sects and to prevent any national ecclesiastical establishment."[10]

The Supreme Court itself can be quoted to much the same effect. In an 1891 case, Justice David Josiah Brewer wrote simply: "[T]his is a Christian nation."[11]

Let quarrel with the facts who will, such amounts to the "original intent," shown by the original practice. If the Founders had erected a "wall of separation between church and state," the barrier was hardly impermeable to Christianity as would later be claimed. They rejected an established church like the Church of England. But beyond that, far from shutting out Christian influence or exhibiting a suspicion of the Christian majority, they left Christianity dominant, leaving toleration up to the states, presumably up to the democratic process. We might even recall those so neglected words also in the Bill of Rights, where the 10th

Amendment says: "The powers not delegated to the United States by the Constitution ... are reserved to the states respectively, or to the people." Under the principle of federalism, the people through the states "reserved" the right to decide on the place of Christianity, indeed, of religion, in the national life.

The Founders' views on religion – By embodying these religious clauses in the Constitution, the Founders attempted to learn from history, but drew not quite the lesson so often attributed. Customarily we hear stressed their *separation* of church and state, yet this emphasis neglects their actual practice, which as seen left America very much a "Christian Nation," and deliberately so. Such Founders as Jefferson or Madison may have shared the more skeptical tone of the Enlightenment, of which more in a moment, but by far the greater number, such as prominently Washington, adhered to their Christian heritage, especially as an ethical source and force. Whatever their personal beliefs, they lived in a nation where Christianity mattered, where as Justice Story said: "an attempt to level all religions would have created universal disapprobation, if not universal indignation." Not a universal church, rather a collection of churches, yet this Christian institutional set rivaled the government and economic sets in importance. Christianity stayed a defining national trait, perceived as foundational.

That insightful French observer, Alexis de Tocqueville, who visited this country in 1831 and 1832, recorded the prevailing view: "Religion in America takes no direct part in the government of society, but nevertheless it must be regarded as the foremost of the political institutions of that country; for if it does not impart a taste for freedom, it facilitates the use of free institutions. Indeed, it is in this same point of view that the inhabitants of the United States look upon religious belief. I do not know whether all Americans have a sincere belief in their religion, for who can search the human heart? But I am certain that they hold it to be indispensable to the maintenance of republican institutions. This opinion is not peculiar to a class of citizens or to a party, but it belongs to the whole nation, and to every rank of society."[12]

In other words, Americans thought Christianity central to their way of life, the substratum bearing up the social order, indeed, bearing up the government. The Father of his Country, George Washington, exemplified this outlook in his famous Farewell Address, delivered September 19, 1796, on leaving the presidency: "[L]et us with caution indulge the supposition, that morality can be maintained without religion. Whatever may be conceded to the influence of refined education ... reason and experience both forbid us to expect that National morality can prevail in exclusion of religious principle."[13]

The religious conflicts of the Reformation – Such views about the indispensability of religion possess a long history, stretching back centuries and across cultures. Old Testament prophets like Jeremiah ceaselessly dinned the message into the ears of Jewish kings, calling upon them to maintain strict Jewish tradition, foretelling doom if they backslid. Socrates suffered death for the crime of impiety, which the Athenians saw as a threat to their polis. So perceptive an historian as Polybius attributed Roman triumph not just to their superior constitution, but to faithful adherence to their religious rites. At the fall of that ancient world, the Catholic Church was the last institution standing, and as the new nations of Europe emerged that religion was inseparable from their design. In late medieval Europe, no one conceived society or government without Catholicism, as witness Dante's *Divine Comedy*, which blended society, government, and the church in a grand theory, incomprehensible without Christianity, which gave ultimate meaning and ethical value. Yet at the dawn of modernity during the Reformation, something went radically wrong between church and state. To America's founding generation, those disastrous events were recent and well-remembered history, whose passionate faith still stirred men's souls, whose costs still haunted their fears.

Whether or not in 1517, Martin Luther actually, physically nailed his *Ninety-Five Theses* to the door of All Saints Church in Wittenberg, the actual, physical costs of the Reformation were not a matter of speculation. But how the two relate may puzzle. How did a theological controversy turn into a tipping point, an argument over papal indulgences precipitate crises across a continent? Yet so it was. During this era, European societies looked like modern chaos theory in action, changes in the initial circumstances causing unpredictable and dramatic system-wide swings. Altering the religious item on the social agenda triggered epic meltdowns. Apparently economics, class, culture, politics, all teetered on the brink of a chasm, unaware, but fraught with potential energy. In a way hard to fathom, religion intertwined with the other strands. Luther and his colleagues saw themselves as reformers, but as they tugged on the religious' cord, the connectedness of the entire system unraveled, a totally unforeseen consequence.

Nation after nation crashed down the incline, dashing in ruins at the bottom. Virtually every European country went through a series of civil wars, the sanguinary "Wars of Religion," spreading, recurring, self-sustaining cycles of violence. From 1642 to 1651, the English Civil War rang up a casualty list of perhaps 190,000, leaving out Ireland, which suffered even more. But when compared to others, these figures showed proverbial English self-restraint. In France from 1562 to 1598, the Catholics and Protestant Huguenots convulsed that kingdom with assassinations, massacres, and battles. Only in 1598, after three decades of fratricide, did the Edict of Nantes finally restore an uneasy truce, signed on the graves of an estimated 2,000,000 to 4,000,000. From 1618 to 1648 in Germany, the Thirty Years War claimed even more, between 15% and 30% of the population. Somehow or other while calling on God, they had summoned up the very devil.

In the end, societies re-organized at the bottom, which became the new ground level. All contrived some sort of religious settlement. The monolith of the medieval Catholic Church had splintered, as had the Protestants, who began as protestants against Catholicism, but ended as often protesting against each other. Of crucial significance to American history, in England this inter-Protestant schism pitted the Church of England against the Puritans, who came in a variety. Back in the 1530s while quarrelling with the papacy over his first divorce, Henry VIII had carried his point by carrying his country out of the Roman communion, nationalizing the physical plant and clergy, replacing the pope with the monarch, and renaming the new entity the Church of England. But he failed to distance himself sufficiently from Rome for some, later known as Puritans, who wished to "purify" the church, adopting more Protestant doctrine and practice. The later English Civil War featured a three-way fight between the Catholics, the Church of England, and the Puritans, the last of whom won the battles, but lost the peace. England separated permanently from Rome, leaving off executions, confiscations, and forcible conversions, but also leaving the Church of England an "established" church. But dissenters and nonconformists rejected this religious settlement, dissatisfied with their share.

A similar pattern emerged across most of the Old World, the institutional cathedrals of state-affiliated churches still towering over those nations, dominating dissenters and nonconformists. But in the New World, the English colonies unevenly mirrored a reverse image. The official Church of England stood on a narrow foundation, her edifice non-existent over much of the map, largest in the South. Rather, America had served as the refuge for all sorts of dissenters and nonconformists, especially the Puritans in New England, the Presbyterians in the Middle Colonies, and the Quakers in Pennsylvania, but you could locate an enclave devoted to almost any Protestant sect, as well as Catholic redoubts. The trans-Atlantic religious migration resulted in a bazaar-like collection of churches, turning European arrangements upside down.

The emergence of religious toleration – During the Reformation, enforced religious conformity began as the default position of all the major controversialists, but losers increasingly sought to dial up another solution, and everybody lost somewhere and through the constant wars. The idea of calling a religious truce promptly occurred. To end a war you negotiate a peace. Then why not sign a treaty on religion, agreeing to mutual religious toleration, leading to peaceful coexistence? Naturally enough this notion appealed to smaller sects, who bore the brunt of persecutions, but as total victory proved elusive, their bigger brethren began to see the light as well. Catholicism might dictate in Spain, but not in England. So as little as toleration appealed to them in Spain, such greatly appealed to them in England. While in nations like England, the strong dissenting and nonconformist sects threatened stability, tinderboxes ready to ignite revolutionary fires. Repression seldom extinguished their smolder, so why not let them burn openly, dissipating their enthusiasms in the air, rather than tamping down the coals until they exploded? Nor did the spectacle of mutual Christian slaughter much edify, being more than a little hard to square with Christ's injunction: "Love thy neighbor as thyself." It seemed time to recall about "turning the other cheek." We cannot doubt the religious fervor of those times, since so many gave the last full measure, resolute to martyrdom. Yet undoubtedly many would have settled for less zeal, preferring to get on with their lives, marrying and giving in marriage, tending to material interests in this world. In the end, religious toleration offered something for everyone except the most intransigent, presumably a permanent minority.

A memorable quote from America's own Roger Williams gives an example of the sort of arguments for toleration made by the dissenters and nonconformists: "[W]hen they have opened a gap in the hedge or wall of separation between the garden of the church and the wilderness of the world, God hath ever broke down the wall itself, removed the candlestick, and made His garden a wilderness, as at this day. And that therefore if He will ever please to restore His garden and paradise again, it must of necessity be walled in peculiarly unto himself from the world; and that all that shall be saved out of the world are to be transplanted out of the wilderness of the world, and added unto his church or garden."[14]

No one more persistently dissented than Williams, who having rejected the orthodoxy of every community in which he ever lived, finally moved beyond the fringe of settlement, ending up founding his own colony, Rhode Island. His antique imagery conveys an intensely religious vision, "the garden of the church walled in peculiarly unto himself from the world," and "all that shall be saved are to be transplanted out of the wilderness of the world." While not such extreme personalities, yet many contemporaries aspired to the same extreme spirituality, and so they rested their pleas for religious toleration on similar grounds, basically the idea of direct contact between the believer and God, unpolluted by outside influence, which amounts to freedom of conscience. Not that they proved by any means consistent. When they came to occupy the secular power, say in the Massachusetts Bay Colony, they often conveniently forget their own logic, persecuting in their turn. Nor did many imagine universal toleration, let alone secularization. Rather again as Story put it, their thoughts carried no further than: "to exclude all rivalry between Christian sects and to prevent any national ecclesiastical establishment," having no purpose "to level all religions." Only by taking their words out of the living context can we misapprehend them in this respect, as proved by the practices they adopted.

However, by the American Revolution, more secular thinkers were deploying similar arguments with a more secular slant. Succeeding to the Reformation, the Age of Reason and the Enlightenment originated in multiple, connected causes, demographic, technological, economic, and political, but as an intellectual current followed the course of the scientific revolution, whose successes challenged faith and authority with empirical methodology. Many of the leading figures moved away from Christianity, some toward deism, which replaced a personal God with a rational mechanism, some going the distance to skepticism, such as David Hume, the atheistic Scotch philosopher. In part, too, their social and political ideas reacted against the disasters of the Reformation and the Wars of Religion, sometimes placing much of the blame on Christianity. In part, they reacted against autocracy in church and state, which they perceived irrational and oppressive. Then naturally enough, virtually all these men advocated separation between church and state, but not so much to free up religion as to free up thought. In America their most influential member was John Locke, whose 1689 *Letter Concerning Toleration* popularized their views this way: "[T]he care of souls cannot belong to the civil magistrate, because his power consists only in outward force; but true and saving religion consists in the inward persuasion of the mind, without which nothing can be acceptable to God. And such is the nature of the understanding, that it cannot be compelled to the belief of anything by outward force. Confiscation of estate, imprisonment, torments, nothing of that nature can have any such efficacy as to make men change the inward judgement that they have framed of things."[15]

Thus, Locke makes an argument like that heard from Roger Williams, but clothed in more secular garb. Both based themselves upon freedom of conscience, a personal relationship between the believer and God, "the inward persuasion of the mind" not "compelled to the belief of anything by outward force." But in his more secular way, Locke went on to expound a more pragmatic program: "I esteem it above all things necessary to distinguish exactly the business of civil government from that of religion and to settle the just bounds that lie between the one and always arising between those that have, or at least pretend to have, on the one side, a concernment for the interest of men's souls, and, on the other side, a care of the commonwealth."[16]

Yet it is easy to exaggerate the secular bent of the Enlightenment, since many of these intellectuals did not break with Christianity at all. Locke again demonstrates. If we continue to read, we find his concept of toleration did not extend to atheists, since: "Promises, covenants, and oaths, which are the bonds of human society, can have no hold upon an atheist."[17] Nor did it even extend to Catholics, since: "all who enter into [that church] do thereby *ipso facto* deliver themselves up to the protection and service of another prince."[18]

The initial American "religious settlement" reflected all these influences. No rationale statesman wished to relive the Reformation or the Wars of Religion. Nor could any pragmatic politician suppose the "establishment" of a national church, where so many regional churches already ruled, all fiercely committed to their autonomy. Mainly dissenters, nonconformists, and disciples of the Enlightenment, the Founders shared the idea of "religious toleration." But like Roger Williams or John Locke, few rejected Christianity or advocated secularization. Like Washington, most perceived Christianity as fundamental to social order and morality. So they left Christianity largely where they found it. The 1st Amendment did not so much change things, as institutionalize an existing situation. Christianity stayed dominant, but no church dominated. Christianity continued to diffuse the society, exercising influence not only through the churches, but through the states. America stayed a "Christian Nation."

Religion in the schools – Christianity in the schools deserves as word to itself, since the topic attracted later litigation like a lightning rod. Again the facts are uncontested. Christianity and the schools began in tandem, each mutually reinforcing the other. The Revolution, the Constitution, and the 1st Amendment affected this connection not at all. But in the mid-nineteenth century, fresh immigration and the rise of common schools put a strain on the relationship. In particular, the influx of Irish Catholics wanted their own parochial schools, while the rise of common schools, compulsory and tax-supported, drew government into the activity, raising the separation of church and state in an unanticipated setting. In the initial response, states and school boards re-designed the curriculum, Christianity receding from the core to no more than an ancillary.

In 1647, Massachusetts had passed the first American law on education with an overtly Christian purpose, her aptly named "Old Deluder Satan" Act. The preamble began: "It being one of the chief projects of that old deluder Satan to keep man from the knowledge of the scriptures."[19]The act established education as a counter-measure, the primary goal being literacy to read the Bible. With that as the starting point, America founded her colonial schools with an avowedly religious agenda. These schools meant to make Christians.

For almost the entire eighteenth century, the *New England Primer* served as the national textbook. Samples from its pages illustrate the Christian nature of colonial education. The text asked students questions like: "What is the chief end of man?" Answer: "Man's chief end is to glorify God, and to enjoy him forever." Another question: "What rule hath God given to direct us how we may glorify and enjoy him?" Answer: "The Word of God which is contained in the Scriptures of the Old and New Testament, is the only rule to direct us how we may glorify and enjoy him." In sum, the themes of Christianity infused every lesson.

In the 1830s, the movement for "common schools" picked up momentum, free to everyone, tax-supported, and compulsory, what we now call "public schools." This was an idea whose time had come, today an educational system taken for granted. This same era witnessed the demise of the last established state churches, and the two phenomena bear some relation. In these years the flood of immigrants, as said particularly the Catholic Irish, undermined the prior consensus beneath the old state-funded churches. By the same token, millions of immigrant children now needed an education to make their way in a new homeland. But how accommodate the increased religious variety among the pupils in these common schools?

Almost every city has a school named after Horace Mann. A reformer in his day, Mann stands as the most famous exponent of the common school system. During his tenure as superintendent of schools for Massachusetts in the late 1830s, he built a model largely copied around the country. His extremely influential ideas came to represent the accepted solution on religion in schools. Mann wrote "that government should do all that it can to facilitate the acquisition of religious truth, but shall leave the decision of the question, what religious truth is, to the arbitrament, without human appeal, of each man's reason and conscience." He went on: "religious instruction in our schools ... was indispensable to [the students'] highest welfare, and essential to the vitality of moral education." But he did not mean by "religious instruction" the intensive indoctrination of the *New England Primer*. Rather, he proposed the Bible itself be read without comment. His curriculum welcomed "the religion of the Bible" and "all the doctrines which the Bible really contains." Mann thought reading of the Bible without comment in school allowed it "to do what it is allowed to do in no other system, --- to speak for itself."[20]

In nineteenth century America, these views turned into standard practice. Eventually, about 75% of the schools opened the day with reading a few verses from the Bible, often accompanied by a prayer and the singing of a hymn. Entering the twentieth century the American Law Reports provide a snapshot of the law on this issue. These reports print a case of interest and annotate all the other cases across the nation on the same topic. In 1920 under the annotation "Sectarianism in schools," we find this summary: "It might be stated as a broad general rule, deducible from the cases, that while Bible reading and exercises which merely tend to inculcate fundamental morality in pupils, and quiet them for their studies, are not prohibited, such exercises may be carried so far as to emphasize the teachings of a particular sect or denomination, and thus come within a constitutional inhibition."[21] In 1941 another annotation updating this topic appeared in these Reports,[22] showing things had stayed the same.

But over this same run of time, another side of the issue presented, the controversy over state aid to sectarian schools. Somewhat inconsistently, states that saw no problem with prayer or Bible reading in public schools often had laws prohibiting public assistance to sectarian schools. As we heard Justice Holmes say, the life of the law is not so much logic as the felt convenience of the times. In this instance, the felt convenience was the still smoldering hostility between Protestant and Catholic. At the time, to say sectarian school was the same as to say Catholic parochial school, and so whatever the neutrality on their face, such laws were far from neutral in purpose, being crafted to hurt the Catholics. This antagonism reached the height of a proposed constitutional amendment, the Blaine Amendment, offered in 1875 by Republican Congressman James G. Blaine of Maine, which read in material part: "No public property and no public revenue, nor any loan of credit by or under the authority of the United States, or any State, Territory, District, or municipal corporation, shall be appropriated to or made or used for the support of any school, educational, or other institution under the control of any religious or anti-religious sect, organization, or denomination, ...

This article shall not be construed to prohibit the reading of the Bible in any school or institution, ..."

This amendment passed the House easily, 180 to 7, but failed the two-thirds needed in the Senate, never going on to the states for ratification. However, all except eleven states later incorporated some such provision in their constitutions. There the matter rested, prayer and Bible reading approved, aid to sectarian schools generally disapproved.

Perhaps further reform was in order. Opening the school day with Bible reading and a prayer smacked of a Christian ceremonial, while serving only as a perfunctory introduction to either Christianity or the larger topic of religion. As for aid to sectarian schools, perhaps true toleration involved one of those difficult problems thrown up by real-world complexity, of which more in a moment. One interesting idea was to move religion back to the curriculum as a serious subject of study, taking the time and effort to teach from the sources. A prominent scholar puts the rationale this way: "If we are to take any point of view --- secular or religious --- seriously, we must let its advocates tell their own stories. No textbook can convey what Jeremiah or Paul or Martin Luther King, Jr., had to say as well as they themselves can. The one- or two-page excerpts of primary source readings found in many textbooks help, but not much, for the power of a position depends on seeing it in the context of supporting evidence and assumptions, and this requires a more substantial dose of material than the few excerpted paragraphs can provide. Anthologies and supplementary primary source material ... are essential. ... Students should read Jewish accounts of the Holocaust, fundamentalist arguments against abortion, papal encyclicals on economic justice and much else."[23]

But whether the states or local school boards might have adopted this or any other reform belongs to speculative history, since precisely at this point the Court intervened, taking the matter out of their hands.

The complexities of religious toleration – Surely the Founders' religious settlement assured a remarkable religious openness, surely an advance on what went before. As the living proof, later in the nineteenth and early twentieth centuries, millions of immigrants entered this country, religious freedom often among their motivations. Not to say all went smoothly, avoiding all tension and strife, for an extreme example the well-remembered anti-Catholic riots in Boston. But these new arrivals survived and flourished. At the same time, the already native species underwent a significant evolution. By 1775 at the end of the colonial period, probably 80% of the population affiliated with three churches tracing to English ancestry, the Anglicans in the South, the

Presbyterians in the Middle Colonies, the Congregationalists in New England, while a strong contingent of the Dutch Reformed Church held forth in New York and New Jersey, and Catholics and Jews together accounted for less of .1% of the population. But by the early twentieth century, only 40% claimed a religious affiliation, the largest Protestant denominations the Baptists, Methodists, and Lutherans, Roman Catholicism the largest single denomination, and Jews 3.2% of the population.[24] Such a proliferation and alteration must demonstrate a friendly legal environment, laws well adapted to assure a wide toleration.

Yet "religious toleration" continued and will continue to present enumerable practical difficulties, as usual when fitting an abstract ideal onto real-world complexity. Absent renouncing the world and removing to a mountaintop, religion never stays a private affair, rather compelling the devout to works as well as faith, engaging them with the public and political spheres. Only false toleration would expel their participation, yet true toleration must mediate between their discordant voices, lest the loudest shout down the rest. Nor does toleration ever mean absolute toleration, only reasonable toleration; whatever a man may believe, not every belief will authorize a practice. While however spiritual the message, religion seldom sloughs off earthly coils, churches inhabiting corporal bodies, possessing property and funds, subject to the ills of the flesh which plague such encumbrances. In some way, religion must remain subject to the ordinary civil and criminal law, otherwise becoming a law unto itself. Sorting all this out sets the lawgiver a never-ending task, never yet performed to universal approbation.

The interface between religion and law – As the cases show, difficulties creep in and multiply. Some early examples in American legal history concern schisms. When a congregation splits, who owns the meetinghouse? In 1820, the Massachusetts case of Baker v Fales[25] tangled the courts in just such a controversy. While not originally set up as a formal legal entity, the Congregational Church in Dedham, like numerous others across the state, was governed by a board of deacons and owned some property, either privately donated or granted by the colony. Back in 1754, the legislature had regularized that relationship, passing a law that made the deacons "a corporation with the power of holding the property." However, the Declaration of Rights in the Massachusetts Constitution provided: "that the several towns, parishes ... or religious societies, shall at all times have the exclusive right of electing their public teachers." Now a "parish" was something different than a church, consisting of all the inhabitants, not just those attending the church. And in 1818, the Dedham parish elected a new minister, a

Reverend Alvan Lamson, a Unitarian. But the deacons and most actual church members were Congregationalists. They refused to attend his services, maintaining they continued the real Dedham Church. Then who owned the church property, the parish or the deacons on behalf of the actual church members?

Without going into more detail, the Massachusetts Supreme Judicial Court held for the majority in the parish and against the majority in the old Congregational church, that is, the Unitarians got the property and the Congregationalists were dispossessed. Of course, the judges professed to determine the case as a matter of property rights, not to take sides in a theological dispute. Yet they could have ruled the other way with just as much reason. The claim of the deacons looks as good as the claim of the parish. The law made the deacons "a corporation with the power of holding the property." The Declaration of Right said that "parishes ... shall at all times have the exclusive right of electing their public teachers." Between such contradictory claims one looks as good as the other. Moreover, undoubtedly devout Congregationalists had donated some of this property, and the judges had now alienated their gifts to benefit a doctrine contrary to their faith. Even assuming the best intentions, the state had been forced to thrust a hand through the "wall" into the "garden," favoring one denomination over another.

A raft of similar cases filled the courts after the Civil War, which had split denominations North and South, the rival sides both claiming the physical plant and treasury. In 1871 one of these cases, Watson v Jones,[26] reached the U.S. Supreme Court, which summarized a well-reasoned rule over the state's role in such controversies. Basically, the rule said that the churches should settle their internal affairs by their own established procedures, the courts doing no more than holding them to follow those established procedures. This rule keeps the churches faithful to their own rules, while keeping the state from running the churches.

But in numerous ways, religious toleration continues to raise difficulties. The Thuggee cult famous in cinematic lore murdered and robbed wayfarers, the Aztecs carried out human sacrifice, Hindu suttee emulated the widow on her husband's funeral pyre. Such alien and deadly rites fall outside the pale of toleration. Yet closer to home the application becomes less obvious. Can a religion sacrifice animals? Can American Indians ingest peyote in their ceremonies? Can the Mormons practice polygamy? If the parents believe in faith healing, can the authorities force medical treatment for a sick child? Can religious pacifists avoid military service? Can government funding go to a hospital run by Catholic nuns or the Seventh Day Adventists? Can such funding assist a religiously based drug rehab center? Can government funding support a mission ministering to the homeless? Can a state appropriate tax money to aid sectarian schools? Can Congress give parents a tax deduction for the costs of such schools? Can federal grants for education help pay tuition to study theology at a religious college? Can Congress allow a charitable tax deduction for donations to churches? Can Congress exempt churches from taxes? Can a minister preach politics from the pulpit, say endorsing a candidate for public office? Can a church lobby for a political cause, say for or against abortion? How exactly do you distinguish a church from related organizations, say a political action committee not affiliated with a specific church, but drawing support and advocating for a religious viewpoint? Such a list appears capable of endless extension.

The complexities of religious toleration in the schools – Nothing better illustrates the complexities than the public schools. On one side stands the laudable goal of universal public education, on another the freedom of parents to raise their children in their faith, traditions, and culture. Both look perfectly legitimate concerns, yet they stumble into conflict. Autocratic regimes, such as the Soviet Communists or Nazis, starkly demonstrate the problem, using the schools to indoctrinate their ideology. American public education has avoided such extremes, yet bound up in the very process, education teaches not just facts and skills, but socializes in culture and values. Only what distinguishes socialization from indoctrination? Does a high school civics course that praises American democracy socialize or indoctrinate? The line between these two appears nothing more than consent. We regard socialization as consensual, but indoctrination as imposed. Yet consent must be somehow manifested, which we would say takes place through the elected legislatures and schools boards, features conspicuously lacking in the Soviet and Nazi regimes.

Yet looking back at the nineteenth century and the conflict over aid to sectarian schools, did America cross this line? In those days, the Catholics had argued they were being coerced. They wanted to socialize their children in their own religion and traditions, but felt themselves forced into the public schools. Look, their argument ran, we agree on universal education, but let us educate our children in parochial schools, keeping our religion and values alive, passing our torch to the next generation. By taxing us for the public schools, the government makes us pay twice, shoving us toward the public schools, there to socialize our children in alien values, tending to extinguish our religion. Our parochial schools are an integral part of our church, essential to its survival, and by putting a price on our schools, the government denies us religious toleration. At the least, pay some money back through public aid to sectarian schools.

Certainly, they had one thing right. Those laws against aid to sectarian schools often reflected an anti-Catholic bias. Yet perhaps their argument pushed too far. By this time, the public schools no longer taught from the New England Primer, no longer inculcated Protestantism, but at most said a non-denominational prayer and read a few Bible verses, which hardly amounted to intolerance toward Catholics. And so their opponents responded the government not promoting an anti-Catholic agenda, just not assisting the Catholic agenda. All paid taxes alike for the public schools, Catholics not selected out. Yet perhaps these comebacks did not entirely deflect the Catholics' point. They weren't asking for aid, they said, only exemption from coercion, not being forced into the public schools by taxation. Moreover, few Protestants churches had schools, almost all the sectarian schools being Catholic. So while impartial on their face, in fact the taxes fell disproportionately on them.

But there was still another aspect to this argument. In those days, the public schools served as vital to the American "melting pot," socializing millions of immigrants in a common culture, starting with the English language, going on to instill attitudes favorable to democracy and free-markets. Religious toleration may have been a value, but many saw a competing value, socialization in a common culture, thus promoting a basis for cooperation, while canceling out the antagonisms immigrant groups cherished for each other, antagonisms transported from their homelands. In this view, the Catholic Irish asked too much, refusing to join in the common culture, holding themselves excessively apart, not amalgamating, perpetuating the conflicts of the Reformation. In the end, then, did toleration prohibit government assistance to sectarian schools or require it? Both sides possessed a certain justice.

Then take the same argument over shifting ground. As we will see, shortly the Supreme Court will thoroughly secularize the public schools, expelling all religions alike. Surely this remedy looks fair to everyone, not favoring one religion over another. Yet while secularism not a formal ideology, rather a viewpoint, and may be neutral among religions, it is far from neutral toward them, always at odds, often hostile to their beliefs. Then to stick with the Catholics for a moment, secularizing the public schools answered their old complaint not at all, leaving them still forced into the public schools by taxation, still forced into a process of socialization in an uncongenial viewpoint.

And as secularism took over the public schools, many Protestants suddenly discovered they shared the grievance. The familiar controversy over evolution versus creationism illustrates. Secularists say biology a science, evolution an accepted theory of that science, creationism not, and therefore, creationism lacks any place in a biology course. All well and good, but does that mean creationism can have no place in the curriculum whatsoever, that to teach about creationism except to condemn the falsity endorses religion, violating the separation of church and state? If so, then the public schools can only teach the secular viewpoint. But doesn't that amount to government endorsement of secularism, government condemnation of religion? While the secularists may claim the result "neutral" and religious toleration, who doubts the existence of underlying motives, a motive as suspect as the old Protestant hostility to Catholics, which drove the old movement against aid to sectarian schools? Who doubts a scheme of many secularists to socialize all children in secularism, thus defeating all religion, secularizing the society?

All of which should make evident the complexity. Whatever the stated general rule on religious toleration, logic will not answer such questions, any more than logic solved the Dedham Church schism in 1820. Real-world complexity demands a detailed application, which will depend upon a choice between competing values. Then as a matter of law, some institution must state the general legal rule, and some institution must carry out the detailed application, making the value-laden choices. So as always with political science, the issue comes back to which institution gets the power. As seen, the Founders largely left this authority with the state legislatures and democratic processes. But shortly the Court will seize that authority, and in the familiar pattern, the judicial process will reach very different conclusions about religious toleration.

The politics of religion – Religious affiliation cannot but reflect in a myriad of other affiliations, helping form the basis for cooperation, but at the same time entangling with cultural alignments and political factions. In a perfectly natural way, people carry their religion into the political arena, doctrine supplying the value-laden arguments, the churches institutional coherence. But once in that partisan boxing ring, the ritualized rules brutalize the fight. Inside those ropes, the pugilists cannot resist aiming low blows at their foes' underbelly, acting on the maxim that to kill the body will kill the head, and religion got the same rough treatment. To take a defunct and graphic example of this style: Don't elect a Catholic president because he will take orders from the Pope. Such artful punches hit below the belt, looking to unman the opponent, calling in question his fundamentals. Gradually such attacks accumulated, religion getting drawn into the free-for-all, punched like any other part of the anatomy that came to hand.

Really, history was repeating itself, reminiscent of those earlier brawls over the Church of England, much for the same reasons, employing much the same tactics. In those bygone days in England, the dissenters and nonconformists had been a growing force, at odds with the "established" church and each other, facing off on all sorts of fronts, the then current political, economic, class, and cultural antagonisms. Now in present-day America, religious diversity was on the rise, similarly in conflict over current political, economic, class, and cultural antagonisms. Just as the argument for religious toleration came in handy then, it came in handy now, as a way to hurt the other guy, while claiming the ethical high ground.

We should be only too familiar with how all this works. In small town America, the local Presbyterian, Baptist, or Methodist church likely voted as a clique, often highly influential in the town, tending to excite a degree of hostility in the breasts of other factions. In the cities, a Catholic parish likely corresponded with an Irish or Polish precinct, which voted a party line, tending to excite a degree of hostility in the other party. And so it went, Protestants, Catholics, Jews, secularists, all facing off, lending their support to factions, parties, and coalitions, exciting mutual enmity. It was only a step to raising the hue and cry "separation of church and state" against the foe. Protestants opposed parochial schools as violating the principle; Catholics demanded assistance on the same principle; Jews and secularists stood against both on the same principle. But these conflicts were not merely over religion, but over politics and power.

Yet no mobs swarmed out of the *banlieues* to storm the Bastille of the old Protestant "establishment" nor would crowds march in the streets, as for example rallied for desegregation. Nevertheless, backing was out there, non-Christians happy enough to see Christianity taken down a peg, Christians a house divided, various players anxious to kick the Christian props out from under their adversaries.

But this movement went forward very much top-down, not bottom-up, the driving force a collaborative effort between academic, intellectual, and legal elites, who generated the agitprop and propelled the cause through the courts. Nor were their motives or choice of venue hard to understand. Leaving aside some survivals, universities had long left behind their Christian origins, having become secular institutions, competing with rather than promoting religion, and universities had multiplied mightily in number and influence. For at least as long, free-floating intellectuals have been in the business of constantly re-inventing the latest worldview, habitually at odds with any nostrums other than their own, and so pervasively hostile to religion. Academia, the intelligentsia, and the religious, these organize in separate camps, but the first two as generally allied by their disagreements with the third. Not surprisingly, then, they made common cause, standing shoulder to shoulder to shove against the Christians. The lawyers formed still another camp, which took the same side for equally obvious reasons: First, their ranks contained a strong contingent of those same academics and intellectuals; second, lawyers are always keen for more judicial power, since judicial power always translated into professional prestige and professional business.

Here was an impressive iron triangle, academics, intellectuals, and lawyers, forged together out of mutual interests. But victory could not come through mass conversion of the electorate, since most of the people stubbornly Christian, which blocked the democratic way. But forcing that barrier was fortunately unnecessary, since entry by the judicial gate offered as an alternative. By a happy coincidence, secularization coincided with the judicial will-to-power. By creating a new doctrine of "religious rights," re-defining religious toleration, the Court would ascend in power. All the pieces in this puzzle fit together in a familiar pattern.

Of course, no one blazoned their banners "anti-Christian" or "anti-religious." Rather they marched under slogans proclaiming "equality" and "religious toleration," claiming to advance even-handedness for all, claiming Christianity suffering disproportionately only due to her prominence. Perhaps all this was not untrue; perhaps those who advocated the change were right. After all, society was no longer as it had been. Measures appropriate to another day might no longer be so appropriate. By the 1930s, the old Protestant establishment was on the wane, Catholics the largest single church, Jews a rising influence, many secular in outlook. Perhaps further change was in order. But our purpose focuses on the political processes, particularly the role of the Court. And so we cannot but notice four things: First, the Constitution in no way mandated the change, which rested on a choice among policy alternatives simply not addressed in the Constitution. Second, the change involved a switch from democratic process to judicial process. Third, this shift in method significantly shifted the outcomes, the Court taking a path the legislatures would never have taken. Fourth, once again the Court took the side coinciding with the judicial will-to-power and acquired more power.

The wall of separation – In 1947, the Everson Case re-interpreted the "establishment clause" of the 1st Amendment and made a highly appealing metaphor part of the language, the "wall of separation between church and state." But if such a wall had earlier existed, Everson re-located the wall and changed the guard. After Everson, the wall kept out not just the national government, but the state governments; after Everson, the wall blocked not just an established church, but any "aid" to religion; and after Everson, the justices now guarded the wall.

As future cases worked out the details, these alterations would permanently alter America's long-standing religious settlement. Christianity lost an influence long exercised through the state legislatures, America becoming a more secularized state through the judicial process. While once again, the Supreme Court ascended in power, leveling the pretensions of the states, leveling, too, the pretensions of Christianity, making clear the Court's supremacy over all comers, even over religion, historically a touchy and potent adversary.

Everson began in New Jersey, where the legislature had passed a law to assist private, non-profit schools with transportation costs, including religiously affiliated schools, which especially benefitted the numerous Catholic parochial schools. This statute read: "Whenever ... there are children living remote from any schoolhouse, the board of education of the district may make ... contracts for the transportation of such children to and from school, including the transportation of school children to and from school other than a public school, except such a school as is operated for profit."[27] Thus, a school board could elect to spend tax monies in such a way as aided a church run school.

Justice Hugo L. Black crafted the opinion for the Court. "The New Jersey statute," he began, "is challenged as a 'law respecting an establishment of religion.' The First Amendment, as made applicable to the states by the Fourteenth ... commands that a state 'shall make no law respecting an establishment of religion or prohibiting the free exercise thereof.'"[28]

In these two sentences, which sound so matter of fact, Justice Black has just re-interpreted settled doctrine, changing constitutional law, in effect amending the Constitution. We see this result by recalling that the "establishment clause" restrained *only the federal government*, while he is saying the clause applies *against the states*. As quoted and discussed extensively, the 1st Amendment does not say "*no state* shall establish a religion," rather saying "*Congress* shall make no law respecting an establishment of religion." But Justice Black has chopped out the key word "*Congress*," substituting the word "*state*." He has ruled that: "The First Amendment ... commands that *a state* 'shall make no law respecting an establishment of religion.'"

By this simple exchange of words, *state* replacing *Congress*, the power moves, transferred from the states to the national government, in practical effect to the Court. If the establishment clause only applies against congressional laws, that clause cannot apply to a law passed by the New Jersey legislature. Ergo, the Supreme Court totally lacks authority to declare unconstitutional the New Jersey statute. As a further absolute corollary, if the Court wanted to declare the statute unconstitutional, first they had to seize the power to do so. Justice Black has just executed such a coup. He has claimed control over church-and-state for his Court.

What about his rationale? Black wrote: "The First Amendment, *as made applicable to the states by the Fourteenth [Amendment]* ... commands that a state 'shall make no law respecting an establishment of religion." He is saying the 14th Amendment made the 1st Amendment applicable against the states, binding them as well as the federal government. To check that assertion, look back at the 14th Amendment, which reads: "*No State* shall make or enforce any law which shall abridge the privileges or immunities of citizens ... nor shall any State deprive any person of life, liberty, or property, without due process of law; nor deny to any person ... the equal protection of the laws."

That looks good for Justice Black, since it says "no state," but at least three difficulties lurk in the way of his conclusion. First comes the evident purpose of the 14th Amendment, which when ratified in 1868, meant to confer civil rights on the freedmen, nothing suggesting an intent to extend the establishment clause against the states. Second comes prior judicial interpretations, which until this very hour never so construed the Amendment, leaving in place the existing religious settlement. Third comes the express wording of the 1st Amendment: "*Congress* shall make no law respecting an establishment of religion," limiting the federal government, not the states.

Once more the discussion tangles with the tortured history of the 14th Amendment. In an earlier chapter, we saw Congress intended to protect the freedmen's rights, as part of that program arguably making the Bill of Rights, including the 1st Amendment, applicable against the states. But we also saw the Supreme Court earlier blocked that purpose, interpreting away the guarantees. In fact, back in 1873 in the Slaughter-House Cases, Justice Samuel Freeman Miller explicitly rejected the very view just affirmed by Justice Black, ruling the 14th Amendment *did not* make the Bill of Rights applicable to the states. But finally in the last half of the twentieth century, the Court has begun to change its mind through a process known as "incorporation." They have gradually begun to reverse their prior rule, finding that the 14th Amendment "incorporates" the Bill of Rights against the states, making select provisions apply to them.

Already in the 1943 Murdock Case,[29] the Court had "incorporated" the "free exercise clause." Here in Everson, we encounter another prime example of this technique, the "incorporation" of the "establishment clause."

And surely all of this is well and good? Let the will of Congress and the people finally go through, at last applying the Bill of Rights across the nation. Of course, one might still argue the establishment clause a bad candidate for such a process, the terms being specifically limited to "*Congress.*" Nevertheless, let plausible reasoning pass muster. None of the states have established churches anyway, none wish to establish a church, none think they should.

Except Justice Black does not stop there. He is hunting bigger game. He next says: "The 'establishment of religion' clause of the First Amendment means at least this: Neither a state nor the Federal Government can set up a church. Neither can pass laws which aid one religion, aid all religions, or prefer one religion over another. ... No tax in any amount, large or small, can be levied to support any religious activities or institutions ... In the words of Jefferson, the clause against establishment of religion by law was intended to erect 'a wall of separation between Church and State.'"[30]

The quote from Jefferson leaps off the page, "a wall of separation between church and state," a potent and appealing metaphor. In an 1802 letter to the Baptists in Danbury, Connecticut, Jefferson had written: "Believing with you that religion is a matter which lies solely between man and his God ... I contemplate with sovereign reverence that act of the whole American people which declared that their legislature should 'make no law respecting an establishment of religion, or prohibiting the free exercise thereof,' thus building a wall of separation between church and state."[31] His words echo the earlier language from Roger Williams quoted above, with which Jefferson was perhaps familiar. And incidentally, Jefferson was a much more radical exponent of separation between church and state than almost any other Founding Father.

But a new meaning back-loaded into the old metaphor does the real work. This occurs when Justice Black says: "Neither [a state or the federal government] can pass laws which aid one religion, aid all religions, or prefer one religion over another." When we unpack the implication, we discover not only has he suddenly applied the "establishment clause" against the states, but as suddenly re-defined what amounts to an "establishment" of religion. The "establishment clause" meant to prevent an established church, an official state church, buttressed as the Church of England by a set of laws. The negative went no further. But abruptly, Justice Black rules the "establishment clause" not only forbids such an established church, but all "aid" to religion. What exactly does this portend?

From Everson itself we hardly know, since after having gone to all this trouble, Justice Black does not strike down the New Jersey law at all. Instead, he passes that statute right through his constitutional portal, saying: "We must ... be careful, in protecting the citizens of New Jersey against state-established churches, to be sure that we do not inadvertently prohibit New Jersey from extending its general State law benefits to all its citizens without regard to their religious belief. ... [W]e cannot say that the First Amendment prohibits New Jersey from spending tax-raised funds to pay the bus fares of parochial school pupils as a part of a general program under which it pays the fares of pupils attending public and other schools."[32]

That is, the "wall of separation" appears a leaky as ever, hardly an impermeable barrier. This perhaps rather surprising result brought forth a memorably amusing dissent from Justice Robert Houghwout Jackson, who wrote: "[T]he undertones of the opinion, advocating complete and uncompromising separation of Church from State, seem utterly discordant with its conclusion yielding support to their commingling in educational matter. The case which inevitably comes to mind as the most fitting precedent is that of Julia who, according to Byron's reports, 'whispering "I will ne'er consent," consented.'"[33]

Raising the wall of separation – Once again the Court had seized without really exercising power, much as back in 1803 in Marbury v Madison, where Justice Marshall claimed judicial review, but put that doctrine too little practical use. But just as in Marbury, a power once asserted will later expand, nor would there be long to wait. In the next years, the Court would quickly clarify what qualified as "aid" to religion, totally re-ordering the prior religious settlement.

In the 1948 McCollum Case, Justice Black again crafts the opinion. The facts originate out of Champaign, Illinois, where in 1940, an interdenominational group of Protestants, Catholics, and Jews formed the Champaign Council on Religious Education. They obtained permission from the board of education to offer religious classes in the public schools, grades four through nine, held during time-release periods to avoid conflicting with regular lessons. Interested parents could sign up their children. The interdenominational group paid for the teachers and supplies. This sounds somewhat like the reform earlier advocated, making religion a subject in the curriculum, letting those viewpoints tell their own story.

But this time Justice Black lowered the boom in a few short words.

"This is beyond all question a utilization of the tax-established and tax-supported public school system to aid religious groups to spread their faith. And it falls squarely under the ban of the First Amendment ... as we interpreted it in Everson."[34]

In dissent, Justice Stanley Forman Reed vainly protested: "Well-recognized and long-established practices support the validity of the Illinois statute ... . That statute ... is comparable to those in many states. ... Cases running into the scores have been in the state courts of last resort ... . Except where the exercises with religious significance partook of the ceremonial practice of sects or groups, their constitutionally has been generally upheld."[35]

Next came the 1962 Engel v Vitale Case out of the great state of New York. In 1951 and again in 1955, the New York State Board of Regents recommended that each school day commence with the Pledge of Allegiance to the Flag and the following prayer: "Almighty God, we acknowledge our dependence upon Thee, and we beg Thy blessings upon us, and our parents, our teachers and our Country."[36]

The New York state courts saw no constitutional defect, but made clear no children should participate against their will. Chief Judge Desmond wrote: "Not only is this prayer not a violation of the First Amendment, ... but a holding that it is such a violation would be in defiance of all American history ... . The 'Regent's Prayer' ... includes an acknowledgment of the existence of a Supreme Being just as does the Declaration of Independence and the Constitutions of each of the 50 States of the Union, including our own. ... No historical fact is so easy to prove by literally countless illustrations as the fact that belief and trust in a Supreme Being was from the beginning and has been continuously part of the very essence of the American plan of government and society. The references to the Deity in the Declaration of Independence; the words of our National Anthem; 'In God is our trust', the motto on our coins; the daily prayers in Congress; the universal practice in official oaths of calling upon God to witness the truth; the official thanksgiving proclamations beginning with those of the Continental Congress and the First Congress of the United States and continuing till the present; ... the directions by Congress in modern times for a National Day of Prayer and for the insertion of the words 'under God' in the Pledge of Allegiance to the Flag; innumerable solemn utterances by our Presidents and other leaders --- all of these make historically inescapable the flat statement [by the Supreme Court itself in the 1952 Zorach Case] that: 'We are a religious people whose institutions presuppose a Supreme Being', which paraphrased the Supreme Court's similar assertion in 1892 in the Holy Trinity Church case."[37]

But up at the Supreme Court, Justice Black again had the last word: "We think that by using its public school system to encourage recitation of the Regents' prayer, the State of New York has adopted a practice wholly inconsistent with the Establishment Clause."[38] Justice Potter Stewart's dissent drew attention to the fact a brief prayer hardly amounted to the establishment of a religion: "I cannot see how an 'official religion' is established by letting those who want to say a prayer say it. On the contrary, I think that to deny the wish of these school children to join in reciting this prayer is to deny them the opportunity of sharing in the spiritual heritage of our Nation."[39]

In the 1964 School District of Abington Case, the issue involved Bible reading in the schools. In 1960, Pennsylvania passed a statute reading: "At least ten verses from the Holy Bible shall be read, without comment, at the opening of each public school on each school day. Any child shall be excused from such Bible reading, or attending such Bible reading, upon the written request of his parent or guardian."[40] As long ago as 1905, Maryland had enacted a similar statute.

Justice Tom Clark writes the opinion: "It is true that religion has been closely identified with our history and government. ... [In a 1952 case] we gave specific recognition to the proposition that '[w]e are a religious people whose institutions presupposes a Supreme Being.' The fact that the Founding Fathers believed devoutly that there was a God and that the unalienable rights of man were rooted in Him is clearly evidenced in their writings, from the Mayflower Compact to the Constitution itself."[41] But he goes on: "We agree ... as to the religious character of the exercises. Given that finding, the exercises and the law requiring them are in violation of the Establishment Clause."[42]

Other cases followed in rapid succession. In 1980, Stone v Graham[43] ruled Kentucky could not post the Ten Commandments on classroom walls. In 1985, Wallace v Jaffree[44] held Alabama could not have a one-minute period of silence "for meditation or voluntary prayer." In 1987, Edwards v Aguillard[45] chastised Louisiana for teaching creationism alongside evolution. In 1992, Lee v Weisman[46] prohibited benedictions at high graduation ceremonies. In 2000, the Sante Fe Case[47] struck down student-led prayer at high school football games.

In these decades the Court articulated several new rules under the "establishment clause," continually striving for a perfect, self-explanatory formula, which as continually eluded. In 1971 in the Lemon Case, the Court set forth what became known as the Lemon Test, which had three prongs: "First, the statute must have a secular legislative purpose; second, its principle or primary effect must be one that neither advances nor inhibits religion; ... finally, the statute must not foster 'an excessive government entanglement with religion.'"[48] In 1984 in Lynch v Donnelly,[49] Justice Sandra Day O'Connor authored an "endorsement test," under which government action must not be perceived as either endorsing or disproving a religion.

It is needless to go into the details, since just as with Everson, the announced doctrines never counted as much as the spirit of the application. While Everson had managed to reason around the new ban against "aid" to religion, approving state funds for sectarian schools, these future cases managed to reason the other way around, looking with disfavor on Christian influence. As usual, not the surface logic, but the logic under the surface counted for more. The working hypothesis became that any mention of Christianity in a public context threatened litigation, where Christianity likely lost, the judges awarding rich fees to the suing lawyers, paid out of the public till. Christianity assumed the posture of a supplicant before the courts, constantly haled before the bar by public-interest lawyers, as constantly rebuked by the judiciary, both professing to act as defenders of "the separation of church and state."

Religious institutions – Coming to compare institutional performance, we find not so much a conflict for power between governmental institutions, as between a branch of government and a set of non-government institutions, the judiciary against the churches. At all levels, the institutional will-to-power continues to operate, while the Court's institutional will-to-power continues to operate at variance with Congress and the states, the judicial process reaching far different outcomes than the democratic process. The federal government aggrandizes more power, acquiring a power initially reserved to the states by taking control over religion, but all the gain goes to the judicial branch. In a unique turn of events, the Court also turns upon a competing power-center outside government, the churches. After all, a more secular state amounts to a more powerful state, one with a traditional rival weakened. Yet no such effort could have succeeded through Congress, where the churches' own institutional will-to-power exerted strong pull, and in fact, Congress voiced some faint protests. The same applied to the states, which endeavored somewhat more resistance. But in a familiar pattern, the Court held the balance-of-power between the competing factions and easily brushed aside this opposition. As a matter of power politics, the justices again took the side coincident with their judicial will-to-power, and their Court once again ascended in power.

Considered from this institutional perspective, while typically described in terms of dogma and doctrine, organized religion obviously rests upon institutional foundations, and Christianity copied from

Judaism a powerful institutional model. Both are religions of the book; both exhort to constant study of the book; both exhort to constant prayer; both set aside a holy day each week; both designate places devoted to worship; both require attendance at services on the holy day; both designate a priesthood; in both the priesthood teaches and deliver sermons; both insist on donations. In combination, these elements weld together a potent and persistent institution form that goes far to explain their influence, not to mention their success and survival.

We hear a great deal about the superior Judeo-Christian ethical message as compared to Greco-Roman paganism, but should also notice this institutional advantage. Paganism lacked similar coherence, relying on a welter of contradictory myths, their theology as confused as their pantheon of gods, their cults locally dispersed, their priesthood irregularly constituted, their festivals scattered days, their rituals no more than libation and sacrifice. By contrast, the Judeo-Christian model delivered a lucid story line, regularly reinforced by priests vested in the plot, the lessons further reinforced by daily prayer, the donations keeping up the priesthood and physical plant. These mutually reinforcing mechanisms bonded the members, the institution solid and self-perpetuating.

As a proselytizing religion, Christianity went still further, copying the Romans as well as the Jews, adapting Roman political organization to grow their church. Just as Rome stretched a governmental hierarchy across the empire, the Christians stretched a church hierarchy. Rome gathered municipalities into provinces, provinces into the empire, all roads leading to Rome. Christianity gathered local churches under bishops, provincial churches under archbishops, the whole church under the pope, also at Rome. No wonder Christianity surpassed Judaism and supplanted paganism, the institutional form more encompassing than the first, more solid than the second.

These Judeo-Christian institutional methods have enjoyed a long run of success. If imitation is the sincerest flattery, Islam long ago paid that compliment, adopting the same techniques with equal success. But while Judaism, Christianity, and Islam promote cooperation internally, just like political institutions they tend to conflict externally, not just with each other, but with any other institution in their way. So quite naturally religion and government have frequently collided. Also in the nature of things, religion and government have frequently found collaboration more convenient, leading to some sort of alliance. An "established" church was no more than such a treaty. But again just as in politics, the partners in such coalitions have proved ready to turn on each other, when one weakens, stronger allies offer, or convenience suggests betrayal.

State and church cooperation and conflict – By now this is an old story. As an example of the conflicts, we might remember Roman persecution of Christianity; as an example of the mutuality, we might remember Constantine's conversion, which whatever the sincerity, co-opted the youthful, vibrant institutions of Christianity to prop up the senile, crumbling institutions of the Roman state. The same conflict and cooperation made up a constant theme throughout the Middle Ages, as monarchs and the papacy alternatively fought and made common cause. In 1077, the Holy Roman Emperor Henry IV stands a bareheaded supplicant in the snow at Canossa, brought to heel by Pope Gregory VII's excommunication, the quarrel over investiture, whether emperor or pope controlled the clergy. In 1303, an army of French King Philip IV seizes the person of Pope Boniface VIII, who is slapped in the face when he refuses to resign the papacy, the argument over the king's right to tax the clergy. But just as often church and state moved together. In 1066, William the Conqueror imposes a Norman regime on England, the church integral to his machinery of government. In 1685, the French King Louis XIV revokes the Edict of Nantes, withdrawing toleration from Protestants, working hand in glove with the Catholic Church to combat their mutually unruly subjects, the Huguenots. But coming to this early modern era, more and more the kings succeed in centralizing their states, and growing stronger, more and more succeed in reducing the church's influence over their governments. During the Reformation, local rulers provided crucial support to the Protestants, turning against the Roman church, using the schism to throw off her authority, so expanding the ruler's authority. As the obverse of that coin, other rulers staunchly upheld Rome, together resisting the Protestants, who menaced the established political order as much as the established church.

What are the Court's religious cases except this same old story, revised edition? Initially, the "Protestant establishment" and the government cooperated, Christianity preaching the value of democracy, the government promoting Christianity. But in the mid-twentieth century, the old establishment weakened, and the Court seized the day. Just as Reformation monarchs took advantage of the attacks on the Catholic Church, the Court took advantage of the attacks on the old establishment. Just as the kings went into alliance with the Protestants, the justices went into alliance with a rising opposition. Just as the kings thereby acquired power, the Court thereby acquired power. In 1947 with Everson, the power moved, not just shifting from the states to the Court, but from the churches to the Court, all religion firmly placed under judicial suzerainty. Christianity had exercised strong influence through the legislative process, but as the future cases would show, from now on the Court trumped the churches, and the Court's values would differ significantly from the churches' values. In whatever sense we might still refer to America as a "Christian Nation," it is certainly not in the old sense. Today America is a secular nation, Christianity far less influential. It is not too much to say that America is no longer "one nation under God," but "one nation under law," and the Supreme Court lays down that law.

Toleration and complexity – But was this change an advance in religious toleration or the reverse? Our conclusions will generally depend upon our preconceptions, which will as generally depend upon our cultural and institutional, not to mention partisan affiliations and interests. Of course, the Court's supporters proclaim toleration their exclusive property. Yet surely the issue never presented quite so starkly, never really tolerance versus intolerance, but competing concepts of toleration. In the first place, Christians might complain everybody knew the rules going in. America was a Christian Nation where that religion enjoyed prominence and influence. So if others emigrated into the existing social contract, they took that clause as part of the bargain. Nor were the terms onerous, such things as prayer in school or celebrating Christmas hardly amounting to persecution. Then too, democracy was another clause in the social contract. So if you wanted to re-negotiate, you negotiated with the people, rather than suing them; the parties could mutually re-define the religious covenants at any time. Whence then the need for the lawyers to do what they do so well, cleverly re-interpreting the language, re-writing the original contract with judicial interpretation?

In the last analysis, a diversity of religions flourished, as did secularism. American already ran as a religiously tolerant nation. If we confess so much plausible, the Court's supporters lose their claim to self-evident righteousness, and instead we see in the Court's cases a combination of less laudable motives, a desire to strike at political opponents, delegitimizing Christian participation, and on the part of the secularists a scheme to thoroughly expunge religion from the public sphere, leaving her with a mark of disapproval on her forehead, presumably to wither away through impotence. In this light, we see in the Court's cases another species of intolerance. The Court was not really neutral; the Court condemned Christianity. It held Christians had acted unconstitutionally, violating fundamental constitutional values, attempting to deny religious freedom to others. By expelling all religion from the public schools, as much as possible from the public square, it gave victory to the secularists.

What America had in hand was a complex social and political

problem, caused by demographic shifts, technological innovation, and the rise of new institutions. Recall what Washington said: "[R]eason and experience both forbid us to expect that National morality can prevail in exclusion of religious principle." He might be taken to mean only fear of an omniscient God keeps people to the straight and narrow. But his concern also reflects a commonplace observation: Traditionally religion served as a primary mechanism of ongoing socialization. In the language of modern sociology, religion socialized in culture and ethical values. In Biblical times, what was a Jew except someone socialized by the Jewish religion into the Jewish culture? In medieval Europe, Catholicism similarly inculcated culture. In America in Washington's day, the churches still performed this function. When we also recall how Jewish and Christian institutions work, we see how this identity comes about, those institutions socializing in the culture, getting everybody on the same page, keeping them there. If religion weakened, no longer performing that function of socialization, Washington felt the morality of the culture would similarly weaken.

But over time, the old Protestant establishment had in fact weakened as a force in socialization. At the time of the Constitution, Protestant churches filled the landscape. No other institutions significantly competed; few schools existed, fewer universities; government performed few tasks. By the 1930s, a diversity of religions crowd in, Catholicism the largest denomination, Jews highly influential; public schools cover the nation, as do universities; government fills up much more space. And another totally unanticipated force appears on the scene, the new technological media, radio, movies, and shortly television, which deliver a steady stream of highly persuasive messaging. All are game changers. In that earlier time, Protestants had the playing field almost to themselves, now Catholics and Jews field sides, the public school and universities suit up teams, the government referees everything, and media inserts in the lineup a four-hundred pound gorilla. Then how do all these players fit together to play the game?

In American history the three most important institutional sets had been representative democracy, free-markets, and Christianity. This is no more than descriptive, and it is also no more than descriptive to say that these three sets were woven together in mutually supportive ways. All three promoted cooperation, cooperated with each other, and avoided conflict. But the situation alters. Gradually a diversity of religions comes to speak with somewhat discordant voices, tending to a degree of conflict. Public schools and universities fail to deliver the same coherent, life-long socialization as offered by Judeo-Christian methods. Media lack any values not supplied by the profit-motive. Then how do all these cooperate or conflict? How does socialization get done? How does "national morality prevail?"

The answer was that no one knew, and whatever their protestations, no one could know. Due to the complexity, the system eludes predictability. Nor did the 1st Amendment address such unforeseen issues. But the Constitution did contain an algorithm to churn out the solution. Having prohibited an "established church," the Constitution left the answers up to the democratic process. Then if Everson was anything, it was imposing a top-down solution upon complexity, purporting to deduce from the "establishment clause" a response simply not given there, not only changing the original intent about religion, but changing the original intent about democracy, transferring power from the elected legislatures to the unelected judiciary.

CHAPTER 12

The Judicial Revolution

Brown and Everson launched the "judicial revolution." In a whole series of cases, the Court revolutionized the law, as already seen about race and religion, but soon about a lengthening list of individual and minority rights. And "revolution" a revealing term. Proclaiming "rights," revolutions seize power, but only the rights that justify the seizure, not other rights. Nor did the judicial revolution fail in this respect, being really a counter-revolution, where the Court re-claimed lost powers, proclaiming rights, but only the rights that justified re-claiming the lost powers, not other rights. During the judicial revolution, whenever a right triumphed, the Court triumphed, and no right otherwise triumphed.

The longing for judicial supremacy – Already back in 1938, Footnote Four had issued the cautiously worded, lawyerly manifesto for a counter-revolution. Even as the justices bent the knee to the New Deal, they could not but regret the lost freedom. Having long ago emancipated themselves from the chains of "clear-cut" cases, having long enjoyed the freedom to void laws at will, reluctantly they fit back on those rusty fetters, pledging to "presume" laws constitutional in future. Giving into the iron of political expediency, they submitted to the superior force so masterly gathered into President Roosevelt's hands, who was running a successful revolution of his own. In the Carolene Case, they stayed as good as their word, upholding a congressional law. Yet with Footnote Four they appealed against the servitude, while prudently putting off further confrontation, speaking with studied indirection.

To re-read Justice Harlin Fiske Stone's careful words: "There may be narrower scope for operation of the presumption of constitutionality when legislation appears on its face to be within a specific prohibition of the Constitution, such as those of the [Bill of Rights.]

"It is unnecessary to consider now whether legislation which restricts those political processes which can ordinarily be expected to bring about repeal of undesirable legislation, is to be subjected to more exacting judicial scrutiny ... Nor need we inquire whether similar considerations enter into the review of statutes directed at a particular religion ... or national ... or racial minorities ... whether prejudice against discrete and insular minorities may be a special condition, which tends seriously to curtail the operation of those political processes ordinarily to be relied upon to protect minorities, and which may call for a correspondingly more searching judicial inquiry."

This looked to the future, saying "there may be" and "it is unnecessary to consider now," but longed for the past. All the Court's earlier great and famous cases had claimed to repeal "undesirable legislation," claimed to defend some "prohibition in the Constitution," claimed to defend individual and minority rights. Except since such rights not clear-cut, they had all had to rely on "a narrower scope for the operation of the presumption of constitutionality," that is, not to presume laws constitutional, but freely engage in implication. From 1857 in Dred Scott all the way to the New Deal, such freedom had let the Court repeatedly imply rights. But now they had just pledged to presume constitutionality again, leaving off such implication. Then when Justice Stone mused "there may be narrower scope for operation of the presumption of constitutionality," what could "narrower" contemplate, if not a return to what the Court had done all along, a return to the freedom of implication? He was imagining a way back to the future, back to such judicial freedom in the future.

But Footnote Four not only longed for lost freedom, the idea sought to recruit support, appealed to habitual ways of thought and doing politics and offered potent incentives to join the cause. People like deductive, top-down logic, particularly ethical logic, and they like deductive, top-down politics when the deductions go their way. Throughout American history, no one ever failed to deduce their rights, then demand their rights. Except democracy works inductively, bottom-up, sorting out rights through elections, much to the dismay of losers, who continue to believe in their deductions. But the Court had come to offer an alternative. Losers could appeal to the Court, which could side with them, deducing their rights from the Constitution, reversing inductive loses with deductive wins. Who would not prefer such top-down, deductive politics when the top sides with their deductions and forces their conclusions down?

Look no farther than the great and famous cases to see the logic. Before the Civil War, the South deduced a right to slavery, but looked likely to lose the electoral induction. So they appealed to the Court, which rescued their deduction by deducing a right to slavery from the Constitution. During Reconstruction, the Republicans won outright through induction, enacting the freedmen's rights into amendments and laws. But the Court reversed the induction, deducing separate but equal from the Constitution, enacting segregation. In the era of industrialization, when the inductions moved the reformers way, the Court blocked the inductions by deducing rights against the reforms.

Footnote Four floated a prospectus to re-open this well-worn proscriptive right-of-way, inviting fresh litigation to find a way around the sudden closure of the easement. If the gate of substantive due process blocked, find other gates, go through the Bill of Rights, go through other minority rights. So attractive such shortcuts, the public interest lawyers shortly swarmed to file their cases, assisting the Court to level new super-highways, running back to judicial supremacy. So enticing such detours, huge constituencies signed up, putting their causes behind the litigation. Even those who suffered severely in the past showed willing to forgive and forget, as long as the deductions went their way in the future. Picking up momentum, the cases drove toward the judicial revolution. The political traffic grid re-set, going back to top-down, deductive politics.

The need for new legal doctrines – But after the New Deal defeat, after publicly renouncing substantive due process, the Court needed fresh legal doctrines. Nor did such creation prove beyond judicial competence. The Court had given away some of the gears of their power, but kept the engine. By avoiding institutional reform, they kept lifetime tenure, kept judicial review, kept judicial supremacy. Nothing inserted an effective override. Now during the judicial revolution, they only needed to fire back up those cylinders, releasing the horsepower in a fresh direction. So just as in the past they had invented substantive due process, now they invented a doctrine called incorporation, which used the due process clause to "incorporate" the Bill of Rights against the states, that is, make the Bill of Rights applicable against the states, which extended the Court's power over them. Next they invented a doctrine of "fundamental" or "preferred rights," which designated certain rights as worthy of "heightened protection." In turn that worthiness triggered a new requirement for "more exacting scrutiny." That meant the law had to serve a "compelling interest" and in the "least intrusive way." Since no precise standards defined any of these terms, they gave the Court a renewed facility, letting them again void laws at will.

A full enumeration of the cases would demand a treatise, so let a short-list serve, selecting typical and prominent cases, enough to show the method and the scope. In 1957 with the Roth Case, the Court begins to do away with the earlier laws that had restrained obscenity. In 1966 with the Miranda Case, the Court changes the law on confessions, the leading case in the "criminal procedure revolution." In 1969 with Shapiro v Thompson, the Court defends the rights of welfare recipients, one of several cases putting a new type of rights, "entitlements," under strict judicial protection. In 1976 with Elrod v Burns, the Court virtually eliminates patronage, mandating a thorough-going civil service system, replacing legislative and executive authority to hire and fire bureaucrats with a constitutional right to employment. While in 1973 with Roe v Wade, the Court holds the Constitution protects a right to an abortion, enhancing the concept of a constitutional right to privacy under judicial control.

Through such cases the Court won the judicial revolution, re-gaining their lost judicial freedom, re-ascending in power. To win they would simply follow the same formula they had followed to win their earlier successes, the same formula they followed during Reconstruction, industrialization, and segregation. As the first step, the factions in the democratic arena conflict over some right. As the second step, one side wins the electoral contest over the right. As the third step, the losers appeal to the Court. As the fourth and final step, the Court rules for the losers, reversing the outcome by finding the losers' rights implied in the Constitution. But the Court only takes the fourth step, only reverses the outcome, when the implied right also increases judicial power. By this winning formula, the Court sorts out winners and losers, while the Court never loses, and Congress and the states never win.

Defining obscenity – Obscenity seems to require no introduction, since all think they know it when they see it. But like all definitions outside the pure sciences, obscenity eludes a precise definition. One may find a working formula, but not a perfect rule. Moreover, what's the harm? Some might think to know the harm as well, except they can't prove that either with scientific precision. Massive studies assayed the effort, but where one researcher found harm, the next researcher found no harm, back and forth, which strongly suggests bias throwing off objectivity, a familiar effect when a lot on the line, and so a lot must be on the line. While if no one could demonstrate the harm of obscenity, no one really tried to demonstrate the benefits.

So in attacking the obscenity laws, free speech advocates preferred to attack the definition, seldom contending for the benefits of obscenity. Their argument went this way: Since no exact definition of obscenity possible, any law against obscenity stays inexact. As a practical result, obscenity laws constantly condemn works with social or artistic merit. Therefore, the only effective remedy is to eliminate the vagueness by eliminating the laws, thus guaranteeing free speech.

If this logic was flawed, yet it had a point. They insisted obscenity not sufficiently identifiable to convict, yet insisted social and artistic merit sufficiently identifiable to acquit, but then how did such merit stand out in the lineup? Nevertheless, surely we should favor less restraint on free speech rather than more, erring on the side of caution. Traditionally censorship marks repressive regimes. If as traditionally, dissent and artistic expression go to extremes, better to indulge them, letting the public decide for themselves.

But their arguments never quite convinced the majority, who stubbornly persisted in thinking they knew obscenity when they saw it, a working definition good enough, and backed laws against it. The public persisted in thinking to know the harm as well, thinking obscenity threatened morality, threatened the right to live in a virtuous society. They thought obscenity possessed little if any redeeming social value, obscenity laws not a real hindrance either to a serious social and political dialogue or artistic expression. But the free speech movement would have none of it. While still not usually defending obscenity as such, they came close, portraying such laws as no more than fear, unnaturally repressing natural human sexuality. They repeatedly claimed actual persecution and as repeatedly churned out works that challenged previous limits to prove their point. They demanded the right to live in an open society, free from such irrational restraint.

The 1st Amendment and obscenity – Whoever had the best of this argument, what did the Constitution say? What did the Founding Fathers think about obscenity? And they thought very little of it, since they still thought they knew it when they saw it, and when they thought they saw a pornographer or panderer, they gave short shrift, jailing and fining malefactors. Yet the 1st Amendment memorably said: "Congress shall make no law ... abridging the freedom of speech, or of the press." Did those words not protect obscenity? Not at all, since what they thought obscene outside the guarantee. So much amounted to settled constitutional law, all the way from the Founding to the 1950s. All across America, laws outlawed what thought obscene.

To call upon authority, as late as 1942 in the Chaplinsky Case, the Supreme Court espoused this long-accepted rule, that is, obscenity not protected by the 1st Amendment. Justice Frank Murphy wrote: "Allowing the broadest scope to the language and purpose of the [1st Amendment], it is well understood that the right of free speech is not absolute at all times and under all circumstances. There are certain well-defined and narrowly limited classes of speech, the prevention and punishment of which have never been thought to raise any Constitutional problem.

These include the lewd and obscene, ... It has been well observed that such utterances are no essential part of any exposition of ideas, and are of such slight social value as a step to truth that any benefit that may be derived from them is clearly outweighed by the social interest in order and morality."[1]

But what defined obscenity? In Anglo-American jurisprudence, the best-known definition traced to the 1868 English case, Regina v Hicklin, where Lord Chief Justice Cockburn pronounced: "[T]he test of obscenity ... whether the tendency of the matter charged ... is to deprave and corrupt those whose minds are open to such immoral influences, and into whose hands a publication of this sort may fall."[2]

But increasingly this definition came under attack. Juries sometimes handed down verdicts against works with perceived artistic or social merit. In 1928, one Mary Dennett suffered conviction over a birth control pamphlet, although her conviction later overturned. In 1930, Massachusetts' courts declared obscene Theodore Dreiser's *An American Tragedy* and D.H. Lawrence's *Lady Chatterly's Lover*. However, in 1934 James Joyce's *Ulysses* avoided this fate in federal court, declared non-obscene. The judges expressed concerns over the old rule, as passing judgment upon the effect of isolated passages on the most susceptible, instead suggesting a better standard would measure the effect of the work as a whole upon the average reader.

Defining obscenity away, the Roth Case – Perhaps such a reasonable change, and in 1957, the Supreme Court obliged with the Roth Case, ruling the prior definition unconstitutional. But a definition going so far back, embodied in so many laws, enforced by so many courts, carries a strong presumption of constitutionality. So to drop that long-standing definition, the Court first had to drop that pledge about "the presumption of constitutionality." In short, the Court needed to apply newer rules, which conferred more facility, more power to declare laws unconstitutional. They needed the new doctrines of incorporation and preferred rights.

Nor would the re-definition of obscenity pause at this initial proposal. As later cases quickly re-defined the re-definition, obscenity underwent a complete reversal of fortune. People might still think they knew it when they saw it, but shortly the lack of a perfect legal definition led to a virtual renunciation of all legal definition. Becoming legally un-definable, obscenity virtually ceased legal existence. As a logical consequence, nearly all works previously defined obscene, previously defined outside constitutional protection, now re-defined as inside constitutional protection, re-defined as guaranteed free speech.

The facts in Roth consolidated two cases from the East and West Coast. In New York, one Samuel Roth lent his name to posterity by taking a jury conviction under federal obscenity law, which made a crime out of mailing any "obscene, lewd, lascivious, or filthy book, pamphlet, picture, paper, letter, writing, print, or other publication of an indecent character." In Los Angeles, one David S. Alberts took the fall for violating the California Penal Code, which provided: "Every person who ... "[w]rites, composes, ... prints, publishes, sells, distributes, keeps for sale, or exhibits any obscene, indecent writing, paper, or book" guilty of a misdemeanor.[3]

Up at the Supreme Court, Justice Brennan writes the opinion, beginning: "The constitutionality of a criminal obscenity statute is the question in each of these cases. In Roth, the primary constitutional question is whether the federal obscenity statute violates the provisions of the First Amendment. ... In Alberts, the primary question is whether the obscenity provisions of the California penal code violate the freedoms of speech and press as they may be incorporated in the liberty protected from state action by the Due Process Clause of the Fourteenth Amendment."[4]

Of course, Brennan will hold the due process clause of the 14th Amendment does incorporate the 1st Amendment free speech guarantee against the states. Thus, we see the doctrine of incorporation in action. As the 1st Amendment now applies against the states, the Court's power over the 1st Amendment now applies against the states. Nor should any quarrel with this much, since all agree the states should regard the 1st Amendment.

Next, Justice Brennan acknowledges the long-accepted rule that obscenity not protected speech, writing: "[E]xpressions found in numerous opinions indicate that this Court has always assumed that obscenity is not protected by the freedoms of speech and press."[5]

He amplifies, finally referring, indeed, to the above cited Chaplinsky Case: "The protection given speech and press was fashioned to assure unfettered interchange of ideas for the bringing about of political and social changes desired by the people. ... All ideas having even the slightest redeeming social importance --- unorthodox ideas, controversial ideas, even ideas hateful to the prevailing climate of opinion --- have the full protection of the guaranties, ... But implicit in the history of the First Amendment is the rejection of obscenity as utterly without redeeming social importance. This rejection for that reason is mirrored in the universal judgment that obscenity should be restrained, reflected in the international agreement of over 50 nations, in the obscenity laws of all the 48 States, and in the 20 obscenity laws enacted by the Congress from 1842 to 1956. This is the same judgment expressed by this Court in Chaplinsky v. New Hampshire."[6]

Nothing new appears, as he concludes: "We hold that obscenity is not within the area of constitutionally protected speech or press."[7]

But then he turns to a somewhat obscure explication of fundamental or preferred rights doctrine: "The fundamental freedoms of speech and press have contributed greatly to the development and well-being of our society and are indispensable to continual growth. Ceaseless vigilance is the watchword to prevent their erosion by Congress or the States. The door barring federal intrusion into this area cannot be left ajar; it must be kept closed and opened only the slightest crack necessary to prevent encroachment upon more important interests."[8]

In other words, "the fundamental freedoms of speech and press" amount to fundamental or preferred rights. The "door barring federal intrusion into this area cannot be left ajar; it must be keep closed and opened only the slightest crack." In other words, any legislation must be subject to "heightened judicial scrutiny," not "presumed" constitutional. Having set out this new standard, he turns to the application.

First, he notes the problem with the old rule: "The early leading standard of obscenity allowed material to be judged merely by the effect of an isolated excerpt upon particularly susceptible persons. Regina v Hicklin." Next, he formulates an entirely new rule: "Obscene material," he writes, "is material which deals with sex in a manner appealing to prurient interest." The test is "whether to the average person, applying contemporary community standards, the dominant theme of the material taken as a whole appeals to prurient interest."[9]

Well, then, we have a demonstration of the doctrines, incorporation and fundamental or preferred rights, but nothing much alters. Obscenity still falls outside the shield covering free speech, only we have a fresh definition for obscenity. The Court actually affirmed the convictions of both Roth and Alberts.

Defining obscenity away, Fanny Hill and beyond – Except within a decade, Justice Brennan grew dissatisfied with this initial effort and taking up his pen again tilts at the definition of obscenity. Writing for the majority in the 1966 Fanny Hill Case, he devises a newer, three-pronged test. Material is obscene if: "(a) the dominant theme of the material taken as a whole appeals to a prurient interest in sex; (b) the material is patently offensive because it affronts contemporary community standards, ... and (c) the material is utterly without redeeming social value."[10]

Again nothing looks much altered, obscenity still condemned. But as so often, it is not so much the formal rule as the informal attitude that infuses the application. The work at issue, Fanny Hill, more precisely titled *Memoirs of a Woman of Pleasure* by one John Cleland, dated so far back as 1750, had long occupied a niche on the shelves reserved for erotica. If Fanny's fictitious memoirs not obscene, the author failed in his purpose. Yet Justice Brennan finds the book non-obscene, passing his new test, ushered through the constitutional portal, entitled to constitutional protection. Now something had certainly changed, since if Fanny Hill not obscene, then almost nothing else was either. As Justice Tom Clark wrote in dissent: "[Q]uotations from typical episodes would so debase our Reports that I will not follow that course."[11]

Justice Brenan himself would shortly fall out with his own, second re-definition, coming to regard obscenity as non-definable. Dissenting in the 1973 Paris Adult Theatre Case, he wrote: "I am forced to conclude that the concept of 'obscenity' cannot be defined with sufficient specificity and clarity ... I would hold, therefore, that, at least in the absence of distribution to juveniles or obtrusive exposure to unconsenting adults, the First and Fourteenth Amendments prohibit the State and Federal Governments from attempting wholly to suppress sexually oriented materials on the basis of their allegedly 'obscene' contents."[12]

The majority on the Court never formally agreed, yet in effect, Justice Brennan won that argument, as he won so many others. Today, obscenity might still rank as technically outside the law, but what might be called the Brennan rule applies. Perhaps as unbiased authority the *Oxford Companion to the Supreme Court* may serve: "Subsequently, the Court began to overturn virtually every obscenity prosecution it encountered unless the material was sold to minors or advertised salaciously."[13] But perhaps authority not needed, since all may satisfy themselves from the empirical data, works previously regarded as obscene widely available on bookshelves, magazine counters, showing in the theaters, filling the airwaves and the internet.

The winners and losers – The free speech advocates triumphed, and they could have only so triumphed through the Court, since none can imagine Congress or state legislatures going so far. Naturally enough, the victors applaud themselves and the Court, as vindicating free speech. Yet dare one ask about the defeated? The victors depicted their foes as the aggressors, as violating free speech. But what about the right to live in a virtuous society? The victors certainly recognize such a right, claiming they made society more virtuous and open. What about a right against obscenity? Even Justice Brennan recognized such a right, at least against "distribution to juveniles or obtrusive exposure to unconsenting adults." So some such right must exist.

In 1957 in Roth, Justice Brennan had said: "But implicit in the history of the First Amendment is the rejection of obscenity as utterly without redeeming social importance. This rejection for that reason is mirrored in the universal judgment that obscenity should be restrained, reflected in the international agreement of over 50 nations, in the obscenity laws of all the 48 States, and in the 20 obscenity laws enacted by the Congress from 1842 to 1956. This is the same judgment expressed by this Court in Chaplinsky v. New Hampshire."

But by 1966 in Fanny Hill, he had totally changed his mind. Then if his own mind divided against itself across a decade, perhaps reasonable minds might still divide. In which case, when reasonable men could differ, what made the Court the ultimate authority on obscenity? Surely not the 1st Amendment, which for more than a century and a half commanded no such re-definition of obscenity. Surely not the Constitution as a whole, which when reasonable men might differ, originally left them to Congress and the state legislatures, there to settle their differences.

What had the Court wrought with this celebrated victory in the judicial revolution? If people thought they knew obscenity when they saw it, they saw a great deal more of it. If people thought obscenity harmful, they saw a great deal more harm. But if people thought obscenity laws harmful, that thought prevailed. While whoever thought the Supreme Court not running this show had another think coming. Did obscenity produce harmful effects? No one knew for sure, only thinking they knew. But the Court thought they knew, and all should know by now. Whatever the Court wrought, the Court won.

Criminal procedure – Decided in 1966, the Miranda Case, the most famous by name case in the history of the Court, illustrates the "criminal procedure revolution," a large subset of cases within the judicial revolution. Criminal procedure deals with the investigation, arrest, and prosecution for crime. With these cases the Court changes these rules, much in favor of the accused. Specifically, Miranda changes the rule on confessions, creating the Miranda Rule or Miranda Warnings, the familiar incantation that: "You have the right to remain silent. Anything you say or do can and will be used against you in a court of law. You have the right to speak to an attorney. If you cannot afford an attorney, one will be appointed for you."

To examine criminal procedure, and Miranda as part of criminal procedure, starts with some general principles, which are two: First, criminal procedure should accurately sort out innocence from guilt, since an overriding concern to acquit the innocent, but convict the guilty. Second, criminal procedure should not work as a tool of government repression, since in the past so often abused for that purpose.

Neither of these targets an easy mark, and in combination like trying to hit two marks with one shot, while the competitors try to jerk on the targets, since criminal procedure a contest pitting elemental interests with strong temptations not to play fair. The authorities seek to detect and convict, while the accused, and of course their lawyers, seek to avoid detection and conviction. In this cat-and-mouse game, innocence has every claim, yet guilt does not have the same claim, but guilt hides behind claims of innocence. In their zeal, the authorities tend to play too rough, sometimes so rough as to break the rules themselves, while the guilty and their lawyers play with matching zeal. Criminal procedure must referee impartially, and since the lone individual mismatched against government, should closely call fouls by government, stopping oppression before the start. Much better serves justice imbued with a beneficent mildness, well expressed by that old adage "better to acquit ten guilty than convict one innocent man." Yet not well serve laws that let criminals run roughshod over law-abiding citizens. This even-handedness puts the lawgiver to a task never quite perfectly performed.

The forced oaths – Miranda deals with the law of confessions, a part of this task, since eliciting confessions a procedure of criminal investigation. The basic text comes from the 5th Amendment, which reads: "No ... person ... shall be compelled in any criminal case to be a witness against himself." What exactly do those words mean?

Like so much else, American law transplanted notions against self-incrimination from England, and two stems grew together to form the trunk of the 5th Amendment. The first had a genesis in the 1600s, growing out of English conflicts over religion. The second grew out of English experience in ordinary criminal prosecutions. Untangling these English roots shows how these two stocks entwined in American soil.

In those bygone days, English law established the Anglican Church and heresy stood on the statute books as a crime. Today this looks more like a problem in substantive criminal law than criminal procedure. The substantive law makes a crime, while procedural law merely punishes for crime. Then in legal parlance, heresy looks a 1st Amendment rather than a 5th Amendment problem. The 1st Amendment remedied the wrong by separating church and state. Problem solved, and why need the 5th Amendment, the right against self-incrimination, come into the discussion? Except in the 1600s in England, the idea of toleration fell on deaf ears. So instead, heretics attacked the procedure rather than the substance of the law.

Such a phenomenon often happens in the law. A potent appeal rejected by an ironclad legal doctrine recasts into the form of another, more elastic legal doctrine convenient to hand. The process can achieve a success, but often at the expense of warping the controversy out of shape. This attack on English procedural law shows the technique as well as the complication, somewhat blurring the real issue.

Because if truth stood as the main pursuit, the English authorities had developed an effective criminal procedure. Two courts gained infamy in persecuting heretics, Star Chamber and the Court of High Commission. Not your run-of-the-mill "common law" courts, about which more in a moment, these extraordinary tribunals carried out special missions for the crown, bringing to bear procedures copied from medieval church courts. In either Star Chamber or Court of High Commission, the judges forced an oath upon a suspected heretic and then posed questions, designed to reveal guilt. If he refused to take the oath, the judges punished him for contempt. If he took the oath, but refused to answer, the judges presumed the answers as confessed.

This procedure impaled the heretic on a four-horned dilemma. If he refused the oath, he suffered punishment for contempt. If he took the oath and refused to answer, they took the matter as confessed and punished him for heresy. If he took the oath and confessed, they punished him for heresy. If he took the oath and committed perjury, a sincere heretic condemned himself to punishment in Hell, and in those days heretics sincerely believed in Hell. Only an innocent man faced no such dilemmas, took the oath, purged himself, and so established innocence.

Heretics haled up before these judges, unable to mount a frontal assault on the heresy laws, instead assailed the flanks by throwing themselves against the forced oaths. They argued such a procedure violated the ancient liberties of freeborn Englishmen, exhuming Magna Charta and other texts. Suffice to say such a liberty doubtfully existed. But ultimately they won this fight not in the courts, but on the battlefields of the English Civil War, which took place in the mid-1600's, where the Puritan heretics defeated the Anglican monarchy.

Meanwhile back in 1637, a twenty-three year old clothier's apprentice, John Lilburn, had taken on Star Chamber in a case that agitated the whole nation. "Freeborn" John later described himself as "an honest true-bred, freeborn Englishman that never loved a tyrant nor feared an oppressor."[14] While a contemporary remarked of him, "if John Lilburn were the last man on earth, John would fight with Lilburn and

Lilburn with John."[15] In a career devoted to civil disobedience, he went on trial for his life four times, spent much of that life in prison, and died in banishment. Through it all he possessed a knack to stay in the limelight and a thorn in the flesh of authority.

The old English law books report Lilburn's Case this way: "John Lilburn was committed to prison by the Council of Star Chamber ... on a charge of printing or importing certain heretical and seditious books; on examination, by the Attorney-General, having denied these charges, he was further asked as to other charges, but refused, saying: 'I am not willing to answer you anymore of these questions ... ' Then, when examined before the Chamber itself, he again refused, saying, '... I perceive the oath to be ... against the law of the land ...' Then the Council condemned him to be whipped and pilloried for his 'boldness in refusing to take a legal oath,' without which many offenses might go 'undiscovered and unpunished'; and in April, 1638 ... the sentence was executed. On Nov. 3, 1640, he preferred a complaint to Parliament; and on May 4, 1641, the Commons voted that the sentence was 'illegal and against the liberty of the subject,' and ordered reparation. ... on Dec. 21, 1648, he was finally granted L3000 reparation."[16]

This short, dry, legal account encapsulates the controversy, but omits the momentous political upheaval of these same years. We see Lilburn charged with heresy, with "printing or importing certain heretical and seditious books." When faced with the forced oath, he refuses, saying: "I perceive the oath to be against the law of the land." Held in contempt, he suffers the severe punishment of whipping and being pilloried in the stocks. But beginning in 1640, the Puritans, many whom had suffered as heretics by the same procedure as Lilburn, seized control of Parliament and revolted against the monarchy. These events explain the ultimate parliamentary ruling, which held the forced oaths "illegal and against the liberty of the subject," eventually ordering heavy compensation paid to Lilburn. Having been persecuted by the forced oaths, once in power the Puritans outlawed the procedure. They might have done better to legislate religious toleration. Such a reform would have eradicated the true abuse, which was intolerance. Unfortunately, the time was not yet ripe. Instead, the Puritans went on to persecute their own religious foes, but under other procedures.

But we might ask: Was Lilburn guilty? Of course, he was guilty. Then insofar as criminal procedure seeks to sort out guilt from innocence, the forced oaths worked quite well. But did the forced oaths amount to government repression of dissent? Not really, if we will see the distinction. If the law had not wrongly made heresy a crime, the procedure would not have prosecuted heresy, not in-and-of-itself repressing dissent. The evil resided in the house of substantive criminal law, which makes crimes, not in the house of criminal procedure, which merely punishes crimes. Let us say the authorities had been prosecuting murder, rather than heresy. While society owes an accused murderer a duty, does not an accused murderer owe some duty to society? Leaving out such terrors as whipping and the stocks, which again another problem, that of coercion, why not question the accused about the crime? Why not require him to answer, silence an admission? Such a procedure relates closely to commonsense.

However that may be, the forced oaths disappeared almost one hundred and fifty years before the American Revolution. Yet Lilburn's Case exercised an influence on American law. Many Americans came from dissenting stock. Blurred in the public mind, they preserved some memory of Lilburn's Case. Only the careful legal scholar could have told the precise legal issue settled: No man could be forced to take an oath and testify against himself, punished for refusal to take the oath, silence being presumed as a confession. To most the forced oaths had come to stand for oppression pure and simple.

The common law rule on confessions – This rule against forced oaths formed the first major branch that went to make up the 5th Amendment. The second branch grew up out of English experience over in the "common law" courts. In contrast to Star Chamber or the Court of High Commission, these courts handled your routine criminal cases, housebreaking, robbery, murder, whatever, the surviving reports read like a police blotter. Repeatedly the suspect makes the mistake of confessing to the constable or sheriff, and these unsworn, out-of-court statements later surface in-court, convicting the hapless accused. What rules of criminal procedure governed these confessions?

The English had developed a quite sensible rule, the truer ancestor of most present day litigation about confessions. Their concerns with these unsworn statements centered on their reliability. Torture was long gone. But what if the officers induced a confession by some coercion or making a promise or a threat? Coercion or inducements present an almost irresistible temptation to falsehood, particularly to the weak, ignorant, and inexperienced, tainting the reliability of the confession. The English crafted a precise counterstroke, a rule that any coercion, promise, or threat prevented later use of the confession to convict the accused.

The 1783 Warickshall's Case well states the doctrine: "Confessions are received in evidence or rejected as admissible under a consideration whether they are or are not entitled to credit. A free and voluntary confession is deserving of the highest credit, ... But a confession forced from the mind by flattery of hope or torture of fear comes in so questionable a shape when it is to be considered as evidence of guilt that no credit ought to be given to it, and therefore it is rejected."[17]

Putting Lilburn's Case together with Warickshall's Case sums up the law of confessions taken over from England at the Revolution. The prosecution could not require the accused to take an oath and testify against himself, silence taken as an admission of guilt. But as long as they did not promise or threaten, the authorities could interrogate a suspect. What he said could be used against him. If he declined to answer, the jury could hear about his refusal, drawing what conclusion they wished. This describes the law in effect both before and after adoption of the 5th Amendment. The old law books are full of cases illustrating these rules in operation.

Confessions in American law – Only nothing stays the same. During the nineteenth century, America underwent urbanization. This rise of the city coincided with the rise of a municipal police force. No longer did questioning take place at the hands of a local constabulary or a rough-and-ready justice-of-the-peace. The police haled the suspect down to the station house. This change of venue led to some abuses.

In 1910, recorded as speaking before the seventeenth annual meeting of the International Association of Chiefs of Police held in Washington, D.C., a Major Sylvester, the President of the Association, describes the "third degree:" "We have heard of the other vulgarity, the 'Third Degree,' ... . In police and criminal procedure and practice the officer of the law administers the 'First Degree,' so called, when he makes the arrest. When taken to the place of confinement, there is the 'Second Degree.' When the prisoner is taken into private quarters and there interrogated ... that [is] the 'Third Degree.' The prisoner is cautioned by the reputable officer today that he need not incriminate himself, and, in some places, the authorities have blank forms in use stipulating that what a prisoner states is of his own volition and without coercion. ... There is no justification for personal violence, inhuman or unfair conduct, in order to extort confessions."[18]

Despite the Major's reassurances, the third degree descends with a sinister sound. In 1929, President Hoover set up a commission to study law enforcement, the Wickersham Commission, named after former Attorney General George W. Wickersham, who headed the eleven-man group. By 1931, the Commission churned out some fourteen reports. *No 11* entitled *Report on Lawlessness in Law Enforcement* described the following situation: "After reviewing the evidence obtainable the authors of the report reach the conclusion that the third degree --- that is, the use of physical brutality, or other forms of cruelty, to obtain involuntary confessions or admissions --- is widespread. Protracted questioning of prisoners is commonly employed. Threats and methods of intimidation ... are frequently used ... . Physical brutality, illegal detention, and refusal to allow access of counsel to the prisoner are common."[19]

As far as the law went, this sort of third degree already stood condemned. In their introduction the Commission noted: "The third degree is a secret and illegal practice."[20] So such practices represent not so much a failure of the law as a failure of will to enforce the law. However that might be, the Commission did suggest a reform: "Probably the best remedy for this evil would be the enforcement of the rule that every person arrested charged with crime should be forthwith taken before a magistrate, advised of the charge against him, given the right to have counsel and then interrogated by the magistrate. His answers should be recorded and should be admissible in evidence against him in all subsequent proceedings. If he chooses not to answer, it should be permissible for counsel for the prosecution and for the defense, as well as for the trial judge, to comment on his refusal."[21]

This suggestion should sound like nothing so much as the antique English procedure in Lilburn's Case with some safeguards installed. The examining magistrate does advise of the charges and right to counsel. However, the magistrate does question the individual charged, and while silence not punished as contempt, nor taken as a confession, such refusal may be later used at trial, with the prosecution or the judge allowed to comment, that is, pointedly tell the jury he failed to proclaim his innocence when given the chance.

Whether or not a good idea, such a reform never adopted, apparently the third degree largely eradicated through other instrumentalities. Already illegal and in official disfavor with higher-ups, enforcement of existing law and police guidelines remedied the abuse. Yet later cases do show such tactics sometimes lingered.

Putting all this together, prior to Miranda in 1966, the American law of confessions centered around the "voluntariness test." In a case typical of many, the Supreme Court stated the doctrine this way: "A confession, *if freely and voluntarily made*, is evidence of the most satisfactory character."[22] While based largely on the rationale of Warickshall's Case, this rule also prevented any such procedure as Lilburn's Case. The 5th Amendment said: "No ... person ... shall be compelled in any criminal case to be a witness against himself." The voluntariness test described the understood meaning of that right.

Then how well did this rule on confessions serve those twin goals of criminal procedure, sorting out innocence from guilt and preventing repression of dissent? No real empirical studies exist. Yet neither does the general impression exist American jails and prisons full of innocent men; neither does the general impression exist America repressed dissent. Of course, as to repressing dissent, complaint sometimes sounded. For example, the 1798 the Alien and Sedition Acts made a crime out of publishing "false, scandalous and malicious writing" against the government or officials, leading to the prosecution of several Jeffersonian newspaper editors. More recently in 1940, the Smith Act made a crime out of advocating the overthrow of the government, leading to a series of prosecutions against such as communists. But if such faults, none lie at the door of the voluntariness rule on confessions. All entered through substantive law, not by way of procedural law.

The facts in Miranda – In 1966 with the Miranda Case, the Court changed this long-accepted rule on confessions, super-adding a requirement. The voluntariness rule still applies, but the new Miranda Warnings also required. What exactly caused this change?

To begin with the facts of the case simply put, on the evening of March 3, 1963, the defendant, Ernesto Miranda, kidnaps and rapes an eighteen year old girl in Phoenix, Arizona. In slightly more detail, the girl rides the bus home from work, gets off at her stop, and starts walking to her house. Miranda pulls out in his car from a nearby lot, driving so close she jumps back. Exiting the car, he grabs her, puts his hand over her mouth, and dragging her to the car, shoves her in the backseat. He ties her hands and feet and places something sharp against her neck, saying, "Feel this."[23] He then drives around for about twenty minutes, during which time the girl lays in the backseat crying. When he stops the car, he unties her hands and feet, and tells her to take off her clothes. When she says no, he starts to remove them. Although she tries to push him away, after one unsuccessful attempt, he rapes her. Miranda then drives the girl to a location, during which time she dresses, and releases her. She runs home and tells her family. They call the police.

Ten days later officers apprehend Miranda at his residence and take him to the police station. The victim picks him out of a lineup, and "two officers then took him into a separate room to interrogate him." Although "at first denying his guilt, within a short time Miranda gave a detailed oral confession and then wrote out in his own hand and signed a brief statement admitting and describing the crime." Altogether this took about two hours. The officers used no force, threats, or promises, nor gave him any warnings. He is 23 years old, indigent, and dropped out of school in the ninth grade. According to a doctor who later examined him, Miranda had an "emotional illness" of the schizophrenic type, was "alert and oriented as to time, place, and person," was "intelligent within normal limits, competent to stand trial, and sane within the legal definition."[24]

An Arizona jury convicts him of kidnap and rape. On appeal, the Arizona Supreme Court affirms, approving use of the confession against him, saying: "The facts and circumstances in the instant case show that the statement was voluntary, made by the defendant of his own free will, that no threats or use of force or coercion or promise of immunity were made; and that he understood his legal right and the statement might be used against him."[25]

In other words, these judges applied the voluntariness test. But Miranda's lawyers take an appeal to the U.S. Supreme Court. In a five to four decision, the justices reverse Miranda's conviction, changing the law on confessions, promulgating the Miranda Rule. Chief Justice Earl Warren writes for the majority: "[W]e hold that when an individual is taken into custody ... and is subjected to questioning, the privilege against self-incrimination is jeopardized. Procedural safeguards must be employed ... . He must be warned prior to any questioning that he has the right to remain silent, that anything he says can be used against him in a court of law, that he has the right to the presence of an attorney, and that if he cannot afford an attorney one will be appointed for him prior to any questioning if he so desires. ... After such warnings have been given, and such opportunity afforded him, the individual may knowingly and intelligently waive these rights and agree to answer questions or make a statement."[26]

Furthermore, if these warnings not given, nothing the suspect says can be used in court against him. If at any time the suspect indicates a wish to stop talking or wants a lawyer, the questioning must immediately cease. If the suspect refuses to speak, the ultimate jury cannot be informed of this fact.

The stakes in Miranda – What goes on here? To the man-on-the-street, if anyone's rights look violated, the girl looks like the victim, not Ernesto Miranda, who whatever his misfortunes or harsh fate, looks like a dangerous character who needs to be off the street. But a potent minority experienced this conviction quite another way. In trial after endless trial, the criminal defense lawyers sat at counsel table next their hapless clients, hearing such confessions read from the witness stand, and as routinely hearing guilty verdicts read back from the jury box. So whether or not familiar with the remote precedents, over and over these lawyers were re-living Lilburn's Case. No more than Lilburn could they prove their clients' innocent. No more than Lilburn could they assault the underlying, substantive criminal law, the law making murder, robbery, or rape a crime. So history repeated itself and they presently did what Lilburn did so long ago. They threw themselves against the procedure. They got up a cause claiming a violation of the right against self-incrimination.

Why did their clients persist in confessing? However good for the soul, these lawyers knew confession bad legal strategy, convicting of crime. By confessing their clients acted against self-interest. But law enforcement had learned an effective procedure. If they could interrogate a suspect in isolation, preferably as soon as possible after the crime, confession routinely resulted. A number of psychological factors appear at work. Under the immediate emotional stress of crime and arrest, suspects feel a need to tell the story, often an actual need to confess, but only within a degree of intimacy. A man alone in small room with two detectives and a tape recorder will confess, but draws back when led into a courtroom with a judge on the bench and a court reporter. He recedes into himself not only from the publicity, but the formal legal setting threatens with formal legal terrors, which the privacy of questioning minimizes. Alone with a suspect, the skillful interrogator may play upon the need to tell the story, the actual need to confess, which often proves enough. Alone the suspect flatters his mind with hopes and fears, not quite sure how the evidence stands, not quite sure about consequences. The skillful interrogator may play upon these doubts as well, for example saying the case strong, so he might as well make a clean breast of it, or perhaps even playing a trick, for example falsely saying a co-conspirator confessed, but blames everything on him, so unless he wants to take the whole fall, he better tell his side of the story. The scenario plays out in variety of scripts, but isolation crucial to persuade the suspect to speak his part, coming to confess.

Just like those old English authorities in Lilburn's Case, if truth the main pursuit, the American authorities had developed a reliable procedure. So just like Lilburn, the defense lawyers needed to break up this procedure, first convincing themselves of the unfairness, then convincing others. They were not hard to convince, and they capacity in forensic argument ready to hand to convince others. Look, they said, everyone knows what's going on. Leave aside the sincerely penitent man, a negligible number, and who confesses except the weak or ignorant? Law enforcement takes advantage of this weakness or ignorance, carefully crafting the setting of isolation. Never mind no overt coercion, the isolation inherently coercive, overcoming the suspect's will to resist.

Then such confessions as Miranda's are not truly voluntary and violate the spirit of the 5th Amendment, if not the existing letter of 5th

Amendment law. The letter should expand to meet the spirit. Reinterpret the 5th Amendment and expand the voluntariness test. Put an end to isolation and stop inherent coercion. How? Mandate "station-house lawyers" available around the clock and mandate their presence during interrogation. Being neither weak nor ignorant, such lawyers will put the suspect on a level with the police. Having a lawyer would protect the right against self-incrimination, assuring truly voluntary confessions.

Predictably enough, this scheme brought howls of anguish from law enforcement. Any defense lawyer "worth his salt" never tells his client to confess, unless actually innocent and able to prove it. Station-house lawyers would effectively end interrogation period, as effectively end a great deal of detection and conviction. They urged the defense lawyers' professional outlook took a biased view, obsessing over their clients' rights, while overlooking individual responsibility and the interests of society. If criminals capable to carry out crimes without legal counsel, what made them incapable of interrogation without legal counsel? By doing the one, they assumed the risk of the other, as an aspect of individual responsibility, a burden justly shifted by society. Transferring more weight to law enforcement's shoulder would tip the scales of justice, coming down against society, regularly freeing the criminal. The voluntariness rule already measured a fair balance, no one forced to answer anything, confessions generally truthful, government not repressing dissent. The 5th Amendment right against self-incrimination demanded no more.

For once an appeal to empirical methods looks practicable, the data available, but not yet analyzed. Comb through all the cases and break out the statistics. How many convictions rested on a confession, sufficient evidence otherwise lacking? A percentage should come out, say 1% or 10% or 50%. This figure calculated the cost of changing the law, stopping confessions. Even the most ardent defense lawyer failed to advocate complete immunity from prosecution, tacitly recognizing a mean, an equilibrium point between the rights of the accused and the rights of society. Then let the theory about confessions consult the facts about confessions. Let abstractions about the rights of the accused intersect with pragmatic constraints, taking account of the rights of society, really the rights of the victims of crime. Crossing some line might go too far, putting too many of the guilty beyond the reach of punishment. One might argue about locating this crossover point, but unless placed on a graph with numbers, the argument took place in thin air.

The opinion in Miranda – Coming then to the Court's opinion in

Miranda, we understand what at stake. Chief Justice Warren writes for the five-man majority, and sides with the defense lawyers against law enforcement. Yet perceiving the want of real data on the actual impact, he goes not as far as the lawyers wanted. Cautiously, the ruling mandates not station-house lawyers, mandates not a lawyer at every interrogation, but only the Miranda Warnings, advising of the right to counsel. In practical effect, the ruling turned out short of the lawyers' hopes.

The following sums up the core of Warren's rationale: "A valuable source of information about present police practices, however, may be found in various police manuals and texts which document procedures employed with success in the past, and which recommend various other effective tactics. ...

"The officers are told by the manuals that the 'principle psychological factor contributing to a successful interrogation is privacy --- being alone with the individual. ...

"It is obvious that such an interrogation environment is created for no other reason than to subjugate the individual to the will of the examiner. This atmosphere carries its own badge of intimidation. To be sure, this is not physical intimidation, but it is equally destructive of human dignity. The current practice of incommunicado interrogation is at odds with one of our Nation's most cherished principles --- that the individual must not be compelled to incriminate himself. Unless adequate protective devices are employed to dispel the compulsion inherent in custodial surroundings, no statement obtained from the defendant can truly be the product of his free choice. ...

"These precious rights were fixed in our Constitution only after centuries of persecution and struggle. ... We sometimes forget how long it has taken to establish the privilege against self-incrimination, the sources from which it came and the fervor with which it was defended. It roots go back into ancient times. Perhaps the critical historical event shedding light on its origins and evolution was the trial of one John Lilburn. ... These sentiments worked their way over to the Colonies and were implanted after great struggle into the Bill of Rights. ... We cannot depart from this noble heritage. ... [T]o respect the inviolability of the human personality, our accusatory system of criminal justice demands that the government seeking to punish an individual produce the evidence against him by its own independent labors, rather than by the cruel, simple expedient of compelling it from his own mouth."[27]

This rationale seems to go a long way in several ways. It seems a long way from John Lilburn and Star Chamber to two officers in a room with Ernesto Miranda. It seems a long way from the third degree to no more than interrogation in isolation. It seems a long way from Miranda's questioning to an "atmosphere of intimidation." It seems a long way from the original intent of the 5th Amendment to the Miranda Warnings. It seems a long way from the rights of Miranda's victim to "justice demands that the government produce the evidence against him by its own independent labors, rather than by the cruel, simple expedient of compelling it from his own mouth." Along the way, the victim's rights seem somehow to drop away. Along the way, the right against self-incrimination seems to lose the aspect of a pragmatic rule in criminal procedure, sorting out innocent from guilt and guarding against repression of dissent, and seems to assume another aspect altogether, as guarding "the inviolability of the human personality." As a "precious right fixed in our Constitution only after centuries of persecution and struggle," as a "noble heritage," the right seems to take on a semi-sacred nature, worthy of almost any sacrifice in and of itself.

Yet despite the stirring peroration, Justice Warren goes not all the way. By his rationale why not stop confessions altogether, mandating station-house lawyers? But cautiously, Warren draws back, sensing possible peril ahead. No empirical studies exist, but stopping all confessions would be an experiment sure to produce empirical proofs. But how big might the impact be? A really high number might generate a heat not even the justices' lifetime insulation could fade. If half the murders started standing on the books unsolved, the public audit might blame the Court. Then as so often, why not go by careful increments? Rather than mandate station-house lawyers, just mandate the Miranda Warnings, advising of the right to counsel, throwing in some other safeguards.

Warren thought he could consult an empirical source about the likely effect. He writes: "The limits we have placed on the interrogation process should not constitute an undue interference with a proper system of law enforcement. ... Over the years the Federal Bureau of Investigation has compiled an exemplary record of effective law enforcement while advising any suspect or arrested person, at the outset of an interview, that he is not required to make a statement, that any statement may be used against him in court, that the individual may obtain the services of an attorney of his own choice and, more recently, that he has a right to free counsel if he is unable pay."[28]

Now this took a risk, but looked a manageable risk. In the first place, the FBI practice differed materially from the Miranda Warnings. Even if a suspect did not wish to talk, the Bureau did not necessarily cease questioning nor did failure to give this caution automatically exclude a confession as evidence. Secondly, drawing an analogy between the FBI and other law enforcement ignores a vast discrepancy in resources and types of crime investigated. For example, most murder cases start with a call to the local police dispatcher, and the homicide detectives hit the ground running. With the other prime witness eliminated by the crime, their investigation must rely heavily on questioning the suspect. The FBI generally handles less abrupt crimes, such as bank fraud or ongoing criminal conspiracies, which drag a longer tail. Investigation frequently can follow a paper trail, and techniques like surveillance and penetration serve in place of confessions.

Warren took the risk, and events bore out both his concerns and confidence. Miranda did hurt law enforcement. Empirical studies showed some drop in confessions, which some maintained a crucial loss, freeing too many of the guilty. Yet the figures rose not so high as to threaten the Court with a serious backlash. In practical effect, most still confessed, even when advised of their rights. The jail and prisons stayed full of suspects who made the mistake of confessing. But if some justices had in mind pushing on to the next level, going on to mandate those station-house lawyers, they never made the push.

And so it came to pass. The Miranda Rule entered the culture. But almost as a footnote, whatever happened to Ernesto Miranda? He received a new trial with all reference to his confession excluded, yet suffered through another guilty verdict. Enough other evidence existed to reconvict, including the victim's identification. Eventually released from prison, in 1976, an unknown assailant stabbed Miranda to death in a Phoenix bar fight.

But Miranda was only the most prominent case in the criminal procedure revolution. In other cases, the Court expanded numerous other rights of the accused. Space prohibits examination. Yet Miranda shows the method of constitutional interpretation used in all. Nothing is clear-cut. The constitutional interpretation assumes an aspect close to legislation, the Court promulgating detailed rules of criminal procedure, carefully supervising every aspect of investigation, arrest, and prosecution.

CHAPTER 13

The Judicial Revolution Continued

The welfare state – In 1969, Shapiro v Thompson showed the judicial revolution coming to the defense of other rights, this time the "right" to "welfare assistance." This term the Court's, but while accurate enough, perhaps carries an unfortunate connotation. Many respond negatively to the notion of a "right to welfare," a tendency existing to regard welfare as paying over other people's money, too often to the undeserving, who in any case should be grateful for what they get, rather than aggressively asserting their rights. But such a view overlooks the fact that modern nations, including America, run as welfare states, and the generic term "welfare" not only describes redistributions to the poor, but vast programs more properly called "social insurance," where people pay in to earn the benefits, the most notable being Social Security retirement. As for the poor, poverty far from limited to the undeserving, for instances people with disabilities or children not fairly blamable for falling into that fate. As for social insurance, people justly expect their payments under such programs as Social Security. In either case, the law must zealously guard these "entitlements," preventing arbitrary denial or cutoff, seeing the benefits regularly paid.

Yet the welfare state displays disturbing trends, a sort of will-to-power all its own. Starting with deserving appeals, but appealing to less deserving motives, the welfare state has grown inexorably. In the same way interests operate throughout government, interests operate upon welfare programs, attracted to not just the money doled out, but to the power available. People surge toward the money, while interest group entrepreneurs ride if not generate the wave, using the swell to propel themselves. For their part, the welfare bureaucracy scarcely raises a voice other than to call for more funds and bigger staffs. Gradually the accumulating costs have begun to crowd out other crucial government functions, such as national defense. Gradually the accumulating taxes have begun to crowd out the free-market, lacking whose dynamism taxation collapses, leaving government unable to pay either for the welfare state or such mundane items as roads and bridges. The welfare state threatens to become so massively expensive as threatens national bankruptcy.

Welfare rights – In 1969, Shapiro v Thompson came while the welfare state only in late adolescence, not yet the 400-pound gorilla in the room, but already the case shows these twin concerns, fairness and costs. Back in the 1930s in the time of the Great Depression, the states ran a variety of welfare programs, somewhat hit and miss, many states much in advance of others. The New Deal sought to regularize and widen such a social safety net, the Depression having dramatically "exposed the inadequacies of state and local welfare programs," as Chief Justice Warren will say in dissent. With this goal in mind, Congress stepped in with the 1935 Social Security Act, opening the purse of the national treasury. But rather than opting for federalization, Congress left the states as the basic units of administration, still bearing some of the costs, with the feds infusing massive funds through grants.

And during the congressional hearings, an issue surfaced over a waiting period to collect the benefits. States had imposed such waiting periods, often quite lengthy, and states with more generous benefits wanted such delays kept in place, seeking to discourage a migration of the needy, that is, to prevent welfare shopping. But welfare advocates pointed out the impact upon people who moved with quite innocent motives, say to take a job, but where the plant unexpectedly closed, or where they fell too ill to work. Congress compromised, letting states impose residency requirements, but no more than one-year.

In 1969 in the Shapiro v Thompson Case, this one-year waiting period became the bone of contention. Justice Brennan will again write for the Court. His statement of the facts sums up the basic issue: "[T]he Connecticut Welfare Department ... den[ied] the application of Vivian Marie Thompson for assistance under the program for Aid to Families with Dependent Children (AFDC). She was a 19-year-old unwed mother of one child and pregnant with her second child who changed residence in June, 1966, from Dorchester, Massachusetts, to Hartford, Connecticut, to live with her mother, a Hartford resident. She moved to her own apartment in Hartford in August, 1966, when her mother was no longer able to support her and her infant son. Because of her pregnancy, she was unable to work or enter a work training program. Her application for AFDC assistance, filed in August, was denied in November, solely on the ground that, ... she had not lived in the State for a year before her application was filed."[1]

Her lawyers challenged this denial as violating her constitutional rights. Using the now familiar doctrine of fundamental rights, Justice

Brannan agrees with them. His rationale follows the three steps of the doctrine. First, he concludes the right fundamental. Second, he subjects the congressional law to enhanced scrutiny. Third and finally, he concludes the majority again violated individual rights.

But what fundamental right relates to a one-year waiting period for collecting welfare? To locate such a right Justice Brennan starts at what may seem a distance away, saying: "The Court long ago recognized that the nature of the Federal Union and our constitutional concepts of personal liberty unite to require that all citizens be free to travel throughout the length and breadth of our land uninhibited by statutes, rules, or regulations which unreasonably burden or restrict this movement." He quickly admits: "We have no occasion to ascribe the source of this right to travel interstate to a particular constitutional provision."[2] So we have an implication, but no one doubts a right to travel around the country.

Upon this first implication, Justice Brennan adds his next implication, dubbing the right to travel fundamental. Therefore, under fundamental rights doctrine, any law touching travel now subject to enhanced scrutiny, that is, must show a compelling state interest. And he fails to find the waiting period meets this standard, saying: "Since the classification here touches on the fundamental right of interstate movement, its constitutionality must be judged by the stricter standard of whether it promotes a *compelling* state interest. Under this standard, the waiting period requirement clearly violates the Equal Protection Clause."[3]

Of course, he buttresses these conclusions with other convincing arguments needless to detail, since other, equally convincing arguments remain on the other side, as shown by the dissents. In an unusual break between Justice Brennan and Chief Justice Warren, the later will write: "The congressional decision to allow the States to impose residence requirements ... was the subject of considerable discussion. Both those favoring lengthy residence requirements and those opposing all requirements pleaded their case during the congressional hearings on the Social Security Act. Faced with the competing claims of States that feared that abolition of requirements would result in an influx of persons seeking higher welfare payments and of organizations that stressed the unfairness of such requirements to transient workers forced by the economic dislocation of the depression to seek work far from their homes, Congress chose a middle course. It required those States seeking federal grants for categorical assistance to reduce their existing residency requirements to what Congress viewed as an acceptable maximum. However, Congress accommodated state fears by allowing the States to retain minimal residence requirements. ... I am convinced that Congress does have the power to enact residence requirements of reasonable duration or to authorize the States to do so and that it has exercised this power."[4]

Then unless the three justices who dissented somehow less rational than the five who joined Justice Brennan, we must conclude convincing reasons on both sides of the argument. In turn this rational split reveals the loose nature of that doctrine of fundamental rights. In Shapiro the Court defends no clear-cut constitutional meaning, no clear-cut individual rights. Rather the doctrine lets the majority on the Court simply void laws at will, replacing legislative judgment with judicial judgment. We see fundamental rights doctrine in action, how the doctrine lets the Court void laws at-will.

A three-fold wider significance appears. First, the Court has re-gained dominance over Congress. Second, the Court infuses welfare with a new right, and in other cases in the same timeframe, the Court would infuse welfare with other rights, hedging entitlements with careful judicial safeguards. So as to welfare, in one sense the Court expands rights, the right to collect welfare. But in another sense, the Court shows much less concern for rights, the right of Congress and the states to decide fairness and contain costs. Third, the welfare state becomes more rigid, encumbered with rules handed down from the top, made constitutional rules, unchangeable except by the Court. While the effect on the overall system of government incalculable, generally agile, responsive systems perform better in the real world.

Bureaucracy, the fourth branch – The Founders gave not much thought to bureaucracy, which in their day counted for not much. Article II, Section 2, says: "[T]he Congress may by Law vest the Appointment of such inferior Officers, as they think proper, in the President alone, in the Courts of Law, or in the Heads of Departments." In keeping, the First Congress created three cabinet departments, State, Treasury, and War, giving the president authority to appoint their heads and officials. Something of a controversy then appeared over authority to un-appoint, but Washington dug in his heels against a cabinet effectively outside his control, and his prestige and commonsense prevailed. The chief executive started out with authority to hire or fire the bureaucrats, who served "at will."

From such a humble seedling grew the huge "fourth branch," today bureaucracy overtopping in sheer size the other three branches, often competing with them for significance. In 1789, Washington's cabinet held only the three departments and about 3,000 officials; two centuries later in 2001, President George W. Bush looked out over hundreds of agencies with some 2.8 million civilian employees. But not only their numbers grew, their authority grew. In Washington's day, officialdom consisted mainly of clerks engaged in such routine tasks as keeping ledgers or issuing vouchers. By the late twentieth century, the bureaucracy carried out numerous, ongoing, and complex missions. Think of sending a man to the moon or sending out millions of Social Security checks, assigned respectively to NASA and SSA. Think of regulating the monetary supply or regulating nuclear energy, assigned the FED and the NRC. The list of projects runs longer than the list of acronyms, and the inertia that drives their burgeoning continues to drive, whether already gone too far or not. Congress, the president, and the courts cannot hope to meet all the demands made by modernity. The response has generated a great deal more bureaucracy, while thrusting down the line a great deal more authority, empowering the bureaucracy. Bureaucracy became the "fourth branch."

In this way, modern government came to face a problem not evident in the Founders' day: How assure the efficiency and accountability of the bureaucracy? In the first place and perhaps disturbingly, the answers must leave behind straightforward democratic methods. For reasons too obvious for detail, electing bureaucrats fails as a workable solution. Rather, the solutions fall into three institutional forms: a patronage system, a civil service system, or some middling system. Each of the first two possesses virtues and corresponding vices, while finding a golden mean in the last an elusive endeavor.

Patronage – In the mouths of late nineteenth century reformers, "patronage" became a dirty word, yet boiling away that aftertaste, at bottom patronage did no more than leave the bureaucracy under the chief executive, serving at-will. Such described the original setup, which seemed natural at the time, indeed, no other suggestion being made. Since the chief executive responsible, give him power to hold them responsible, which had the obvious virtue of binding bureaucracy beneath democracy. The voters enforced accountability upon the chief executive; the chief executive enforced accountability among the bureaucracy. Only as reformers came loudly to complain, certain vices attended the virtue.

From the outset of the Republic, lamentation sounded against any criteria for public office except merit. The Founders cherished an ideal that public esteem would reward superior attainments, conceiving elections as spontaneously elevating the best men to office, selecting for moral and intellectual excellence. Thinking in this way, they conspicuously failed to anticipate the rise of political parties, yet parties quickly generated in the soil they prepared, which many regarded like the weeds choking the garden. They saw parties as supplanting disinterested public service and merit with an unholy alliance in pursuit of office. This hostility ran so deep Thomas Jefferson, that great originator of party politics, felt compelled to publicly deny what he privately did, glossing over partisan motives with other pretenses, such as the outrages perpetuated by his opponents. Nor has the cry against partisanship entirely died out and for good reason. Party loyalty overrides a dispassionate view, weighing candidates and issues by partisan labels, identifying partisan victory with the public good, surely not a reliable standard for either men or causes.

Yet if Americans possess a practical genius for politics, nothing better exemplifies the genius than inventing parties. The idea of elections as spontaneous generation, bringing the best and brightest to life in office, rests on partial truth. Elections open a career to talents, letting the more vigorous thrive. But without parties, democracy breeds an incoherent mass, not an organized body politic. Without parties, the electorate cannot organize and move together, rallying behind causes and leaders. Without parties, leaders cannot connect across the country and inside government. Without parties, Congress cannot organize. Without party leaders in Congress, the president cannot deal with Congress. Whatever their downside, parties knit together a nervous system with a brain, put muscle and bone beneath the flesh, arise and walk.

And patronage fit party politics like hand in glove, although it took a while to find the fit. While filling the some 3,000 places under the new government, Washington stressed ability over faction, helped by the fact parties did not yet quite exist. But even Washington picked men who shared his viewpoint, who had supported ratification and were gravitating toward the emerging Federalist Party. Then in 1801, Republican Thomas Jefferson carried out the first hostile take-over of the presidency, and in an obvious coincidence, made the first significant use of patronage as a party device. Jefferson found officialdom totally populated by the adherents of his predecessor, the Federalist John Adams, an inequity he rectified by appointing a number of his followers to their places.

In the heated election of 1828, Democrat Andrew Jackson triumphed over the incumbent, John Quincy Adams, and patronage picked up speed and heat. Jackson's partisan appointments raised the old hue and cry, opponents claiming men of merit turned out, replaced by no more than party hacks. Actually, careful studies reveal rather restrained partisanship. In eight years, Ole Hickory removed no more than one-fifth of federal employees for partisan purposes, perhaps nearer a tenth.[5] Yet a negative appellation attached. In a speech defending his chief, Senator William L. Marcy made the frank remark that "to the victor go the spoils." However justified the logic, the other side turned his words against him. The label "spoils system" stuck ever after to patronage.

In 1861, Abraham Lincoln used patronage much more profoundly, perhaps to better purpose. Finding in officialdom a nest of hostile Copperhead Democrats, some suspected of spying and sabotage, many Confederate in sympathy, Lincoln sent them packing. Appointing faithful Republicans in their stead, he replaced 1,457 out of 1,639 direct presidential appointees, subordinate employees suffering in proportion.[6] How win the Civil War working through a lukewarm and obstructive bureaucracy? Lincoln looks justified.

His experience graphically illustrates that initial virtue of patronage, executive control over the bureaucracy, assuring obedience. Nor did patronage lack other virtues. If parties serve as useful to democracy, patronage serves as useful to both, exciting participation. However altruism may motivate in politics, a division of the loaves and fishes motivates as well. The prospect for employment raised commitment. People involved themselves, served in the party, went to precinct meetings, gave money, knocked on doors, and voted en masse, all with some hope of earthy reward. Turnout is never higher than when jobs on the line. Then too, patronage gave party leaders sticks and carrots, ways to control their followers, not always a bad thing, if we believe any wisdom may sometimes reside in leadership.

But if Americans possess a native genius for politics, they also possess a native genius for business, and not a few saw the main chance in a merger. These entrepreneurs converted politics into a business run at the public expense, creating "machine politics." Local parties operated like political factories, the bosses rewarding workers' labor and donations with official posts, some quite lucrative, such as Collector of the Port of New York. By so doing, they outcompeted their rivals, managing to win elections. But whatever they then did for the public, and they did some, they could not resist the siren call to milk the profits, not confining themselves to the legal side of the business. They bribed voters and stuffed ballot boxes; they handed out public projects to their cronies, pocketing bribes and kickbacks; they avoided justice by corrupting prosecutors and courts. Boss Tweed in New York, Tom Pendergast in Kansas City, their names and exploits make up a colorful, but overall an inglorious chapter in the history books.

But eventually, the larger democracy reformed them out of business. Criminal prosecutions targeted the more egregious. Tweed died in

Ludlow Street Jail, Pendergast spent time. Institutional reform sought to put their machines out of business permanently and went after patronage as a root cause of the evil. As a replacement, reformers touted civil service or a merit system. European nations had already tried this alternative with success, especially the British.

Civil service reform – Later, German sociologist Max Weber would formally identify six elements making up a civil service system: First, officials within the bureaucracy must be selected and promoted on merit and dischargeable only for cause; second, officials must be paid fixed salaries; third, a clear hierarchy or chain of command must reach from top to the bottom of the organization; fourth, within the bureaucracy a clear division of labor must define relationships and responsibilities; fifth, clients of the bureaucracy must be dealt with impersonally based upon the merit of their cases; and sixth, the entire structure must be governed by express laws and regulations.

Together, these elements re-designed the bureaucracy, reforming a timeless institution of government into a modern type. Past experience showed a remedy needed, and future experience showed this model a useful and powerful mechanism. Patronage suffered not only from gross abuse, but haphazard nature. Modern social and economic conditions demanded size, continuity, and expertise. Turning over officialdom on the electoral tide upsets stability nor did party loyalty select well for other qualifications. To recall as instances NASA or the NRC, building rockets ships or nuclear reactors long-term projects, requiring highly technical skills. Decapitating the staff after each election interrupts the work, and the school of political hard knocks educates not scientists and engineers, who toil for knowledge in far other schools. As well as doing away with the faults of cronyism, civil service saw to these other defects, set up a regular assembly line, tested applicants to fill the jobs, and churned out quality products. To recall as instances the FED and SSA, how would Americans pay for their daily bread without a regulated monetary supply and social security checks? Today such governmental services stretch toward an earlier unimagined horizon, the distance already traveled as unimaginable without prodigious feats of bureaucratic management and manufacture. For all the present execration heaped upon their name, bureaucrats might well complain as victims of their own successes. Having done so much for so many, they are expected to do all for all, and do it now. Doubtfully could the amateurs from patronage have carried the nation as far and fast as the professionals from civil service.

Yet American political genius did not fail to perceive that these good civil servants potentially bad masters. History does not lack instances of bureaucracies that effectively took over the government, running things for themselves. Which comes back to the initial question: How assure the efficiency and accountability of the bureaucracy? The answer looked simple. Just keep them under the elected officials, Congress and the president. Congress must pass the laws setting up agencies with sufficient specificity, confining agencies to a mandate. Then Congress must keep them to their mandate, using oversight and budgetary control. The president serves as CEO, keeping their eyes focused on the job, noses to the grindstone. Here patronage still had a part to play, since whom the president fires, the president runs. As for the courts, they kept the bureaucrats to the law, not just their agency mandate, but all the other laws as well.

Of course, in those bygone days patronage being near and dear to the hearts of practicing politicians, they ceded not willingly the power, the annals of this fight long and bloody, but falling outside the scope, needing only to know the outcome. That came in 1883, when Congress finally passed the Pendleton Act changing to a federal civil service system. Generally, the states fairly quickly followed suit. By 1939, Congress forced all states to initiate civil service for programs aided by federal funds.

Yet by no means did all patronage disappear, not all government employees being made civil service. In pursuit of purposes good, bad, or indifferent, Congress left a lot of jobs at-will, as did state legislatures. In those enclaves an elected official could still decimate his staff either to enforce policy or reward retainers. Parties still retained an amount of patronage for distribution, attracting cupidity and stimulating engagement. Thus, rightly or wrongly Congress and the states continued to recognize the claims patronage made to virtue, while hopefully winnowing out the vices. Above all, Congress and the states still had the power to change the system, either to enforce their will or perhaps in response to unforeseen circumstances or emergencies.

In short, there was a compromise. The law moved toward a predominantly civil service system, but patronage stayed around. Whether this hybrid struck the proper balance remained a question, shortly to be answered by the Supreme Court in the negative, which brings up the next case in the judicial revolution. Once more the Court begged to differ with Congress and the states.

Civil service as a right – In 1976 with Elrod v Burns, the Supreme Court made civil service a constitutional right except for a few tip-top jobs. Seen the other way around, the Court revoked the long-stranding constitutionality of patronage. But exactly how did this reversal of fortunes occur? How did the unquestioned practice of Washington, Jefferson, Jackson, and Lincoln, down to that present day, suddenly come to violate the Constitution? To reach the result, the case tacks together that pair of new legal doctrines, incorporation and fundamental or preferred rights. The conclusion followed from the easy facility conferred.

The facts of Elrod v Burns come out of Chicago, a city notable for a lurid past in machine politics, her old ways still strongly attracting. In 1970, one Richard Elrod, a Democrat, wins election as Sheriff of Cook County, displacing a Republican. The sheriff's office employs some 3,000. The Illinois legislature had put roughly half under civil service, leaving the rest patronage. Under the routine practice of many years, the new Sheriff set about dismissing at-will employees with the wrong party ticket, and the end of the line loomed for three men, John Burns, Frank Vargas, and Fred L. Buckley. According to the dissenting opinion, they "apparently accepted patronage jobs, while fully familiar with the 'tenure' practice long prevailing in the Sheriff's office."[7] Nevertheless, all three sued.

The case reaches the Supreme Court, where Justice Brennan writes for the plurality, a majority agreeing on the outcome, but split on the rationale. Justice Brennan rules: "We hold, therefore, that the practice of patronage dismissals is unconstitutional under the First and Fourteenth Amendments."[8]

To unpack that, recall the 1st Amendment says: "Congress shall make no law ... abridging the freedom of speech, or of the press; or of the people peaceably to assemble." The 14th Amendment has been so often quoted as to render further repetition monotonous. But the joined reference to "the First and Fourteenth Amendments" serves as shorthand for the doctrine of incorporation. The 1st Amendment says, "*Congress* shall make no law," saying nothing about the states. Then for the Court to find the Illinois law unconstitutional, first the 1st Amendment requires extension, made to apply to the state of Illinois as well as Congress. Earlier cases have already accomplished this feat, holding the 14th Amendment incorporates the 1st Amendment against the states, giving the Court power over them as well.

All right, so much for doctrine number one, incorporation. But one might still wonder, given that the 1st Amendment now binds the states, how such bonds make "patronage dismissal unconstitutional?" This further reach calls for doctrine number two, fundamental or preferred rights.

Justice Brennan lays this doctrine down as follows: "It is firmly established that a significant impairment of First Amendment rights must survive exacting scrutiny. ... The interest advanced must paramount, one of vital importance, and the burden is on the government so show such an interest. ... Moreover, it is not enough that the means chosen in furtherance of the interest be rationally related to that end. ... The gain to the subordinating interest provided by the means must outweigh the incurred loss of protected rights. ... In short, ... it must further some vital government end by a means that is least restrictive ... and the benefit gained must outweigh the loss of constitutionally protected rights."[9]

All this possesses a pleasing aspect. What more sacred that the people's rights? That government is best which governs least. Keep the government out. All his language looks right in step with long-standing American values, appealing to a rational commitment, appealing to the very ideal of freedom. Yet the rhetorical sugar covers a doctrine of power as much as restraint, the doctrine of fundamental or preferred rights. Power moves to the Court, away from Congress or the states. Certain rights become "fundamental" or "preferred," and in protecting those rights, the Court need not defer to the judgment of Congress or the states. Rather than that the old clear-cut limit on judicial review, the Court employs other criteria without clear-cut limits.

Re-reading what Brennan said, look how indefiniteness collects. He says "a significant impairment of First Amendment rights." He says "exacting scrutiny." He says "vital importance." He says, "outweigh the incurred loss of protected rights." He says "means that is least restrictive." What standards govern all these terms? All these phrases display the same easy facility as that old "unreasonableness" test of substantive due process. Such ample vagueness lets the Court drop in and out their preferred meaning, the Constitution once again saying whatever they want to say.

Justice Brennan demonstrates in practice: "The cost of patronage is the restraint it places on freedoms of belief and association. ... It is not only belief and association which are restricted where political patronage is the practice. The free functioning of the electoral process also suffers. ... Patronage, therefore, to the extent it compels or restrains belief and association, is inimical to the process which undergirds our system of government and 'is at war with the deeper traditions of democracy embedded in the First Amendment.'"[10]

After thus establishing patronage "a significant impairment of First Amendment rights," Brennan goes on to the next step, an "exacting scrutiny," asking first for some government policy of "vital importance," then weighing that policy against the "incurred loss of protected rights" and whether the "means that is least restrictive." He sits up three possible justifications for patronage, knocking down each in turn, beginning: "One interest which has been offered in justification of patronage is the need to insure effective government and the efficiency of public employees." But, "fundamentally ... the argument does not succeed because it is doubtful that the mere difference of political persuasion motivates poor performance, nor do we think it legitimately may be used as a basis for imputing such behavior."[11]

Next he disposes of a second argument: "A second interest advanced in support of patronage is the need for political loyalty of employees, ... to the end that representative government not be undercut by tactics obstructing the implementation of policies of the new administration policies presumably sanctioned by the electorate. The justification is not without force, but is nevertheless inadequate to justify patronage wholesale. Limiting patronage dismissals to policymaking positions is sufficient to achieve this governmental end."[12]

Thus, the very tip-top position, the "policymakers" can remain patronage, although he quickly adds that: "No clear line can be drawn between policymaking and nonpolicymaking positions." As a practical matter, such a gray area left elected officials to the perils of future litigation, and not a few suffered the consequences, finding themselves accused of patronage dismissals in doubtful cases, mulched of embarrassment, expense, and sometimes damages. But leaving this dismay behind, Brennan turns to the third and final argument.

"It is argued that the third interest supporting patronage dismissals is the preservation of the democratic process. According to the petitioners, 'we have contrived no system for the support of party that does not place considerable reliance on patronage.' ... But however important preservation of the two-party system or any system involving a fixed number of parties may or may not be, ... we are not persuaded that the elimination of patronage practice ... will bring about the demise of party politics."[13]

All looks reasonable enough. How did the three dissenting justices counter? Quoting from Justice Lewis Powell: "The Court holds unconstitutional practices as old as the republic, a practice which has contributed significantly to the democratization of American politics. This decision is urged on us in the name of First Amendment rights, but in my view the judgment neither is constitutionally required nor serves the interests of representative democracy. ...

"[W]e deal here with a highly practical and rather fundamental element of our political system, not the theoretical abstractions of a political science seminar. In concluding that patronage hiring practices are unconstitutional, the plurality seriously underestimates the strength of the government interest --- especially at the local level --- in allowing some patronage hiring, and it exaggerates the perceived burden on First Amendment rights.

"It is against decades of experience to the contrary, then, that the plurality opinion concludes that patronage hiring practices interfere with the 'free functioning of the electoral process.' ...

"The judgment today unnecessarily constitutionalizes another element of American life --- an element certainly not without its faults but one which generations have accepted as on balance having merit. We should have heeded instead the admonition of Justice Holmes that '[i]f a thing has been practiced for two hundred years by common consent, it will need a strong case for the Fourteenth Amendment to affect it .... .'"[14]

Who has the better side of this argument? No one can say with logical or scientific exactness. All depends on a sliding scale of values. Perhaps Justice Brennan right "mere difference of political persuasion" relates little to "poor performance." Yet at-will employees have motives to good performance, motives absent in employees surrounded by the near insurmountable barriers to discharging civil servants. Perhaps Brennan right "political loyalty" not needed in employees below the policymaking level. Yet already we have seen civil servants obstruct presidential policy, working with public interest lawyers and through the courts. Brennan certainly right the case did not bring about the "demise" of parties, yet did the ruling contribute to their present weakness, and if so, does that carry negative consequences? On the other hand, Justice Powell certainly right patronage a "practice as old as the republic." Powell looks right, too, that over "decades of experience," existing practice did not seem to overly "interfere with the free functioning of the electoral process." America seemed a robust democracy, chock full to bursting with free speech and association. After the case, free speech and association stayed about the same.

But whoever right or wrong, the judicial revolution made progress, deductive, top-down politics made progress. The bureaucracy turned into a monolithic meritocracy, came more nearly to resemble the federal judiciary. The hand of democracy receded from control. Safe within the cocoon of their rights, the bureaucracy spin out their lives, a vast pyramid of officialdom with the Court at the pinnacle. Whether this structure more accountable and efficient than the hybrid form, which mixed patronage with civil service, leaving politicians on top, not self-evident. But the system is evidently more deductive, less inductive. And this system looks quite a bit more rigid, much less flexible.

The most controversial case – Decided in 1973, Roe v Wade

continues the Court's most controversial case. Writing for the majority, Justice Harry A. Blackmun will find implied in the Constitution a right to abortion. Remarkable as creating a new constitutional right, remarkable as reversing laws a century old, remarkable as near total victory for abortion advocates, remarkable as a great triumph of the judicial revolution, yet this case sits not as easy in the saddle as others, continually in fear of being bucked off in the next go round. Operating at the limits of human understanding, the case operates at the limits of judicial power, and together these operate unsteadily.

Best let the case speak for itself. Justice Blackmun sets out the basic issue: "This Texas federal appeal ... present[s] constitutional challenges to state criminal abortion legislation. The Texas statutes under attack here are typical of those what have been in effect in many States for approximately a century. ... The Texas statutes ... make it a crime to 'procure an abortion,' ... except with respect to 'an abortion procured ... by medical advice for saving the life of the mother.' ... Jane Roe, a single woman who was residing in Dallas County, Texas, instituted this federal action ... She sought a ... judgment that the Texas criminal abortion statures were unconstitutional ... Roe alleged that she was an unmarried and pregnant; that she wished to terminate her pregnancy by an abortion."[15]

Thus, the lawyers for the plaintiff, Jane Roe, a pseudonym for the young woman, who at that time wished to remain anonymous, were challenging the long-standing laws against abortion as violating the Constitution. But while the legal issue may be so clearly framed, the underlying questions appear not capable of being so clearly answered. Justice Blackmun writes: "Our task, of course, is to resolve the issue by constitutional measurement, free of emotion and predilection."[16] But where to find such measurement may bemuse, since the questions stubbornly resist answers not based upon emotion and predilection.

First, when does life begin? Second, who possesses what rights? Labeling themselves "pro-choice," one side insists the woman possesses a choice, a right to an abortion. Labeling themselves "pro-life," the other side insists the unborn possesses a right to life, a right against an abortion. But these opposites don't exhaust the alternatives. Does a women possess a right to an abortion, but only up to a point, say when the fetus viable, capable of independent life? Or does the fetus possess a right to life from the moment of conception? Does a woman possess a right to an abortion in limited cases, say when pregnancy results from rape, say when tests show birth defects, or say when the pregnancy threatens the mother's own life?

As to that initial question, when life begins upon which so much else seems to depend, Justice Blackmun frankly renounces a final answer, writing: "We need not resolve the difficult question of when life begins. When those trained in the respective disciplines of medicine, philosophy, and theology are unable to arrive at any consensus, the judiciary, at this point in the development of man's knowledge, is not in a position as to speculate as to the answer."[17] Yet such an admission looks at odds with his earlier statement that: "Our task, of course, is to resolve the issue by constitutional measurement, free of emotion and predilection." When neither scientific objectivity nor consensus exists, how answer the questions "free of emotion and predilection?"

To learn how Justice Blackmun claims to have pulled off this task, let us plunge into the legal thicket of his opinion. Here is the heart of it, expressed in language no one but a lawyer could love: "The Constitution does not explicitly mention any right to privacy. In a line of decisions, however, going back as far as Union Pacific R. Co. v. Botsford (1891), the Court has recognized that a right of personal privacy, or a guarantee of certain areas or zones of privacy, does exist under the Constitution. In varying contexts, the Court or individual justices have, indeed, found at least the roots of that right in the First Amendment, Stanley v. Georgia (1969); in the Fourth and Fifth Amendments, Terry v. Ohio (1968), Katz v. United States (1967), ... in the penumbras of the Bill of Rights, Griswold v. Connecticut; in the Ninth Amendment ... or in the concept of liberty guaranteed by the first section of the Fourteenth Amendment, see Meyer v Nebraska (1923). These decisions make it clear that only personal rights that can be deemed 'fundamental" or 'implicit in the concept of ordered liberty,' ... are included in the guarantee of personal privacy. They also make clear that the right has some extension to activities relating to marriage, Loving v Virginia (1967); procreation, Skinner v Oklahoma (1942); contraception, Eisenstadt v Baird; family relationships, Prince v Massachusetts (1944); and childrearing and education, Pierce v Society of Sisters (1925), Meyer v Nebraska, supra."[18]

With no other intervening words, he reaches his implication and draws this conclusion: "This right to privacy ... is broad enough to encompass a woman's decisions whether or not to terminate the pregnancy."[19]

Untangling the legal logic – Now in the first place Blackmun says: "The Constitution does not explicitly mention any right to privacy," so already we enter the land of constitutional implication. In the second place, we know this right of privacy did not previously include a right to an abortion, so we also enter the land of double constitutional implication, one implication loaded onto the back of another. Then how does he reach these implications? To untangle the mass of his legal logic, let us take a piece at a time.

Blackmun says: "In a line of decisions, however, going back as far as Union Pacific R. Co. v. Botsford (1891), the Court has recognized that a right of personal privacy, or a guarantee of certain areas or zones of privacy, does exist under the Constitution." Now if we go back and read the cited case, we find a lady had sued the railroad for injuries, and the railroad lawyers demanding a surgical operation to determine the extent of her injuries. While an individual alleging injury must submit to medical examination, demanding they undergo surgery goes too far, and the Court so ruled. Next he says: "[T]he Court or individual justices have, indeed, found at least the roots of that right in the First Amendment, Stanley v. Georgia (1969)." Of course, the 1st Amendment guarantees freedom of speech, and the cited case had overturned a conviction for possessing reels of pornographic material turned up in the search of a bookmaker's house. By so doing, the Court established a right to possess pornography in one's home. Next he says: "the Fourth and Fifth Amendments, Terry v. Ohio (1968), Katz v. United States (1967), Boyd v. United States (1886) ... ." Of course, the 4th and 5th Amendments guarantee against unreasonable search and seizure and self-incrimination. In 1968, Terry v Ohio held a police officer needed reasonable suspicion to stop and frisk an individual on the street. In 1967 in Katz v U.S., the FBI attached an eavesdropping device to the outside of a public phone booth, listening as a suspected gambler transacted business. The Court held this violated his right against unreasonable search and seizure. While way back in 1886, Boyd v U.S. simply held the authorities could not search a house without a warrant.

Next Blackmun cites Griswold v Connecticut (1965), which stands out from the other cases, not so much for the holding as the language. This case dealt with a statute Justice Potter Stewart in dissent called an "uncommonly silly law,"[20] passed by Connecticut back in 1879, which banned the sale of contraceptives even to married couples. The Court turned lose Justice William O. Douglas to write the opinion, and he turned lose some memorable phraseology in striking down the law, saying: "The First Amendment has penumbras where privacy is protected from governmental intrusion." He amplified that "specific guarantees in the Bill of Rights have penumbras, formed by the emanations from those guarantees that help give them life and substance."[21] Now the dictionary defines "penumbra" as "a surrounding or adjoining region in which something exists to a lesser degree ... a surrounding atmosphere" and defines an "emanation" as "a flowing forth." So Douglas' words quickly attained legal renown, generally conceded to exceed any prior notion of constitutional interpretation. If the Court interprets the Constitution on a "surrounding atmosphere" which "flows forth," the process stands revealed as little more than a rational pretense covering the nakedness of judicial will.

But returning to Justice Blackmun's list of authorities, the 9th Amendment provides that: "The enumeration in the Constitution, of certain rights, shall not be construed to deny or disparage others retained by the people." In 1928, Meyer v Nebraska held unconstitutional a state law requiring public education in only the English language. In 1967, Skinner v Oklahoma ruled unconstitutional compulsory sterilization as a punishment for crime. In 1972, Eisenstadt held unconstitutional a law against possession of contraceptives by unmarried individuals. In 1944, Prince v Massachusetts involved a Jehovah's Witness minister who used a child to distribute religious literature, which Massachusetts' law prohibited. Upholding the conviction, the Court held states had broad to regulate the actions and treatment of children.

Such sums up the authorities upon which Blackmun's implications rely. From these authorities he implies a "right to privacy." From this right he implies a "right to abortion." To repeat his operative words: "This right to privacy ... is broad enough to encompass a woman's decisions whether or not to terminate the pregnancy."

Granting this conclusion perfectly reasonable, which a great many critics fail to grant, yet the deduction appears far from compelled. On the contrary, honesty would rather compel an admission: The conclusion reaches an implication not "free of emotion and predilection." When neither scientific objectivity nor consensus available, the logic must take a leap of faith, and that leap of faith will rest upon reasons most convincing to the reasoner, nothing more. In other words, Justice Blackmun's perfectly reasonable conclusion takes a perfectly reasonably side, but no more. Nothing in the Constitution compels him. Rather to be free of hypocrisy, we must admit he compelled the Constitution.

But to follow Justice Blackmun's opinion to the end, having implied a new right to abortion, he shortly finds this a "fundamental" right, which a state can only limit for a compelling interest, only limit in the least restrictive way. He writes: "Where certain 'fundamental rights' are involved, the Court has held that regulation limiting these rights may be justified only by a "compelling state interest'... ."[22] This brings to his ultimate holding.

With respect to abortion, he finds that fundamental right not absolute, the state with a compelling interest. He says: "[A] State may properly assert important interests in safeguarding health, in maintaining medical standard, and in protecting potential life. The privacy right involved, therefore, cannot be said to be absolute." Then he sets out two situations where he finds the right to abortion properly limited:

"With respect to the State's important and legitimate interest in the health of the mother, the 'compelling' point, in the light of present medical knowledge, is at approximately the end of the first trimester. This is so because of the now-established medical fact ... that until the end of the first trimester mortality in abortion may be less than mortality in normal childbirth. ... With respect to the State's important and legitimate interest in potential life, the 'compelling point' is at viability. This is so because the fetus then presumably has the capability of meaningful life outside the mother's womb. State regulation protective of fetal life after viability thus has both logical and biological justifications."[23]

So effectively, Roe v Wade allows abortion in the first trimester of pregnancy. Any more elaborate analysis of the case serves no purpose here. Suffice to say, one may agree or disagree with Roe v Wade, but how not agree, how disagree the case operates at the farthest limits so far seen for judicial power? "Everything's up to date and they've gone about as far as they can go." Roe v Wade reaches at least to the limits of rational implication. The ascent to power complete for the moment, the Court need do no more than enjoy the perquisites.

Classifying revolutions – To classic political science, winning revolutions come in just three types, just as governments come in just three types. The one follows from the other, since winning revolutions end as governments. A winning revolution ends as a monarchical, an aristocratic, or a democratic government. While to democratic theory, such seems an easy way to tell a "good" from a "bad" revolution. Disregard the ideological façade and regard the institutional structure. Unless a revolution erects a democracy, the rest is no more than propaganda and lies.

But if such the rule, the judicial revolution must claim an exemption. They deny nothing more vehemently than their type. Never expressly rejecting the fundamental right to democratic process, yet they deem other rights even more fundamental, in essence their ideological version of individual and minority rights. Next they subsume their ideology under their definition of "democracy." Then by protecting and enhancing those "rights," they assert to protect and enhance "democracy." Yet their revolution ends in aristocratic, not democratic government. The unelected Court rules, not the people through elections. Then if their revolution "good," not "bad," what explains the exceptionalism?

To consider the difficulty, compare the history of modern revolutions, consider the failures against the successes. Invariably the failures redefined democracy into their ideology, then in the name of democracy, imposed their ideology. Invariably the successes actually set up a working democracy. As archetypes, compare the 1917 Russian Revolution with the 1991 fall of the Soviet Union. In 1917, the Communists used Marxist ideology to redefine democracy. Marx had proclaimed democracy the "truth," saying: "All forms of the state have democracy for their truth, and for that reason are false to the extent that they are not democracy."[24] But he could not heap enough scorn upon "bourgeois" democracy, like in Britain or the United States. Instead, true democracy demanded: *"From each according to his ability, to each according to his needs,"*[25] and as the first step *"abolishing private property."*[26] Once accomplished, "In place of the old bourgeois society ... we shall have an association in which the free development of each is the condition for the free development of all."[27] But this laudable end forced a violent means. "Between capitalist and communist society there lies the period of the revolutionary transformation of the one into the other. Corresponding to this is also a political transition period in which the state can be nothing but *the revolutionary dictatorship of the proletariat.*"[28] Consequently, true democracy required a dictatorship. What an appealing idea to so many revolutionaries. To bestow true equality and true democracy, they had to assume dictatorial powers. Lenin and Stalin loved this theory. More surprisingly, a great many European and American intellectuals loved the theory, too. But the results in practice greatly disappointed the later. Eventually the ideological promise separated farther and farther from the institutional reality, so far that only willful blindness could conceal the contradiction. Almost by consensus in 1991, the next Russian revolution actually tried to set up a working democracy. If the effort somewhat disappointed, who doubts the 1917 revolution a catastrophe, the 1991 reforms a step in the right direction?

These same phenomena kept recurring, profoundly non-democratic revolutions masquerading under the name of democracy, over and over with the same disastrous results. After World War I, the fascists came up with "authoritarian democracy," where a great leader expressed the people's true and highest democratic will. While after World War II, People's Republic became a synonym for totalitarian regime. China became the People's Republic of China, neighboring North Korea the Democratic People's Republic of Korea. The Stalinist puppet states across Eastern Europe all became People's Republics. If not for the tragic costs, such mislabeling would qualify as farce. In a classic in the genre, the Libyan tyrant, Muammar Ghadafi, told the world in his little *Green Book*: "Political struggle that results in the victory of a candidate with, for example, 51 per cent of the votes leads to a dictatorial governing body in the guise of a democracy." While no more coherent, the further logic found "the solution to democracy" in his personal and arbitrary rule. How could one make up such absurdities, truth once again stranger than fiction?

With these compare the successful revolutions, the ones that actually set up a democracy. We might go back as far as the Glorious Revolution of 1688, which by finally winning sovereignty for Parliament, gave the world a working model for representative democracy. Almost exactly an hundred years later in 1787, the Constitutional Convention closely followed the model with the Constitution. In the next century and a half, France with many stops and starts finally became a real democracy. After World War II, the victors frankly imposed democracy on West Germany, Italy, and Japan. In 1947, India gained independence with a democratic constitution. With the fall of the iron curtain in 1989, the nations of Eastern Europe rapidly democratized. In 1998, Indonesia, the world's fourth most populous country, replaced a military junta with a democratic government. Others joined and continue to join the ranks. What people cannot count themselves fortunate from the day their name heard upon the roll call of working democracies?

But why should non-democratic revolutions turn out badly and democratic revolutions well? Democratic theory sees basically four causes. First, real freedom comes only from a working democracy, where the people actually elect and retain sufficient checks upon the officials, since otherwise the people do not really rule themselves, but somebody else rules the people. Second, no one's rights being any better than anyone else's, only an elected legislature takes into account the rights of all the people. The English historian A.F. Pollard has well made this point: "If the interest of the community is the supreme consideration, it must be superior to the liberty of any section; and any differentiation must be based, not on the absolute right of any class, but on the value which concessions to a particular class may have for the community as a whole. ... The only criterion of such issues is the common sense and conscience of the community expressed by means of parliament. On that all liberty must depend."[29]

Third, only the people rule in the public interest, since when somebody else rules, they rule in their interests, not the public interest. Fourth, more recent theorists stress the openness and bottom-up nature of democratic systems, as compared to the closed, top-down nature of monarchy or aristocratic systems. Democracies rapidly transmit information back and forth, while elections serve as a feedback mechanism, constantly correcting the course of the laws and government. As a result, democracy far out-performs at innovation and diffusion, churning out all sorts of useful knowledge, maximizing creativity, efficiency, and adaptability, getting far more out of available resources, responding far more agilely to change.

If such briefly sums up the natural history of revolutions, what grants the "judicial revolution" an exemption from the natural laws? Revolutionary life forms aspire to power, much as plants aspire to light. The natural life of the judicial revolution displayed such an attraction through every cycle of growth. The Court acquired more power like trees grow annual rings, driven to greater width and height by the inner chemistry. So far the biology matches with the DNA of any revolution you can name, good or bad. But when you come to typing the genome, the judicial revolution types as non-democratic, not sitting up a working democracy. Elsewhere all the species under that genus matured as noxious weeds, not the pride of the garden. Then had the judicial revolutionaries succeeded in breeding a new hybrid, which flowered as new and improved government? The journals of other revolutions had repeatedly announced such inventions, advances such as the Rights of Man or Communism. But these heralded breakthroughs all turned out unreliable science, biased not a little by the ambitions of the researchers. Yet had the judicial revolutionaries finally re-written the formula, achieving that longed for feat of scientific immortality, shifting the paradigm? The peer review must start with the natural history of the judicial revolution itself.

Classifying the judicial revolution – And in the first place, a "judicial revolution" sounds a contradiction in terms. Courts uphold the laws, while revolutions overthrow governments. How do both at the same time? The revolutionary elite, the intellectuals, academics, lawyers, judges, whoever came up with the phrase, undoubtedly enjoyed this play on words, which let them display their usual ingenuity. While claiming to do the one, they would actually accomplish the other. While claiming to uphold the constitutional law, they actually overthrew the constitutional law, seizing more power for themselves. Proving the pen as mighty as the sword, rather than mobs in the streets and heads on pikes, the justices calmly pronounced judgment from the bench, acting under all the forms of law, doing no more violence than to coerce the words. While in this way unique, yet they carefully complied with the first law of revolutionary action: Seize the power of the government.

Nor did the judicial revolutionaries vary much from the typical ideological script, describing their cause in idealistic terms, describing their goals as "democratic." They always explained and justified themselves as vindicating "rights." As Justice Warren wrote in Miranda: "These precious rights were fixed in our Constitution only after centuries of persecution and struggle. ... We cannot depart from this noble heritage." They often specifically referred to such "rights" as "democratic." For example, Justice Brennan was heard above to say in the Elrod v Burns, the case outlawing patronage, that: "Patronage, therefore, to the extent it compels or restrains belief and association, is inimical to the process which undergirds our system of government and 'is at war with the deeper traditions of democracy embedded in the First Amendment.'"

So there are "deeper traditions of democracy embedded" in such rights as the 1st Amendment. So if the democratic process reaches outcomes like patronage, the Court will protect the "deeper traditions of democracy." So democracy becomes something other than democratic process, becomes the "deeper traditions" apprehended by the Court. How can this thesis not remind of those other revolutions, which re-defined democracy into something else, then claimed that in advancing that something else, they advanced democracy?

But also as typical, since "rights" rest upon ethical reasons, the judicial revolution shortly came up against the trouble with ethical reasons. One can state an ethical rule clearly enough, even apply the rule clearly enough, solving an easy case, but more detailed application leads to harder cases, not so easily solved. Take "thou shalt not kill." All agree that means not commit murder, but not all agree capital punishment falls outside the commandment. In the same way take "all men are created equal." All agree that means "equal rights," but not all agree equal rights command affirmative action. The lawyers have a saying that bad cases make bad law. A corollary might be that hard cases make even good laws hard to apply.

But again typically, revolutionaries can begin with the easier cases. Failed governments never in short supply, reform routinely long delayed, they can begin with the real grievances. In 1789, the French Revolution could begin by crying out against the abuses of the *Ancien Regime*, proclaiming the Rights of Man. In 1917, the Russian Communists could begin by pulling down the centuries old autocracy of the czars, proclaiming the rights of the proletariat. In 1954, the judicial revolutionaries enjoyed just such an advantage. They could begin with the Brown Case, assailing the evils of segregation, proclaiming equality and fairness.

But just as typically, revolutions shortly come to the harder cases, not untypically losing their way. Somehow in France, the Rights of Man led to the Reign of Terror and the reign of the Emperor Napoleon. Somehow in Russia, the rights of the proletariat led to Stalin's terror and the terror of the Soviet Empire. But few revolutionaries ever admit to losing their way. They keep insisting to apply the people's rights clearly enough, only fewer and fewer people believe them. The judicial revolution, too, shortly came to the harder cases, and the judicial revolutionaries, too, kept insisting to apply equality and fairness clearly enough. But while Brown had commanded a consensus, the later cases commanded no such consensus.

We saw the cases get harder. Accepting segregation in education violates equality, yet why did desegregation demand massive busing rather than neighborhood schools? Accepting religious toleration, why did toleration demand a new wall of separation between church and state rather than the prior religious settlement? Accepting free speech, why did free-speech demand protection for obscenity rather the earlier restraint on obscenity? Accepting the rights of the accused, why did their rights demand the Miranda Warnings rather than the existing voluntariness rule on confessions? Accepting the right to entitlements, why did entitlements demand welfare shopping? Accepting government employees' rights, why did their rights demand a monolithic civil service? Accepting even a dubious right to privacy, why did privacy demand a right to abortion?

We saw the consensus erode. The majority backed Brown, Congress passing the Civil Rights Act of 1964 and Voting Rights of 1965. But a majority more seldom backed the later cases, which all overturned congressional or state laws. In fact, Congress and the states often sought to fight back, albeit unsuccessfully. For an example since Miranda just mentioned, that case received harsh criticism, and in 1968, Congress actually passed a law purporting to reverse the ruling. After being ignored for some thirty years, in 2000, the Court finally struck down this law in Dickerson v. U.S.[30]

Then how not see: To explain and justify the judicial revolution as vindicating "rights" an argument with a dubious presumption. When others no longer went along, you had to presume the revolution kept getting it right. Most went along at the start, went along with Brown, the easy case, agreed segregation violated equality and fairness. But shortly the argument came to the harder cases, equality and fairness harder to apply, agreement harder, consensus harder. Eventually, you reached the parting of the ways. Either people agreed, or they disagreed. But since the Court kept overthrowing majority legislation, apparently fewer and fewer agreed. Then at this parting of the ways, what settled the argument, unless you presumed the revolutionaries simply got it right, even when the majority got it wrong?

Then how not also see: Precisely at this parting of the ways, the judicial revolutionaries parted with democracy, parted at precisely the point so many other revolutions parted, precisely at the point where consensus lost. As that pathway fades before the eye, the true believer still sees the path clearly in his mind's eye. So guided with an inner certitude, the judicial revolutionaries took a familiar turning in the road. They imposed authority on the argument. But rather than go down that broad and beckoning avenue with open violence, like the *sans-culottes* storming the Bastille or the Bolsheviks the Winter Palace, the judicial revolution found a subtler work-around. They pulled off more a palace coup, where one government ministry seizes power from another government ministry. When "the consent of the governed" no longer rallied behind the revolutionary elite, the elected branches as quickly fell out of sympathy with the revolution. So the revolutionary elite proposed a deal to that other elite, the unelected branch, the lifetime justices. In the name of the revolutionary ideology, let the Court overthrown Congress and the states, taking power for itself. Not only would the ideology provide the pretext, the revolutionary vanguard would provide the necessary outside support, sufficient to block any counter-revolution in Congress and the states. By this strategy both won. The judicial revolutionaries imposed the Court's authority on the argument, winning for themselves. The Court re-gained the authority lost by their institutional defeat during the New Deal, winning for themselves. Moreover, the Court's adherence lent an air of complete legitimacy, conforming to accepted judicial procedure, where both sides received a hearing. Yet no show of hands counted except on the lifetime Court. While no one guillotined, no one sent to the gulag, yet the final orders like the *lettre de cachet* or ukase, no appeal to the people, backed by all the force of the state.

Dare one commit the ancient crime of *lese-majesty*, violating the majesty of a reigning sovereign in the intellectual realm? The judicial revolutionaries have now ruled so long their account official, written in the textbooks, orthodox in the law schools and universities. They have always explained and justified their cause as vindicating "rights" and "democracy." Yet if one might make so bold as to look this intellectual monarch in the face, her features bear a strong familial resemblance to the dynasts of failed revolutions. Her speeches from the throne sound much like their speeches. Clever she may be, but does the public not hear the same old revolutionary rhetoric? She promises to vindicate their rights. She promises democracy. But the lady carefully pre-selects the promised rights, selecting for rights adapted to vindicate her rule, not rule by the people.

Very different would be the reign of classic political science and democratic theory, intellectual traditions with strong claims to rule in this realm themselves. If we would but obey their sovereignty, rather than endless arguments over "rights," never able to agree, we might put the argument into another form, which might permit wider agreement. If we must appeal to authority, which finally we must, since political arguments must end with some authority laying down the law, we might also agree how best to make that appeal to authority.

Democratic theory holds that the most fundamental right "the consent of the governed." Classic political science holds that the only way to consult such consent through the democratic process. Will most not agree they have such a right to consent to their government and also not agree others have the same right? Will most not further agree only democracy consults this primary right? Then most will have agreed how to settle all the other arguments over "rights." Most will have agreed the only legitimate appeal to authority an appeal through democratic process.

But the judicial revolutionaries will not agree. They continue to deny nothing more vehemently than their revolutionary type. They continue to proclaim their cause vindicates "rights" and "democracy." They continue to rule through the Court. The judicial revolution continues.

CHAPTER 14

Judicial Ideology

Having traveled the Court's cases with a companion who professed some political science, as well as some more recent social science, a reader who glances into the standard guidebooks finds the journey otherwise described. We might label our traveling companion the Institutionalist, since he kept pointing to the institutions. While we might label these standard guides the Idealists, since they point to the ideas, when formalized the ideologies. The Institutionalist kept insisting on the influence of institutions, while the Idealists insist on the influence of ideas. The Institutionalist saw the cases as monuments to institutional power, but the Idealists see the cases as monuments to the power of ideas.

A traveler in a strange land should not neglect to take the standard tour, and so we need to re-visit the cases with the standard guidebooks in hand. But let the Institutionalist come along as well, speaking up when of a mind. In this way, let us set up a dialogue. Since there seems some variance, let both sides express their views, the readers hopefully the impartial audience, judging between them, not compelled except by inner conviction, the prerogative of gentlemen since the days of Socrates in all his glory.

The standard guides to the Court – Let the standard guides speak in their own way, so far as practical in their own words. Nor are they reluctant. Their books fill a daunting length of shelves in the law library. Who could read all, let alone keep all in mind? But the more one reads, the more a pattern emerges. In a long and well-established tradition, they study the lives of the justices and set them in their time and place. Then they tirelessly follow all the twists and turns of legal doctrine, which they as painstakingly trace to what Justice Holmes called, in another famous turn of phrase, "the felt necessities of the time, the prevalent moral and political theories, intuitions of public policy, avowed or unconscious, and even the prejudices which judges share with their fellow-men."[1]

Let us briefly look at such treatments of the three longest-running

Courts, which cover most of the ground to the New Deal. These would be the Marshall Court (1801 to 1835), the Taney Court (1836 to 1864), and the Fuller Court (1888 to 1910). Then let us cover the new ground broken by the Warren Court (1953 to 1969), which led the judicial revolution and whose legacy looms largest today. Along the way, let us witness how ideological contests play out between the justices, glancing inside the Warren Court at such a contest. Let us pause to notice how elevation to the Court often affects the thinking of the elevated. Finally, let us hear how these guides sum up the Court.

The Marshall Court – At the source looms up the towering figure of John Marshall, whose long life (1755 to 1835) spanned the formative years of the Republic and who served as Chief Justice longest (from 1801 to 1835). A biographer sums up Marshall's central ideology this way: "He believed in a strong central government, the supremacy of the constitution, the necessity for an independent judiciary, and the inalienable right to possess, enjoy, and augment private property."[2] Another puts the matter slightly differently: "The Federalist Party, to which Marshall belonged, favored a strong central government, encouragement of industry, protection of property, and a well-ordered society."[3]

The Marshall Court's great cases are seen as flowing from these central tenets. Marbury v Madison (1803) claimed the power of judicial review, flowing from the belief in an "independent judiciary." Fletcher v Peck (1810) for the first time held a state statute unconstitutional, asserting federal supremacy, flowing from a belief in a "strong central government." Martin v Hunter's Lessee (1816) and Cohens v Virginia (1821) overturned state court decisions, again asserting and flowing from the same belief. McCulloch v Maryland (1819) expansively read the "necessary and proper clause," approving congressional creation of the Second Bank of the United States, not only asserting wide federal authority, but as Marshall saw it, providing "encouragement of industry." The Dartmouth College Case (1819) strictly construed the "contract clause" against the states, providing "protection of property." Gibbons v Ogden (1824) construed favorably to federal authority the "commerce clause," again as Marshall saw it, providing "encouragement of industry."

The Taney Court – Taking office in 1836, his successor, Roger Brooke Taney, served the second longest tenure, lasting until his death in 1864. A biographer sums up his ideological pattern this way: "In some respects, particularly its general willingness to grant more authority to state governments to regulate in the public interest, the Taney Court's record represented a departure from the Marshall era. In other ways, however, the Taney Court built on the Marshall legacy, especially in preserving the significant role of the Supreme Court and the federal courts generally in the American constitutional system. Moreover, even if Marshall and Taney differed in what they believed was the better method of promoting economic growth and development, the two chief justices shared a forward-looking belief in American entrepreneurship and the capitalistic market."[4]

This ideology is then seen as working out through the cases. The belief in "entrepreneurship and the capitalistic market" marked a series of cases that fostered the business corporation, then a new form of doing business and which responded to the needs of a national market and the technological acceleration leading to industrialization. The Charles River Bridge Case (1837) allowed more state regulation of corporations, a decision that actually encouraged the corporate form, since states were more willing to create corporations when they could control them. Bank of Augusta v Earle (1839) held a state could not stop an out-of-state bank from doing business in their state, assuring all sorts of corporations could do business across state lines. Bronson v Kinzie (1843) held unconstitutional a state law restricting foreclosures, thus preventing states from discriminating against out-of-state lenders. Louisville v Letson (1844) opened the federal courts to corporations under "diversity jurisdiction," letting them remove cases to federal court when they were sued in another state, affording an important protection to corporations against local animus. Swift v Tyson (1842) began the creation of a federal common law to govern commercial transactions, which replaced state laws that discriminated against out-of-state corporations and so promoted a national marketplace.

As for the unpleasantness surrounding Dred Scott, over and over we find expressed such views as the following: "If the political results of *Dred Scott* were monumental, the constitutional and legal impact of the decision was minimal. As a matter of law, the opinion had a short life.... The Thirteenth Amendment [ratified in 1865] abolished slavery in the United States. ... In short, although it had helped bring about the Civil War, the *Dred Scott* decision had had virtually no effect on American constitutional law."[5]

"Of all the cases decided by the Marshall and Taney Courts, hardly more than a hundred dealt with slavery, and most of these did so indirectly. Only a handful of these cases are remembered; not one including *Dred Scott v. Sandford* (unless one counts the unintended lesson on judicial humility), contributed any lasting principle to

American law."[6]

Yes, the Institutionalist breaks in, I find this very odd. They see Dred Scott as important in immediate effect, helping bring on the Civil War, yet otherwise hardly matters, no more than a relic of discarded doctrine, since the formal doctrine about slavery later discarded. Yet surely the case contains not just a doctrine about slavery, but a new doctrine of unrestrained judicial review, which greatly enhanced judicial power. But in the same way Justice Taney failed explicitly to discuss that question in the case, his modern critics go right by that same question. But excuse my interruption and let them go on with what they were saying.

The Fuller Court – Chief Justice Melville Westin Fuller (who lived 1833 to 1910) served the third longest tenure (from 1888 to 1910). The leading modern scholar on the Fuller Court sums up the ideological bent this way: "Fuller and his colleagues believed that individual liberty and property rights were interdependent. The Fuller Court was therefore dedicated to economic liberty as the preeminent constitutional value. The jurisprudence of the Fuller era was characterized by the principles of limited government, state autonomy, and respect for the rights of property owners."[7]

These values are then seen as motivating the cases. Chicago, Milwaukee, and St. Paul Railway Co. v Minnesota (1890) and Smyth v Ames (1898) limited government regulation of railroads and other businesses. Of course, the more famous Lochner v New York (1905) threw out the New York law that tried to limit work to no more than 60 hours a week. So that case was regarded as limiting government regulation by protecting freedom of contract. On the other hand, unions were regarded as inimical to economic liberty and property rights. So In re Debs (1895) approved the use of injunctions against unions. As we saw, the Danbury Hatters Cases (1908) turned the Sherman Anti-Trust Act against them. Adair v United States (1908) allowed yellow-dog contracts, which made an employee pledge not to join a union. In a rather striking instance of their care for the "rights of property," the Pollock Case (1895) held an income tax unconstitutional, a decision later overturned by the 16th Amendment (1913). Their concern with limited government also showed with ICC v Cincinnati, New Orleans, and Texas Pacific Railway Co. (1897) and ICC v Alabama Midland Railway Co. (1897), which limited the authority granted the ICC to regulate railroads. Of course, that same concern had shown in E.C. Knight (1895), which had so narrowly read the Sherman Anti-Trust Act of 1890 as to negate the effort to outlaw monopolies, although it must be noted that the Northern Securities Case (1904) backtracked slightly.

As for Plessy v Ferguson (1896), we find the Fuller Court portrayed as no more than "majoritarian," as going along with the majority. The following serve as typical: "[The] Fuller Court's acquiescence in the relegation of the Negro to second-class citizenship represented accommodation to the facts of turn-of-the-century America."[8] Or, "As public opinion in the North abandoned Reconstruction, white supremacist sentiments gained ascendency in southern politics. With the acquiescence of northerners, southern Democrats restricted black suffrage and imposed formal racial segregation on many social institutions."[9] Or, "Perhaps one should conclude that *because* the Negro was abandoned by Congress and the President he was also repudiated by the courts."[10] Or finally, "All the same, perhaps, one should not be too harsh judging the Fuller Court for a decision that mirrored its own time and place."[11]

Well, again I cannot forbear, the Institutionalist breaks in, I just cannot see how constitutional amendments and congressional laws enacted by the majority do not represent the will of the majority. I do not see how when the Court interprets these away, it expresses the will of the majority. But let them go on to the Warren Court.

The Warren Court – Earl Warren's tenure ran from 1953 to 1969, if less long not less influential than the others. Professor Bernard Schwartz, who law clerked for Warren, later taught for many years at New York City Law School, and wrote a biography of the man he obviously so greatly admired, describes Warren's approach this way: "Throughout his tenure on the Court, the Chief Justice tended to use 'fairness' as the polestar of his judicial approach. ...

"The Warren approach ... left little room for deference to the legislature, the core of the restraint canon. Warren never considered constitutional issues in the light of any desired deference to the legislature. Instead, he decided those issues based on his own independent judgment, normally giving little weight to the fact that a reasonable legislator might have voted for the challenged law.

"For Chief Justice Warren, the issue on judicial review was not *reasonableness* but *rightness*. If the law was contrary to his own conception of what the Constitution demanded, it did not matter that a reasonable legislator might reach the opposite conclusion. ... For the Chief Justice ... legislative reasonableness was irrelevant when the practice conflicted with his own interpretation of the Constitution.[12]

"[H]e was the paradigm of a 'result-oriented' judge, who used his power to secure the result he deemed right in the cases that came before his Court.[13]

"Employing the authority of the ermine to the utmost, he never hesitated to do whatever he thought necessary to translate his own conceptions of fairness and justice into the law of the land."[14]

But what more specifically defined "fairness" and "rightness" in his mind? Professor Mark Tushnet, a leading constitutional scholar, tells us: "The Warren Court was a liberal Court. After 1962 it was one institution in a unified government dominated in both Congress and the presidency by liberal Democrats." But again, what more precisely defined "liberal" or "liberal Democrat?" Professor Tushnet elsewhere tells us the "Warren Court implemented the modern liberal agenda, enforcing norms of fair treatment and racial equality."[15] Then generally, we may conclude the "liberal agenda" included "norms of fair treatment and racial equality," and for a detailed list of items may simply look at the cases which "implemented" the agenda.

In 1954, Brown v Board of Education changed prior precedent, finally ruling segregation unconstitutional. The 1962 and 1964 cases of Baker v Carr and Reynolds v Sims changed prior precedent about legislative apportionment, going to the "one-man, one-vote" rule, requiring U.S. House and state legislative districts of equal size. A series of cases such as Yates v U.S. and Service v Dulles (both 1957) changed prior precedents against advocating revolutionary violence, in essence allowing anything except "incitement to imminent lawless action." The Roth Case (1957) began to change the prior precedent on obscenity, in essence eventually allowing almost all obscenity. Engel v Vitale (1962) and Abington School District (1963) changed prior precedent on religion, finding prayer and Bible reading in the public schools unconstitutional. Such cases as Gideon v Wainwright (1963) and Miranda (1966) changed prior precedent on criminal procedure, vastly increasing the rights of the accused.

All of this true enough, the Institutionalist puts in, but I believe there were internal ideological struggles in the Warren Court, as generally happens, since with the exception of the Marshall Court, justices frequently dissent. Would they discuss an instance to show how such conflicts play out?

An ideological conflict in the Warren Court – Then let us turn to an example, which takes us behind the scenes into the inner workings of the Warren Court. Let us start with Justice Felix Frankfurter (who lived 1882 to 1965). From an earlier generation, he went on the Court earlier (1938), but served through much of Warren's tenure (until 1962). Before going on the Court, Frankfurter taught at Harvard Law School and was a leading voice for the progressive movement. He was friendly to labor, advocating such reforms as the minimum wage, and helped found the ACLU. He condemned the Palmer Raids in 1919 and 1920, which sought to arrest and deport radical leftists, and defended in print the anarchists Sacco and Vanzetti. Close to Franklin Roosevelt, Frankfurter served as a loyal and trusted advisor throughout the New Deal, and Roosevelt appointed him to the Court in 1939. He retired in 1962 after a debilitating stroke.

With such a background, many expected Frankfurter to lead the Court's progressive wing, but events proved otherwise. Having seen so many progressive reforms thwarted by the Court had made him into a faithful adherent to the doctrine of judicial restraint. One of his biographers records what happened when he went on the Court. "McReynolds and Company" refers to the so-called Four Horsemen on the Court (Justices McReynolds, Butler, Sutherland, and Van Devanter), who adamantly opposed the New Deal.

"Frankfurter did in fact frequently disappoint his 'liberal friends' and was quickly disowned by them. He spelled out his explanation in a letter to another friend: 'For twenty-five years,' he said, 'my preoccupation as a student of American law was protest against undue assumption of power by judges. I protested when judges declared law unconstitutional, not because they were laws I favored, but because it was a denial of the democratic process to have our society ruled by judges outside the democratic process.

"'After I became a judge,' he continued, 'I could not change my convictions of what I conceive to be the proper function of a judge and nullify legislation simply because I may not like it. But I find that too many of my friends who protested against McReynolds and Company, acting as a super-legislature, now want me to be a McReynolds for the things they don't like --- that is, to be indifferent to the limits that properly should confine a judge, leaving the remedy for foolish legislation where it mostly belongs, in the hands of an enlightened electorate. I had supposed that that was the best kind of "liberal" doctrine, but as Holmes said long ago, people on the whole don't want justice, they want you to decide cases their way.'"[16]

Well, then, the Institutionalist says, if Frankfurter's career on the Court shows anything, it shows how ideology can decisively influence a justice's performance. You have provided a very convincing example. First and foremost, Frankfurter believed in judicial restraint. Having made the commitment, his intellectual honesty kept him to the vow. But what about Frankfurter's opponents?

Let us turn to them and the outstanding example, Justice William Joseph Brennan, Jr. (on the Court 1956 to 1990). Although perceived as a moderate conservative by the president (Eisenhower) who appointed him, one of his biographies would later dub Brennan the "liberal champion." Just as ideology decisively influenced Frankfurter, ideology decisively influenced Brennan. But he reversed the priorities. Rejecting Frankfurter's pleas for judicial restraint, he led the charge to the judicial revolution.

Professor Schwartz described Brennan's approach this way: "The Brennan approach to law has been called 'instrumental rationality.' Under it the judge reflects upon the values and ideals underlying the legal system, seeks to understand what those ideals requires in the practical world, and molds his decisions to accomplish the desired result. The end is to ensure that proper values prevail and that the decision adopts the best means for attaining that goal. In achieving the goal, the judge is not to be deterred by logic or even a mass of precedent the other way. The Brennan jurisprudence was in large part based upon rejection of the formal logic and case law that stood in the way of giving effect to the Justice's scale of values. Once Brennan determined what the desired end should be, he never had any difficulty in fashioning the legal means to achieve that end."[17]

Late in life after retirement from the Court, Brennan himself would write an essay, *My Life on the Court*, in which he would say: "As I have said many times and in many ways, our Constitution is a charter of human rights and human dignity. It is a bold commitment by a people to the ideal of dignity protected by law. The vision is deeply moving. ...

"I approached my responsibility to interpret the Constitution in the only way I could --- as a twentieth century American concerned about what the Constitution and the Bill of Rights mean to us in our time. The genius of the Constitution rests not in any static meaning it may have had in a world that is dead and gone, but in the adaptability of its great principles to cope with current problems and present needs. ...

"At the heart of each drama was a person who cried out for nothing more than common human dignity. In each case, our Constitution intervened to provide the cloak of dignity. ...

"If I have drawn one lesson in my ninety years it is this: To strike another blow for freedom allows a man to walk a little taller and raise his head a little higher. And while he can, he must."[18]

Of course, Frankfurter lost the power struggle within the Court, and of course, saw Brennan and the other liberals quite differently, as he once made clear in letter to another well-known jurist, Judge Learned Hand. A close friend of Frankfurter's, Hand sat for many years on the U.S. Circuit Court of Appeals in New York (1924 to 1961), where his acute legal mind and trenchant writing style made him an ornament of the American bench. But while many admirers such as Frankfurter actively promoted him for the Supreme Court, the political stars never quite aligned. In this letter Frankfurt refers to Justice Benjamin Cardozo, who sat on the New York Court of Appeals before elevation to the Supreme Court, thus being "brought down from Albany." The 1936 Tipaldo Case refers to the Supreme Court decision voiding the New York minimum wage law for women. Cardozo dissented in that case, and Frankfurter, who didn't go onto the Court until 1939, strongly supported the law. The four "hard-core" on the Court again refers to the Four Horsemen.

"In counting your blessings you [should] rank high that you were not one of the Nine! I happened to see Ben Cardozo after the *Tipaldo* decision in 36 and with tears in his eyes, I'm being literal and direct, he deprecated that he was 'brought down from Albany.' 'This is not a Court now --- this is a political body' he moaned. In his day there were four who were the 'hard core' of the Court. They were narrow-minded economic sectarians. No such doctrinal cohesion binds together the present 'hard core' 'liberal' wing of the Court. Their common denominator is a self-willed, self righteous power-lust, conditioned by different causes, internal and external, undisciplined by adequate professional learning and cultivated understanding."[19]

Yes, the Institutionalist puts in, isn't that usually the way with ideological disputes? The two sides lodge in mutual antipathy, each claiming to dwell on the ethical high ground. Brennan feels that: "To strike another blow for freedom allows a man to walk a little taller and raise his head a little higher. And while he can, he must." But Frankfurter sees in Brennan "a self-willed, self righteous power-lust." How resolve such disparity? But as a practical matter, Justice Frankfurter's ideology of judicial restraint lost out, and Justice Brennan's liberal ideology won out. Quite simply, the liberal wing had the most votes where it counted, on the Court. But let me ask a question: Has not this same outcome repeated over and over in the history of the Court? Not that the liberals have always won, but whatever the ideological arguments, hasn't judicial restraint constantly lost? But something else interests me about this story, the mention that Justice Brennan disappointed the ideological hopes of the president who appointed him. I believe such sorrow not an isolated incident. Perhaps that a topic appropriate to explore in more detail?

Changes in judicial ideology – In his classic *The Supreme Court in United States History*, published in 1921, the great legal scholar Charles Warren remarked: "[N]othing is more striking in the history of the Court than the manner in which the hopes of those who expected a Judge to follow the political views of the President appointing him have been disappointed."[20] Let us illustrate with some memorable instances.

Thomas Jefferson displayed a well-known antipathy for Chief Justice John Marshall, an antipathy highly connected with the schism between Jefferson's Republican Party and Marshall's Federalist Party. If the Federalists stood for one policy, Jefferson routinely came up with an attractive alternative. After all, the loyal opposition does just that, opposes the party in power, and until 1801 when sworn in as president, Jefferson loyally performed this duty. So if the Federalists supported a strong national government, his Republicans supported less centralization, claiming the national government threatened the people's liberty. As president, he took vacancies on the Court as chances to nominate justices from his party, counting on them to rein in Marshall. But lo and behold, his appointees kept turning coat. His first appointee, Justice William Johnson, furnished the most prominent example, ruling against the Jefferson administration in a number of cases. Jefferson's Attorney General, Caesar A. Rodney, remarked, "You can scarcely elevate a man to a seat in a Court of Justice before he catches the leprosy of the bench."[21] Other Jefferson appointees caught the malady as well, which also spread to those of Jefferson's lieutenant and successor as president, James Madison. During Madison's administration, the Republicans actually made up a majority on the then seven-judge court. But in such cases as Cohen v Virginia in 1821, the four Republicans (Johnson, Livingston, Todd, and Duvall) joined the three Federalists (Marshall, Washington, and Story) to uphold federal over state power, Federal ideology over Republican ideology.

This case led to a notable public assault upon the Court, when Judge Spencer Roane published a series of articles in *Richmond Enquirer*. Roane sat on Virginia's highest court, the Court of Appeals, and was a prominent member of the Richmond Junto, which controlled that state's politics in the name of Jefferson's Republican Party. As customary for the time, Roane wrote under a pseudonym, Algernon Sidney. harking back to a leader against royal tyranny in the England. "Calling the Court's holding 'a most monstrous and unexampled decision,' Roane said that 'it can only be accounted for from that love of power which all history informs us infects and corrupts those who possess it.' ... The Republican justices who had concurred with Marshall were denounced ... . 'How else is it that they also go to all lengths with the ultra-federal leader who is at the head of their court? ... He must be equally delighted and *surprised* to find his *Republican* brothers going with him.' ... Roane said it was because there were 'on the side of the government that feeds them.'"[22]

The Jeffersonian Republicans shortly turned into the Jacksonian

Democrats. In 1829, President Andrew Jackson appointed Justice John McLean of whom a later commentator would observe: "By the end of his career, John McLean had strayed about as far as possible from the values associated with Andrew Jackson, the president who nominated him."[23] In 1830, Jackson appointed Justice Henry Baldwin, who returned the favor by siding against Jackson in the momentous fight over the Second Bank of the United States. In 1835, Jackson tried again with Justice James Moore Wayne, whose main claim to fame rested on marching in zealous lockset with Jackson's drumbeat through three terms in Congress. But "it was not long before the new justice demonstrated that he ... would be independent of the president who appointed him."[24]

Lincoln's selections proved no more loyal to their party, the new Republican Party. As Secretary of the Treasury in Lincoln's cabinet, Salmon P. Chase supported the Legal Tender Act, which made greenbacks, that is, paper money, legal tender, a measure greatly facilitating the war effort. But after succeeding Taney as Chief Justice in 1864, Chase voided the same act as unconstitutional. Other Republican justices (Swayne, Miller, David, Strong, Bradley, Hunt, and Waite) helped overthrow their party's Reconstruction program.

So illustrious a justice as Oliver Wendell Holmes, Jr., disappointed so illustrious a president as Theodore Roosevelt, who appointed him to the Court in 1902. Dedicated to the concept of judicial restraint, Holmes failed to support many of the president's progressive reforms. When Holmes dissented in the Northern Securities Case (1904), Roosevelt quipped: "I could carve out of a banana a judge with more backbone than that."[25]

Appointed in 1910 by Republican President William Howard Taft, "[Justice Willis] Van Devanter's conservative judicial philosophy was not immediately evident. Indeed, he could have been mistaken for a progressive at the outset of his tenure."[26] But he ended up one of the Four Horsemen, who later so adamantly opposed the New Deal. In 1914, progressive Democrat Woodrow Wilson had no better luck with Justice James McReynolds. "Some Court observers expected McReynolds to join the liberal wing of the Court, but by the end of his tenure, he had become its most conservative member."[27] By contrast, in 1925 conservative Republican Calvin Coolidge picked Justice Harlan Fiske Stone, who later allied with the liberals in support of the Democrat's New Deal initiatives.

Moderate Republican Dwight Eisenhower appointed both Earl Warren (1953) and William Brennan (1956), neither of whom had given prior evidence of their liberal course on the Court. Eisenhower later supposedly remarked these the two biggest mistakes of his presidency.

Justice Harry Blackmun, the author of Roe v Wade, provides a recent and outstanding instance of such an ideological shift. President Richard Nixon, a Republican, appointed Blackmun to the Court in 1970. Back in 1959, Eisenhower had previously appointed Blackmun to the Eighth Circuit Court of Appeals, where he established a solid reputation as moderately conservative. Blackmun also claimed a close and a lifelong friendship with conservative Chief Justice Warren Burger, whom Nixon had appointed to succeed Earl Warren in 1969. Undoubtedly, Nixon thought of Blackmun's nomination as sending reinforcements to Burger.

Blackmun himself later recorded that during the job interview, which took place at the White House: "[Nixon] took my arm, however, and led me to the window overlooking the Rose Garden. He said, Judge, when you come down here, you will be completely independent. That is the way it should be. I should warn you, however, that the 'Georgetown crowd' will do their best to elbow in on you. You will be wined and dined and approached. I suspect that two of the Justices have fallen victim to this kind of thing. Can you resist the Washington cocktail party circuit? My response was that I could and, in fact, that I had to in order to maintain my ability to work and my health. He then asked whether Mrs. Blackmun could resist it. I told him that I thought she could. He said it was very important."[28]

This account sounds very much like Nixon asked Blackmun to swear featly on the party banner, and Blackmun clasped the banner and took the oath. Yet gradually another loyalty dawned. During his first five terms (1970 to 1975), he voted with the conservative Chief Justice Burger in 87.5% of closely-divided cases, and with Brennan, the Court's leading liberal, only 13% of the time. But in the next five terms (1975 to 1980), Blackmun joined Burger in only 45.5% of divided cases, Brennan in 54.5%. During the last five years they served together, Blackmun sided with Burger in only 32.4% of the close cases, with Brennan in 70.6%. From the 1981 through 1985, Blackmun went with Brennan 77.6% of the time, with the liberal Thurgood Marshall 76.1%. From 1986 to 1990, his rate of agreement with these two most liberal justices climbed to 97.1% and 95.8%.[29] By his retirement in 1994, Blackmun claimed title as the Court's most liberal justice.

Clearly then, the Institutionalist says, a strong tendency exists for a man elevated to Court to migrate across the aisle, leaving behind former friends. Then what explains such conversions? Did the law make them do it? How say so, since the law so seldom compels the justices, while the justices so often compel the law. Well, then, did the better values carry an inherent conviction, working these transformations? How say so, since those who applaud say Blackmun's switch decry Van Devanter or McReynolds, and vice versa. But I cannot help noticing that no justice named ever transferred allegiance to Justice Frankfurter's judicial restraint, but always toward Justice Brennan's judicial activism. But what about an overall view of the Court across time?

Ideologies over time – Very well then, another illustrious Harvard Law professor, Laurence H. Tribe, may serve as typical, his widely used textbook, *American Constitution Law*, organizing all the cases into ideological "models." He writes: "I have [organized] the constitutional principles, rules, and theories that are this book's subject in terms of the seven basic models that, ... have represented the major alternatives for constitutional argument and decision in American law from the early 1800's to the present. The models to be described are those of (I) separated and divided powers; (II) implied limitations on government; (III) settled expectations; (IV) governmental regularity; (V) preferred rights; (VI) equal protection; and (VII) structural justice."

He adds: "Representing approximate tendencies, emphases, and approaches rather than precise formal systems, these models are not put forth as mutually exclusive; constitutional discourse in any given period can thus be expected to draw on ideas and categories characteristic of more than one model."[30]

More specifically, he says that: "Model I played its most pervasive role from the era of the Marshall Court to the Civil War."[31] By "separated and divided powers" the model thought to maintain liberty by separating and dividing power between the nation and state governments and between the three branches of government. The next model, Model II, "held sway through the first quarter of the twentieth century,"[32] and by enforcing "implied limitations on government," sought to protect freedom largely by limiting government regulation of economic activity. Model III, "settled expectations," sought to protect "certain 'vested rights' in property and contact."[33] Model IV, "governmental regularity," tried to set forth clear legal norms and procedures, especially in criminal prosecutions. Model V, "preferred rights," thought to identify and protect "certain 'preferred' rights from all but the most compellingly justified instances of government intrusion,"[34] especially in such areas as free speech, religion, and the right of privacy and personhood. Model VI, "equal protection," centered around even-handedness. While Model VII, "structural justice" thought to assure the basic ingredients of a democratic structure, but also refers to a not yet realized aspiration, a longing summed up by Professor Tribe's surmise that: "The day may indeed come when a general doctrine under the fifth and fourteenth amendments recognizes for each individual a constitutional right to a decent level of affirmative government protection in meeting the basic human needs of physical survival and security, health and house, work and schooling."[35]

Standard views of the Court – The standard guides regard the Court from standard views. Let us return to that eminent scholar, Charles Warren. He published his great work, *The Supreme Court in United States History*, as long ago as 1921. Yet he still well sums up one such view of the Court: "'The Judiciary of the United States --- independent of party, independent of power, and independent of popularity' was a toast given at a dinner in Washington in 1801; these words have expressed the aim, and substantially the achievement, of the Court, in the one hundred and twenty years which have since elapsed."[36]

Thus, the Court is applauded as "independent of [partisan] party [politics], independent of [outside] power, and independent of popularity [the majority]."

Professor Schwartz, whom we quoted earlier, expresses another view: "'Human history,' says H.G. Wells, 'is in essence a history of ideas.' To an American interested in constitutional history, the great theme in the country's development is the idea of law as a check upon governmental power. The institution that best embodies this idea is the United States Supreme Court."[37]

Thus, the overarching theme in American constitutional history is seen as "the idea of law as a check upon government power" and the Supreme Court "the institutions that best embodies this idea."

Professor R. Kent Newmyer, who teaches at the University of Connecticut Law School, in his excellent *Supreme Court Under Marshall and Taney*, expresses still another view: "[F]ew would deny that the structure of the Court and its mode of operation are uniquely suited for the chore in hand. ... [T]he Court is neither too small to preclude an enlightened clash of opinion nor too large to stifle debate or prevent agreement. The science of jurisprudence, bound up in the time-honored tradition of the Court, supplies the intellectual rules of the game. The responsibility of meting out justice to real people restrains careless speculation. Secrecy of conference invites open and candid deliberations, just as the publication of opinions encourages responsibility and excellence of craftsmanship. By giving minority justices a voice --- and a chance to pioneer new law --- dissents and concurrences work to keep the majority on its toes. Probably no other institution of government is better suited to speak to the rationality and morality of the American people."[38]

Thus, the Court is seen as an ideal forum to conduct the national dialogue, "no other institution better suited to speak to the rationality and morality of the American people."

All the standard guides to the Court organize the cases into some such ideological models, all take some such view of the Court as independent, as checking government power, and as reaching rational and ethical decisions.

The Institutionalist's response – You labeled the standard guides the Idealists, the Institutionalist says, and that label appropriate. Professor Schwartz quoted H.G. Wells: "Human history is in essence a history of ideas." All these gentlemen appear to agree, since first and foremost, they study the ideas, especially ethical ideals and ideologies. Nor are they entirely wrong. Some ideals possess a power over men's minds, such as the ideal that "all men are created equal." But you labeled me an Institutionalist, and that as appropriate, since my conceit that institutions also possess a power over the human mind. So the Idealists see that men control the political institutions, and conceiving that the ideals control the men, conceive the men's ideals control the institutions. But my argument is that the exact opposite more nearly true, that the institutions more nearly control the men's ideals and ideologies.

Political institutions get inside people's heads. A man wearing a crown thinks very differently from an elected politician, and a nobleman, whether of the sword or the robe, thinks very differently from either. Not that their motives differ. All relentlessly pursue their interests, all demonstrate the same will-to-power, all seek to impose their will on others. But everyone thinks in the institutional box. They make up ideologies as needed to justify their institutional power, taking them down divergent mental paths. Monarchs rationalize their rule, say as the divine right of kings; aristocrats convince themselves as well, say as "rationally and morally" superior. Democratic enthusiasts have been known to persuade themselves to cut off the king's head and massacre the aristocracy. The magnetic needle of interest points in conflicting directions, depending on a man's institutional location.

This same tendency works upon the legal mind as much as any other. Lawyers constantly think about their clients' rights, rather than their clients' duties and responsibilities, since they can sue over the first, but not the second, and the more rights they can sue over, the more business they have and the more money they make. When elevated to the bench, they take along this professional mindset, where the judicial will-to-power seconds the motion, since the more the lawyers can sue over, the more the lawsuits, and the more the lawsuits, the more the judicial power. When put together with the judges' capacity to make law, including constitutional law above and beyond check, the systemic inertia explains itself.

The previously mentioned and noted English historian A.F. Pollard once remarked: "It has been the supreme good fortune of England that her constitutional history and her liberties started from service and duty, and not from the rights of man. These were the natural product of an impious generation which ignored man's obligations, and looked upon him as an anarchist to be judged by the liberties he seized and not by the services he rendered."[39]

But American lawyers have reversed this start. To them the "rights of man" are sacred, meaning their clients' rights, that is, rights they can sue over. To them "service and duty" seldom means the service and duty their clients owe others, but much more usually the service and duty owed their clients by others. To them, individual responsibility means mainly other individuals' responsibility to their clients. They never cease exalting rights, but always a special sort of rights, the rights that let them sue others on behalf of their clients. That is, the rights that confer business, money, and power on themselves.

Thus, the lawyers and judges have gradually come to exalt the Bill of Rights, an afterthought to the Founders, over the rest of the Constitution, since those Amendments confer rights they can sue over, while the original text merely set up the government, conferring few rights except democratic participation. In the same way, they have gradually turned the Reconstruction Amendments into a whole new set of rights, using say the "due process clause," making up still more rights to sue over. The working of their will has gradually altered the entire system, moving away from democratic process, always toward judicial process, almost the only right neglected that original most fundament right, the right of the people to govern through democratic process.

Whether they write biographies of the justices or histories of the Court, the standard guides fail to account for such judicial interests upon judicial ideology. They regard the justices' ideology as controlling the institution, but in truth, the institution more nearly controls the justices' ideology. The judicial psychology behind the judicial ideology turns out no more than another instance of an aristocracy creating a set of values to justify their dominance.

By failing to deal with judicial interests, the standard, ideological approach deals with the surface, not penetrating to the core. Consider Professor Tribe's seven ideological models. While accurate enough, yet they do not really tell us what is going on at the deeper level. For example, Model II was "implied limitations on government," which "held sway through the first quarter of the twentieth century," But describing the doctrine does not tell us why the Court adopted it. The same holds true for his other models. In reality, formal ideologies often serve as little more than disguises, assumed as needed to justify the real motives. Then what are the real motives?

An analogy from somewhat far afield – Let me further illustrate by going what may seem somewhat far afield, taking another historical topic altogether, the rise of fascism after World War I. This phenomenon has generated a body of work rivaling that on the Court. And just as the scholarship on the Court focuses on judicial ideology, we find these historians focus upon fascist ideology. But since fascist ideology scarcely coherent, they have a hard time. Il Duce and the Fuhrer shared a great deal, and both regarded consistency a fault for smaller minds, a trait the lesser fascists copied. Let us turn to a recognized authority, Professor Stanley G. Payne in his *History of Fascism*, who candidly confesses this difficulty up front, making even a definition of fascism problematic: "At the end of the twentieth century *fascism* remains probably the vaguest of the major political terms."[40]

So Professor Payne set out to find a definition: "If fascism is to be studied as a generic and comparative phenomenon, it has first to be identified through some sort of working description. Such a definition must be deprived from empirical study ... It must be developed as a theoretical construct or an ideal type, ... Thus no single movement or group under observations would necessarily be found to have announced a program or self-description couched in the exact terms of this definition."[41]

In pursuit of this program, Professor Payne exhaustively reviews all the fascist source materials, then summarizes the characteristics that mark fascism in a table as follows:

A. Ideology and Goals: Espousal of an idealistic ... philosophy, normally involving the attempt to realize a new modern ... and secular culture. Creation of a new nationalistic authoritarian state ... Organization of a new highly regulated ... integrated national economic structure, ... Positive evaluation and use of ... violence and war. The goal of empire, expansion, ... B. The Fascist Negations: Antiliberalism Anticommunism Anticonservativism

> C. Style and Organization
> Attempted mass mobilization with militarization of political relationships and style and with the goal of a mass party militia.
> Emphasis on aesthetic structure of meeting, symbols, ... stressing emotional and mystical aspects.
> Extreme stress on masculine principle and male dominance ...
> Exaltation of youth ...
> Specific tendency toward an authoritarian, charismatic, personal style of command ...[42]

The depth of scholarship must command our admiration. Professor Payne turns over the huge lexicon of the fascist archives. He deduces a theory that accurately accounts for all the facts. Yet this table reminds of nothing so much as those complex assemblages of globes and wheels that pictured the Ptolemaic universe in visible form. "The sun also ariseth, and the sun goeth down," but what explains the rise and fall? Since the ground stays steady beneath our feet, but the sun travels across the sky, what more natural than to regard the earth as steady and the sun in motion? By the same token, in the political world all hide their interests beneath ideological justifications, and so what more natural than for them to talk about their justifications rather than their interests? But the political scientist should not fall into the same fault. Newton found a simpler, more elegant explanation for the rising and setting of the sun, the force of gravity throughout the universe. In the same way, the political scientist can find a simpler, more elegant explanation for the political universe, the force of institutional interests throughout. With this perception, suddenly all the political planets align.

Rather than defining fascism by the irregular ideological features, let us define fascism by the regular feature, the institutional structure. Fascism always aspired to dictatorship, all power to the dictator. Il Duce and the Fuhrer were never inconsistent about that. Power being their real concern, they simply seized on ideologies ready to hand or made up ideologies useful to hand, logical consistency their least concern, anything to justify dictatorship. Rather than their ideologies explaining their lust for power, their lust for power explains their ideologies. Fascists wanted "a new nationalistic authoritarian state" because they wanted power. Fascists wanted "a highly regulated economic structure" because they wanted power. Fascists were "antiliberal, anticommunist, and anticonservative'" because they didn't want to share power. So to define fascism, why resort to all these ideologies, all this complexity? Why not simply define fascism as dictatorship? By all means study what may distinguish fascism from say communism. But in the end, dictatorship describes fascism, indeed, the same thing that in the end describes communism, which differ only in superficials, not essentials.

A critique of the standard guides – Why should not the same principle apply to any political institution, including the Supreme Court? Instead of Professor Tribe's seven ideological models, let us merely look at the Court's institutional will-to-power. Suddenly the models all converge, all justifying the Court's ascent to power.

But that is exactly what the standard guides to the Court go to a great deal of trouble to avoid. Instead they claim the Supreme Court a political institution unique in history, an aristocracy that works better in the public interest than a democracy. We have heard this claim take several forms.

Professor Warren toasted the Court as "independent of party, power, and popularity." But one could say the same about any run-of-the-mill monarch, who rules above party, power, and popularity. Then whence the allure of this image as applied to the Court? Why would we prefer an "independent," hence unaccountable judiciary, rather than an elected, hence responsible government? Even in 1921 when Warren wrote, how well had such "judicial independence" served the American people? The Court had already interpreted away congressional Reconstruction, enacted segregation, and thwarted progressive reforms. They would shortly throw out virtually the whole New Deal. One wonders what Professor Warren would have said if he had lived through the judicial revolution, when the Court enacted the agenda of "liberal Democrats." Was that independent of party, or merely independent of power and popularity?

Turning to Professor Schwartz, let me quote him again to put the words in front of our eyes: "To an American interested in constitutional history, the great theme in the country's development is the idea of law as a check upon governmental power. The institution that best embodies this idea is the United States Supreme Court."

But while "the idea of law as a check upon government power" a great theme, what about other great themes? Wasn't democracy as great a theme to the Framers? While as much as checking government power, the Constitution released government power. The Framers wanted to put government to work, doing such essential tasks as setting up a national marketplace, regulating interstate and international commerce, conducting foreign policy, and providing a national defense. In fact, if we read him further, we find as much as wanting to check government power, Professor Schwartz very much wants to put governmental power to work in his own causes, which turn out basically the "liberal agenda."

Moreover, how does history show the Court "the institution that best embodies the idea of law as a check upon government power?" Does that describe the Marshall Court, which rather than checking, constantly added to the federal government's power? Does that describe the Warren Court, which as much as checking the government's power further added to government power, ordering such government programs as massive busing? How exactly do such events show "the idea of law as a check upon government power?"

Professor Newmyer makes a much more serious effort to justify the institution. Let us recall what he said: "[F]ew would deny that the structure of the Court and its mode of operation are uniquely suited for the chore in hand. ... [T]he Court is neither too small to preclude an enlightened clash of opinion nor too large to stifle debate or prevent agreement. The science of jurisprudence, bound up in the time-honored tradition of the Court, supplies the intellectual rules of the game. The responsibility of meting out justice to real people restrains careless speculation. Secrecy of conference invites open and candid deliberations, just as the publication of opinions encourages responsibility and excellence of craftsmanship. By giving minority justices a voice --- and a chance to pioneer new law --- dissents and concurrences work to keep the majority on its toes. Probably no other institution of government is better suited to speak to the rationality and morality of the American people."

Yet what does this really say and where are the proofs? He says: "the structure of the Court uniquely suited for the chore in hand." But that's no more than a subtle way of saying an aristocratic form of government better than a democracy. Then whether "uniquely suited" or not, that must mean the people lose the right to govern themselves. And where's the proof "the Court uniquely suited?" He says: "Probably no other institution of government is better suited to speak to the rationality and morality of the American people." But again where's the proof? Did the Court do better over slavery, Reconstruction, industrialization, segregation, and the crisis of the Great Depression? No, not at all. Then what has changed? The justices still go about their business just as they did in the past. Then finally what makes the Court "uniquely suited" or better at "rationality and morality?"

Understanding history – To sum up my argument, if you want to understand history, you cannot just think about the ideas. You have to account for all the following factors: First, geography and demography. Where a society puts it foot to the ground has a lot to do with its fate, as do the size and makeup of the population. Second, human psychology. Human needs drive human history. Third, individuals. Not just as statistics, but as individual shakers and doers whose choices change the course of history. George Washington and Abe Lincoln made a difference, as did the choices of millions of nameless people who did the right thing. Fourth, knowledge. Human understanding alters human history, which easily seen by the influence of science and technology on events. Fifth, ethical ideals. Such ideals as "all men are created equal" lead influential lives of their own. Sixth, groups. The most important groups are culture and class. And seventh, institutions, the most neglected influence, yet all sorts of institutions, religious, economic, political and so forth, exert an undeniable influence. And it is just here that the standard approach to the Court, indeed, the standard approach to history goes awry. And finally, let us never to ask like the old Roman lawyers, *Qui bono*, Whose Good? Interests dominate throughout.

Habitually we engage in one-step thinking about government. We think that that if someone gets their values right, then a government run by them will get its values right. We fail to see the need for an intervening step. Such an "ethics first" way of thinking deeply ingrains political thought. And it's even right, but not completely right. First we have to get out values right. But to get the problem completely right, our thinking has to take a second step. We have to get our political institutions right. Otherwise the political institutions will warp the ethical values.

In conclusion, you asked for a dialogue with the reader the impartial judge. And from Socrates to now, a dialogue asks for willing assent. You seek to persuade your opponent by reasons, not compel him. In the political sphere, democratic process comes the closest to this method, letting everyone into the dialogue, seeking their consent to the conclusion. But the Supreme Court practices another method, excluding everyone from real participation except the nine justices. They impose their conclusions on everyone else. Then how say that "no other institution of government is better suited to speak to the rationality and morality of the American people?" Apparently the American people are best spoken to when they have no effective voice.

CHAPTER 15

A Summing Up

What holds together the great and famous cases in the history of the Supreme Court? Such a question suggests an endeavor to frame a coherent explanation, not less than a reliable tendency, sufficient to account for the course, covering all the cases and good across time. Unless the Court reflects no more than a place and a time, some such coherence must run throughout.

The logic of the legal doctrines – Faced with such a request, the legal mind goes from habit to explanations built on legal doctrines. From beginning to end, we saw the Court start each case by laying down some legal doctrine, say "due process of law" or the "establishment clause." So in Lochner (1905) they started with the doctrine: "No state can deprive any person of liberty without *due process of law*." Then they built on that foundation, saying: "The right to purchase or to sell labor is part of the liberty *protected by this Amendment*." Next they erected another level, saying: "The [Bakeshop Law] interferes with *the right of contract* between the employer and employees, concerning the number of hours in which the later may labor in the bakery of the employer." Finally, they topped off the structure by ruling that the Bakeshop Law was unconstitutional. Or in Everson (1947) they started by laying down the doctrine of *"the establishment clause* of the First Amendment," on which they raised the ruling that: "The *'establishment of religion' clause* of the First Amendment means neither a state nor the Federal Government can set up a church."

In this familiar way, the legal doctrines stand beneath the cases, offering explanations. In this same way and through all their long generations, Anglo-American judges have explained their rulings as "following the law," as resting on and reasoned from the legal doctrines. In this same way and through all their same generations, the lawyers have argued before these same judges: "Your Honor, the law says that," meaning a legal doctrine says that, meaning that explains why the judge should rule for them. In this same way, the law schools teach the students, teaching the doctrines to explain the cases. In this same way, the legal scholars think, analyzing the doctrines to explain the cases. For an example, recall the previous passage from Professor Tribe, whose widely used textbook, *American Constitution Law*, began: "I have [organized] the constitutional principles, rules, and theories ... in terms of the seven basic models that, ... have represented the major alternatives for constitutional argument and decision in American law from the early 1800's to the present. The models to be described are those of (I) separated and divided powers; (II) implied limitations on government; (III) settled expectations; (IV) governmental regularity; (V) preferred rights; (VI) equal protection; and (VII) structural justice." In other words, his ingenuity has organized all the lesser doctrines, "the constitutional principles, rules, and theories," under more general doctrines, "the seven basic models." These general doctrines "[represent] the major alternatives for constitutional argument and decision in American law."

Throughout all the years, the judges, lawyers, and scholars have analyzed and argued in this same way, seeking to explain the cases. Nor do they seek entirely in vain. In the English common law inheritance, respect for precedent the deepest courtesy, so younger cases bow to their elders, acknowledging their authority. This etiquette sets up an orderly relationship between the cases, sufficiently logical that their legal doctrines, as the lawyers say, "descend" from each other. One may trace these lines of descent with no more trouble than reading through centuries of cases, drawing the family tree as one goes, carefully following all the branches of doctrine. While with the same decorum, precedent sets up a stately inertia, since established doctrine carries weight, often enough to tip a case, seldom rudely ignored. With such becoming formality the common law gathered the doctrines into an orderly array, while giving steadiness and stability to them. Anglo-American jurisprudence relied on precedent to help achieve a renowned commitment to the "rule of law," furnishing predictability and dependability, allowing reliance on the laws. The legal profession justly takes pride in this accomplishment, justly insist on the usefulness and value, and resist meddling with their time-honored forms.

The limits of precedent – But the "rule of law," as the rule of doctrine guided by precedent, reaches only so far. In the first place and as a recognized privilege, the higher a judge in the hierarchy, the less respect owed to judges lower on the scale, and as the highest of all, the justices have often extended this discourtesy to their predecessors as well. A justice so inclined may observe a mannerly "judicial restraint," as Justice Frankfurter urged. But a justice may as easily take the attitude ascribed to Justice Brennan: "[T]he judge is not to be deterred by ... even a mass of precedent the other way."

In the second place, about the Supreme Court one might state a contradictory rule: The greater the case, the less the respect for precedent. Today the lawyers revere nothing more than judicial review, but in 1803, Marbury v Madison rested on no real precedent at all, since never before had the Court voided a congressional law. The Court's most notorious case, Dred Scott (1857), simply ignored clear precedent, refusing to regard the "clear-cut" limit on judicial review. Another case of unpleasant memory, Plessy v Ferguson (1896) enacted "separate but equal," then an unprecedented doctrine. While perhaps the Court's greatest case, Brown v Board of Education (1954), turned upside-down the long-standing precedent of Plessy. The justices in Lochner (1905) relied on substantive due process, a doctrine with dubious precedents, while by 1963, a justice could reject Lochner as easily as writing: "The doctrine that due process authorizes courts to hold laws unconstitutional has long since been discarded."[1] Under the pressure from Roosevelt's "court-packing plan," precedents departed in numbers and haste. For example, in 1935, Tipaldo held unconstitutional a wage and hour law, but a mere year later in 1936, West Coast Hotel held constitutional a like law. During the judicial revolution, precedent almost carried the disrepute of out-of-date. So for example, as long ago as 1845, the Permoli Case held the "establishment clause" not applicable to the states, but in 1947, the Everson Case held the same clause now applicable, raising a wall of separation between church and state. As recently as 1942, Chaplinski approved restraint on obscenity, but as soon as 1957, Roth disapproved most restraint. Patronage as old as the Republic, but in 1976, Elrod v Burns suddenly found civil service a constitutional right.

Such events more than embarrassed the old-fashioned "legal formalism," which somehow regarded "the law" as a closed system of thought, where remote from the world around them, judges deduced their rulings from their prior rulings. But the explanation that the cases "follow the law," that is, follow from the legal doctrines, never worked very well anyway. No one ever really believed that the legal doctrines generated from themselves, rather everyone quite familiar with their human progenitors, whose features clearly recognizable in the offspring. Nor did anyone believe the justices thought in legal doctrine, rather like everyone else, they thought in a more personal language, which greatly influenced their translations into the formal language of the law. Instead and more forthrightly, present legal scholarship never pretends the legal doctrines fully explain the cases, freely admitting something else beneath and mixed with the doctrines. One often hears Justice Holmes quoted about "the felt necessities of the time, the prevalent moral and political theories, intuitions of public policy, avowed or unconscious, and even the prejudices which judges share with their fellow-men." A founder of "legal realism," Holmes accepted such realities.

The evolution of law – As students of the common law, the legal scholars already knew the latest cases no more than the recent turnings in a far longer road. The case law made by Anglo-American judges stretches back centuries, and while they usually travel slowly, the judges have constantly altered the legal doctrines as the journey went along. In Holmes' words, they had responded to the "the felt necessities of the time," and with the rise of evolutionary theory in the late nineteenth century, Holmes and others began to regard the genealogy of doctrines as tracing an evolution, as creative adaption to altered circumstances. So for example, one might think of the Taney Court as adapting the corporate doctrines of the Marshall Court, altering the law to better fit the changed economic environment. Holmes' great work, *The Common Law* (1881), carried out such a project in lengthy detail, showing an evolution across the law from the earliest times. Such a view suggested the common law not only gave order and stability, but gave adaptability and flexibility as well. Although just as the order and stability reached only so far, this claim of adaptability and flexibility might reach too far. Doubtlessly the judges have adapted the law to "the felt necessities of the time," yet whose felt necessities? Some of the Court's felt necessities appear all to the good, say the Marshall Court's nationalism, but others perhaps not so good, say the Fuller Court's substantive due process.

At any rate, if the order and stability failed to explain the Court's cases, next the legal mind turned to the adaptability and flexibility. Today, by far the larger body of legal scholarship puts the cases into an evolution or progression. They view the Court as leading away from the errors of the past, leading toward an ever more enlightened present. Brown v Board of Education serves as the model case, showing how the process works. But a stubborn core of dissident scholars refuses to go entirely along, accepting Brown as positive movement, but not accepting other cases move quite the right way. To avoid entangling in this learned dispute, let us leave behind their reservations, taking the Court's present enlightenment as a given. Yet how does even such a concession make the explanation work? How does a better present explain a worse past? In other words, how does the present doctrinal correctness explain the past doctrinal errors? In evolution the fittest survive, but in the earlier era, the doctrines now deemed fittest failed to survive before the Court. Nor did the progress now deemed better happen through the Court.

To illustrate with a well-known textbook, written by two well-known law professors, Melvin Urofsky and Paul Finkel, they make the thesis of evolution or progress obvious in their very title, *A March of Liberty: A Constitutional History of the United States.*[2] But if the Court was leading a "march of liberty," how did the justices manage to select the rather odd route for the parade? How come they marched away from congressional Reconstruction and toward segregation? How come they marched against progressive reforms and the New Deal? Presuming the Court now marching along the high road to the right music, how explain their earlier counter-marching and dead-end detours, leading down the wrong road while playing out of tune?

Originalism and the living Constitution – For their part, virtually all the present legal scholarship stays in the wide causeway worn by the common lawyers. They continue to argue over doctrines, presently the dominant schools "liberal" versus "conservative." The liberals maintain a doctrine of constitutional interpretation, "the living constitution," which typified the majority on the Court during the judicial revolution. Those justices asked: "What do the words of the text mean in our time?"[3] For them an answer was "the implementation of contemporary American values in constitutional cases."[4] Of course, as Professor Tushnett told us, the Warren Court, which began this revolution, a "liberal court," and so "contemporary American values" turned out liberal values. Less than convinced, conservatives retreated to another doctrine of constitutional interpretation, "originalism," maintaining that the Court should not go beyond the original intent of the Constitution. What the text didn't say back then, it cannot say now, and it certainly did not say the judicial revolution. Developed in excruciating detail and elaborated in variations, these rivals firmly set the context for the ongoing scholarly debate.

Then who has the best of it? For our purpose neither side, since neither tries to explain the Court, rather both try to persuade the Court. Each catches at sound reasons. The liberals' "living constitution" catches the need for a living government. That noted conservative jurist, Justice Antonin Scalia, may say the Constitution "dead," but a body politic seized into a constitutional rigor mortis can only go on to decay. In the life of a nation, the constant changes what never changes, the unexpected the expected. Think of industrialization, the crisis of the Great Depression, or World War II. Unless the organic laws allow creative adaptation, the government cannot respond. While the conservatives' "originalism" catches the Founders' intent in this respect, which made the elected Congress the dynamic organ of government, not the unelected Court. But either side turns their better reasons to serve their partisan purposes. Either doctrine turns out to justify a preconceived agenda. In the recent past, the "living constitution" served to justify the Court's enactment of the liberal agenda, and liberals can hardly wait to have another such go. In the more recent present, "originalism" served to justify the enactment of some items on the conservative agenda, and they somehow think that this may last. Then self-evidently, neither side offers to explain the Court, but merely tries to persuade the Court. As seems best to them, the justices have and can pick and choose between these competing agendas. So nothing about either doctrine tells why they go one way or the other.

In their histories of the Court, which make up the standard canon, these same scholars gather the legal doctrines into ideologies, which they use to label the Court. But as explanations, such ideological labels carry an expiration date. One can say the Marshall Court "favored a strong central government, encouragement of industry, protection of property, and a well-ordered society." One can say the Taney Court still favored "entrepreneurship and the capitalistic market," later favored slavery. One can say the Fuller Court "characterized by the principles of limited government, state autonomy, and respect for the rights of property owners" and "served conservative interests." One can say the Warren Court "a liberal Court." But there seems no way to say some ideological label sticks throughout, that is, explains all the Courts. So conservatism may explain the Fuller Court, liberalism the Warren Court, but neither explains both. Nor does any other ideology look capable of such a feat across time.

The Court relative to Congress – But another aspect of the great and famous cases forces a way upon our minds: Over time the Court has regularly differed with and overruled Congress. Then relative to Congress, the cases present a more regular appearance. Even though the Court has changed ideological fronts more than once, sometimes radically, yet relative to Congress, the Court has regularly faced the same way, presenting a hostile front. Over the more than two hundred years, Congress was passing laws every session, responding to their own "felt necessities of the time." While asserting to act constitutionally, their real concern was to act effectively, not least with regard to winning the next election. But somehow over all these years, new and crucial congressional law stayed out of synch with the Court's changing ideology, although never so much before as after the fact. Congress having moved, the Court would move to block them. Congress must have begun to wonder how to avoid giving such repeated offense.

Their first crime looked no more than a misdemeanor, coming over an insignificant part in the Judiciary Act of 1789. The Constitution had left to Congress the details for a federal court system, saying: "The judicial Power ... shall be vested in one Supreme Court, and in such inferior Court as the Congress may from time to time ordain and establish." The Judiciary Act filled up this space by "ordaining and establishing" the "inferior courts." The Constitution also set forth the federal courts' jurisdiction, but "with such Exceptions, and under such Regulations as the Congress shall make." The Act went on to confirm this jurisdiction, and almost incidentally gave jurisdiction to the Supreme Court over a particular type of case, petitions for mandamus. But in 1803 with Marbury, Chief Justice Marshall rejected this last, rather minor proffer of authority as unconstitutional. Now arguably, Congress had not strayed outside the Constitution at all, which said: "with such Exceptions, and under such Regulations as Congress shall make." Nor does Marbury resonate for limiting the Court's jurisdiction, rather for quite the opposite reason. But on any view, Congress hardly seems guilty of malice aforethought, hardly seems to have deliberately trampled over a bright-line marking out a constitutional crime.

But the second offense amounted to a major felony on someone's part, being over slavery, the hottest topic of the day. If Congress the guilty party, once more they could make a strong argument to act within the Constitution. In 1820, they had passed the Missouri Compromise, prohibiting slavery in the territories. In so doing, they could point to Article IV: "The Congress shall have the Power to ... make all needful Rules and Regulations ... respecting the Territory ... belonging to the United States." Even under the Articles of Confederation, that Congress had passed such a law, the Northwest Ordinance of 1787, which outlawed slavery north of the Ohio River. Under the U.S. Constitution, the very First Congress re-enacted that law intact. Nineteen members of that First Congress had attended the Constitutional Convention. George Washington, who as president signed into law the new Northwest Ordinance, had presided at the Convention. Apparently, all these gentlemen thought Congress possessed such authority. The Missouri Compromise had stood on the books for over thirty years. But suddenly in 1857 with Dred Scott, the Court declared Congress had been in violation of the Constitution all along. If so, might they not appeal at least against the *ex post facto* proceedings, as making their act a crime only after the fact? Might they not also appeal to their good intentions, which sought to hold the union together, not to mention prevent the spread of slavery?

During Reconstruction, Congress went the extra mile, not only passing laws, but constitutional amendments which the people ratified.

The overriding question was how to fit the freedmen into society. Congress answered with the Reconstruction Amendments. The 13th Amendment (1865) freed the slaves; the 14th Amendment (1870) guaranteed their civil rights; the 15th Amendment (1875) granted them the franchise. If all this sounded reasonable enough, it also sounded like Congress avoided any constitutional violation, since they wrote their new laws into the Constitution itself. Yet the Supreme Court proved they could go the extra mile, too. Unable to punish Congress for violating the Constitution, instead the Court punished Congress by interpreting away the meaning of their amendments. The Slaughter-House Cases (1873) gutted the "privileges and immunities" clause; the Reese Case (1876) edged around the guarantee for the franchise. The Court handed down their final verdict with Plessy v Ferguson (1896), which read "separate but equal" into the Constitution, a doctrine which permitted segregation, effectively repealing the intent of the Reconstruction Amendments.

Congress must have begun to feel like a prisoner in the dock, facing a judge with a hanging countenance. Their laws were continually hauled off to the condemned cell. During industrialization, the E.C. Knight Case (1895) narrowed to nothing the Sherman Anti-Trust Act of 1890, which sought to outlaw monopoly. The Danbury Hatters Case (1908) turned the same Act against unions, a wholly unintended target. When Congress tried to counter with the Clayton Act of 1914, coming to the aid of unions, the Duplex Printing Case (1921) simply ignored them. Coming to the crisis of the Great Depression, the Court resolutely passed sentence against the whole initial round of New Deal laws. The Schechter Case (1935) executed the National Industrial Recovery Act of 1933; the Butler Case (1936) sent to the same fate the Agricultural Adjustment Act of 1933.

President Franklin Roosevelt finally came to their aid, pleading their cause with some success, and reversed the trend of guilty verdicts for a while. But shortly, the indictments against Congress once more populate the docket. The Roth Case (1957) condemns a long-standing law that restrained obscenity; Miranda (1966) condemns a similarly long-standing law about confessions; Shapiro v Thompson (1969) condemns limits on welfare shopping; Elrod v Burn (1976) condemns the congressional law on patronage. More widely than any of these, the Swann Case (1971), together with other cases, finds guilty for errors of omission the Civil Rights Act of 1964, as not going far enough to desegregate the schools. This time the justices sentence Congress to a sort of closely supervised court probation, where federal judges direct and monitor their programs. With the Adams Case (starting in 1970 and going on for twenty years) the judiciary takes control over the bureaucratic program for school desegregation, the judges running the agency themselves, rather than Congress or the president.

But might not Congress complain about the fundamental fairness of these prosecutions? A maxim of the common law, so ancient as to descend from the Roman, was *nemo iudex in cause sua*, "no man should judge in his own cause." James Madison gives the reason in the *Federalist, No. 10*: "No man is allowed to be a judge in his own cause, because his interest would certainly bias his judgment, and, not improbably, corrupt his integrity." Then recall that "jurisdiction" the power in the court to hear a case. A "plea to the jurisdiction" challenges such power. Ironically, Marbury, the very first case in the lexicon, went off on such a plea. Congress had passed a law giving the Court a jurisdiction over mandamus, but Justice Marshall voided the law as unconstitutional, and the Court then lacking power, dismissed the case. Of course in the process, he claimed a much greater power, judicial review. But in each and every case which followed, what made up the first and essential question, if not the jurisdiction of the Court? Under the theory, the separation of powers gives each branch their proper powers. In every case Congress claimed to act within their proper powers, while the Court claimed to act within its proper powers. Power being the most valuable commodity in the political market place, did the justices not have an interest in the possession? If so, then in every case they had a conflict of interest with Congress. In ruling on the first and essential question, they were sitting as judges in their own cause. Might not Congress claim a real grievance?

The graph of judicial power – And the grievances collect. The justices constantly rule for themselves. Their jurisdiction as constantly goes up. Drawn on a graph, this power side of the cases would steadily incline. Put the passage of years on one pole and judicial power on the other. Locate the cases on the grid. The upward trend would clearly appear. While another coincidence also appears. The Court's ideological shifts look scattered, unconnected by any ideological line, yet chronologically, these same shifts fit with the upward arc for judicial power. The conflicts with Congress fit as well.

Let us plot the numbers as these would appear on such a graph, but where place the first mark? America inherited her legal system from England, and English judges had no power to void parliamentary laws. Rather judicial review originated with a royal prerogative. To keep tight control over the Empire, the monarchy retained an authority to void acts of the colonial legislatures, either as conflicting with their charters or British law. With the Revolution, this crown prerogative lapsed. But as the royal mantle slipped away, some American judges reached out to catch for this loose fold, which they wrapped around themselves, but rearranged to suit the fashion of the times. Henceforth, they proclaimed, the courts would wear this remnant of the purple, but not to protect the sovereign's rights, rather to protect the sovereign rights of the people. They would void laws that violated the new state constitutions. But their boldness met with controversial success, since many thought "the doctrine that the judiciary have authority to set aside Acts [of the legislature] anti-republican."

Nor did the Constitution expressly delegate the power of judicial review to the Supreme Court. At the Convention, some delegates thought like Elbridge Gerry: "[The judiciary] will have a sufficient check against encroachments on their own department by their exposition of the laws, which involved a power of deciding their Constitutionality." But others thought like John Francis Mercer: "He disapproved of the Doctrine that the Judges as expositors of the Constitution should have authority to declare a law void." But whatever their views, they wrote nothing on the face of the Constitution.

Such leaves to Chief Justice Marshall the honor of marking the number [1] on the graph. Marbury v Madison (1803) claims the power of judicial review. But under this "original doctrine of judicial review," the power stays highly limited. The judges repeatedly pledge never to void a law except in a clear-cut case, where all reasonable men would agree. Since Congress almost never lacks a reasonable argument, the Court looks highly restrained.

[2] Dred Scott (1857), after waiting half a century, voids a congressional law for only the second time, the Missouri Compromise of 1820. But since that conclusion far from clear-cut, Chief Justice Taney had to abandon the original limits on judicial review. In effect, the case creates a new paradigm, "unrestrained judicial review," no longer limited to clear-cut cases.

[3A] The Slaughter-House Cases (1873) interpret away the "privileges and immunities clause" of the 14th Amendment, doing away with a guarantee for black rights. [3B] U.S. v Reece (1876) begins to interpret away the 15th Amendment, which meant to guarantee blacks the franchise. Being unrestrained in voiding congressional laws, judicial review now as unrestrained in voiding the clear-cut meaning of constitutional amendments.

[4A] The Civil Rights Cases (1883) interpret away much of the Civil Rights Act of 1875, doing away with the protection against individual discrimination. [4B] E.C. Knight (1895) severely narrows the Sherman Anti-Trust Act of 1890, which had meant to outlaw monopoly. Neither being clear-cut, both cases re-affirm unrestrained judicial review as applied to congressional laws.

[5] Plessy v Ferguson (1896) enacts into the Constitution "separate but equal," opening the way for legal segregation. The Court not only interprets away clear constitutional meaning, but interprets in a wholly unexpected meaning. Judicial review turns into a much more dynamic power, since the justices cannot just prevent Congress from violating the Constitution, but can insert novel doctrines into the Constitution, letting them intervene much more directly.

[6] Williams v Mississippi (1898) holds that the 14th Amendment did not prevent black disenfranchisement. Again judicial review interprets away clear constitutional meaning.

[7] Lochner (1905) assists at the invention of "substantive due process," a doctrine that let the judges void laws deemed "unreasonable." Since "unreasonable" lacks any clear definition, the judiciary acquires an even greater facility in voiding laws.

[8] The Danbury Hatters Case (1908) turns the Sherman Anti-Trust Act against unions, a wholly unintended target, authorizing wide-ranging injunctions against them. Not being limited by clear-cut constitutional meaning, neither is the Court limited by the clear-cut statutory meaning, but can put congressional laws to wholly unintended purposes.

[9] The Duplex Printing Case (1921) further disregards the principle of legislative primacy, which requires courts to carry out the legislative intent of a statute. After the Danbury Hatters Case, Congress had passed the Clayton Act (1914), which came to the aide of unions by forbidding injunction against them. The Court simply ignores the clear intent of the statute, letting judges carry on with the same anti-union injunctions.

[10A] Schechter Poultry (1935) and [10B] the Butler Case (1936) show unrestrained judicial review on a fully national scale, voiding the central New Deal laws passed in response to the crisis of the Great Depression.

[11A] However, in the face of Roosevelt's court-packing plan, West Coast Hotel (1937) and NLRB v Jones & Laughlin (1937) abruptly reverse course, approving laws similar in all respects to those just voided. [11B] The Carolene Products Case (1938) goes so far as to say: "the existence of facts supporting the legislative judgement is to be presumed." Such appeared to pledge a return to the original limits on judicial review. For once the Court's power declines.

[12] But within a decade, Everson (1947) returns to unrestrained judicial review, using another novel doctrine, "incorporation." By "incorporating" the Bill of Rights to apply against the states, the justices reverse their own prior clear-cut constitutional rulings. The Court

acquires another far-reaching power, soon employed in as far-reaching a way.

[13] Brown v Board of Education (1954) re-asserts the power to change clear-cut constitutional meaning. Back in 1896 Plessy had enacted "separate but equal," but now the Court enacts the opposite. The Court has shown the full-blown power to unmake, make, and remake the Constitution. They have unmade the Reconstruction Amendments, they have made "separate but equal," and finally they have remade "equal."

[14] Brown II (1955) creates the "new model judicial supremacy." Using a few words in the Constitution, say "equal protection of the laws," the Court recasts a policy choice as a constitutional commandment, thus replacing congressional authority under the Constitution with judicial authority over the Constitution. Next, they use another wide-ranging power, "equitable remedies," whose "plastic remedies are molded to the needs of justice," whatever that may mean. Finally, they use the class action to extend the reach of litigation to cover national constituencies. Judicial review becomes the power to order and directly carry out vast social programs across the whole nation.

[15] The Roth Case (1957) interprets away the prior constitutional restraint on obscenity and exemplifies another new doctrine, "fundamental or preferred rights." Designating some rights as "fundamental or preferred," the Court applies a "heightened scrutiny." Since nothing clearly defines which rights or what scrutiny, the doctrine confers an easy facility to void laws at will.

[16] Miranda (1966) rejects the old "voluntariness test" on confessions, instead ordering the Miranda Warnings. Once again the Court reverses a clear meaning given the Constitution, then interprets in a wholly new meaning.

[17] Shapiro v Thompson (1969) reaches out to assert judicial power over an entirely new set of growing rights, "entitlements." Once again the doctrine of "fundamental or preferred rights" shows the easy facility, letting the justice intervene at will.

[18] Green (1968) re-interprets the policy choices over school desegregation as constitutional commandments, transferring power from Congress to the Court. With the Civil Rights Act of 1964, Congress opted for "neighborhood schools," but the Court used those five words in the Constitution, "equal protection of the laws," to hold the law inadequate.

[19] Swann (1971) replaces the congressional policy on school desegregation with a more thoroughgoing judicial policy, including massive busing. The federal judges directly run the program, excluding Congress.

[20] The Adams Case (starting in 1970 and running for twenty years) stretches nationwide. Once again ignoring the clear meaning of a congressional statute (again the 1964 Civil Rights Act), which gave the president discretion to cut off federal funds in aid of school desegregation, the federal judge takes this power unto himself. In the same breath, he seizes control of the bureaucracy charged with overseeing the funding cut offs, running the agency beyond congressional or executive controls. Judicial review now includes the power for judges to directly run administrative agencies.

[21] Roe v Wade (1973) reaches the farthest from "clear-cut" of any case mentioned. The Court finds a "right to privacy," located among other places in the "penumbras" and "emanations" of the Bill of Rights, and including a right to an abortion. Whether good or bad as policy, unrestrained judicial review reveals the full potential.

[22] Milliken v Bradley (1974) shows the potential size to which the class action can reach, sweeping across 2000 square miles and over 4,000,000 people. Although the Court signaled a pause, yet a similar size would soon occur in other cases, while the Adams Case would take on a national size, showing the full scope.

[23] Elrod v Burns (1976) again uses the doctrines of incorporation and fundamental or preferred rights, this time holding patronage unconstitutional. Dispensing with a practice as old as the republic, the Court now mandates a monolithic civil service system.

[24] The Kansas City Case (1977) shows the potential size of equitable remedies, ordering the building of new schools and facilities in aid of desegregation. When the enormous expense exceeds the school budget, the judge simply orders taxes raised, disregarding the fundamental principle of "no taxation with representation."

The Court's power goes up relentlessly, the lone hiccup the institutional defeat over the New Deal. While we should also easily see the ideological changes coincide. The Marshall Court "believed in a strong national government," which served to justify aggrandizing power to the federal government, incidentally including the federal courts. The Taney Court approved of slavery, which served to justify forgetting the clear-cut limits on judicial review. The Fuller Court "was characterized by the principles of limited government [and] state autonomy," which served to justify the enactment of "separate but equal." The Fuller Court was also "dedicated to economic liberty," which served to justify the invention of substantive due process and "served conservative interests." The Warren Court was a "liberal court," which served to justify the new model judicial supremacy, served as well to justify the doctrines of "incorporation" and "preferred or fundamental rights." The ideologies change, even reverse course, but continue to justify more judicial power. Obviously, the conflicts with Congress also coincide. The Court constantly clashes with Congress and wins more power in the process.

The Court's present powers – To summarize how far the power has moved, start with the original doctrine of judicial review, whose narrow limits Chief Justice Marshall himself set forth in Fletcher v Peck (1810): "The question, whether a law be void for its repugnancy to the constitution, is at all times of much delicacy, which ought seldom, if ever, to be decided in the affirmative, in a doubtful case. The Court, when compelled by duty to render such a judgment, would be unworthy of its station, if it were unmindful of the solemn obligation which that situation imposes. ... The opposition between the law and the constitution should be such that the judge feels a clear and strong conviction of their incompatibility with each other."

How do the Court's present powers have anything to do with such restraint? To summarize those present power: 1) The Court may void congressional laws at will; 2) The Court may disregard the clear intent of congressional laws, either ignoring or turning them to entirely unintended purposes; 3) The Court may ignore or change the clear meaning of the Constitution itself; 4) The judiciary may order and directly carry out vast social programs across the whole nation; 5) The judiciary may directly control bureaucratic agencies and programs; and 6) The judiciary may even order taxation.

The explanations of political and social science – What explains the great and famous cases making up the history of the Supreme Court? Not the doctrines. Not the ideologies. Rather the judicial will-to-power. The justices have altered the legal doctrines out of recognition. The Court has switched ideologies. Yet their power ascended. Then not the ideals proclaimed, but the power claimed, not the rationalizations, but the motivations coherently explain the cases. The judicial will-to-power gives the reliable tendency, running through all the cases and good across time, accounting for the course.

Political science stands not amazed, while democratic theory stands violated. To political science, the Court did nothing more and nothing less than the standard model predicts. Being an aristocratic institution, the Court aggrandized power. To democratic theory, the standard model predicts the same. Being an aristocratic institution, the Court aggrandized power over the people.

Political science does no more than observe and describe. People attract toward their interests. Government organizes around this attraction, coming in three available types, monarchy, aristocracy, or democracy. Each sets up a political process to control the power, the ability to impose one's will. The government performs in the interests of whoever predominates. They exert a force throughout, aligning all other interests, bringing about cooperation if not coercion. Motivated by hope and fear, people get in line, stay in line, and push toward the head of the line. The better strategy suggests to get along, go along, taking available advantage while avoiding threatened harm. But the maximum strategy suggests to seize control. All striving for their interests, all seek the rewards and safety of power. Nor does anyone ever rest content, since constantly offered fresh opportunities and faced with renewed challenges.

In the language of the social sciences, these tendencies amount to social facts, reliable observations and predictions about an aggregate of individual choices or behaviors. In politics, individuals demonstrate a will-to-power and institutions a corresponding institutional will-to-power. Not to say that better nature never prevails, say ethical values or altruism. Rather to say self-interest the gravitational force. One can no more design a political institution while ignoring interests than build a bridge while ignoring the weight suspended over the chasm.

Democratic theory – Being committed to observation and description, political science, seconded by the other social sciences, tells how and why government works, but makes no choice between governments, not telling which to prefer. That depends on what you want to accomplish. But democratic theory makes such a choice, starting with a choice among ethical values. The Declaration of Independence best states this start: "We hold these truths to be self-evident: that all men are created equal, that they are endowed by their Creator with certain unalienable rights, that among these are life, liberty, and the pursuit of happiness. That, to secure these rights, governments are instituted among men, deriving their just powers from the consent of the governed."

Having made the choice, democratic theory holds that only democracy realizes the values. For the proofs, they turn back to political science, the other social sciences, and history.

What can "equality" mean, if not first and foremost, equality in the political process? That process controls the power, the ability to impose one's will. If one man can arbitrarily impose his will upon another, the second man not equal to the first. Only a political process that prevents such arbitrariness can prevent such inequality. Only democracy sets up such a process. In the periodic elections, each citizen has the same vote, the same eligibility for office, and the majority rules. Arbitrary government gives way to responsible government, the officials held responsive to the people's will. Then what can "unalienable rights" mean, if not first and foremost, that very right to democratic process? Finally, what can "the consent of the governed" mean, if not just that?

By their very natures, monarchy and aristocracy reject these democratic values. The officials hold permanent offices, letting them impose their will. All other rights wait upon their right to rule, and the only consent comes from them. Whatever their virtues, they practice not the democratic virtues.

While if we may appeal to interests, only democracy reflects the people's perception of their interests. The periodic elections constantly refract the officials' self-interest to mirror the people's views. To win and stay in office, they must image the will of the people. While this same feedback mechanism keeps the system stable and adjusted. The people resist meddling with their established interests, especially their interest in control over the system. But as the people's interests change, they will demand changes in line. Thus, the power relationships stay stable, and the adjustments coincide with the people's views. Consider as the outstanding example the British, whose government since the Glorious Revolution of 1688 has stayed remarkably stable. Yet their system has constantly adapted to changes in public attitudes. For instances, they moved toward socialism with Clement Atlee (Prime Minister 1945 to 1951) and back toward a free-market with Margaret Thatcher (Prime Minister 1979 to 1990).

Reversing this image, non-democratic governments mirror the rulers' interests, and the feedback adjusts in line. Their apparent stability no more than the rulers' longevity, their adjustments tend to add to their power, and so the power relationships never really stay stable. While resisting efforts to wrest control away, they make every effort to wrest still more control, and since already in control, generally succeed. Consider as an example the Roman Empire, where merely the ceremonials showed an ever more onerous authority. When Augustus seized imperial power in 27 B.C., he called himself no more than *Princeps Civitatis* (First Citizen) and preferred to manage behind the scenes, not openly stepping on stage garbed in the purple. By the time of Trajan (96 to 117 A.D.) an old woman could still approach the emperor, pluck the sleeve of his toga, and demand a hearing for her petition. But by the time of Diocletian (284 to 305) the emperor "had become an absolute monarch and was elevated above all his subjects" and "hardly ever appeared in public, but if he did he wore a diadem of pearls and beautiful clothes embroidered with jewels. In his presence people had to prostrate themselves (*adoratio*) and only a few senior officials were allowed to kiss the hem of his robe. Anything that was linked to the emperor ... was regarded as sacred."[5]

Practical proofs for democracy – These contrasts appear nowhere more familiarly than with the freedoms under democracy as compared to the repression under autocracy. Most of history shows the wider effects of the less attractive alternative. Concerned with nothing so much as their own right to rule, authoritarian regimes grant few rights to anyone else. To force their power down, they set up a narrow, stovepipe like chain-of-command. Their orders go down this chain easily enough, since the current of incentives runs that way. But since the links insulated from other interests, requests from below transmit slowly, uncertainly, or not at all. Their ascendency resting on an established order, they enforce conformity from above. Censorship locks down and rigidity sits in. In a classic instance, in the fifteenth century, the Ottoman sultans outlawed the printing press, rightly fearing Guttenberg's recent invention a danger to their set ways. People resent most the subordination, but the heavy chain-of-command binds not just the body, but weighs down the mind. The human intellect itself goes about in fetters, ingenuity and human potential strangled by the system. To stay with the Ottomans, for how many centuries did their empire stagnate? For exactly the same reasons, for how many centuries did how many peoples stagnate in frustration, borne down by the dead hand of authority and repression?

But while autocracy leads to a top-down, closed system, democracy leads to a bottom-up, open society. The incentives reverse. Elected officials open their mail and answer their phone calls, which says it all. Information flows back and forth with speed and accuracy. The top responds to the bottom. The people win their rights. Every imaginable interest finds a way into the legislative lobby and executive corridors. The society opens. Innovation takes off. Knowledge takes off.

The effects appear dramatically in economics, where the rise of democracy coincides with the rise of free-markets. Autocracy expropriates wealth, leaving the marketplace high and dry. Democracy lets people protect their interest in property, floating the free-market. This dichotomy stands out with the English Civil War, which culminated with Glorious Revolution of 1688. The king had sought to heighten the royal authority, trying to tax without parliamentary consent. But for once the people resisted with success. Recall the rationale later provided by Locke. Property being the product of labor, a man possessed an inherent right to his property. Taxation required consent through an elected legislature. As later reduced to a motto by the American colonists, "no taxation without representation." In other words, democracy would protect the people's interests in their property. Indeed, so it proved. The Glorious Revolution gave the world a workable model for modern democracy, and that working model gave the British a free-market. Who can imagine what came after without this first step? Who can imagine the rise of British commerce, who can imagine the British leading the industrial revolution, who can imagine the British Empire, if the monarchy could have taxed and expropriated to heart's content? All depended upon their free-market, which depended upon their democracy.

The same holds true in reverse. Democracy leads to free-markets, which lead to enormous wealth and amazing innovations. But autocracy stagnates economically, often going in reverse. Look to the Soviet Union, Communist China, or the kleptocracies of the under developed world. The autocrats kept strangling the goose that could have laid the golden eggs. So forcible the evidence, even they finally became convinced. When the fall of the Soviet Union dashed their last hopes for socialism, which let them own it all, they began to open up their markets. The most remarkable example turned our China, where the GDP took an astounding leap. Yet the long run has yet to tell if an authoritarian state and a free-market can co-exist. More likely one will consume the other. The English scenario may play out in other climes and times, the propertied interests winning the protections of democracy. Either that or the power elite will sooner or later give into temptation, raking off the profits and gaming the system, causing the market to run at some partial speed or collapse. Meanwhile, Europe and the U.S. have transformed into welfare states, where the interests in the entitlements may prove heavier than the old propertied interests, laying on a weight of taxation that will bear down the market from below. Any more detail falls outside the present scope, which no more than to show the decisive influence of interests within any political system, especially as related to economics.

In sum, the democratic true believer makes an ethical claim. He demands his right to democracy, come what may. But he makes practical claims as well. Whether measured by the index of freedom or Gross National Product, democracy decisively outperforms. If the choices freedom and prosperity, democracy must be the choice. The reasons appear as clear as the evidence.

The same analysis applied to the Court – All of this looks familiar enough, but while not so familiar, why not look at the Court in this familiar way? Why not see the justices for what they are, a *noblesse de robe*, a judicial aristocracy? They also qualify as that rarity, a real aristocracy of merit. As for powers, not resembling an absolutism, the Court contends with significant restraints. Ruling within their domain outside democratic controls, yet they are forced to share the government and confined by their institutional nature. Congress commands the vastness of legislation, giving them an initiative and a facility denied the Court. The president commands the broad reach of executive action, giving him a centrality and directness denied the Court. While as a court, the justices must wait for a case and act only through a case, the procedures careful, complex, and time-consuming. As a collegial body, they must first muster a majority among themselves. Nor can they entirely ignore public opinion, since existing in a surrounding democracy, where sufficient popular outrage threatened in the past and may still threaten.

Yet their lifetime offices set them apart, denoting an aristocratic body, putting them above and beyond electoral restraints. While this single lack of restraint has gone far to overcome all the other restraints. Typical of aristocracy, their power has not stayed stable, but step-by-step, they have leveraged their position to acquire still greater power. They have adeptly played their institutional strengths against their institutional weaknesses. Recalling their present powers, what have they not accomplished that feasible to accomplish? Today they virtually own the Constitution. Their interests own as much. American has become "the litigious society," where almost anybody can be sued for almost anything. A business model nourished by friends in high places, litigation has spread vertically and horizontally, growing ever more profitable.

Looking back over this long struggle, the Court's gains came at the expense of its rivals, especially Congress, but also the presidency and the states. But they altered more than the balance-of-power. Their pursuit of power changed the course of history. Their successes re-directed events in line with their interests. So Congress laid out a route for Reconstruction. Give blacks the vote and let the electoral compass steer from there. But to take the power, the Court re-routed the program, finally ending up at "separate but equal." During industrialization, Congress and the states took the path to progressive reforms. But to take the power, the Court invented substantive due process, blocking the path. Congress searched for a way out of the Great Depression. But not to cede the power, the Court stood resolutely in the way. Rudely shouldered aside by President Roosevelt, they left behind some acquired powers, substantive due process and a narrow reading of the commerce clause. But they carefully carried away their essential powers, lifetime tenure and judicial review. Soon returning to reclaim their lost power, with Brown they finally reversed themselves on segregation, thus creating the new model judicial supremacy, which let them order and control vast social programs across the nation. To take still more power, they led the charge with judicial revolution, creating incorporation and preferred rights, which let them drop in and out their own constitutional meaning. What might have been belongs to the dubious realm of alternative history, but what happened not in doubt. The Court decisively influenced the national destiny, guiding the nation down the way that favored judicial power.

What a more familiar story? What famous or infamous hero, what collection of characters ever varied from this plot? The hero in romantic literature pursues a love interest, but in politics the heroes and villains pursue the love of power. Think of the great protagonists in the genre. For love of power, Julius Caesar changed Rome from a failing republic into a fledgling despotism. With the same love, Napoleon changed the soaring republican hopes of the French Revolution into the short-lived glory of the Napoleonic Empire. But such men with their grand passions pursued this mistress no more eagerly than the common folk. In her pursuit, the parliamentary forces changed history with the Glorious Revolution of 1688. After the same lady's daughter, the Founding Fathers changed history with the American Revolution in 1776. "It's still the same old story, a fight for love and glory." Being but men, the justices on the Supreme Court love no differently.

The Madisonian Compromise – But the dominant view about the Court follows the lawyers and legal scholars, who as leaders of this vanguard make their case on a different argument. In a familiar form, they start by posing a paradox and conclude with a shared solution. This Madisonian Dilemma not better stated than by a distinguished federal jurist in a recent book: "The Constitution establishes a government around two principles that necessarily exist in tension: majority power and minority freedom." In other words, the "democratic paradox," the majority threatens to oppress the minority. The Madisonian Compromise sets forth the shared solution, again not better stated than by this same judge: "The task of maintaining the balance between majority rule and minority rights falls to the courts."[6]

Variously expressed, the Court itself has often claimed and given content to this task. For a well-remembered example, Justice Robert H. Jackson wrote in Barnette (1943): "The very purpose of the Bill of Rights was to withdraw certain subjects from the vicissitudes of political controversy, to place them beyond the reach of majorities and officials and establish them as legal principles to be applied by the courts. One's right to life, liberty and property, to free speech, a free press, freedom of worship and assembly, and other fundamental rights may not be submitted to vote; they depend on the outcome of no elections."[7]

This argument rests on a basic truth. Amidst the drama or melodrama of every case, the courts must act as the guardian not just to minority rights, but to all legal rights. Let no one attempt to write them out of this proper role, which judges well-adapted to play. Yet the Madisonian Compromise alters the original script much to their prominence. Consider the underlying assumption: "The Constitution establishes a government around two principles that necessarily exist in tension: majority power and minority freedom." Well, yes and no. Yes, the Constitution concerned with "majority power and minority freedom," but no, did not solely "establish a government around [those] two principles." Rather, the Constitution established a government around republican principles, where elected representatives govern. Next consider the conclusion: "The task of maintaining the balance between majority rule and minority rights falls to the courts." Well, again yes and no. Yes, a "task of maintaining ... minority rights falls to the courts," but no, originally not the task as now carried out.

The Madisonian Compromise projects onto the past events in the future. The Founders could not have intended what never yet conceived. In their day some held the original, limited doctrine of judicial review, where the Court would void congressional laws in a clear-cut case. But in their day none could have held the present doctrine of judicial supremacy, since none could have imagined the Court's present powers. The Compromise fails to draw this distinction over time, simple saying: "The task of maintaining the balance between majority rule and minority rights falls to the courts." But the "task" has radically changed from then to now. Even assuming all the Founders agreed that the "task ... falls to the courts," none could have agreed to the present "task," since in that day, the present powers of the Supreme Court did not exist, not even in speculation.

The underlying dilemma – Thus, the Madisonian Compromise makes a false appeal to the Founders' authority, a false appeal to "original intent." But any appeal to authority should ask for reasoned assent as well. Then if the authority fails, what about the other reasons? Basically, the argument goes as we heard Justice Jackson say that: "One's ... fundamental rights may not be submitted to vote; they depend on the outcome of no elections." What a pleasing theory, except like so many pleasing political theories, practice proves the impracticality. As a prohibitive hurdle, which the "fundamental rights?" We might name some as Justice Jackson did with "free speech" and "freedom of worship." Yet no one has ever been able to agree on a complete enumeration, let alone the details, all of which a work in progress. Then who settles the list, fills in the details, and carries on the work? As a practical matter, some political institution must get the job. Then also a practical matter, how say some worthy rights should "depend on the outcome of no elections?" Either the majority elects the worthy rights or someone else elects the worthy rights.

That's the true dilemma. You cannot avoid a political process. You have to choose between the available types of political institutions. That leaves the only live question: Which institution gets the power? The Madisonian Compromise does not escape this dilemma, but simply makes a choice between the institutions, choosing the Court. To sort out the operative words: "The task of *maintaining the balance* between majority power and minority rights *falls to the courts.*" Now *maintaining the balance* may sound like something less than *shall have the power*, but means nothing less, and *falls to the courts* means *the courts shall have the power*. Then what has the formula accomplished except to take the power from the majority and give it to a minority, specifically the Supreme Court?

The evidence of history – Then what justifies the choice? Surely the great and famous cases must justify the choice, that is, actual performance must provide the empirical proofs. The Madisonian Dilemma says that: "two principles ... necessarily exist in tension: majority power and minority freedom." Of course, the further argument goes that "majority power" not trustworthy around "minority freedom," so we must put "minority freedom" under the guardianship of a non-majoritarian institution, the Supreme Court. What can serve as evidence other than the great and famous cases?

But recall that British judges have never attained judicial supremacy. Nevertheless, that country stayed as free as America. Then if the British system has not judicial supremacy, yet guarantees freedom as well as the American system, whence the need for judicial supremacy to guarantee freedom in the American system? A *"necessary* tension" may exist between "majority power and minority freedom," but as the British example shows, a well-designed democracy can release this tension without the need to introduce a judicial *deus ex machine.*

Madison's name being so much bandied about, he spoke to this very issue in an oft-quoted passage from *Federalist No. 10*: "Among the numerous advantages promised by a well constructed Union, none deserves to be more accurately developed than its tendency to break and control the violence of faction. ... The smaller the society, the fewer will probably be the distinct parties and interests composing it; the fewer the distinct parties and interests, the more frequently will a majority be found of the same party; and the smaller the number of individuals composing a majority, and the smaller the compass within which they are placed, the more easily will they concert and execute their plans of oppression. Extend the sphere, and you take in a greater variety of parties and interests; you make it less probable that a majority of the whole will have a common motive to invade the rights of other citizens; … ."

In other words, "extend the sphere" to the size of the proposed United States and "take in a greater variety of parties and interests." As a result, "majority power" will stand on no more than the shifting sands of a coalition of minorities, and no one will be able to get enough traction "to concert and execute their plans of oppression." Did his prediction hold true? Did American demography combine with American democracy in a "well constructed Union," breaking majority power to protect minority rights?

What do the great and famous cases show? Does their evidence support Madison's prediction in favor of democracy, or does their evidence support the compromise that also bears his name, the Madisonian Compromise? Take first the greatest failure, segregation. Many fathers claim success, failure an orphan, but the Court's friends claim success by blaming the illegitimacy of segregation on "majority power," then claiming legitimacy for the Court as the father of Brown. To remember one quote earlier heard to express this blame: "With the acquiescence of northerners, southern Democrats restricted black suffrage and imposed formal racial segregation on many social institutions." Yet Madison's prediction in favor of democracy did not fail over segregation. Rather during Reconstruction, the "white" majority divided Democrat versus Republican, and the one party showed willing to bid for black votes. The working majority enacted the Reconstruction Amendments, surely monuments to "majority power" as protecting "minority rights." What failed was the Madisonian Compromise. Not that the Court failed to protect "minority rights." Rather they protected a minority, the segregationists, by interpreting away the Reconstruction Amendments. Except today, everyone concedes they choose the wrong minority. Not "majority power," but a minority and the Court "imposed formal racial segregation on many social institutions." Nor does Brown save the argument. For all the inestimable service, Brown corrected the Court's own earlier errors.

Next, take the other great and famous cases where opinion settled by historical consensus. Through industrialization, the Progressive Era, and the New Deal, democracy did better, the Court worse. Which leaves the remaining cases, the cases from the last half of the twentieth century, the cases making up the judicial revolution. Other than Brown, these remain contentious. But can their evidence be made to speak to the question?

First take Brown. The case commands a consensus, which must say that "majority power" supports the case. The diehard segregationists fought to the end, but bereft of the Court's crucial aid, their minority lost decisively in the public forum. Congress made no effort to repudiate Brown, rather the opposite. Previously, judicial supremacy had set "separate but equal" in constitutional concrete. But after Brown, Congress could again legislate, and they did exactly that. The Civil Rights Act of 1964 and the Voting Rights Act of 1965 worked to finally make civil rights and voting a reality for blacks. Such a response hardly shows majority power a negative force in this equation, which the Court needed to cancel out. Rather, once the Court canceled itself out, the math soon added up to a better solution.

Take the rest of the cases in the judicial revolution. How exactly does their evidence run the other way? Everson (1947) raised the wall of separation between church and state, but if a flourishing variety in the religious garden any test, did not American soil already richly nourish religious toleration? Roth (1957) gave protection to obscenity, but if the right to free speech "fashioned to assure unfettered interchange of ideas," did not the people already have free speech? Miranda (1966) ordered the Miranda Warnings, but did not the voluntariness test already prevent coerced confessions? Shapiro v Thompson (1969) threw out the waiting period to collect welfare benefits, but did not passing the welfare laws evince a generous spirit, and why not let the states stop welfare shopping? Elrod v Burns (1976) mandated a monolithic civil service, but had not Congress and the states already passed civil service reform, and good reasons existed to keep some flexibility in the system? Roe v Wade (1973) ruled for a right to an abortion, but had not several states already legalized abortion, and so apparently the majority at least willing to listen?

Finally, then, what holds up the Madisonian Compromise except a willing suspension of disbelief? The reasoned arguments turn out empty. They say the Founders gave such powers to the Court, but the Founders never conceived the present judicial supremacy. They say that our fundamental rights should depend on the outcome of no elections, but a vote of five to four on the Court has repeatedly changed our fundamental rights. They say the unelected Court serves to protect the minority, but Madison's well-designed democracy better serves. What left except the pleasures derived from the Court's performance by those who derive the pleasures? They accept the conventions of the theater to enjoy the entertainment. They accept judicial supremacy, since that contrives the plot to suit their tastes. Their glowing reviews persuade the public that the Court the best show in town. Not for the first or the last time, the *claqueur* carries along the crowd.

The Court's future – What does the future hold for the Court? Likely more of the same and their power will continue to ascend. A "second judicial revolution" looks in the offing. While the first round played out, the justices have retreated on nothing, made some more gains, and need wait only for reinforcements. Already the legal doctrines stand poised, fraught with potential energy. Incorporation, fundamental rights, strict scrutiny, the right to privacy, such doctrines can be made to mean almost anything. Already calls sound to release the potential, putting the energy to work behind newer causes. When the interests of a sufficient coalition thereby served, the time will grown ripe for the Court. With allies able to block any backlash in the democratic arena, the justices can go forward in the familiar way, granting the people such further rights as grant the Court further power.

Tellingly, they have reversed none of the cases of the judicial revolution. Despite severe attacks, Roe v Wade survives intact. Despite a congressional attack, Miranda was re-affirmed. While more recent cases show the revolutionary doctrines still very much alive and well. McDonald v City of Chicago[8] (2010) "incorporated" against the states the 2nd Amendment right to bear arms, finding in the moribund provisions a right to possess handguns. In Citizens United v FEC[9] (2010) the Court, referring to "strict scrutiny," struck down a part of the 2002 Bipartisan Campaign Reform Act, which had banned corporations and unions from spending money on "electioneering communication." With Brown v Plata[10] (2011), they ordered a sweeping injunction, releasing some 46,000 inmates from the California penal system, finding their conditions of confinement violated the "cruel and unusual punishment" clause of the 8th Amendment. All of which goes to show the revolution not in retreat, but consolidated, ready to push on to the next level.

The Second Bill of Rights – An obvious line of advance suggests for the Court to take up the Second Bill of Rights. Also called an "economic bill of rights," this idea harks back to President Franklin Roosevelt's State of the Union Address, delivered January 11, 1944.

"It is our duty now to begin to lay the plans and determine the strategy for ... the establishment of an American standard of living higher than ever before known. We cannot be content, no matter how high that general standard of living may be, if some fraction of our people—whether it be one-third or one-fifth or one-tenth—is ill-fed, ill-clothed, ill-housed, and insecure.

"This Republic had its beginning, and grew to its present strength, under the protection of certain inalienable political rights—among them the right of free speech, free press, free worship, trial by jury, freedom from unreasonable searches and seizures. They were our rights to life and liberty.

"As our nation has grown in size and stature, however—as our industrial economy expanded—these political rights proved inadequate to assure us equality in the pursuit of happiness.

"We have come to a clear realization of the fact that true individual freedom cannot exist without economic security and independence. 'Necessitous men are not free men.' ... .

'In our day these economic truths have become accepted as self-evident. We have accepted, so to speak, a second Bill of Rights under which a new basis of security and prosperity can be established for all—regardless of station, race, or creed.

"Among these are: ... The right to earn enough to provide adequate food and clothing and recreation; ... The right of every family to a decent home; The right to adequate medical care and the opportunity to achieve and enjoy good health; The right to adequate protection from the economic fears of old age, sickness, accident, and unemployment; The right to a good education.

"... [W]e must be prepared to move forward, in the implementation of these rights, to new goals of human happiness and well-being."

Roosevelt makes a powerful appeal worded in familiar language, but aspiring toward something not nearly as familiar at the time. He appeals to "true individual freedom" and "an American standard of living higher than ever before known." But he is not saying, Hands off liberty and raise the per capita GDP. He is saying, Guarantee "economic security and independence." In other words, he is aspiring toward the American version of the welfare state, a work now well along, if still a work in progress. But notice he laid out not just aspirations, but called for "rights." He called these rights "self-evident" and called for "a second Bill of Rights" just like the original Bill of Rights.

Now as Justice Jackson just heard to say: "The very purpose of the Bill of Rights was to withdraw certain subjects from the vicissitudes of political controversy, to place them beyond the reach of majorities and officials and establish them as legal principles to be applied by the courts. One's right to life, liberty and property, to free speech, a free press, freedom of worship and assembly, and other fundamental rights may not be submitted to vote; they depend on the outcome of no elections."

Then why not make the "second Bill of Rights" the same? Why not "withdraw [these rights] from the vicissitudes of political controversy" as well? Why not "place them beyond the reach of majorities and officials and establish them as legal principles to be applied by the courts?" Let the Supreme Court guard these newer rights with the same care bestowed upon the older rights.

Such an endeavor remains part of the unfinished business left over from the first judicial revolution. Although unable to carry the day, the dissenters in Dandridge v Williams[11] (1970) sought to invigorate "the Equal Protection Clause as a constitutional principle applicable to the area of welfare administration."[12] The dissenters in Lindsey v Normet[13] (1972) would have done the same for housing. In San Antonio School District v Rodriguez[14] (1973) they would have done the same for public education. In the past, the Court has often returned to dissents, finding their reasons now convince the majority, and why not this time?

The attraction of the proposal – To understand the attraction, understand the aspiration. Back in 1938, Footnote Four made a proposal. Let the Court turn away from defending property rights, instead turn to defend the Bill of Rights, racial minorities, religion, and political processes. During the judicial revolution, the Court took up this proffer, extending their power across much of the national life. The Second Bill of Rights offers just such another proposal. Let the Court take up the new rights to "economic security and independence," that is, the rights of the welfare state. Let them defend the rights to employment, housing, health care, education, retirement, and disability. Regard the vista that opens. The Court need only exploit a natural synergy. As the rights of the welfare state grow, so can judicial power grow by defending those rights. In fact, one can help along the other.

To conceive this future more precisely, recall the new model judicial supremacy. Recall how the school desegregation cases developed the model. Congress had passed the Civil Rights Act of 1964, basically opting for neighborhood schools. But many thought this program went not far enough. The Court sided with them, rejecting the congressional program as constitutionally insufficient. The justices declared a more thoroughgoing program as constitutionally mandated. They ordered racially gerrymandered school districts, massive busing, new facilities, co-opted bureaucratic agencies, even raised taxes. In this way, the judiciary came to directly run a massive social program across the whole nation.

Next put this same model together with the welfare state. Take the rights Roosevelt mentioned, employment, housing, health care, education, retirement, and disability. Congress and the states have already passed laws, already made policy. Huge programs already exist. But who cannot point out the shortfalls and inequities? Large and well-led constituencies remain dissatisfied. Bureaucrats regard their mandate as overly narrow, their agencies under staffed and under funded. The situation exactly resembles the earlier situation over school desegregation. Then let them follow the model. Let the public interest lawyers file their lawsuits. Let the judiciary declare "economic security and independence" as constitutional rights. Let them declare the existing programs constitutionally insufficient. Let them declare more thoroughgoing policies as constitutionally commanded. Finally, let them order the needed remedies, make up for the shortfalls, fix the inequities. In this way, the judiciary will come to directly run all these huge programs across the nation. While the constituencies, their leaders, and the bureaucracy will have their reward, being released from legislative restraint.

What item on the domestic agenda would the Court not come to dominate? But why stop at the border? Traditionally the justices have shied away from foreign policy and the war powers. The Constitution clearly assigns these closely connected missions elsewhere, mainly to the president. Moreover, frequent failure attends such hazardous undertakings as diplomacy and war, and judicial prudence surely suggests the blame better left elsewhere as well. Over time, this reluctance has drawn something of a line in the sand, marking off the separation of powers. For the Court to step across might excite adverse comment.

Yet in the present state of things, the distinctions blur, trying judicial self-restraint, while widening their openings and narrowing their risks. Numerous national security concerns tread on the Court's sensibilities. Surveillance, detention, interrogation, and trial of suspected terrorists, all impinge on their established prerogatives. When and how can the authorities monitor, search, arrest, or interrogate? Such questions not only affect national security, but also present as questions of liberty, privacy, and criminal procedure. In providing answers, the Court may easily assert to do nothing more than jealously watch over cherished freedoms, stopping heavy handed and oppressive official conduct. At the same time, such matters lend themselves to intervention in detail, letting the Court go step-by-step, often a useful tactic in the past. Going case-by-case and issue-by-issue will avoid the appearance of excessive interference. They can claim not to direct foreign policy, not to hinder military or covert action, only to defend constitutional rights. As part of this, they will likely open the way for more lawsuits against the government and government officials, widening their liability for the conduct of internal security, foreign intelligence gathering, and the use of deadly force. Similarly, the conduct and deep pockets of large, multinational corporations beckon for more liability, allowing more lawsuits over human rights violations in foreign lands. By such means, the Court may come to crucially structure foreign policy and the war powers, setting limits and foreclosing options, exerting a great deal more control than in the past.

The winning system – If the institutional will-to-power exerts the usual attraction, the Court will respond. Just as in the past, they will take the power. Just as in the past, they will change history in the process. Just as in the past, the winning side will celebrate their victories, sure they got it right, got the ideology right, especially got the ethical values right. Yet since in the past they so seldom got it right, how much confidence should their assurances inspire this time around? Are they getting it right like Brown, or wrong like Reconstruction and substantive due process? How know for sure? Are their truths self-evident to all or even most? Apparently not, or they would not need the Court, having won over the majority and passed the laws in the first place. Which says one thing for sure. Such a future will not win out through democracy. Rather, the Court will select the winners. So in this future, democratic values will turn out losers. The winners will turn out the values most valued by the judiciary, and what more valuable to the judiciary than judicial interests? So in the future as well as the past, judicial interests will turn out the winners. But what proves judicial interests get it right?

Notice, too, that top-down replaces bottom-up government, making the system much less adaptable. As more and more turns into a constitutional right, less and less stays open to change through mere legislation. Judicial rigidity replaces legislative flexibility. Whatever the complaints or inconveniences, the justices need not respond, so will not respond until their interests benefited or threatened. By comparison, elected legislators respond with agility, since their interests immediately affected. Recall how the justices handed down Reconstruction, segregation, and substantive due process. Until they reversed themselves after waiting for decades, nothing could change. Now the Court will hand down these newer constitutional rights. Whatever the complaints and inconveniencies, change will again wait upon the Court.

Nor will judicial supremacy in aid of the welfare state work like democracy and the free-market. The former will center on righting the inequities of the later. The free-market releases economic innovation and production, but unevenly distributes. The few come out ahead, leaving the majority with every incentive to redistribute, and democracy looks the perfect vehicle. But over the years, the wealthy minority resisted, often with more than success, leveraging their money to influence the democratic marketplace. In the bad old days of substantive due process, the Court joined forces with them, protecting their property rights, protecting their minority rights. But the newer arrangements re-align the forces. Slowly but surely, the welfare state has gained momentum through the democratic process. Each new program raises a pyramid of new interests. The broad base rests on the direct beneficiaries, say recipients of Social Security or food stamps. Next come the layers of bureaucracy and outside service providers, who draw a livelihood from the programs, say dispersing or receiving the billions paid out by Medicare, the millions food stamps put in consumers' pockets. At the pinnacle sit the politicians and interest group entrepreneurs, who promote the causes, drawing support from below. In essence, the entitlements have created a new type of property. Just as earlier a host gathered around the older property interests, now a host has gathered around these newer property-like interests. Just as earlier the Court allied with the first, now the Court will enter in an alliance with the second. The combination looks an imposing array, able increasingly to bear down the wealthy minority. But while the free-market serves as an engine for economic production, the welfare state serves as an engine for redistribution. Past a certain point, fueling the one starts to take fuel away from the other. Axiomatically, excessive taxation becomes self-defeating, stifling the source of the taxation. So just as industrialization brought massive benefits, accompanied by massive ills, the welfare state grants massive benefits, threatens massive ills. So just as the remedies for the first called for ingenuity, the remedies for the second will call for similar ingenuity. But just as the Court blocked Progressive reforms in the name of constitutional rights, will they not again block reforms in the name of constitutional rights? It will be hard enough to make things come right. How much harder when the Court dominates the proceedings, replacing bottom-up with top-down government, replacing legislative flexibility with judicial rigidity?

The lessons of history – What chance a reversal of fortune? What chance reform of the Court? Habit and interests look disinclined to relax their grip. Yet set ways may grasp better ways, and interests may grasp their better interests. If the values and benefits of democracy carry sufficient conviction, the Court sits not entirely beyond fear from revolt. But unless the lessons of history correctly seized, an insurrection against the judicial aristocracy might easily make the wrong heads roll, doing more harm than good. In political science, even the best intentions *gang aft aglay*. Nothing better illustrates such unintended consequences than the Court's own history.

Centuries ago the English Parliament cut the lead strings by which the monarch made their judges jump. Before they sat at the royal pleasure, now they sat during good behavior. This precise counterstroke stood the test of time. Given "judicial independence," their judges well upheld the rule of law. The Founding Fathers stuck with this proven reform. The Constitution said that: "The Judges, both of the supreme and inferior Courts, shall hold their Offices during good Behaviour."

They also closely followed the English way of choosing the judges. The president assumed the royal prerogative, nominating the candidates with confirmation from the Senate. "He ... by and with the Advice and Consent of the Senate ... shall appoint ... Judges of the supreme Court." The historical record conclusively shows the process elevates highly qualified judges.

The Founders meant to give the federal courts at least the powers of English courts. Article III said: "The judicial Power shall extend to all Cases, in Law and Equity, arising under this Constitution, the Laws of the United States, ..." And they well-understood that English judges made laws, even laws of constitutional magnitude. Such authority proves both necessary and useful. Unless judges can fill in the gray areas, respond to unforeseen circumstances, and deal with constant changes, the letter of the law dies to the spirit. Interpreting the law, even the constitutional law, demands a dynamic power.

But the English constitution had evolved over centuries, not written down in any one document. American circumstances forced an immediate act of constitutional creation, which forced a single and written document. Seeing in necessity a virtue, the Founders thought a written constitution a great and overdue advance, a way to etch the fundamental laws clearly and indelibly. By such solidity, they hoped to "secure the Blessings of Liberty to ourselves and to our Posterity," as Lincoln later said, with a Constitution "which it was hoped and is still hoped will endure forever."

In this pursuit, they left behind the English "parliamentary sovereignty," where parliamentary laws could change the constitution. Congress could not amend the Constitution by mere legislation. Instead, amendments wend through an arduous, and as turned out, largely unworkable process. But no similar reason appeared to deny the judges' traditional authority to interpret the law. Some even thought to give them the newer, added authority of judicial review. By letting them void unconstitutional laws, they would maintain the Constitution in perpetuity.

So with the very best intentions, the Founders altered the initial conditions of the system. The law of unintended consequences took over from there. After claiming judicial review, the Court slowly claimed ever-greater powers. Congress could not amend the Constitution, and judicial review kept Congress from edging around. But nothing kept the Court from edging around. Gradually, the Court turned judicial review into a power to amend the Constitution itself, as well as the other present powers of judicial supremacy. In the result, the British and American systems diverged in their very natures. The British remained fully democratic, where the elected House of Commons dominate. But the American altered into a mixed form, where the unelected Court widely dominates over Congress and the president, not to mention the states.

Judicial reform – To restore a true democracy would ask for a careful cure. Do no harm to a healthy judicial power, whose vitality essential to a healthy body politic. Do no harm to a proper judicial independence, since as shown by English experience, a judiciary dependent on the executive cannot uphold the rule of law. Do no harm to the method of selecting judges, since that method works well. Do no harm to the judges' power to interpret and to make laws, even constitutional laws, since otherwise the letter of the law dead to the spirit. Do no harm even to class actions and equitable remedies, since a justice that goes one-by-one goes at too halting a pace, and since without "a practical flexibility in shaping remedies," many a wrong goes un-remedied.

Rather, a careful reform would attempt to repudiate no more than judicial supremacy, which raises the Court beyond responsibility to the people. In the manner of the Founding Fathers, a careful reform would seek to follow a proven model. And what better model than the British Constitution? Their judiciary well enforces the rule of law, well protects the people's rights. Then go back to the fork in the road that unexpectedly led to judicial supremacy. Take the other fork, accepting the principle of parliamentary sovereignty, in the American context, congressional sovereignty. Leave behind judicial review and formally recognize that the Court must defer to Congress, since Congress responsible to the people. No lesser reform meets the minimum requirement, restoring the dominance of a democratic institution. But as a caveat, a prospective looks better than a retrospective reform, leaving in place existing constitutional meaning. Otherwise, the constitutional law would be thrown into utter confusion. But for the future, let Congress make such changes as seem best to them. As heard suggested in the debates at the Constitutional Convention by Mr. John Francis Mercer: "He thought the laws ought to be well and cautiously made, and then to be uncontroulable." If we must trust someone with the power, and we must, let us thrust the people through their elected representatives.

Effective judicial reform – But if the history shows anything, it shows mere words not enough, a doctrine however formal not enough. Just as elections enforce congressional accountability, some similar effective mechanism must enforce judicial compliance. But such a necessity reaches a complex and vexing topic, where if anywhere, the law of unexpected consequences likely to rear its dreaded head.

Some might run to the nostrum of term limits, say limiting the judges to twelve-year terms. But such medicine would excite the virulence of another disease. Judges limited to a single term would display much less institutional loyalty than lifetime judges, that interest weakening in favor of personal ambition. Likely they would spend their judicial careers building their professional resumes, accrediting their credentials with an eye on future employment, and the more imminent their departure, the more pressing this concern. As they stepped down from the bench, who would wait for them with open arms? Who would offer them a partnership in the best law firms, a comfortable professorship in elite academia, a lucrative seat on corporate boards? Surely whomever they had championed in their opinions, whichever faction, cause, or interest. With such motives the judges might well lose their institutional bias, but would acquire a worse bias, descending to serve as the mere tools of outside influences.

Others might suggest the nonpartisan judicial retention election, an innovation used in a number of states. Appointed for a term of years, a judge must later stand for retention in office. With no party affiliation listed and no opponent on the ballot, the judge wins successive terms with a simple majority, fifty percent plus one vote. But leaving aside how well this system may work in the states, lifted to the federal level, especially to the level of the Supreme Court, such elections could not but pull the judges into the partisan maelstrom. However much against their will, how could they avoid campaigning for office? As a practical matter, how could they avoid calling on the parties and interests groups for support, and how call for such support without some sort of pledge of allegiance? And how finance such campaigns? Perhaps give the judge some public financing. But could the opposition not spend? If not, the opposition silenced. Yet if enemies can spend, why cannot friends? Otherwise, the support silenced. There appears no way to keep the partisan money out. And if the partisan money in, the justice would have to make a partisan appeal for the money. The judiciary would become politicized.

Then to go back to the British model, the better alternative looks a check in the hands of Congress. Simply provide some careful way for Congress to remove a judge. Under such a threat, likely the power would seldom if ever be needed. The British judiciary and their parliament seem to co-exist well enough. The judiciary recognizes the primacy of the legislature, and the legislature respects the independence of the judiciary. Why should not a similar truce hold within the American constitutional system?

But if reform out of reach, let us recall that back at the very start, in the very first of the *Federalist Papers*, Alexander Hamilton wrote: "It has been frequently remarked that it seems to have been reserved to the people of this country, by their conduct and example, to decide the important question, whether societies of men are really capable or not, of establishing good government from reflection and choice, or whether they are forever destined to depend, for their political constitutions, on accident and force."

Then let us confess that question not answered by our "conduct and example" the way we like to think. True, the American people thought to establish "good government from reflection and choice" when they ratified the Constitution, thought to establish a republic. But "accident and force" account for the Court's present powers in the government. Across time, the "accident" of events gave the justices their chances, and their "force" seized upon judicial supremacy. They changed the very nature of the government. Neither do they consult the peoples' "reflection and choice" nor does a true democracy remain.

END

INDEX

A
abortion, 349
Adams Case (Adams v Richardson), 258
Agricultural Adjustment Act, 189
Alien and Sedition Acts, 86
aristocracy, 5, 13, 15, 405
  Supreme Court as, 13, 235, 410

B
Black Codes, 108
Black, Justice Hugo L.
  opinion in Everson Case, 292
  opinion in McCollum Case, 296
  opinion in Engel v Vitale, 296
Blackmun, Harry A., 19, 377
  opinion in Roe v Wade, 349
Blackstone, Sir William
  nature of a court, 25
  parliamentary sovereignty, 54
Berea College Case (Berea College v Kentucky), 212
Bradley, Justice Joseph P., opinion in Civil Rights Cases, 121
Brennan, Justice William Joseph, Jr., 18
  opinion in Green v County Board of Education, 249
  opinion in Roth Case, 314
  opinion in Fanny Hill Case, 315
  dissent in Paris Adult Theater Case, 316
  opinion in Shapiro v Thompson, 336
  opinion in Elrod v Burns, 345
  judicial philosophy, 373
Brewer, Justice, opinion in Louisville, New Orleans, and Texas Rail Company v Mississippi, 166
Bolling v Sharpe, 224
Brown, Justice Henry Billings, opinion in Plessy v Ferguson, 168
Brown v Board of Education, 217
Brown II, 226
bureaucracy, 12, 186, 248, 259, 339, 349

see patronage
see civil service
Burger, Chief Justice Warren Earl
  opinion in Swann v Charlotte-Mecklenburg Board of Education, 251
  opinion in Milliken v Bradley, 256
Bushell's Case, 27, 146, 159
busing, 239, 241, 244, 251
Butler Case (U.S. v Butler), 190

C

Calhoun, John C., 88, 154
Cardozo, Justice Benjamin, opinion in McPherson v Buick Motor Co., 30
  Carolene Products Case (U.S. v Carolene Products), 37, 204
  Catron, Justice John, opinion in Permoli Case, 271
  Chaplinksky Case (Chaplinsky v New Hampshire), 312, 314
  Civil Rights Act of 1875, 119
  Civil Rights Act of 1964, 243
    definition of desegregation in education, 244
    prohibition on busing, 244
  Civil Rights Cases, 121
  civil service, 259, 310, 343, 345
    Pendleton Act, 344
  class actions, 229
  classic political science, 5
  classical liberalism, 41
  Clayton Act, 139
  Commerce Clause, 131, 132, 141, 163, 166, 187, 201
  common schools, 281
  Compromise of 1820, see Missouri Compromise
  Compromise of 1850, 85
  confessions
    forced oaths, 319
    Lilburne's Case, 320
    common law rule, 322
    voluntariness rule, 325
    Miranda Warnings, 327
  consensual democracy, 88
  Constitution of the Confederate States, 81

Constitutional Convention, 57
Contract Clause, 30
Corfield v Coryell, 110, 113
court, nature of, 25
court packing plan, see Roosevelt, President Franklin D.
criminal procedure, 318
Cumming v Richmond Board of Education, 209

D

Danbury Hatters Case (Loewe v Lawlor), 135
Declaration of Independence, 41
democratic contradiction (paradox), 43, 412
desegregation in education
  competing definitions, 218
  Civil Rights Act of 1964, 243
De Tocqueville, Alexis, on religion in America, 274
democracy, 5, 6, 7, 11, 13, 43, 47, 48, 308, 355, 356, 408, 409, 413
  Disenfranchisement, 155
    U.S. v Reese, 116
    Williams v Mississippi, 157
  Douglas, Justice William O., opinion in Griswold v Connecticut, 353
  Dred Scott Case (Scott v Sandford), 89
  Due Process Clause, see Fourteenth Amendment
    origins, 145
    definition in Murray's Case, 145
    Alexander Hamilton on the meaning, 146
  Duplex Printing v Deering, 140
  Durkheim, Emile, 10

E

equitable remedies, 228
Elrod v Burns, 345
enfranchisement, see Fifteenth Amendment
Engel v Vitale, 296
Equal Protection Clause, see Fourteenth Amendment
Everson Case (Everson v Board of Education), 291

F

factual issue, 28
Fanny Hill Case (Memoirs v Massachusetts), 315

fascism, 303
Federalist Papers, 59, 171, 398, 414, 427
Fifteenth Amendment, 115
First Amendment, see religious toleration, freedom of speech
Fletcher v Peck, 72, 404
Footnote Four, see Carolene Products Case
forced oaths, 319
Fourteenth Amendment, 109
　Privileges and Immunities Clause, 109
Fourth Amendment, 33
Frankfurter, Justice Felix, 371, 374
freedom of speech
　First Amendment, 312
　see obscenity
Fuller, Chief Justice Melvin Weston
　opinion in U.S. v E.C. Knight, 132
　opinion in Danbury Hatters Case, 136
　ideology, 368
Fuller Court, the, 368
fundamental rights doctrine, see preferred rights doctrine

G

grandfather clause, 118
graph of the Court's power, 403
Great Depression, 179
Green v County School Board, 249
Gompers, Samuel, 139

H

Hall v De'Cuir, 162
Hamilton, Alexander
　on judicial review, 59
　on due process of law, 146
　on the judiciary as the least dangerous branch, 171
　on the taxing power, 192
Harlan, Justice John Marshall
　dissent in Civil Rights Cases, 122
　dissent in Lochner v New York, 148
　dissent in Plessy V Ferguson, 169
　opinion in Cumming v Board of Education, 212
Holmes, Justice Oliver Wendell, Jr., 53, 349, 365, 372, 392

dissent in Lochner v New York, 148
Howard, Senator J.M., on the "privileges and immunities" clause, 109
Hughes, Chief Justice Charles Evans
  on the Constitution, 131
  opinion in Schechter Poultry Case, 186
  opinion in West Coast Hotel v Parrish, 199
  opinion in National Labor Relations Board v Jones & Laughlin Steel Corporation, 202
Hume, David, 7
Humphrey, Senator Hubert, on the Civil Rights Act of 1964, 244

I

incorporation doctrine, 38, 294, 310, 314, 346, 417
industrialization, 125
injunctions, against unions, 138
institutional will-to-power, 6
integration, 238

J

Jackson, Justice Robert Houghwout
  opinion in Wickard v Filburn, 202
  dissent in Everson Case, 295
  purpose of the Bill of Rights, 412
Jefferson, Thomas
  on judicial review, 70
  on the wall of separation between church and state, 294
judicial reform, 425
judicial retention election, nonpartisan, 426
judicial review, 34, 35
  origins, 54
  at the Constitutional Convention, 57
  Marbury v Madison, 62
  original, limited doctrine, 70
  distinguished from action under the supremacy clause, 73
  new paradigm of Dred Scott, 93
judicial revolution, 307
judicial supremacy, 34
  justifications, 38

K

Kansas City Case (Missouri v Jenkins), 257
Kentucky and Virginia Resolutions, 86
L
law, 26
  judge made law (case law), 29
  least dangerous branch, the, 170
  legal issue, 28
  legislative primacy, 31
Lemon Case (Lemon Test) (Lemon v Kurtzman), 298
Lilburne, John, 320
Lincoln, Abraham
  on slavery in the Constitution, 81
  response to Dred Scott, 96, 98
  use of patronage, 342
living constitution, the, 393
Lochner v New York, 142
Locke, David Ross (Petroleum V. Nasby), 155
Locke, John, on religious toleration, 279
Loewe v Lowler, see Danbury Hatters Case
Louisville, New Orleans, and Texas Rail Company v Mississippi, 165
Lynch v Donnelly (endorsement test), 298
M
Madison, James, 57, 59, 61, 79, 270, 273, 398, 414
Madisonian Compromise (Dilemma), 411
management theory, 10
Mann, Horace, 281
Marbury v Madison, 59
Marshall, Chief Justice John
  opinion in Marbury v Madison, 62
  on the limitations on judicial review, 72
  on the doctrine of executive discretion, 263
  ideology, 366
Marshall Court, the, 366
McCollum Case (McCollum v Board of Education), 296
McCulloch v Maryland, 88
McKenna, Justice Joseph, decision in Williams v Mississippi, 158
Memoirs v Massachusetts, see Fanny Hill Case

Miller, Justice Samuel Freeman, opinion in Slaughter-House Cases, 113
Milliken v Bradley, 255
Miranda Case (Miranda v Arizona), 325
Missouri Compromise (Compromise of 1820), 84
Missouri v Jenkins, see Kansas City Case
monarchy, 5, 6, 13, 19, 357, 405
monopoly, 112, 128
Murphy, Justice Frank, opinion in Chaplinsky Case, 312

N

Nasby, Petroleum V., see David Ross Locke
National Industrial Recovery Act, 181
National Labor Relations Act (Wagner Act), 201
National Labor Relations Board v Jones & Laughlin Steel Corporation, 202
neighborhood schools, 240
New Deal, 180
new model judicial supremacy, 235
Newmyer, R. Kent, 381
Northwest Ordinance, 78, 84, 272, 396

O

obscenity
  original limitations on (Chaplinsky Case), 312
  original definition (Regina v Hicklin), 312
  redefinition (Roth Case), 313
  further redefinition (Fanny Hill Case), 315
originalism, 393

P

Paris Adult Theater Case (Paris Adult Theatre v Slaton), 316
parliamentary sovereignty (parliamentary supremacy), 54
patronage, 340
  spoils system, 342
  machine politics, 342
Payne, Stanley G, 383
Peckham, Justice Rufus Wheeler, opinion in Lochner v New York, 143
Pendleton Act, 344
penumbras and emanations of the Bill of Rights, 353
Permoli Case (Permoli v Municipality No. 1 of the City of New

Orleans), 271
Pitney, Justice Mahlon, decision in Duplex Printing v Deering, 141
Plessy v Ferguson, 167
Pollard, A.F., 174, 357, 382
Powell, Justice Lewis, dissent in Elrod v Burns, 348
precedents, 391
preferred rights doctrine, 38, 310, 315, 346, 379
Privileges and Immunities Clause, see Fourteenth Amendment
products liability, 30
progressive movement, 125

R

Reconstruction, Congressional, 44, 102, 106
Reconstruction Amendments, 106, 107
Reed, Justice Stanley Forman, dissent in Engel v Vitale, 296
Regina v Hicklin, 312
religion in the schools
  history of, 280
  complexities of religious toleration in, 286
religious toleration
  establishment and free exercise clauses of the First Amendment, 269
  original meaning of the religious clauses of the First Amendment, 269
  complexities of, 283
Roberts, Justice Own Josephus, opinion in Butler Case, 191
Roe v Wade, 349
Roman Senate, 8
Roosevelt, President Franklin D.
  on the National Industrial Recovery Act, 183
  on the Agriculture Administration Act, 189
  court packing plan, 195
  radio address on court packing plan, 196
  Second Bill of Rights, 417
Roth Case (Roth v U.S.), 313

S

Schechter Poultry Case (Schechter Poultry Corp. v U.S.), 184
Schwartz, Bernard, 370, 373, 380, 386
Scott v Sandford, see Dred Scott Case

Second Bill of Rights, 417
segregation
  in education, 209
  de jure segregation, 238
  de facto segregation, 238
self-interest, 6
separate but equal, see Plessy v Ferguson
Shapiro v Thompson, 336
Sherman Anti-Trust Act, 27, 129
  use against union, 134, 136
Sherman, Senator John, on the Sherman Anti-Trust Act, 130
sick chicken case, see Schechter Poultry Case
Slaughter-House Cases, 111
slavery
  before the Constitution, 78
  at the Constitutional Convention, 79
  in the Constitution, 80
  abolition of, see Thirteenth Amendment
Smith, Adam, 15
Social Darwinism, 127
social facts, 9
Spencer, Herbert, 127, 148
state rights, 86
Stewart, Justice Potter, dissent in Engel v Vitale, 297
Stewart, Senator William M., on the Fifteenth Amendment, 115
Stewart, T. McCants, 153
Stone, Justice Harlan Fiske, Footnote Four to the Carolene Products Case, 204
Story, Justice Joseph
  on the taxing power, 192
  on the religious clauses of the First Amendment, 272
substantive due process, 2, 125, 142, 147, 224
  Lochner v New York, 142
Supremacy Clause, 73
Swann v Charlotte-Mecklenburg Board of Education, 251
T
Taft, Chief Justice William Howard, 135
Taney, Chief Justice Roger Brooke
  opinion in Dred Scott, 93

ideology, 367
Taney Court, the, 367
term limits, judicial, 426
Thayer, James Bradley, Ch. 3, n 4,14,16
third degree, 323
Thirteenth Amendment, 108
Tribe, Lawrence, 378, 390
Dartmouth College Case (Trustees of Dartmouth College v Woodward), 30
trusts, 128

U

U.S. v E.C. Knight, 131
U.S. v Reese, 116

V

voluntariness test, 325

W

Waite, Chief Justice Morrison Remick
  opinion in U.S. v Reese, 116
  opinion in Hall v De'Cuir, 163
Wagner Act, see National Labor Relations Act,
Warickshall's Case (King v Warickshall), 323
Warren, Charles, 375, 379
Warren, Chief Justice Earl
  opinion in Brown v Board of Education, 219
  opinion in Bolling v Sharpe, 224
  opinion in Brown II, 226
  opinion in Miranda Case, 330
  dissent in Shapiro v Thompson, 338
  judicial philosophy, 370
Warren Court, the, 370
Watson v Jones, 285
welfare state, 181, 335, 420, 423
West Coast Hotel v Parrish, 199
Weber, Max, 343
White, Justice Bryon, opinion in Kansas City Case, 258
Wickard v Filburn, 202
Wickersham Commission, 324
Wilkinson, Judge J. Harvie, III, Ch. 15, n 4,6,12
Williams, Roger, on the separation of church and state, 277

Williams v Mississippi, 157
Winthrop v Lechmere, 55

FOOTNOTES

Chapter 1
1 David Hume, *Essays*, "Of the Independency of Parliament"
2 Adam Smith, *An Inquiry into the Wealth of Nations*, Chap. X, Part. 2

Chapter 2
1 Sir William Blackstone, *Commentaries on the Laws of England*, Book III, Ch. 3 (1768)
2 26 Stat. 209 (1890)
3 Bushell's Case, 124 E.R 1006 (1670)
4 Winterbottom v Wright, 10 M. & W. 109 (Exch. 1842)
5 McPherson v Buick Motor Co., 217 N.Y. 382, 389 (1916)
6 Weeks v U.S., 232 U.S. 383 (1914)

Chapter 3
1 Oliver Wendell Holmes, Jr., *The Common Law*, Lecture 1
2 Blackstone, Bk. I, Ch. 2
3 Winthrop v Lechmere, 4 Conn. Hist. Coll., 94n; 5 Mass. Hist. Soc. Coll. (6th Series) 440-511 (1728)
4 James Bradley Thayer, "The Origin and Scope of the American Doctrine of Constitutional Law" (Harvard Law Review, Vol. VII, No. 3) 132 (October 25, 1893)
5 Id. 132-134
6 James Madison, *Notes on the Debates in the Federal Convention of 1787* (Norton) 61, 64, 462, 463 (1969)
7 Marbury v Madison, 5 U.S. 137, 162 (1803)
8 Id. 175, 176
9 Id. 177, 178
10 Id. 176, 177
11. Letter to William C. Jarvis (Sept. 28, 1820) Paul Leicester Ford, ed., *The Works of Thomas Jefferson* (G.P. Putnam's Sons) Vol. XII, 162 (1905)
12. Hylton v U.S. 3 U.S. 171, 175 (1796)
13. Cooper v Telfair, 4 U.S. 14, 19 (1800)
14. Thayer 140
15 Fletcher v Peck, 10 U.S. 87, 128 (1810)
16. Thayer 140, 142, 143
17. Sinking Fund Cases, 99 U.S. 700, 718 (1878)

Chapter 4
1. Madison 286, 410, 411, 502, 503, 532
2. Paul M. Angle, ed., *The Complete Lincoln-Douglas Debates of 1858* (University of Chicago Press) 384-385 (1991)
3 Aristotle, *The Complete Works of Aristotle, Politics,* Bk. I, Sec. 5

(Princeton University Press) 1991 (1995)
[4] Thomas E. Schott, *Alexander H, Stephens of Georgia* (Louisiana State University Press) 334 (1988)
[5]. Don E. Fehrenbacher, *Slavery, Law and Politics: the Dred Scott Case in Historical Perspective* (Oxford University Press) 51 (1981)
[6]. Id. 78, 81
[7] McCullough v Maryland, 17 U.S. 316 (1816)
[8] Gibbons v Ogden, 22 U.S. 1 (1824)
[9]. Don E. Fehrenbacher, *The Dred Scott Case: Its Significance in American Law and Politics* (Oxford University Press) 240 (1978)
[10] Rachel v Walker, 4 Mo. 350, 351, 354 (1837)
[11] Scott v Emerson, 15 Mo. 576, 582, 586 (1852)
[12]. Charles W. Smith, *Roger B. Taney: Jacksonian Jurist* (University of North Carolina Press) 144 (1936)
[13] Scott v Sandford, 60 U.S. 393, 403 (1857)
[14] Id. 404
[15] Id. 427
[16] Id. Id. 451
[17] Id. 452
[18] Id. 405
[19]. Fehrenbacher, *The Dred Scott Case* 417, 418
[20]. Id. vii
[21]. Id. 438
[22]. Roy P. Basler, ed., *Speeches and Presidential Addresses: by Abraham Lincoln, 1859 - 1865* (Lincoln Centenary Association) Vol. V 142, 143 (1907)

Chapter 5

[1] Justices who participated in the Reconstruction cases discussed in this chapter were Nathan Clifford appointed by Democratic President James Buchanan and who served from 1858 to 1881; Noah Haynes Swayne appointed by Lincoln who served from 1862 to 1881; Samuel Freeman Miller appointed by Lincoln who served 1862 to 1890; David Davis appointed by Lincoln who served 1862 to 1877; Stephen Johnson Field appointed by Lincoln who served 1863 to 1897; Salmon P. Chase appointed by Lincoln as Chief Justice who served 1864 to 1873; William Strong appointed by Grant who served 1870 to 1880; Joseph P. Bradley appointed by Grant who served 1870 to 1892; Ward Hunt appointed by Grant who served 1873 to 1882; Morrison Remick Waite appointed Chief Justice by Grant who served 1874 to 1888; John Marshall Harlan appointed by Hayes who served from 1877 to 1911; William Burnham Woods appointed by Hayes who served 1881 to 1887; Stanley Matthews appointed by Garfield who served 1882 to 1902; and Samuel Blatchford appointed by Garfield who served 1882 to 1893.

Thus, all except one were appointed by Republican presidents. That one,

Clifford, was a New Englander with Southern sympathies. Swayne was a Virginian by birth who moved to Ohio because of his anti-slavery views. Originally a Jackson Democrat, he later joined the Republican Party and on the Court strongly supported the constitutionality of Lincoln's war measures. Miller was a Kentuckian who moved to Iowa because of his anti-slavery views and became active in Republican politics, also on the Court supporting Lincoln's war measures. David Davis was from Illinois, a Republican, a close friend of Lincoln, and his campaign manager in 1860. Field was California lawyer who although a Democrat was a strong Unionist during the war. Chase was from Ohio and an early and ardent anti-slavery Republican who served as Lincoln's Secretary of the Treasury prior to his appointment as Chief Justice. Strong was a Pennsylvania lawyer who became a Republican in the 1860s. Bradley was a New York lawyer and an early Republican. Hunt was also a New Yorker and helped organize the Republican Party in that state. Waite was from Ohio and helped organize the Republican Party in that state. Harlan was from Kentucky and had actually been a slaveholder, served with the Union during the Civil War, became a Republican, and on the Court often stood up for the civil rights of the freedmen. Woods was an Ohio lawyer who moved to Alabama after the War and switched to the Republican Party. Matthews was an Ohio lawyer who served in the Union army during the Civil War and had been an abolitionist. Blatchford was a New Yorker who practiced law with William Seward, one of the founders of the Republican Party.

2. Walter L. Fleming, ed., *Documentary History of Reconstruction* (McGraw-Hill) I, 286 (1966)
3. Corfield v Coryell, 6 F. Cas. 546 no. 3,230 (C.C. E.D. Pa. 1823)
4. *Congressional Globe* (39th Cong., 2nd Sess.) 2765 (May 23, 1866)
5. Id. 2765
6. Id. 2765
7. *Id.* 2766
8. Slaughter-House Cases, 83 U.S. 36, 76
9. Id. 76, 78
10. Id. 79
11. Id. 71
12. *Congressional Globe* (40th Cong, 3rd Sess.) 668 (January 28, 1869)
13. Enforcement Act of 1870, 16 Stat. 140
14. U.S. v Reese, 92 U.S. 214, 217
15. Id. 218
16. Id. 218, 220
17. Louisiana Const., Art. 197, Sec. 3 (1898)
18. Civil Rights Act of 1875, 18 Stat. 335
19. Civil Rights Cases, 109 U.S. 3, 4, 5
20. Id. 20
21. Id. 24
22. Id. 10, 11

[23]. Id. 26
[24]. Id. 35

Chapter 6
[1]. Herbert Spencer, *"General Aspects of the Special Creation Hypothesis – Principles of Biology"* vol. I. part III, Ch. 2
[2]. quoted in Hans B. Thorelli, *The Federal Antitrust Policy: Origination of an American Tradition* (John Hopkins Press) 14 (1955)
[3]. Albert H. Walker, *History of the Sherman Act*, (Greenwood Press) 2 (1980)
[4]. 21 Cong. Rec. 3: 2457 (51st Cong., 1st Sess., March 21, 1890)
[5]. Id.
[6]. Id. 2462
[7] Walker 45, 46
[8]. Sherman Anti-Trust Act, 26 Stat. 209
[9]. Speech May 3, 1907, quoted in Lockhart, Kamisar, Choper, Shiffrin and Fallon, *Constitutional Rights and Liberties* (West Publishing) 8 (1996)
[10]. 21 Cong. Rec. 3: 2459
[11]. 21 Cong. Rec. 3: 2726 (emphasis added)
[12]. U.S. v E.C. Knight, 156 U.S. 1, 12 (1895)
[13]. Id. 12
[14]. Henry F. Pringle, *The Life and Times of William Howard Taft* Archon Books) Vol. 2, 967 (1964)
[15]. Loewe v Lawlor, 208 U.S. 274, 284 (1908)
[16]. Loewe v Lawlor, 148 F. 924, 925 (1906)
[17]. Loewe v Lawlor, 208 U.S. 274, 301
[18]. Louis B. Boudin, *The Sherman Act and Labor Disputes*, Columbia Law Review, Vol. XXXIX, No. 8, 1285 (December, 1939)
[19]. Loewe v Lawlor 208 U.S. 274, 297
[20]. Kermit L. Hall, ed., *The Oxford Companion to the Supreme Court* 490 (1992)
[21] Clayton Act, 38 Stat. 730
[22]. Duplex Printing Press Co. v Deering, 247 F. 192, 196 (1917)
[23]. Duplex Printing Press Co. v Deering, 252 F. 722, 748 (1918)
[24]. Duplex Printing v Deering, 254 U.S. 443, 471 (1921)
[25]. Id. 472
[26]. Id. 471
[27]. N.Y. Laws, chap. 415, art. 8, sec. 110 (1897)
[28]. Lochner v N.Y., 198 U.S. 45, 52 (1905)
[29]. Id. 53
[30]. Magna Charta, ch. 29 (1215), reprinted in A. Howard, *Magna Charta, Text and Commentary* (University of Virginia Press) 43 (1964)
[31]. 28 Edw. III, ch. 3 (1354)
[32] cited in Hurtado v California, 110 U.S. 516, 522 (1884)
[33]. Murray's Lessee v Hoboken Land & Improvement Co., 59 U.S. 272, 277

(1856)

34. H.C. Syrett and J.E. Cooks, eds. *The Papers of Alexander Hamilton* (Columbia University Press) IV, 35 (1962)

35. *Oxford Companion* 509

36. Lochner 75, 76

37. Hammer v Dagenhart, 247 U.S. 251 (1918)

38. Bailey V Drexel Furniture Co., 259 U.S. 20 (1922)

39. Adkins v Children's Hospital, 261 U.S. 525 (1923)

40. Employers' Liability Cases, 207 U.S. 463 (1908)

41. Jay Burns Baking v Bryan, 264 U.S. 504 (1924)

42. Weaver v Palmer Brothers, 270 U.S. 402 (1926)

Chapter 7

1. C. Vann Woodward, *The Strange Career of Jim Crow* (Oxford University Press) 33 (1974)

2 Gunnar Myrdal, *An American Dilemma: the Negro Problem and Modern Democracy* (Harper and Brothers) 630 (1944)

3 Otto H. Olsen, *The Thin Disguise: Plessy v Ferguson* (Humanities Press) 25-27 (1967)

4 Woodward 38-41

5. William Gillette, *The Right to Vote: Politics and the Passage of the Fifteenth Amendment* (John Hopkins Press) 134 (1969)

6. *Congressional Globe* (40th Cong. 3rd Sess.) 1629 (February 26, 1869)

7. Williams v Mississippi, 170 U.S. 213, 219 (1898)

8. Id. 219, 224

9. Woodward 85

10. Hall v DeCuir, 95 U.S. 485, 486 (1878)

11. Id. 486

12. Id. 487

13. Id. 488

14. Id. 489

15. Louisville, New Orleans and Texas Railway Company v Mississippi, 133 U.S. 587, 588 (1890)

16. Id. 591

17. Plessy v Ferguson, 163 U.S. 537, 540 (1896)

18. Charles A. Lofgren, *The Plessy Case: A Legal-Historical Interpretation* (Oxford University Press) 29 (1987)

19. Plessy v Ferguson 542, 543

20. Id. 544

21. Id. 552-564

22 A.F. Pollard, *The Evolution of Parliament* (Longman, Green) 166 (1934)

Chapter 8

1. William E. Leuchtenburg, *Franklin D. Roosevelt and the New Deal: 1932*

- *1940* (Harper & Row) 5 (1963)
2. B.D. Zevin, ed., *Nothing to Fear: The Selected Addresses of Franklin Delano Roosevelt, 1932-1945* (Houghton Mifflin) 12 (1946)
3. National Industrial Recovery Act, 48 Stat. 195
4 Gene Smiley, *Rethinking the Great Depression* (Ivan R. Dee) 92 (2002)
5. *The National Recovery Administration: An Analysis and Appraisal* (Brookings Institution) 3 (1935)
6. Home Building and Loan Assn. v Blaisdell, 290 U.S. 398 (1934)
7. Nebbia v New York, 291 U.S. 502 (1934)
8. Panama Refining Co. v Ryan, 293 U.S. 388 (1935)
9. R.R. Retirement Board v Alton R.R. Co., 295 U.S. 330 (1935)
10. Schechter Poultry Corp. v U.S., 295 U.S. 495, 542 (1935)
11. Id. 542, 543
12. Edward G. Nourse, Joseph S. Davis, and John D, Black, *Three Years of the Agricultural Adjustment Administration* (Brookings Institution) 424 (1937)
13. Id. 17
14. Id. 286
15. Id. 431, 432
16. U.S. v Butler, 297 U.S. 1, 62 (1936)
17. Id. 65, 66
18. Id. 66
19. Id. 66
20. Id. 66, 67
21. Id. 68
22. Id. 68
23 Carter v Carter Coal Co., 298 U.S. 238 (1936)
24. Dean Lloyd K. Garrison, "The Constitution and the Future" (The New Republic, January 29, 1936)
25. Robert H. Jackson, *The Struggle for Judicial Supremacy: A Study of a Crisis in American Power Politics* (A.A. Knopf) 329, 330, 332 (1941)
26 Id. 340 – 347
27 Morehead v N.Y. ex rel. Tipaldo, 298 U.S. 587 (1936)
28. West Coast Hotel v Parrish, 300 U.S. 379, 391, 392 (1937)
29. Virginia Railway Co. v Railway Employees, 300 U.S. 515 (1937)
30. Sonzinsky v U.S., 300 U.S. 506 (1937)
31. Wright v Vinton Branch Mountain Trust Bank, 300 U.S. 440 (1937)
32. Louisville Joint Stock Land Bank v Radford, 295 U.S. 555 (1935)
33. National Labor Relations Act, 49 Stat. 449
34. National Labor Relations Board v Jones & Laughlin Steel Corporation, 301 U.S. 1, 36, 37 (1937)
35. Wickard v Filburn, 317 U.S. 111, 125 (1942)
36. U.S. v Carolene Products, 304 U.S. 144, Footnote 4 (1938)

Chapter 9

[1] Cumming v Richmond Board of Education, 175 U.S. 528, 529 (1899)
[2] Id. 530
[3] Id. 530, 531
[4] Id. 532
[5] Id. 532
[6] Id. 532
[7] Id. 533
[8] Id. 533
[9] Id. 535
[10] Id. 542
[11] Id. 545
[12] Id. 544
[13] Loren Miller, *The Petitioners: The Story of the Supreme Court of the United States and the Negro* (Pantheon Books) 197 (1966)
[14] Berea College v Kentucky, 211 U.S. 45, 46 (1908)
[15] Missouri ex rel. Gaines v Canada, 305 U.S. 337 (1938)
[16] Henderson v U.S., 339 U.S. 816 (1950)
[17] Brown v Board of Education, 347 U.S. 483, 496 (1954)
[18] Id. 496
[19] Id. 496
[20] Id. 489
[21] Id. 489, 490
[22] Id. 490
[23] Id. 490, 491
[24] Id. 493
[25] Id. 494
[26] Id. 495
[27] 494, 495
[28] Bolling v Sharp, 347 U.S. 497, 500 (1954) (emphasis added)
[29] Brown v Board of Education (Brown II), 349 U.S. 294, 300, 301 (1955)
[30] 27 Am. Jur. 2nd 624, 625

Chapter 10

[1] Stephen C. Halpern, *On the Limits of the Law: the Ironic Legacy of Title VI of the 1964 Civil Rights Act* (John Hopkins University Press) 43 (1995)
[2] Briggs v Elliot, 132 F. Supp. 776, 777 (1955)
[3] Stephan and Abigail Thernstrom, *America in Black and White: One Nation Indivisible* (Simon and Schuster) 333, 334, 337 (1997)
[4] Civil Rights Act of 1964, 78 Stat. 241
[5] Id.
[6] 110 Cong. Rec. 13821 (88th Cong., 2nd Sess., June 15, 1964)
[7] Id. 12714 (June 4, 1964)
[8] Civil Rights Act of 1964
[9] Thernstrom 319
[10] Report of the White House Conference "To Fulfill These Rights" 63

(June 1-2, 1966)
[11]. Price v Denison Independent School District Bd. of Ed., 348 F.2d 1010, 1016 (5th Cir. 1965)
[12]. Id. 1013
[13]. 45 C.F.R. 181.54 amending 45 C.F.R. 181.5 (Supp. 1966)
[14] Halpern 52
[15]. 112 Cong. Record 18709 (89th Cong. 2d Sess., August 9, 1966)
[16]. Green v County Sch. Bd. of New Kent County, 391 U.S. 430, 432 (1968)
[17]. Id. 435, 436, 438
[18]. Swann v Charlotte-Mecklenburg Bd. of Educ., 402 U.S. 1,6,7 (1971)
[19]. Id. 8
[20]. Id. 9, 10
[21]. Id. 17
[22]. Id. 18
[23]. Id. 23, 25
[24]. Id. 27
[25]. Id. 30
[26]. Milliken v Bradley
[27] Milliken v Bradley, 418 U.S. 717, 722 (1974)
[28] Id. 729
[29] Id. 745
[30] Missouri v Jenkins, 495 U.S. 33, 59, 60 (1990)
[31]. Id. 61, 77
[32] Id. 51
[33] Thernstrom 346
[34] "New Approach to Integration: Interview with the Secretary of Health, Education and Welfare" (U.S. News & World Report, March 10, 1969)
[35] Report of the United States Commission on Civil Rights, "Federal Enforcement of School Desegregation," Appendix C (September 11, 1969)
[36]. Halpern 89
[37]. Id. 89
[38]. Id. 95
[39]. Marbury 170 (emphasis added)
[40]. Id. 165, 166
[41]. 78 Stat. 241
[42]. Adams v Richardson, 356 F. Supp. 92, 97 (D.D.C. 1973)
[43]. Adams v Richardson, 480 F.2d 1159, 1162 (D.C. Cir. 1973)

Chapter 11
[1]. Jonathan Elliot, ed., *The Debates in the Several State Conventions on the Adoption of the Federal Constitution* (Washington) III 330 (1836)
[2] 1 Annals of Congress 451
[3] Id. 757
[4]. Id. 755
[5]. Permoli v Municipality No. 1 of the City of New Orleans, 44 U.S. 589,

609

6 Sydney E. Ahlstrom, *A Religious History of the American People* (Yale University Press) 380 (1972)

7. Id. 759

8. J. Richardson, ed., *A Compilation of the Messages and Papers of the Presidents, 1789-1897* (Government Printing Office) I, 64 (1897)

9 Northwest Ordinance, 1 Stat. 50

10 Joseph Story, *Commentaries on the Constitution of the United States* (Carolina Academic Press) 700, 701 (1987)

11. The Church of the Holy Trinity v United States, 143 U.S. 457, 471 (1892)

12 Alexis de Tocqueville, *Democracy in America* (Schocken Books) Vol. 1, 362 (1961)

13. *George Washington: Writings* (Library of America) 971 (1997)

14 Roger Williams, *The Complete Writings of Roger Williams*, "Mr. Cotton's Letter Lately Printed, Examined and Answered" (Russell & Russell) Vol. 1, 392 (1963)

15 John Locke, *A Letter Concerning Toleration* (Encyclopedia Britannica) 3 (1952)

16 Id. 2, 3

17 Id. 18

18 Id. 18

[19]. Warren Nord, *Religion and American Education: Rethinking a National Dilemma* (University of North Carolina Press) 64 (1995)

20. Id. 72

21 5 ALR 866

22. 141 ALR 1144

23. Nord 230

24 Ahlstrom 517, 518

25 Baker v Fales, 16 Mass. 492 (1820)

26 Watson v Jones, 80 U.S. 679 (1872)

27. Everson v Board of Education, 330 U.S. 1, 3 (1947)

28. Id. 8

29. Murdock v Pennsylvania, 319 U.S. 105 (1943)

30. Everson 15, 16

31. Letter to Nehemiah Dodge and Others, A Committee of the Danbury Baptist Association, in the State of Connecticut (January 1, 1802) Merrill D. Peterson, ed., *The Portable Thomas Jefferson* (Penguin) 303 (1983)

32. Everson 16, 17

33. Id. 19

34. McCollum v Board of Education, 333 U.S. 203, 210

35. Id. 250, 252

36. Engel v Vitale, 370 U.S. 421, 422 (1962)

37. 176 N.E.2d 579, 581

38. Engel v Vitale 424

39. Id. 445
40. School Dist. of Abington Tp., 374 U.S. 203, 205 (1963)
41. Id. 212, 213
42. Id. 223
43. Stone v Graham, 449 U.S. 39 (1980)
44 Wallace v Jaffree, 472 U.S. 38 (1985)
45 Edwards v Aguillard, 482 U.S. 578 (1987)
46 Lee v Weisman, 505 U.S. 577 (1992)
47 Sante Fe Independent School District v Doe, 530 U.S. 290 (2000)
48 Lemon v Kurtzman, 403 U.S. 602, 612, 613 (1971)
49 Lynch v Donnelly, 465 U.S. 668 (1984)

Chapter 12
1 Chaplinsky v New Hampshire, 315 U.S. 568, 571, 572 (1942)
2 Regina v Hicklin, L.R. 3 Q.B. 360, 368 (1868)
3 Roth v U.S., 354 U.S. 476, footnotes 1, 2 (1957)
4 Id. 479
5 Id. 481
6 Id. 483-485
7 Id. 485
8 Id. 488
9 Id. 487, 489
10 Memoirs v Massachusetts, 383 U.S. 413, 418 (1966)
11 Id. 441
12 Paris Adult Theatre I v Slaton, 413 U.S. 39, 103, 113 (1973)
13 *Oxford Companion* 603
14 Leonard W. Levy, *Origins of the Fifth Amendment: the Right Against Self-Incrimination* (Oxford University Press) 272 (1968)
15 Id. 272
16 The Trial of John Lilburn and John Wharton, 3 How St Tr 1315 (1637)
17 King v Warickshall, 168 Eng. Rep. 234, 235 (K.B. 1783)
18 Minutes, 17th Annual Meeting, International Association of Chiefs of Police (Washington, D.C., 1910)
19 *Wickersham Commission Reports, No. 11: Report on Lawlessness in Law Enforcement* (Patterson, Smith) 4 (1968)
20 Id. 21
21 Id. 5
22 Sparf and Hansen v U.S., 156 U.S. 51, 55 (1895) (emphasis added)
23 State v Miranda, 401 P.2d 721, 723 (1965)
24 Miranda v Arizona, 384 U.S. 436, 518 (1966)
25. State v Miranda 733
26. Miranda v Arizona 478, 479
27 Id. 442, 448, 449, 457-460
28 Id. 481, 483

Chapter 13
[1] Shapiro v Thompson, 394 U.S. 618, 622, 623 (1969)
[2] Id. 629, 630
[3] Id. 638
[4] Id. 646, 655
[5] Ari Hoogenboom, *Outlawing the Spoils: A History of the Civil Service Reform Movement 1876-1883* (University of Illinois Press) 6 (1968)
[6] Id.
[7] Elrod v Burns, 427 U.S. 347, 380 (1976)
[8] Id. 373
[9] Id. 362, 363
[10] Id. 355, 357
[11] Id. 365
[12] Id. 367
[13] Id. 368, 369
[14] Id. 376, 381, 382, 385, 386, 389
[15] Roe v Wade, 410 U.S. 113, 117, 118, 120 (1973)
[16] Id. 116
[17] Id. 159
[18] case citations omitted
[19] Roe v Wade, 153
[20] Griswold v Connecticut, 381 U.S. 479, 527
[21] Id. 483, 484
[22] Roe v Wade, 155
[23] Id. 154, 163
[24] Karl Marx, *Critique of Hegel's Philosophy of Right*
[25] Karl Marx, *Critique of the Gotha Program*
[26] Karl Marx, *The Poverty of Philosophy*
[27] Karl Marx and Frederick Engels, *The Communist Manifesto*
[28] Karl Marx, *Critique of the Gotha Program*
[29] A.F. Pollard, *The Evolution of Parliament* (Longmans, Green) 185, 186 (1920)
[30] Dickerson v U.S., 530 U.S. 428 (2000)

Chapter 14
[1] Holmes
[2] Jean Edward Smith, *John Marshall: Definer of a Nation* (H. Holt & Co.) 108 (1996)
[3] John V. Orth, *The Judicial Power of the United States: the Eleventh Amendment in American History* (Oxford University Press) 31 (1986)
[4] Timothy S. Huebner, *The Taney Court* (ABC-CLIO) 115 (2003)
[5] Id. 192
[6] R. Kent Newmyer, *The Supreme Court Under Marshall and Taney* (Harlin, Davidson) 119 (2006)
[7] James W. Ely, *The Fuller Court* (ABC-CLIO) 3 (2003)

[8] John Braeman, *Before the Civil Rights Revolution: The Old Court and Individual Rights* (Greenwood Press) 121 (1988)
[9] James W. Ely, *The Chief Justiceship of Melvin W. Fuller, 1888-1910* (University of South Carolina Press) 59 (1995)
[10] Orth 57
[11] Bernard Schwartz, *A History of the Supreme Court* (Oxford University Press) 189 (1993)
[12] Id. 276
[13] Id. 284
[14] Id. 284, 285
[15] Mark Tushnet, ed., *The Warren Court in Historical and Political Perspective* (University of Virginia Press) 2,12,13 (1993)
[16] H.N. Hirsh, *The Enigma of Felix Frankfurter* (Basic Books) 181 (1981)
[17] Bernard Schwatz, "How Justice Brennan Changed America," in E. Joshua Rosenkranz and Bernard Schwartz, eds., *Reason and Passion: Justice Brennan's Enduring Influence* (W.W. Norton & Company) 40 (1997)
[18] Id. 18-21
[19] Hirsh 181
[20] Charles Warren, *The Supreme Court in United States History* (Little, Brown and Company) I, 2 (1922)
[21] Smith 382
[22] Id. 464
[23] Heubner 55
[24] Heubner 60
[25] Ely, *The Fuller Court* 24
[26] Peter G. Renstrom, *The Taft Court* (ABC CLIO) 54 (2003)
[27] Id. 61
[28] Linda Greenhouse, *Becoming Justice Blackmun: Harry Blackmun's Supreme Court Journey* (Time Books) 48 (2005)
[29] Id. 186, 235
[30] Laurence H. Tribe, *American Constitutional Law* (Foundation Press) 2 (1988)
[31] Id. 3
[32] Id. 8
[33] Id. 587
[34] Id. 770
[35] Id. 779
[36] Warren, *Supreme Court* I, 20-21
[37] Schwartz, *History of the Supreme Court* 3
[38] Newmyer 15
[39] Pollard 185
[40] Stanley G. Payne, *A History of Fascism* (University of Wisconsin Press) 3 (1995)
[41] Id. 4
[42] Id. 7

Chapter 15
1. Ferguson v Skrupa, 372 U.S. 726, 729, 730 (1963) (I have telescoped this quote for readability, but in no way changed the sense.)
2. Melvin I. Urofsky and Paul Finkel, *A March of Liberty: a Constitutional History of the United States* (Oxford University Press, 2002)
3. William J. Brennan, Jr., *The Constitution of the United States: Contemporary Ratification*, 27 S. Tex. L. Rev. 433, 438 (1986)
4. J. Harvie Wilkinson, III, *Cosmic Constitutional Theory* (Oxford University Press) 12 (2012)
5. Olga Tellegen-Couperus, *A Short History of Roman Law* (Routledge) 116, 117 (1993)
6. Wilkinson 36, 37
7. West Virginia State Board of Education v Barnette, 319 U.S. 624, 638 (1943)
8. McDonald v City of Chicago, 561 U.S. 742 (2010)
9. Citizens United v Federal Election Commission, 558 U.S. 310 (2010)
10. Brown v Plata, 563 U.S. (2011)
11. Dandridge v Williams, 397 U.S. 471 (1970)
12. Wilkinson 28
13. Lindsey v Normet, 405 U.S. 56 (1972)
14. San Antonio Indep. Sch. Dist., 411 U.S. 1 (1973)

Made in the USA
Middletown, DE
21 July 2024